Libraries in the Information Age

Recent Titles in Library and Information Science Text Series

LIBRARIES IN THE INFORMATION AGE
An Introduction and Career Exploration

Third Edition

Denise K. Fourie and Nancy E. Loe

Library and Information Science Text Series

LIBRARIES UNLIMITED™

An Imprint of ABC-CLIO, LLC

Santa Barbara, California • Denver, Colorado

Library of Congress Cataloging-in-Publication Data

Names: Fourie, Denise K., author. | Loe, Nancy E., 1954– author.
Title: Libraries in the information age : an introduction and career exploration / Denise K. Fourie and Nancy E. Loe.
Description: Third edition. | Santa Barbara, California : Libraries Unlimited, an imprint of ABC-CLIO, LLC, [2016] | Series: Library and information science text series | Includes bibliographical references and index.
Identifiers: LCCN 2015043486 (print) | LCCN 2016008837 (ebook) | ISBN 9781610698641 (paperback) | ISBN 9781610698658 (ebook)
Subjects: LCSH: Library science. | Library science—Vocational guidance. | Libraries—Technological innovations.
Classification: LCC Z665 .F74 2016 (print) | LCC Z665 (ebook) | DDC 020—dc23
LC record available at http://lccn.loc.gov/2015043486

ISBN: 978-1-61069-864-1
EISBN: 978-1-61069-865-8

20 19 18 17 16   1 2 3 4 5

This book is also available as an eBook.

Libraries Unlimited
An Imprint of ABC-CLIO, LLC

ABC-CLIO, LLC
130 Cremona Drive, P.O. Box 1911
Santa Barbara, California 93116-1911
www.abc-clio.com

This book is printed on acid-free paper ∞

Manufactured in the United States of America

In memory of

Cynthia Graham Hurd (1960–2015),
dedicated librarian,

Charleston County Public Library, South Carolina

Contents

Illustrations

FIGURES

TABLES

Preface for the Third Edition

Ongoing change and innovation are constant themes for those who work in today's libraries and information centers. The ever-expanding ways to access information present both inspiration and challenge to library staff at all levels. The electronic information era directly affects libraries, archives, information centers, media centers, and museums. The promise of instant information is increasingly a reality, transforming the library industry in many specific ways addressed in this book.

The thoroughly revised third edition of this textbook is designed for students and others interested in an overview of the world of modern libraries and information centers in the United States. Earlier editions were widely adopted as a text in Library Technical Assistant (LTA) vocational programs and graduate MLIS or MLS library programs. This edition also addresses these audiences, in particular providing needed fundamentals to students at all levels who have little or no work experience in library settings.

Major additions to this third edition include updated information on current technologies in use across the field; discussion of the re-purposing of library spaces to include features such as learning commons, makerspaces, collaborative learning areas, and art displays; the growth of open access and commercial resources, as well as robust digital collections and archives; the need to engage library communities in participatory learning cultures via outreach, common reads programs, social media, and patron-driven acquisitions.

Other additions include discussion of the Library Support Staff Certification (LSSC) process for paraprofessional library workers; an updated look at traditional and emerging ethical issues facing library workers; and dynamic tools for the job seeker.

Besides serving as a textbook for LTA or MLIS curricula, this book is also used in continuing education courses for staff and as a resource for on-the-job reference work. This book provides a sound foundation of library fundamentals, upon which one can began to build a rewarding career path. In crafting this revised third edition, we have used input from students and instructors who have used the text at all academic levels of coursework, as well as from reviewers, general readers, coworkers, and colleagues. All chapters and accompanying resource sections have been updated to reflect new trends, events, products, services, and links to resources about the ever-evolving library and information industries.

Libraries in the Information Age: An Introduction and Career Exploration begins by examining the redefined and revitalized role of libraries in the era of electronic information, then provides historical background on the evolution of libraries. Job opportunities in a variety of library and information center settings are discussed, followed by a detailed look at the typical major library activities of collection building, materials processing, reference services, and circulation and access. The critical role of resource sharing networks is examined, along with the ethical issues surrounding information access, and an overview of basic job-hunting skills. The text concludes with a look at the continuing impact of digital innovation and customer demand upon library services.

Overall, the book introduces the novice to trends and issues that affect the contemporary library agency. This textbook also helps readers and those contemplating entering the library field to identify key aptitudes, skills, and attitudes needed for success and to alert them to job niches within the industry that may appeal to their individual interests. At the end of each chapter, references to significant electronic and print resources are provided to further guide the reader in learning and information gathering. A good textbook represents the initial step in assimilating knowledge about a course of study or, in this case, a potential career path. But going beyond the text is both necessary and an enriching second step. Especially helpful to students is the opportunity to communicate electronically with others via e-mail, listservs, blogs, social media, and websites. Our world is more connected than ever and it is easier than ever to tap into a supportive network of practitioners, advocates, and mentors as you build a collegial support system for your career.

Acknowledgments

The authors wish to acknowledge the following persons and entities for their valuable assistance and support toward the publication of this revised third edition.

Emma Bailey
Robin Bedenbaugh
Elisabeth Blaikie
Kevin Bontenbal
Joanne Britton
Johanna Brown
Richard Brumley
Del Chausse
Helen Chu
Cuesta College
Jennifer Correa
Hiram Davis
Kathy DeCou
Dave Dowell
Frances Edwards
Elisa Feingold
Marya Figueroa
Terri Fishel
Martha Greene
Nancy Guidry
Kathy Headtke

Ellen Jagger
Cathy Jenkins
Ruth Jordan
Ken Kenyon
Rita Kindle
Tina Lau
Mary Ann Laun
Heidi Lewin-Miller
George Libby
Caroline Lilyard
Carina Love
Ron Maas
Nancy Meddings
Leslie Mosson
Dominik Muggli
Mike Multari
Cathe Olson
Nancy P. O'Neill
Jenny Paxson
Marisa Ramirez
Jennifer Sawyer

Larry Smith   Rebecca True
Laura Sorvetti   Sohair F. Wastawy
Mary Speidel   Peggy Watson
Mark Stengel   Beth Wimer
Betty Stout   Blanche Woolls

Chapter 1

Redefining the Role of Libraries

The millennium ushered in a new era for libraries and information centers. These momentous changes began in the 1990s, when the advances of the World Wide Web made it possible to share digitized information in innovative ways, while offering individuals greater ease of use. Recent developments in mobile computing and social media have led to massive changes in the ways information, both old and new, is created, used, and shared. These technological advances, and the ways in which librarians have integrated them, affect all libraries, whether rural or urban, campus or community, small or large.

Full-text databases, e-books, online public access catalogs (OPACs), digital resource sharing, cloud data storage, electronic periodical indexes, and digitized archives have penetrated to the far corners of the globe, facilitating the exchange of information. No longer are libraries defined by the size of their physical collections, but rather by the amount of information to which they can provide access.

The skills and abilities of librarians and library staff are also evolving, just as the role of libraries within their respective communities is being altered. Will the printed book and the e-book coexist? How will physical library buildings change? How will these changes provide new opportunities to shape the public perception and use of libraries? And, ultimately, what does this mean for people employed in the library profession in the 21st century?

Some trends are discernable in the midst of persistent technological change. The Pew Research Center's Internet and American Life Project conducts ongoing research on libraries in American society. Its 2014 report suggests that the future of libraries lies in three areas:

- The library as a place
- The library as a connector of people
- The library as a platform for getting patrons the information and the contacts they seek.[1]

THE EVOLVING LIBRARY

As we in the profession embrace all aspects of the evolving library, we are also moving beyond the traditional conception of library as repository. The reality of smaller physical collections provides new opportunities to reevaluate the role of the library building itself in the community. Increasingly, the physical library is seen as a *third place*—that is, somewhere other than work or home/classroom, as defined by Ray Oldenburg, in his book *The Great Good Place*.[2] Some of these characteristics include a neutral and welcoming atmosphere, free or inexpensive services, and highly accessible space where users feel a sense of belonging. Physical libraries—within their respective communities of campus, neighborhood, or school—are increasingly and deliberately being positioned to offer elements of Third Places.

A vibrant example of the library as a Third Place occurred during the racial unrest sparked by the police shooting of unarmed teenager Michael Brown in Ferguson, Missouri, in 2014. Just a few blocks from the clashes between protesters and police, Director Scott Bonner placed a sign on the library doors saying, "Stay Strong Ferguson. We Are Family." Offering the public library as a haven for everyone in the community, Brown worked with volunteers, church groups, and local teachers to provide educational programming for up to 200 children a day, while racial tensions were "at a boiling point." Responding to congratulations on Twitter, where he was described as a superhero, Bonner wrote: "Ha! Thanks. But, if I'm a superhero, then so is any local librarian, so go to the library and let them teach you to fly."[3]

Libraries provide materials that help individuals imagine, envision, create, motivate, and inspire themselves and others. Acquiring and sharing information among all citizens instead of a privileged few is referred to as the *democratization of knowledge*. The growth and development of free public libraries in the United States over many generations have been essential to this process.

In a 2013 survey by the Pew Research Center, 90 percent of the respondents indicated that libraries are important to their communities. Seventy-six percent of library visitors also found librarians "very helpful," while 49 percent of unemployed and retired respondents say librarian assistance in finding information is "very important." Fifty-six percent of Internet users without home access say public libraries' basic technological resources (Internet access and computer hardware) are "very important" to them and their families. More than half of library users were assisted by library staff to find needed resources.[4]

Helping Users Evaluate Information

Traditionally, library staff members who work directly with patrons have been facilitators: helping users with research tools and recommending relevant resources. Now, as print and digital information continues to proliferate, librarians and staff must also teach users how to find the *right* information. As award-winning British author Neil Gaiman has said, "Google can bring you back 100,000 answers. A librarian can bring you back the right one."[5] Librarians not only serve as Internet trainers in all library settings, but also are guides to the *Deep Web*, the vast majority of the Web that is not retrieved by search engines and remains largely unknown to casual Internet users.

Before digital publishing, books and other materials first went through a rigorous editing and publishing process. Then, from the many print resources competing for a library's scarce acquisition dollars, librarians acquired materials that met collecting policy guidelines and the needs of that library's users.

With the advent of the World Wide Web, the *democratization of knowledge* has advanced as barriers to publication have been virtually eliminated. Self-published authors were once reliant on vanity publishers to create physical books; now online e-book packagers, such as Lulu; e-book apps, such as iBook; and publishing on demand have altered the publishing landscape forever. Drag-and-drop Web design sites, like Weebly, and blogging applications, such as WordPress and Tumblr, provide additional ways for individuals to express themselves.

By 2006, *crowdsourcing*, or content created by large and random groups of people rather than from traditional sources, entered our lexicon. In his 2004 book, *The Wisdom of Crowds: Why the Many Are Smarter Than the Few and How Collective Wisdom Shapes Business, Economies, Societies and Nations*, writer James Surowiecki argues strongly that decisions made by a group are often better than decisions made by an individual in the group.[6]

The theory that group consensus provides a better analysis of content than a single expert is the foundation of Google's search algorithms, which return search query results based on use, rather than quality. Wikipedia is another example of both crowdsourcing and the democratization of knowledge. This real-time reference tool permits anyone to update its encyclopedia articles at any time, which is both its strength and its weakness. Thus Wikipedia can be a reliable source of information in certain areas, but not necessarily in others. As a consequence, users are left to evaluate the accuracy and reliability of its information themselves.

The rising challenge today for library workers is to help users not only find information, but also become skillful evaluators of its usefulness and reliability from the ocean of resources available. Critical thinking skills are also essential. In school and academic libraries, this responsibility is shared with classroom teachers. Staff members in special libraries have a responsibility to sift through and evaluate data for their colleagues. For public librarians and staff, helping users find and evaluate information is central to their mission. In all cases, the library worker's role as an evaluator is just as important as that of a facilitator. For these reasons, libraries remain alive and well, because the Internet complements libraries, but does not replace them.

Computer Skills Essential

For library workers, the need for proficient computer skills cannot be stressed enough. Although wide reading and a knowledge of and reverence for books is still valued, these alone are insufficient for entering a field that increasingly depends on digital resources and applications. Digital skills unlock the world of electronic resources and transmit information to patrons regardless of location. Skillful use of office productivity tools (word processing, spreadsheets, presentation applications, image editing, e-mail) is fundamental, as is proficiency with dedicated library computer systems, such as OPACs, databases, and circulation and cataloging modules. An understanding of information technology (Web design, metadata, database management) is a growing and valuable part of the toolbox of effective library workers. Social networking in the hands of skillful library professionals and staff offers new vehicles for both outreach and delivery of library services, as well as new ways of engaging library users. Facebook, Google+, Twitter, Pinterest, Instagram, and other social media offer customized ways to reach new and returning users.

As always, library staff members are being called upon to provide basic computer instruction, particularly on search skills, to library users. Whether one is working in an elementary school library or a university research library, the job environment is faster paced than in the past. Few libraries or information centers are tied to any single medium of information storage. Rather, multiple formats are in use simultaneously: paper, archival documents, microforms, digital text, digital images, data sets, infographics, and other visual media. As information storage and retrieval methods evolve and user expectations rise, library workers require continuing education to stay abreast of useful technology. Because of the rate of change, a continuous learning curve now exists not only for library professionals and staff, but also for library users.

The World Wide Web is but one manifestation of the impact of information technology on library work. Over the past five decades, behind-the-scenes processes in libraries have become increasingly automated. Repetitive routines, such as creating bibliographic records, checking in serials, sending overdue notices, filling interlibrary loan requests, and copy cataloging, are increasingly automated or even outsourced to vendors. Since the 1990s, OPACs have been available locally or from remote locations. Catalogs from groups of libraries, once referred to as union catalogs and now commonly known as portals, offer increased ease to locate items across many libraries.

In addition to altering the day-to-day activities of library staff, automation increasingly provides added value for library users. When libraries make public their order, catalog and circulation records, users can determine not only whether the library is acquiring a particular item, but also whether it has arrived or if it is checked out. Other internal library records once reserved for staff, such as in-process files, periodicals check-in files, and location of items in other libraries, are also now available to the public.

During its early stages, some library workers feared that automation would eliminate jobs. In fact, technology often creates new career and support staff positions in libraries maintaining OPACs, delivering databases and full-text documents, and creating and providing access to new digital collections.

CHARACTERISTICS OF LIBRARY WORK

A wide variety of job knowledge and skills are required for any library to operate smoothly. In a small, one-person location, the solo staff member must possess a wide array of library skills. In a large library, these abilities are spread among many different individuals in multiple departments. In general, the size of the library determines whether staff members are primarily specialists or generalists.

Solo Library Worker or Part of a Team

In one-person libraries, a single staff member must do everything. At certain times, the person may perform tasks that would generally be considered professional. At other times, the tasks may be clerical. That single person accomplishes whatever needs to be done. Such staff members must be Jacks and Jills of all trades.

If a person likes a wide variety of very different tasks during the workday, the small library offers such an opportunity. These workers are self-starters, who see what needs to be done, organize and prioritize the tasks at hand, and work through them until they are completed. No supervisor is physically close at hand to advise when difficult situations arise. In fact, no colleague is nearby to assist with any technical matter. Flexibility is an important attribute of a solo library worker because the arrival of a single patron can cause the reordering of the work plan. The main priority is helping the user, whether they are students and teachers using a school library, a professional in a firm using a special library, or a local person using a small public library.

Even if the location is part of a larger library agency, a certain amount of physical processing of materials and database maintenance is required. Other staff members at that location may provide assistance with support tasks such as computer maintenance, Web design, and bookkeeping. They may also be available to assist with difficult-to-please patrons and to provide general moral support and camaraderie. If the small library is a branch of a larger system, advice may be readily available by telephone, e-mail, or a visit. If the site is not part of a larger organization, a sense of isolation may create a morale issue. The solo library worker, in this case, must become a skilled advocate and protector of library turf, as well as a highly skilled technician. This kind of assignment makes good use of general skills, but does not allow the luxury of specialization.

A large library, on the other hand, requires a certain amount of specialization. The larger the library, the more compartmentalized each position becomes. Many levels of staff with different sets of specialized knowledge and skills are employed throughout the organization. In the largest libraries with dozens to hundreds of staff members, job descriptions are carefully defined and everyone is a specialist of sorts. In these settings, keeping track of the larger mission of the library may be difficult. Each person in a large library works as part of a team and must depend on other staff members to accomplish significant projects. Working as part of a team is critical in providing good service to library users.

Public Service or Behind the Scenes

Behind the scenes, a technical services librarian decides which items to purchase for a subject area of the collection; another staff member verifies the bibliographic information, selects the vendor, and places the order; another may receive the order; and yet another may pay the invoice before the item heads to cataloging.

In large libraries, one person may complete descriptive cataloging (the physical description of an item), while another completes the subject cataloging. In very large libraries, the cataloging may be divided among several subject and foreign-language specialists. Yet another person completes physical processing, adding barcodes or RFID tags, ownership markings, and "tattle tape" for theft prevention. Serials, government documents, learning resources, manuscripts, archives, and other special collections usually have separate but parallel workflows to create intellectual access to these special items. These technical tasks require attention to detail, accuracy, and the ability to follow through on complex workflows, and they are often best accomplished away from the distractions of users arriving and telephones ringing.

Once a bibliographic record is created, the materials are discovered by users, or recommended by the library staff members who work with the public. These staff members must be skilled in working with a variety of individuals. Strong oral communication skills—especially intuitive listening ability—top the list of required characteristics. Understanding that individuals have different learning styles (i.e., visual rather than text) also helps library workers reach out to and assist users. Library workers are also using new communications skills with the advent of virtual reference services, where people are assisted remotely rather than in person.

Ability to function without getting frustrated when three patrons are competing for attention and two phones are ringing is also important. Juggling multiple changing priorities often becomes the order of the day at a busy library public service desk. Variety can be great, but some service requests can become repetitive and mundane. However, all requests from patrons must be treated with courtesy, speed, and skill. Successful experience in retail or other services working with the public can be excellent preparation for these library assignments.

LIBRARY JOB CLASSIFICATIONS

To the general public, anyone who sits at a desk in a room where a substantial number of books are shelved is a librarian. Casual use of the term *librarian* is akin to calling anyone who works in a hospital a doctor. To more knowledgeable individuals, the term *librarian* has a much more precise definition.

Within the differing qualifications, knowledge, and skill sets required for effective delivery of library services, there are several career ladders, each with multiple rungs. In the small library discussed previously, workers must possess as many skills as possible. As the size of the library increases, the need for special knowledge and skills also grows.

The following discussion of staff roles in libraries is based on *Library and Information Studies and Human Resource Utilization* (*LISHRU*), a policy statement of the American Library Association.[7] This seminal statement remains an excellent framework for understanding the division of labor in libraries.

In libraries, there are generally four classifications: (1) clerical, (2) paraprofessional, (3) professional, and (4) specialist. Paraprofessionals and clerks may also be grouped as *library support staff,* which commonly refers to all non-librarians, whether they are clerical or paraprofessional, full-time or part-time, working with the public or behind the scenes.

While *LISHRU* provides an important framework, note that libraries are not compelled to follow ALA policy when creating job descriptions and classifications. Library staff members are not certified and regulated as legal, medical, accounting, or other professions are. Although most states prescribe the minimum requirements for certification as a school librarian, standards for other positions in library settings seldom exist. Therefore, libraries may be organized in ways that diverge from this model. However, the *LISHRU* statement provides an important framework, assisting library administrators with balancing the needs of the organization with equitable treatment of library professionals and staff.

Clerical Staff

Libraries are not only places where books and other resources are stored and made available, but are also organizations that must be managed. In this aspect of their activities, libraries have routine tasks similar to any organization. Some of these operational tasks are primarily clerical and mirror those performed by office workers everywhere: data entry, filing, preparing paperwork, paying bills, and greeting and referring patrons are a few examples of clerical tasks performed in libraries. Within larger libraries, there can be several levels of clerical positions, depending on the level of responsibility of the position (e.g., clerical assistant I, II, and III, or account clerk I, II, and III).

Entry into such positions is generally through clerical training, clerical experience, or both. Knowledge of basic library terminology and concepts is usually gained on the job. For such positions, it is almost incidental that they are located in a library.

Paraprofessional Staff

Paraprofessional positions in libraries are generally called library technical assistants (LTAs), library assistants, or library technicians. The LTA classifications defined in *LISHRU* "assume certain kinds of specific 'technical' skills, [but] they are not meant simply to accommodate advanced clerks."[8] Technical skills specifically associated with library work are emphasized, such as bibliographic searching, overseeing circulation and shelving services, or processing materials for public use. Small- to medium-sized libraries may combine these categories into one set of classifications with multiple levels (e.g., LTA I, II, and III or library assistant I, II, III, and IV). These positions are differentiated from clerical positions by requiring library education, training, or experience, or all three, before incumbents are hired.

Prospective LTAs prepare by completing an associate's degree or certification in library technology from a community college program. The ALA-APA (American Library Association's Allied Professional Association) offers two certification programs: the Certified Public Library Administrator Program and the Library Support Staff Certification Program. However, there are currently not enough such programs in the United States to train the number of paraprofessionals needed by libraries. As a result, libraries may hire candidates with general education and provide them with on-the-job training for the knowledge and skills required for their duties.

The *LISHRU* statement also describes an additional paraprofessional classification, usually called library associates, for positions where general education is more important than library knowledge. Usually requiring a bachelor's degree, library associate positions might require foreign-language fluency or knowledge of a specific subject discipline, such as local history. Only the very largest of libraries would use this category.

LISHRU differentiates between the kind of training appropriate for LTAs and that of professional librarians. In general, two-year technical assistant certification programs emphasize applied learning of specific skill sets, while master's degree programs focus on theoretical learning of library concepts, trends, and management.

Astute students of library career development are learning that career progression is now more fluid. The career lattice included in the *LISHRU* statement illustrates many entry points into library employment and internal career pathways once an individual is employed. Options exist for individuals who already have a college degree and perhaps considerable work experience in another occupation before entering the library field. An LTA program may be attractive to a student who already holds an associate's degree, a bachelor's degree, or even a graduate degree. In this case, the student is seeking a credential for vocational credibility. The paraprofessional level may be a worthy final goal; for others it is a first step leading to demonstrable experience as a paraprofessional and, eventually, to a Master of Library Science (MLS) degree and a professional position as a librarian. Still others decide to go directly to a graduate library school to enter the profession as librarians.

Librarians

Graduate school faculty members have debated whether they teach in "l-schools" (library schools) or "i-schools" (information studies). Professional library degrees come in many designations—Master of Library Science, Master of Library and Information Studies, Master of Information Science—depending upon the nomenclature used by various graduate schools. Regardless of name, for those choosing the career of a professional librarian, obtaining a master's degree accredited by the American Library Association is imperative for essential understanding of the field, upholding professional standards, and advancing professionally. Many in the profession find the term *information science* to be a liberating one, emphasizing that librarians deal with the *content* of books and other media, and not just with the physical objects themselves.

Most employers stipulate that the MLS must be from an ALA-accredited school. A teaching credential with a specialization in school library may suffice for entry-level school library assignments in other states. However, individuals who desire the flexibility to move from one type of library to another as their careers unfold would do well to secure an MLS from an ALA-accredited institution.

LISHRU states:

The title "librarian" carries with it the connotation of "professional" in the sense that professional tasks are those which require a special background and education on the basis of which library needs are identified, problems are analyzed, goals are set, and original and creative solutions are formulated for them, integrating theory into the practice, and planning, organizing, communicating, and administering successful programs of service to users of the library's materials and services. In defining services to users, the professional person recognizes potential users as well as current ones, and designs services which will reach all who could benefit from them.[9]

LISHRU also states, "Positions which are primarily devoted solely to the routine application of established rules and techniques, however useful and essential to the effective operation of a library's ongoing services, should not carry the word 'Librarian' in the job title."[10] The job title of professional librarian implies knowledge and leadership relating to current and future technologies.

Both librarians and LTAs may carry out duties that are fairly routine applications of established rules and techniques. The librarian, though, also has a fundamental responsibility to constantly review those established rules and techniques and replace them when they no longer provide the most effective means of delivering services for the unique clientele served by that library. At the Cuesta College Library in California, a librarian was the project manager responsible for implementing the current automation system. After the system was operating well, day-to-day administration was assigned to an LTA. The librarian remains responsible for implementing upgrades, new modules, and major conversions to new systems.

The work librarians accomplish generally falls into the following broad categories:

- **Reference and research librarians** often specialize in specific subjects and possess broad knowledge of professional literature in those fields. They also teach users and groups about effective use of databases and other reference tools. In academic libraries, the subject expertise of these librarians is matched with the curriculum of the university.

- **Outreach librarians** promote library resources and services, often to specific groups of public or library users. In academic libraries in particular, these librarians use social networking forums on campuses to reach students and faculty in specific departments, make visits to residence halls, and partner with teaching faculty using collaborative learning spaces in the library. Excellent communication skills are required to engage students and faculty directly. These responsibilities are often combined with that of research librarians.

- **Public service librarians** work directly with the public answering questions and finding materials; manage specific departments, such as children's and teen services; promote library services; and also promote specific programs and events for library initiatives such as literacy, early learning, makerspaces, and book groups.

- **Technical services librarians** manage acquisitions, collection development, and cataloging. They allocate funds to library departments and programs, select vendors, oversee orders and subscriptions, and cataloging of print and digital resources. They also analyze and assess the library's collections against professional standards and benchmarks, and discard or add materials as indicated.

- **Electronic resources librarians** manage subscriptions and renewals of databases licensed from vendors. They often work in collection development library departments. They also compile and analyze data on use of electronic journals, databases, and e-books, which are shared with research and collection development librarians. They also ensure that electronic resources are used according to the terms of the licensing agreements they have signed with vendors or publishers.

- **Serials librarians** manage magazines, journals, and periodicals that are published at intervals. They oversee subscriptions, renewals, and updating bibliographic records when serials change names or discontinue publishing. As serials continue to migrate from print to digital formats, these librarians increasingly perform the work of electronic resources librarians described earlier.

- **Cataloging librarians** oversee how print and digital materials are prepared for users, from marking library materials with ownership stamps to creating bibliographic records that provide intellectual access for users. These librarians must understand and apply metadata according to professional standards.

- **Systems librarians** manage information technology for libraries. They select and maintain hardware and software, or integrated library systems (ILS), used in the library. They manage servers, operating systems, databases, applications, and upgrades; create and maintain backup systems and disaster recovery plans; and safeguard library systems from malware and attacks. They oversee programmers, digital media librarians, and Web designers who design the ways digital information is delivered to users.

- **Special collections librarians** manage unique and often historical materials, including manuscripts, books, photographs, and documents, collecting by subject, time period, and/or region. These librarians acquire materials, usually by donation; arrange and describe them for public use; and balance the need to protect fragile materials with requests for use by researchers.

- **Digital services librarians** are relatively new positions, focused on creating, implementing, and maintaining digital content created primarily in academic libraries, archives, and special collections. They develop and maintain institutional repositories; implement digital preservation strategies; develop new digital library collections; reach out to teaching faculty to integrate these collections into the curriculum; and help develop technologies in support of digital initiatives on campus.

- **School librarians** work directly with K-12 students to fulfill their educational needs. School librarians (also known as teacher-librarians) also work closely with classroom instructors to identify and provide digital and print materials that complement the official curriculum.

• **Library directors** are administrators who manage a library's human resources, collections, and services. They provide leadership to their organizations regarding trends and developments in the profession, as well as current and future technologies. Directors work with their department heads to develop short- and long-term plans, identify new services and review the effectiveness of existing ones, and prepare and track budgets. Library directors report to upper-level campus administrators, government officials, or library boards. They are also responsible for identifying and securing new streams of funding, from gifts, grants, and other external sources.

Chapter 3 provides an in-depth discussion of the four major library types and their respective responsibilities.

Specialists

One other category in *LISHRU* that deserves attention is that of *specialist.* Specialists in *LISHRU* are found in professions parallel to librarianship in education and in function. Their credentials and education are from their respective fields, rather than library schools. Specialist positions in libraries include human resources managers; accountants; marketing, graphic design, and events management; fundraisers and development officers; and IT professionals, technologists and Web designers.

Specialists meet specific needs, particularly in very large libraries. These specialists work closely with librarians and administrators both on daily management of library functions and new initiatives. Just as their credentials are from disciplines other than libraries, so are the classification levels and job performance reviews based on policies and procedures outside the library.

Effectiveness of Librarians

As *LISHRU* states, "The objective of the Master's programs in librarianship should be to prepare librarians capable of anticipating and engineering the change and improvement required to move the profession constantly forward. The curriculum and teaching methods should be designed to serve this kind of education for the future rather than to train for the practice of the present."[11]

Research has provided support for the value of the MLS. Four dissertations completed in the 1960s relate to this issue. John McCrossan found that MLS holders were likely to perform better in collection development than others.[12] Charles Bunge showed that although the end result might not differ, library school graduates were more efficient in performing reference searches than those with similar library experience.[13] Lucille Wert's study showed that school librarians who held an MLS offered more services and spent less time in housekeeping tasks than did those with similar experience and responsibilities who had an undergraduate minor in library science.[14] In a slightly different exploration, Gordon Baillie found a positive correlation between library school grade point average and successful performance on the job.[15] Since this research, library education has changed, libraries have changed, and the tasks performed by librarians have changed. Similar research needs to be conducted today to see if these results still hold.

As libraries continue to evolve, librarians and library staff should possess the same characteristics that lead to success in other professions—analytical ability, communication skills, intellectual curiosity, and service orientation. In addition, librarians must be committed to continuous improvement of services to the patrons of their libraries.

This book is not theoretical, but instead describes libraries as they now exist and how they might evolve in future. We believe readers will use these ideas and be inspired to become the next generation of library workers and thinkers who will lead our profession as it continues to evolve. Libraries are not just repositories of information about the past and the present, but also agents of change that can help library users imagine and inspire bold courses of action for the future.

NOTES

1. Lee Rainie, "The Next Library and the People Who Will Use It" (conference presentation, AzLA/MPLA Annual Conference, Scottsdale/Fountain Hills, AZ, November 13, 2014), accessed May 15, 2015, http://www.pewinternet.org/2014/11/13/the-next-library-and-the-people-who-will-use-it.
2. Ray Oldenburg, *The Great Good Place: Cafés, Coffee Shops, Bookstores, Bars, Hair Salons, and Other Hangouts at the Heart of a Community* (Cambridge, MA: Da Capo Press, 1989, rev. 1999).
3. Alison Flood, "Librarian Hero of Michael Brown Unrest Wins Lemony Snicket Award," *The Guardian*, March 25, 2015, accessed May 15, 2015, http://www.theguardian.com/books/2015/mar/25/librarian-michael-brown-lemony-snicket-ferguson.
4. Kathryn Zickuhr, Lee Rainie, Kristen Purcell, and Maeve Duggan, "How Americans Value Public Libraries in Their Communities," *Pew Internet & American Life Project*, December 11, 2013, accessed May 15, 2015, http://libraries.pewinternet.org/2013/12/11/libraries-in-communities.
5. Indianapolis-Marion County Public Library, *Neil Gaiman on Libraries*, YouTube video, 1:56, April 16, 2010, accessed March 29, 2015, https://www.youtube.com/watch?v=uH-sR1uCQ6g.
6. James Surowiecki, *The Wisdom of Crowds: Why the Many Are Smarter Than the Few and How Collective Wisdom Shapes Business, Economies, Societies and Nations* (New York: Doubleday, 2004).
7. American Library Association, "Library and Information Studies and Human Resource Utilization: A Statement of Policy," January 23, 2002, accessed May 21, 2015, http://www.ala.org/educationcareers/sites/ala.org.educationcareers/files/content/careers/paths/policy/lepu.pdf.
8. Ibid., paragraph 15.
9. Ibid., paragraph 8.
10. Ibid.
11. Ibid., paragraph 28.
12. John Anthony McCrossan, "Library Service Education and Its Relationship to Competence in Adult Book Selection in Public Libraries" (PhD diss., University of Illinois, 1966).

13. Charles Albert Bunge, "Professional Education and Reference Efficiency" (PhD diss., University of Illinois, 1967).
14. Lucille Mathena Wert, "Library Education and High School Library Services" (PhD diss., University of Illinois, 1970).
15. Gordon Stuart Baillie, "An Investigation of Objective Admission Variables as They Relate to Academic and Job Success in One Graduate Library Education Program" (PhD diss., Washington University in St. Louis, 1961).

RESOURCES

American Library Association—Directory of ALA-Accredited and Candidate Programs in Library and Information Studies. http://www.ala.org/accredited programs/directory.

American Library Association Allied Professional Association—Certification. http://ala-apa.org/certification-news/.

Olin and Uris Libraries of Cornell University Library. Library Vocabulary: Common Terms Defined. https://olinuris.library.cornell.edu/ref/research/vocab .html.

Pew Research Center Internet Science and Tech—Libraries. http://www.pew internet.org/topics/libraries/.

Reitz, Joan M. *ODLIS: Online Dictionary of Library and Information Science.* Westport, CT: Libraries Unlimited, 2004. Also see http://www.abc-clio .com/ODLIS/odlis_A.aspx.

Chapter 2

A Brief History of Libraries

The story of libraries begins with the history of the written record. The oral tradition, which relied on the memorization of history, legends, and folklore, was the earliest form of preserving and transmitting data among people. As humans developed methods of recording data on cave walls, stones, tree bark, and in other formats, the era of written communication began. Whether using pictures, symbols, letters, or language to express themselves, humans made the transition from human memory as the predominant storage device to the written record some 5,000 years ago. With the 21st century has come an era in which most data are increasingly recorded in sophisticated electronic formats. In addition to storing data, the computer also gives us amazing means for composing, transmitting, publishing, and manipulating information.

With the accumulation of written records—whether clay tablets, papyrus rolls, parchment leaves, paper, and now digital format—arose the need to store, preserve, and access them.

THE ANCIENT WORLD

By surveying some of the major inventions, institutions, and technologies of ancient civilizations, one can glimpse the issues that surrounded the development of early libraries. In addition, it is insightful to think about certain common information needs that historians have identified that helped drive the collecting of written materials, then and now. These information needs fall into the following broad categories: government records, religious records, business records, and household records. Tax receipts, property ownership, laws of the land, military intelligence and campaigns, and population censuses are typical examples of government data. Sacred laws, songs and rituals, creation stories, and legends of gods and goddesses typify vital religious records. Successful commerce depends on sales records, accounts, inventories of goods, employee records and salaries, trade routes and explorations, inventions, formulas, and trade secrets. Individual families collect and pass on their genealogical and marriage information, land and property records, personal correspondence, culinary information and recipes, family legends, history, and literature.

The Middle East

The oldest form of writing that survives today is known as cuneiform. This significant contribution to civilization was developed in the Middle East by the ancient Sumerians. They occupied an area once called the Fertile Crescent, a valley bounded by the Tigris and Euphrates Rivers, now within the present-day country of Iraq. Very little stone or wood was available for building in the arid environment, so the Sumerians fashioned houses and structures out of native clay and sticks. Around 3300 B.C., the Sumerians began using a sharpened reed called a stylus to make wedge-shaped marks in damp clay to keep track of grain supplies and other agricultural products. The clay tablets were then dried and baked, leaving a permanent and durable written record.

Contemporary scientists continue to uncover buried collections of these cuneiform tablets.[1] In 1987, archaeologists unearthed a cache of more than 1,000 clay tablets, dating back to about 1740 B.C., that inventoried the royal wine supply, tracked the deployment of spies in warfare, calculated taxes, and contained correspondence between regional kings.[2] Not surprisingly, all of these topics are still vital to humans today.

Throughout the Middle East, libraries arose by about 2700 B.C. to house the tablets of the Sumerians, as well as those of later civilizations, such as the Babylonians and Assyrians. Historians have evidence of significant official libraries at Telloh (southern Iraq) and Nineveh (northern Iraq), each with thousands of clay tablets.

The Ancient Egyptians

At about the same time the Sumerians and others were creating records on clay tablets, in a different part of the ancient world, the Egyptians were making use of the native papyrus plant to develop their writing medium. Sheets of the beaten and pressed central pith of the plant were joined to make long and fragile scrolls. Although easily damaged by dampness or torn because of its brittleness when dry, papyrus paper was economical to produce and easily transported. With a brush-like reed pen, Egyptians recorded information in a hieroglyphic-style of writing. For more than 4,000 years, papyrus remained the standard writing medium in Egypt and along the Mediterranean shore. Use of papyrus continued until about A.D. 300 in parts of Europe and as late as A.D. 1022 in Egypt.[3]

A few papyrus scroll fragments are held at La Bibliothèque Nationale de France in Paris, the Beinecke Rare Book and Manuscript Library at Yale University, and other major museums. Unlike collections of clay tablets, libraries of papyrus scrolls have long disappeared, and the descriptions of their existence are based on second-hand accounts.

Thus, historians know that by about 2500 B.C., large governmental libraries of papyrus scrolls existed, including one at Gizeh near the great pyramids. By 1250 B.C., ruler Ramses II had developed an extensive library at Thebes, an ancient Egyptian capital, that stored rolls of papyrus in clay jars with keywords visible on the end of each scroll to denote the content.

The Greeks

As with many aspects of European civilization, libraries and knowledge reached a pinnacle during the time of the ancient Greeks. Socrates, Sophocles, and Herodotus, great writers and thinkers, were just a few of the scholars active during the period known as the Golden Age (fifth century B.C.).

The noted playwright and scholar Aristotle had one of the great private libraries of the ancient world housed at his school, the Lyceum. His collection was coveted and changed hands many times after his death. Governmental and royal libraries were commonplace throughout the Greek world.

Among the great cultural accomplishments of the Greeks was the founding of the ancient library in Alexandria, Egypt, by Ptolemy I, circa 300 B.C. Part of a large scholarly facility, the library's purpose was to collect every book in the world and translate them into Greek to help the expanding empire better understand the cultures they ruled. The Alexandrian library flourished for approximately 600 years, and was by all accounts the greatest, richest library of the ancient world, with an estimated 700,000 papyrus scrolls.

This academic community functioned like a university, with noted scholars, librarians, and historians being responsible for inventions such as the first encyclopedia and dictionary and the use of alphabetization as an ordering system.[4]

Scribes went to great lengths to copy everything in order to enlarge the Greeks' knowledge and power base. No trace of the fabled library remains today. There are differing opinions among historians as to the degree of destruction sustained by the facility at the time of the Roman conquest in the fourth century A.D.

Today, Egyptian officials and the United Nations Educational, Scientific, and Cultural Organization (UNESCO) have partnered in an ambitious new learning center at the old library site. The new Library of Alexandria emulates its famous ancient namesake by embodying its core concepts and by "reinventing the library and restoring its role as an institute of learning, culture and intellectual interaction," according to Dr. Sohair F. Wastawy, the chief librarian. The new Alexandrian library facility will include multiple specialized libraries, three museums, a planetarium, a children's exploratorium, art galleries, a conference center, and eight research institutes—in addition to being a book repository of over a million volumes.

The Bibliotheca Alexandrina also strives to be a place of dialogue, learning, and understanding between cultures and peoples, thus recapturing the spirit of the ancient library.[5]

In use by both the Greeks and the Romans by the second century A.D. was the codex, a forerunner of the book as we know it today. This storage format used parchment (i.e., sheep's skin) or vellum (i.e., calf's skin) rather than papyrus. Both sides of the parchment could be written upon, and the individual parchment leaves bound or fastened together, forming pages that could be opened flat and read in sequence. The codex represented a more convenient format for both writing and reading.

Although both papyrus and parchment were used in various places throughout the ancient world for centuries, the eventual displacement of papyrus as the standard writing medium was fueled by a rivalry. As Alexandria was accumulating volumes and copies of documents, so was the library in Pergamum. Another important center of scholarship, the Greek kingdom of Pergamum was located in present-day Turkey and was founded in the second century B.C. Not to be outdone by a competitor, Egypt placed an embargo on the export of the native papyrus, thus preventing Pergamum from obtaining the needed writing medium. Cutting off the supply of papyrus only led the scholars in Pergamum to improve parchment and to rely on it as their main writing material. By the waning of the western Roman Empire in 476 A.D., the parchment codex had become the predominant form of the book, replacing the papyrus roll.

The Romans

As the Roman civilization flourished from 650 B.C. to 476 A.D., it was greatly influenced by the Greeks and continued that society's emphasis on learning and literature, science, mathematics, and technology. Throughout the expansion of the Roman Empire, libraries were considered important spoils of war, and Roman army leaders routinely pillaged the contents from collections in fallen cities.

The library as an institution for the general public was a new concept that emerged from the golden days of the Roman Empire. Enumerated on a census of noteworthy buildings in Rome circa 40 B.C. was the first public library, which was based on the private collection of a wealthy donor.[6] Almost 400 years later, the number of libraries increased to 28. Library facilities were part of the Romans' extensive municipal building program, with reading rooms in the lavish public baths.[7] As such, libraries were available to all literate people, whether slaves or free, not exclusively a resource for the wealthy and privileged.

Asia

Although histories of libraries often focus on the evolution of technologies in Europe, many innovations took place even earlier in Asian civilizations. During the time of the creative Han Dynasty, paper was invented (105 A.D.), some 1,000 years before its introduction to European countries.

Wooden block printing was in use throughout Eastern Asia about 700 years before the German Johann Gutenberg was credited with the invention of movable type printing in 1456. First used in China, block printing then spread to neighboring Korea and Japan and became a standard for several hundred years. Baked clay blocks were used from A.D. 1045 in China, and in A.D. 1403 printing with movable metal type was invented in Korea.

The appearance of pictographic writing on bone and other natural materials dates from the Shang period, 1766–1122 B.C., sometime after the advent of the

Sumerian cuneiform. This early Chinese script persisted and formed the basis for modern written Chinese.

Mexico

Although little information survives about whether written works were gathered and organized in libraries in what is now Mexico, a vast array of literature existed in the New World before the arrival of the Spanish. Unfortunately, most of the evidence of these writings soon disappeared "owing to the diligence of church and government officials who rooted out any manifestations of this visible symbol of 'paganism'."[8] The Franciscan bishop Diego de Landa—known for both his detailed accounts of Mayan life in the 1500s and his destruction of their writings—described some of that destruction and the Indian reaction: "We found a large number of books in these characters and, as they contained nothing in which there were not to be seen superstition and lies of the devil, we burned them all, which they regretted to an amazing degree, and which caused them much affliction."[9] Among the few surviving specimens shipped to Europe by early colonists, three survive today. The information in these books was recorded by painting glyphs (pictographs) on paper made from the bark of fig trees.

Fragments of a variety of forms of recorded information have survived and their content indicates that many of the pre-Colombian Indians had a high degree of culture. These include myths, hymns, poetry, drama, history, and other forms of expression. Carbon-dating tests have established that by 600 B.C., sophisticated writing and calendar systems existed. In fact, the Mayan calendar of that era was so accurate that it appeared to have evolved over a long period of time.

LIBRARIES IN THE WESTERN WORLD

Middle Ages

With the decline and subsequent collapse of the western Roman Empire in 476 A.D., that portion of Europe entered a dark period between A.D. 500 and A.D. 1000, when libraries, learning, and scholarship slumbered. Although many Roman libraries were sacked in the fall of the Empire, some collections had earlier been moved east to Byzantium (present-day Turkey) when Emperor Constantine relocated the capital of the empire there and continued the library tradition of the Greeks and Romans. Thus, it is believed that part of Aristotle's renowned private collection survived the fall.

Meanwhile, a continuous stream of barbarians seeking land and resources invaded Western Europe. During the upheaval of the early Middle Ages, Christian monasteries were the main protectors of books, culture, and education in the region. In addition, with the spread of the Muslim empire into Europe, Islamic libraries in Spain, Sicily, and North Africa arose where Christian works were copied and translated into Arabic. In the Middle East, grand Islamic libraries were founded by the caliph al-Ma'mun in Baghdad in the ninth century and by the caliph al-Mustansir in 11th-century Cairo.

In the Christian monasteries of continental Europe, Ireland, England, parts of Asia, and Northern Africa, scribes toiled in their copy rooms or scriptoriums, laboriously hand copying any written document made available to them, whether secular or religious in nature. Because of the labor-intensive effort in producing additional copies of each text, books were very valuable and were literally chained to the shelves. Libraries in the monasteries contained literature on parchment scrolls and codexes. The great works of antiquity—the Bible, Homer's writings, Greek plays, and Roman law—were preserved for humanity through the dedicated copying efforts of the monastic centers.

Additionally, in the late-eighth century during what became known as the Carolingian Renaissance, a culture of learning flourished under Charlemagne, king of the Franks. At his palace in Aachen (present-day Germany), the ruler established a court library and allowed these books to be copied in order to share their contents with other fledgling libraries, thus helping to keep learning alive during this era.

FIGURE 2.1 During Europe's dark ages, the task of preserving written works fell to the scribes in monasteries. Reprinted by permission of Dover Pictorial Archives, Mineola, New York, from *Ready-to-Use Old-Fashioned Illustrations of Books, Reading, and Writing.* Selected by Carol Belanger Grafton. ©1992 Dover Publications.

An especially beautiful art form that flourished primarily in Western Europe from the Middle Ages and into the early Renaissance (about 500–1500 A.D.) was the illuminated manuscript. It combined the hand copying of text (usually religious) with colorful miniature painting. Manuscripts were artfully decorated within the text as well as along the borders and margins with gold and silver paint and vividly colored inks made from lapis, cinnabar, and other sources.

There are many surviving examples available on display for public viewing, including the renowned Book of Kells (ca. 800 A.D.) at the Trinity College Library, Dublin, and the large collection of illuminated manuscripts at the Getty Museum in Los Angeles. (See Resources section at the end of this chapter.)

Early Renaissance

Monasteries remained the primary centers of learning and study until the rise of the modern universities, which began during the 12th century. The Crusades had brought the West in touch with ideas and literature from Asia, and increasing economic stability led to a revival of interest in education.

Among the early universities were those in Bologna, Oxford, Cambridge, and Paris—still major institutions of learning today. Book dealers and professional scribes arose to provide an important service to the urban university community; no longer was the lone monk in his monastic setting the primary copyist of knowledge. In addition to the scribes, lay craftsmen included parchment makers, illuminators, and binders.

To meet the demand for textbooks, authorized texts were copied and then rented to the students. Eventually, the number of students increased, and libraries were formed, with each college of the university maintaining a separate collection to support its scholars.

By the 14th century, the Renaissance, or the rebirth of learning and the classical influences, was stirring in Italy. This marked the emergence of Western Europe from the Middle Ages into a period of incredible discovery, artistic brilliance, technological inventions, and cultural development. With the renewed emphasis on learning, art, and study, the demand for books—books written not only in the scripts of the clergy (which was mostly in Latin) but also in the vernacular languages of the people, such as Italian, French, and German—was great.

Ownership of books was a mark of status, and the ownership of personal libraries among wealthy individuals expanded during this period. But the multiplication of manuscripts by hand copying was too inefficient and unable to keep up with the burgeoning demand. With the fertile climate of the Renaissance as a backdrop, the introduction of a new technology for more easily producing books was imminent and would revolutionize the world.

The Invention of Movable Type

As with many major inventions, several parties were hard at work perfecting the movable type printing press, but Johann Gutenberg of Mainz, Germany, is credited as the first European printer to use the new technology. This was not the birth of the art of printing—wooden blocks and other molds had been used in China since the ninth century. Paper was discovered by the Chinese by A.D. 105 or earlier, eventually making its way to Europe, where it was readily available by the mid-15th century. The convergence of cheap paper and the invention of the printing press combined to make Gutenberg's technology revolutionary.

The Gutenberg Bible, also known as the 42-line Bible or Mazarin Bible, was the first Western full-length book produced using movable metal typeface. Historical evidence suggests that 180 copies of the work were produced around the year 1455. Large, handsomely illustrated, and written in Latin, the Bibles were hand-finished with colorful illumination and underlining. Extant copies of the rare Bibles are held today by the Library of Congress, La Bibliothèque Nationale, the National Library of Scotland, The Huntington Library, and other major research facilities, as well as in private collections.

The significance of Gutenberg's invention was that the mass printing of documents, broadsides, and books became much faster, cheaper, and more accurate. Compared to the previous method for the multiplication of books—laborious and error-prone hand copying—the printing press was an incredible advancement. With this new technique, printers were able to produce a wider variety of reading material, including texts, romances, poetry, travel books, histories, and religious works, for a general audience.

Early examples of books printed after the seminal Gutenberg Bible and up until 1501 are referred to as *incunabula*. In our era, an early leader in the Internet publishing of freely accessible, full text of classic works found in the public domain was appropriately titled Project Gutenberg as a tribute to the innovative European printer. (See Resources section at the end of this chapter for the website address.)

Post-Renaissance Europe

During the 1600s and 1700s, libraries and literacy thrived, with a diverse array of facilities being established or expanded. Great university libraries continued to grow throughout Europe, as did the leading national libraries, such as France's La Bibliothèque Nationale, the British Library, Germany's state library in Berlin, and Catherine the Great's state library in Leningrad. Earlier collections, such as the incredible Vatican Library of the Roman Catholic Church developed during the 15th century, were joined by flourishing Italian state and private libraries. Periodicals and newspapers appeared during this time.

City and town libraries were popular throughout Germany during the 18th and 19th centuries. In the United Kingdom, circulating libraries began to show up in the 1740s, and by the 1780s were important institutions that provided the middle class access to popular reading materials, particularly novels. Another variation on an early type of library, a circulating library was also known as a rental library or lending library. The *Bookman's Glossary* defines such a library as a "collection of books, usually current fiction, for lending at a rental fee for a stated period."[10] Unlike a subscription library—which demanded the outlay of a more substantial membership fee—circulating libraries were more affordable since one could pay a small fee for the loan of just a single item.

In addition, the concept of locally supported libraries had also been evolving in Britain; a much cited early example is the town library in Manchester. Merchant Humphrey Chetham left money in his will to establish this facility in 1653. Both the "pay-to-use" circulating library and the Manchester town model bolstered the cultural foundation for free, public libraries and led to England's instituting the Public Libraries Act in 1850.

NORTH AMERICAN LIBRARIES

Books were highly cherished possessions brought by the first settlers from their homelands to the New World. During the early decades of the colonies, these private book collections were a mark of intelligence and property. Because few printers existed in America, anyone desiring to obtain a book had to purchase it from England. Today, genealogists and other researchers perusing historical insurance policies and estate inventories often note the estimated worth of book collections listed alongside the house, livestock, silverware, china, piano, and other valuables.

The largest private holdings in the colonies formed the nuclei for what would become the fledgling academic libraries at Harvard, Yale, and Princeton. In addition, lending libraries were common among church ministers during the 1600s and 1700s. The Reverend Thomas Bray, an Anglican clergyman, was instrumental in establishing early parochial libraries as he recruited ministers to promote the Church of England in the New World. In 1696, he began his work in the Colony of Maryland, requiring his new clergy to establish libraries for their own education and use; these, in fact, grew to some 30 small libraries throughout the American colonies.[11] Although Bray only visited the colonies for a few months, his efforts on behalf of parish libraries there were sustained.

Early College Libraries

Today, academic libraries pride themselves on their student-centered policies and learning resources, with extended operating hours, computer labs, special collections, and 24/7 remote access to electronic holdings—all considered basic library services. Such offerings are in stark contrast to the limited services found in early American colonial colleges.

Harvard was the site of the earliest college library. It was established in 1638 when clergyman John Harvard donated his theological book collection of about 400 volumes to the young school.[12]

This was typical of most colonial college libraries, which were established with the donation a private collection of books by the libraries' founders or supporters. However, these cherished volumes were hardly available to the toiling students, because college libraries were open only an hour or two a day at best and the books were chained to tables and shelves in poorly lit, cold buildings. Preservation, accumulation, and storage of books, not service to students, were the primary tasks of the academic library. That philosophy did not change much until 1877, when Boston Public Library administrator Justin Winsor became head of Harvard University Library. He brought with him a new philosophy that caused academic libraries to shift to a more customer-service orientation, offering expanded hours, reserve collections, open stacks, and early interlibrary loaning.

Subscription Libraries

Benjamin Franklin—printer, scholar, diplomat, and inventor—at 25 years of age was responsible for starting up one of the first American subscription libraries. Precursors to the concept of the community-funded public library, subscription or social libraries were similar to clubs. In the case of the Library Company of Philadelphia, Franklin gathered together 50 men who shared with him an interest in obtaining significant books on history, political science, agriculture, and other topics of interest. With an initial contribution of 40 shillings each, to be followed by 10 shillings annually, the association was formed in 1731 as an effort to provide a resource for the self-education of its members.

Books were purchased with the collected dues, and members then borrowed the titles at no charge; the association retained ownership of the books. The concept of forming subscription libraries was a popular one until the mid-1800s. Many different types of readers founded such library associations. Women's groups often formed general reading libraries. Merchants and clerks formed mercantile libraries, and tradesmen and apprentices formed mechanics' institute libraries.

Today, serious researchers can study the fine collection of 17th-, 18th-, and 19th-century volumes and manuscripts that are housed in the Library Company of Philadelphia's special collection. The Mechanics' Institute of San Francisco, formed in 1854 as an early subscription library in the gold rush days, and the Charleston Library Society (South Carolina), begun about 1748, are also both examples of extant membership libraries.

National Libraries Established

By 1800, leaders of the new nation realized the need for a designated library collection in the capital to serve their information needs. Thus, the Library of Congress—now the largest library in the world with more than 160 million items—came into being with a start-up budget of $5,000.[13] During the War of 1812, the British burned Washington, DC, and the fledgling legislative collection of 3,000 tomes was destroyed. In 1815, former president Thomas Jefferson sold his private collection—then one of the largest personal collections in the nation—of 6,487 books to Congress for $23,940 as a nucleus from which to rebuild the collection.[14] Housed for many years inside the Capitol building, the Library of Congress moved into its first permanent building, The Thomas Jefferson Building, in 1897.

Figure 2.2 shows the Library of Congress, Jefferson Building. In rebuilding the library around Jefferson's volumes, the Library of Congress also adopted his classification system for the collection, which formed the basis for the first Library of Congress classification scheme. Figure 2.3 shows the modern-day Library of Congress Web page.

At the bequest of British scientist James Smithson, the Smithsonian Institution was founded in 1846 to serve the United States as a scholarly institution. Soon to be included in the research facility were art galleries, lecture halls, and a library. Charles Coffin Jewett, then librarian at Brown University, was hired as librarian of the Smithsonian Institution. As part of his start-up efforts, he advocated the concept of centralized cataloging and conducted a census of libraries. His census count, though probably conservative, indicated that there were 10,015 libraries in the United States in 1850.[15]

FIGURE 2.2 Library of Congress, Jefferson Building. Courtesy Library of Congress.

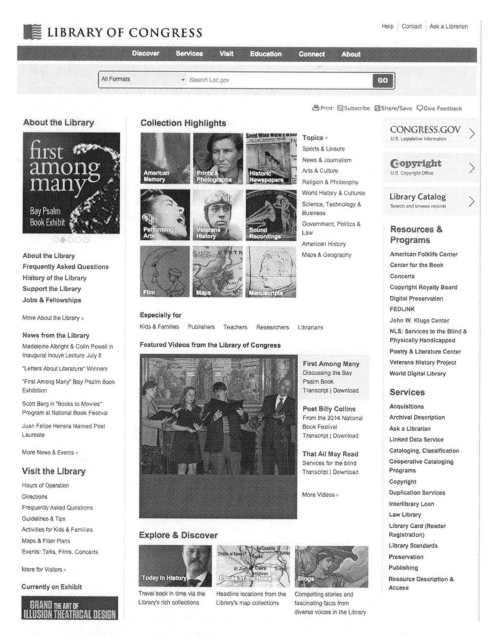

FIGURE 2.3 The Library of Congress provides access to digital collections and to a wealth of information through its website. Courtesy Library of Congress.

Earliest Public Libraries

While New England is credited as the birthplace of public libraries within the new American nation, Charles Town (now Charleston), South Carolina, was the site of one of the earliest public libraries in the American colonies. As a wealthy and cultured regional center surrounded by successful cotton, rice, and indigo plantations, this fourth largest city in the colonies organized a free public library in 1698 by a legislative act.[16]

As the young nation grew, two important events that occurred in New England during the early decades of the 19th century provide evidence of the grassroots momentum that was building in support of public education and for free public libraries. In 1803, educator and bookseller Caleb Bingham established a free library for local youths in his hometown of Salisbury, Connecticut, in an attempt to provide enrichment opportunities and improve the use of the youths' leisure time. After his initial donation of books, the municipality voted to provide some ongoing funds for the purchase of more titles. Then, 30 years later in Peterborough, New Hampshire, the first free, tax-supported public library was established by a vote of the citizens.

Eventually, with Massachusetts leading the way, each state passed its own version of legislation giving cities and other jurisdictions legal authority to collect taxes for library support.

Melvil Dewey

The single most significant contributor to the development of library science in the 19th century, arguably, was Melvil Dewey. A leader and innovator in the emerging profession, Dewey initiated many tools that are still viable today. Most famous for devising his library organizational scheme known as the Dewey Decimal Classification, he also co-founded—along with publishers Frederick Leypoldt and R. R. Bowker—the first periodical devoted to the library field, *Library Journal.* In 1876, he helped establish the American Library Association (ALA), which today is among the oldest and largest library industry associations and well known for its strong advocacy efforts and its resources for members, librarians, staff, and library users. Dewey also started the Library Bureau, a specialized library supply and furnishings company still in existence today.

Dewey's decimal system, which divided human knowledge into 10 main groupings, tackled the major problem of organizing the works that libraries had been accumulating over the centuries, and it remains the standard in K-12 schools and public libraries. Realizing the importance of education for the field, Dewey established the School of Library Economy while serving as librarian at Columbia University in 1887. This program was the first organized training curriculum for library workers in the United States.

Dewey encouraged women to enter the fledgling profession at a time when many of his colleagues opposed women's entry into the field. Efficiency, organization, and time management were his mantras. As a child, he allegedly found delight in arranging the contents of his mother's pantry.[17] Along with Teddy Roosevelt and Andrew Carnegie, he was a proponent of the failed phonetic, reformed spelling movement.

Dewey's life was not without controversy. He was accused of sexual improprieties against young women at an ALA outing and of financial irregularities involving several business ventures. His fervor for new ideas coupled with his sometimes questionable personal behavior resulted in his resignations from library positions during his career.

Despite his faults, Dewey had a major impact on American librarianship with his standardization of library systems and staff education. In addition, he showed great foresight in advocating active library promotion, the consideration of user needs, and the development of new outreach services. The previous passive role of libraries merely warehousing books was insufficient.

John Cotton Dana

Another leader in these formative years of the library profession was a man of many talents, John Cotton Dana. Dana's 44-year career bridged the end of the 19th century and the beginning of the 20th century. Today, he is best known for his advocacy of library promotion. His name graces the annual public relations award jointly sponsored by the H.W. Wilson Foundation, EBSCO and the American Library Association. During his nearly half century in the field, Dana pioneered many other new ideas, including separate children's departments, open stacks (where patrons could help themselves to books), and the use of displays.[18] He also founded the Special Libraries Association in 1909 and established a separate business collection at the Newark Public Library during his tenure as its director, and he collected foreign language materials for the large local immigrant population. Though these seem like standard services today, at the time they were very innovative ideas. A prolific writer, Dana wrote many essays that have been reprinted and still make for thoughtful reading today.[19]

Era of Philanthropy

By the last quarter of the 19th century, American libraries and librarianship were gaining momentum and acceptance. The Boston Public Library, often considered the institution that launched the modern library movement in the United States, opened in 1854. During the 1860s and 1870s, many major cities, including San Francisco, Detroit, Cleveland, and Chicago followed Boston's lead in opening their own public libraries. Dewey's many ideas were taking root, and tangible support for the institutions came in the form of contributions from wealthy philanthropists.

In 1882, wealthy Baltimore merchant Enoch Pratt provided land, a new library building, and $833,000 for library development. A condition of the bequest was that the city set up a $50,000 endowment fund to generate income for annual operating costs and to build four branch facilities. In gratitude, the city named their system the Enoch Pratt Free Library of Baltimore.[20]

Phoebe Apperson Hearst, widow of the senator and mining magnate George Hearst and mother of publisher William Randolph Hearst, selected a variety of educational causes to support, among them early kindergartens, the Parent-Teacher Association (PTA), the University of California, and libraries. At the turn of the century, she outfitted free public libraries to serve miners and their families in the mining communities of her late husband's big strikes in Lead,

South Dakota, and Anaconda, Montana. The Hearst Free Library in Lead was unveiled to the residents as a Christmas gift in 1894, and came fully stocked with materials in English and in foreign languages to serve the many immigrant workers.[21] In addition, Hearst supported the founding of various local subscription libraries in areas where she lived.[22]

Andrew Carnegie

To date, the greatest philanthropist to libraries has been Scottish-born steel millionaire Andrew Carnegie. Born in 1835, Carnegie was the son of a handloom weaver. As the weaving trade became mechanized, his family followed relatives and emigrated to the United States in 1848, searching for improved economic opportunity. They settled in Allegheny, Pennsylvania, near Pittsburgh, where 13-year-old Andrew went to work as a bobbin boy and studied at night. Andrew worked a string of increasingly more responsible jobs, with the young man eventually working for the Pennsylvania Railroad. Shrewd investments in the Pullman sleeping car made him wealthy and were followed by further investments in railroad bridges, iron mills, and oil fields. By the 1870s, the demand for steel to expand the country's infrastructure was high, so Carnegie formed the Carnegie Steel Company. Immensely successful by 1901—when he sold his steel firm for a profit of $40 million—Carnegie was dubbed the richest man in the world. Known as a hard, aggressive businessman among his former partners, he was a controversial figure and very unpopular among labor and trade unions due to his labor policies.

From his own rags-to-riches success story, Carnegie valued the notion of self-improvement and lifelong learning. He also had a theory of philanthropy, which he detailed in essays published in 1889. In Carnegie's "Gospel of Wealth," he speaks of the moral obligation of the rich to distribute their wealth for benevolent purposes.[23] Among his many philanthropic projects were providing funding for public gardens in Scotland and pipe organs for churches, erecting Carnegie Hall and several museums, and creating educational endowments. But Carnegie's richest legacy is his library construction program.

Beginning in 1881, through the Carnegie Corporation, Andrew Carnegie gave more than $56 million for the construction of over 2,500 public library buildings in the English-speaking world.[24] Starting with his birthplace, Dunfermline, Scotland, Carnegie launched a unique effort to help communities construct public libraries. The first city in the United States to benefit from his philanthropy was his adopted hometown, Allegheny City, Pennsylvania. In 1886, the town accepted his offer of $250,000 to build a new facility on the condition that it would be municipally supported. The Carnegie Free Library became the model for the many publicly funded libraries to follow from his construction program.

More than $41 million was distributed to American libraries, both urban and rural, over a 32-year period. By the conclusion of the Carnegie grant program in 1917, communities in nearly every state had received grants for a grand total of 1,679 individual library buildings.[25] Figures 2.4, 2.5, 2.6, and 2.7 are photographs of four Carnegie libraries built in California. Note the ornate architectural styles that are commonly seen in the Carnegie libraries.

FIGURE 2.4 Carnegie Library in Willets, California. Reprinted by permission of Jane A. Kimball.

FIGURE 2.5 Carnegie Library in Gilroy, California. Reprinted by permission of Jane A. Kimball.

FIGURE 2.6 Carnegie Library in Monterey, California. Reprinted by permission of Jane A. Kimball.

FIGURE 2.7 Carnegie Library in Petaluma, California. Reprinted by permission of Jane A. Kimball.

Impact of Carnegie's Program

Carnegie's unique program had a lasting impact on American communities. Until this time, early free public libraries were limited primarily to larger, urban areas. Many communities had subscription libraries but not tax-supported resources. Because of Carnegie's largess, within a couple of decades public libraries for smaller communities became commonplace in the United States. In addition to the educational resources the libraries provided to residents, the surviving edifices themselves are often extraordinary examples of American architecture at the beginning of the 20th century.

In supporting individual communities, Carnegie was attempting to stimulate the movement for more free public libraries. Carnegie's donation to a town was the building only, and formed a cooperative venture with the city that would then need to stock the building with books, staff it, and provide ongoing fiscal support. Carnegie's grants ranged from $5.2 million for the city of New York to $3,000 for smaller, rural towns.

An application process was required for candidate towns requesting a Carnegie library grant. Requirements were that the city not already have a permanent library building, that they had to provide the site on which to build the new library, and that they had to pledge to annually pay an amount equal to 10 percent of Carnegie's gift for upkeep of the facility.

A grand total of 1,412 American cities received Carnegie library building funds.

Today, many areas have outgrown their small, historic Carnegie buildings. As new library facilities are constructed, some, such as Newberg Public Library, south of Portland, Oregon, cleverly find ways to incorporate the original facade into an otherwise modern-day building. Another trend is for the turn-of-the century Carnegie buildings to be converted to new community buildings, such as local history museums, art galleries, city halls, or chamber of commerce offices. Figure 2.8 shows how a community proudly announced its Carnegie library grant.

The 20th Century

Special Populations

Library services for special populations, including children, the visually impaired, rural citizens, and new immigrants, began to develop in the 20th century. Children's departments first appeared in urban public libraries in the 1890s and became a mainstay in the 20th century. The Library of Congress's National Library Services for the Blind and Physically Handicapped (1931) and Braille Institute collections (1934) were originally developed to provide reading materials solely for the blind and visually disabled population; they have since expanded their scope to include people with other disabilities.

Washington County Free Library in Maryland operated the first traveling library service to rural citizens with the advent of its bookmobile wagon in 1905; similar services developed in rural areas throughout the United States.[26] City

CONTRACT FOR CONSTRUCTION OF CARNEGIE LIBRARY IS LET.

Stevens & Maino of This City Take the Job at $8,900---Building to be Done Within 120 Days--Materials Are the Very Best.

The Library Trustees met yesterday according to advertisement and opened bids on the proposition to build a new public library building. The lowest bidders were found to be Stevens & Maino of this city, and the contract was let to them at the price of $8,900. The contractors have 120 days from today to complete the work and it is expected that the building will be occupied by the first of the year.

The library trustees have worked very hard and feel that they have accomplished the most that was possible with the $10,000 donation of Andrew Carnegie. The contract as let does not include electric lighting and some other items which it is expected the balance of the money will provide.

The building will be of one story on a basement of Bishop's Peak blue granite laid in pitch face random rubble. The superstructure will be of the finest stock brick trimmed in Caen stone from the Los Berros quarries. The roof will be of the finest black slate, and the specifications call for the very best material.

The library is thoroughly up-to-date in every particular and will be a perfect institution as near as can be built at the present time. Convenience, utility, light and ventilation are the things which the trustees have kept especially in mind and believe they have incorporated in this structure.

Unless they should be disposed of the stacks, shelving, tables chairs, etc., of the old library will be used in the new building. The library has paid in advance a nine year lease on the present quarters which has not as yet been disposed of. This of course can be made a source of considerable revenue to the new library.

The contract for the new building was signed yesterday and the work will be commenced breaking ground on the site at the northwest corner of north Broad and Monterey streets as soon as the contractors can get their preliminary arrangements made.

FIGURE 2.8 The construction of a Carnegie library was often headline news in communities that were awarded a grant. From the San Luis Obispo, California, *Morning Tribune*, July 7, 1904.

libraries responded to the wave of immigrants in the early decades of the 20th century by providing magazines and book collections in foreign languages.

Nonstop New Technologies

Movable-type printing was the dominant method of printing for 400 years. A major improvement came with the invention of linotype, or machine movable printing, in 1884. Today, the revolution of digital publishing is continually transforming the authoring, dissemination, and access to information as we have known it previously. The venerable printed book is facing serious competition as the dominant format in distributing the written word. However, for many purposes it remains the most cost-effective method for distributing information content.

Microform technology became commonly used in libraries just before World War II. Prior to the advent of electronic information storage, microforms were hailed as the solution to the never-ending library space dilemma. Today, microfiche and microfilm are still in limited use for the archival preservation of large periodical back files and other historical materials, especially those with low usage levels. See Chapter 5, Preparing Materials for Use, for a more detailed discussion of current developments in the area of microform use and digitization.

The Library of Congress developed the MAchine Readable Cataloging (MARC) record in 1966, which became the world's standard format for the communication of bibliographic information between libraries via computer. With the establishment of the MARC standard, computer use and cooperation among libraries has grown tremendously. Most early computer use in libraries was for circulation systems or inventories, in-house functions such as database building and word processing, and union catalogs or cooperative bibliographic databases of library holdings.

Online Computer Library Center (OCLC) has been and remains one of the largest databases of shared library cataloging records and holdings data, with some 17,000 member libraries from around the globe as of 2014.[27] Total holdings records in its WorldCat database—the OCLC "union catalog" or collective catalog—numbered over 2 billion in 2015.[28] Originally founded in 1967, OCLC was then the acronym for the Ohio College Library Center, but now stands for Online Computer Library Center.

Computers and libraries make for a natural match, as libraries have large amounts of data that need to be stored, sorted, retrieved, viewed, printed, and shared. The first generation of automated library catalogs showed up in academic facilities in the 1970s. By the 1990s, most American libraries had automated *online public access catalogs* (OPACs). And according to respected library automation observer, Marshall Breeding, in his "Automation Marketplace 2012" reporting there were few remaining libraries by then who had yet to automate for the very first time.[29] Those exceptions tended to be school libraries (both public and private) and small special libraries (church, museum, historical society) specifically due to limited funding, geographical isolation, lack of participation in any consortium or network, and other issues. In contrast to minority, most libraries are currently focused on major enhancements and upgrades of their platforms to the next phase of technology with strong emphasis on discovery services and mobile applications.

In the early 1990s, another significant technical advance was realized. Although *hypertext markup language* (HTML) was first invented by British scientist Tim Berners Lee in 1989, it wasn't until 1993 that the phenomenon known as the Web fully impacted academic and technical users. The World Wide Web (WWW) revolution exploded, with commercial and consumer use swelling. Wider acceptance and myriad applications continued to emerge through the end of the 1990s. Surveys conducted by the College of Information, Florida State University, found that in 1994 only 20.9 percent of public libraries were connected to the Internet, but a decade later, that figure had risen to include 99.6 percent of all public library outlets.[30]

The use of computers is now pervasive in all library operations and tasks, with the online ordering of materials, full-text and full image retrieval of periodicals, Web-based OPACs, e-books, and online job applications just a small sampling of the automated functions in widespread use, in addition to familiar cataloging and circulation routines.

Increasingly sophisticated innovations that have impacted libraries have included Amazon's "Look Inside the Book" feature, Google Scholar, Google Books, and social networking sites such as Facebook, Flickr, Goodreads, with others emerging on a regular basis. According to Internet World Stats, as of June 2014, over 3 billion users worldwide were connected to the Internet.[31] With its cross-platform environment, speed, ease of use, and 24/7 global access (often free or nearly free), the Web presented amazing advantages for turn-of-the-20th-century information seekers that paralleled the changes brought to 15th-century Europe by the invention of the movable-type printing press.

For libraries, Web technology has had an enormous impact on customers' expectations for overall service and for libraries to provide access to current technology. This has resulted in an increased need for patron instruction and has greatly transformed many internal operations, such as materials ordering, interlibrary loan, and document delivery. In addition, the rapid pace of changes brought about by Web publishing of information has necessitated continued re-evaluation of print collections and the ongoing retraining of staff.

Still, the costs involved in constantly upgrading technology prevent many libraries from keeping pace. Acknowledging this problem, billionaire Microsoft founder Bill Gates—through the Bill & Melinda Gates Foundation—has committed ongoing support to fund technology in public libraries in the United States as well as abroad. Beginning in 1997, Gates grant awards—under their Global Libraries Initiative—have brought computers, Internet access, and staff training to needy public libraries in low-income and other qualifying communities across the United States and since 2002 to worldwide public libraries. The initiative's stated strategy is supporting "the transformation of libraries as engines of development."

Resource Sharing

Since the 1960s, formal resource sharing among libraries and information centers has burgeoned as facilities of all types and sizes realize that in numbers there is strength and increased benefits to customers. Consortia have taken the form of same-type and multi-type library networks, with membership based on geographical proximity, on collection strengths, or on shared customer profiles.

An early example of a powerful and innovative library alliance was Research Libraries Group (RLG), a cooperative formed by Yale, Harvard, Columbia, and the New York Public Library in 1974. An international network with some 150 members, RLG included universities and colleges, national libraries, archives, historical societies, museums, independent research collections, and public libraries. In 2006, RLG was absorbed by OCLC, but still has its own presence for some things under the OCLC brand.

Resource sharing in all its varied forms is the backbone of library services as it enables agencies to share personnel, to centralize cataloging and processing efforts, to lobby for improved purchasing power from vendors, and to provide patron access to a greater number of materials and services.

National Awareness of Libraries

The American Library Association first adopted its "Library Bill of Rights" in 1948 (see Appendix B) to establish guidelines for the rights of library users. Based on our nation's First Amendment to the Constitution, which guarantees the freedom of expression in speech, writing, reading, access to information, and so on, the "Library Bill of Rights" has been supplemented with interpretive statements several times to reflect new issues regarding the freedom to access information, censorship, and multimedia formats. Many libraries formally adopt this statement as part of their official policy.

U.S. libraries of all types benefited from legislation in the 1950s and 1960s that provided financial aid for collection development and facilities building. The nation's Bicentennial Celebration of 1976, with its commemoration of the historical roots of our country, shined a new spotlight on libraries and archives, underscoring the need to preserve documentation of our national, regional, and local history.

The library boom years of the 1950s and 1960s contrasted with later observations made by the National Commission on Excellence in Education in their landmark 1983 report *A Nation at Risk*. This study determined that the educational system in the United States was slipping in terms of quality, effectiveness, and competitiveness, and that publicly supported institutions such as library systems had fallen far behind as well.[32] While industry observers have questioned the overall progress made to improve educational systems and support since then, the study has been credited with focusing the nation's attention on educational reforms.

The American Library Association reports more than 119,000 libraries in the United States as of 2012. Although the funding levels can be counted on to vary widely among these diverse types of libraries, the new technological leaps and fresh challenges of contemporary times promise to keep libraries and information centers in the spotlight as they continue to provide information access, in-demand services, and a sense of community to their clientele.

STUDY QUESTIONS

1. Describe some of the historical information needs that have driven the collecting of written materials.

2. Compare what we know of the Great Library at Alexandria to a modern library facility.

3. What was the impact of Gutenberg's new technology on reading and printing at the time in Europe?

4. Describe the service philosophy of early American colonial college libraries. How does this compare to your current college or university library's philosophy?

5. What were the major contributions of Melvil Dewey to the library profession? How did his accomplishments dovetail with other events in the field in the late 1800s?

6. What impact did Andrew Carnegie's program have on American communities? Are there similar privately funded grant programs in place for helping libraries and information centers today? Name some major ones.

7. Describe the historical rivalry between the writing mediums of papyrus and animal skin. Can you draw any comparisons between the current competition between the printed book and e-books?

8. How do political instability and war—such as World War I or II or the current Middle East conflicts—affect cuneiform collections and other ancient treasures (such as those found in Baghdad's Iraq Museum) that document humanity's common cultural heritage?

NOTES

1. P. J. Huffstutter and Kasri Naji, "Antiquities Stuck in Legal Limbo," *Los Angeles Times*, July 13, 2006.
2. "Large Cache of Mesopotamian Tablets Found," *Los Angeles Times*, December 29, 1987.
3. Jean Key Gates, *Guide to the Use of Libraries and Information Sources*, 7th ed. (New York: McGraw-Hill, 1994): 5.
4. Lionel Casson, "Triumph from the Ancient World's First Think Tank," *Smithsonian* (June): 158–68 (1985).
5. Dr. Sohair F. Wastawy, Chief Librarian Bibliotheca Alexandrina, e-mail to authors, April 29, 2006.
6. Will Durant, *Story of Civilization, Part III: Caesar and Christ* (New York: Simon & Schuster, 1944), 159.
7. Ibid., 360.
8. Sylvanus G. Morley and George W. Brainerd, *The Ancient Maya*, 4th ed. (Stanford, CA: Stanford University Press, 1983), 513.
9. Ibid.

10. Jean Peters, ed., *The Bookman's Glossary*, 5th ed. (New York: R.R. Bowker, 1975), 130.

11. *Encyclopaedia Britannica Online Academic Edition*, s.v. "Bray, Thomas," http://academic.eb.com/EBchecked/topic/78090/Thomas-Bray (accessed January 7, 2015).

12. Elizabeth W. Stone, *American Library Development, 1600–1899* (New York: H.W. Wilson, 1977), 94.

13. John Y. Cole, *Jefferson's Legacy: A Brief History of the Library of Congress* (Washington, DC: Library of Congress, 1993), 12.

14. Ibid., 13.

15. Elizabeth W. Stone, *American Library Development, 1600–1899* (New York: H.W. Wilson, 1977), 153.

16. Ibid., 127, 128.

17. Fremont Rider, *Melvil Dewey* (Chicago: American Library Association, 1944), 6.

18. Ebsco, "John Cotton Dana Library Public Relations Award—About John Cotton Dana," http://www.ebscohost.com/academic/john-cotton-dana (accessed Dec 1, 2014).

19. Carl A. Hanson, ed., *Librarian at Large: Selected Writings of John Cotton Dana* (Washington, DC: Special Libraries Association, 1991).

20. *The Enoch Pratt Free Library of Baltimore City: Letters and Documents Relating to Its Foundation and Organization, with the Dedicatory Addresses and Exercises January 4, 1886* (Baltimore: Isaac Friedenwald, 1886), https://books.google.com/. Google eBook. (accessed January 8, 2015).

21. Richard H. Peterson, "Philanthropic Phoebe: The Educational Charity of Phoebe Apperson Hearst," *California History* 64, no. 4 (Fall 1985): 287.

22. Alexandra M. Nickliss, "Phoebe Apperson Hearst's 'Gospel of Wealth,' 1883–1901," *Pacific Historical Review* 71, no. 4 (November 2002): 585–6.

23. Andrew Carnegie, "Wealth," *North American Review* 148 (June 1889): 653–64.

24. Carnegie Corporation of New York, "About Carnegie Corporation: Biography of Andrew Carnegie," http://carnegie.org/about-us/foundation-history/about-andrew-carnegie/ (accessed January 8, 2015).

25. Abigail A. Van Slyck, *Free to All: Carnegie Libraries and American Culture, 1890–1920* (Chicago: University of Chicago Press, 1995), 22.

26. Nancy Smiler Levinson, "Takin' It to the Streets: The History of the Book Wagon," *Library Journal*, May 1, 1991, 43–45.

27. OCLC, "Advancing Together: Annual Report, 2013–2014," http://www.oclc.org/en-US/annual-report/2014/our-members.html (accessed January 7, 2015).

28. *OCLC Abstracts* 18, no. 1 (2015), e-mail to authors, January 5, 2015.

29. Marshall Breeding, "Automation Marketplace 2012: Agents of Change" *Library Journal*, March 29, 2012, http://www.thedigitalshift.com/2012/03/ils/automation-marketplace-2012-agents-of-change/ (accessed January 15, 2015).

30. John Carlo Bertot, Charles R. McClure, and Paul T. Jaeger, *Public Libraries and the Internet 2004: Survey Results and Finding* (Chicago: Bill & Melinda Gates Foundation and American Library Association, 2005), http://www.ii.fsu.edu/content/download/15106/98626/01_plinternet_exec_summary.pdf (accessed January 15, 2015).

31. World Internet Usage Statistics News and Population Stats, "Internet Usage Statistics: The Internet Big Picture," http://www.internetworldstats.com/stats.htm (accessed January 15, 2015).

32. United States National Commission on Excellence in Education, *A Nation at Risk: The Imperative for Educational Reform: A Report to the Nation and to the Secretary of Education* (Washington, DC: U.S.G.P.O., 1983).

RESOURCES

Books

Battles, Matthew. *The Library: An Unquiet History.* New York: W.W. Norton & Company, 2004.

Campbell, James W.P. *The Library: A World History.* Chicago: University Of Chicago Press, 2013

Casson, Lionel. *Libraries in the Ancient World.* New Haven: Yale University Press, 2001.

Dawson, Robert and Ann Patchett. *The Public Library: A Photographic Essay.* Princeton, NJ: Princeton Architectural Press, 2014.

Harris, Michael H. *History of Libraries in the Western World.* 4th ed. Metuchen, NJ: Scarecrow, 1995.

Jones, Theodore. *Carnegie Libraries Across America: A Public Legacy.* New York: John Wiley, 1997.

Polk, Milbry and Angela M.H. Schuster, eds. *The Looting of the Iraq Museum, Baghdad: The Lost Legacy of Mesopotamia.* New York: Abrams, 2005.

Swerdlow, Joel. "The Power of Writing." *National Geographic,* August 1999, 110–32.

Thorpe, James. *The Gutenberg Bible: Landmark in Learning.* 2nd ed. San Marino, CA: Huntington Library, 1999.

Van Slyck, Abigail A. *Free to All: Carnegie Libraries and American Culture, 1890–1920.* Chicago: University of Chicago Press, 1995.

Wiegand, Wayne A. *Irrepressible Reformer: A Biography of Melvil Dewey.* Chicago: American Library Association, 1996.

Films

The Real National Treasure: An Inside Look at the Library of Congress. (47 minutes). Produced by Actuality Productions, Inc. for History. New York: A & E Television Networks, 2010.

This video provides an overview of the historical development and inner workings of our national library as well as a look at some of its unique holdings

Richest Man in the World: Andrew Carnegie. (120 minutes). Produced and directed by Austin Hoyt. Boston: PBS/WGBH, 1997.

The *American Experience* series looks at the rags-to-riches story of controversial steel magnate Andrew Carnegie.

Websites

Cary Collection: Before the Printing Press
http://library.rit.edu/cary/image-database
(accessed November 30, 2014)

Search the image database from the Cary Graphic Arts Collection at the Rochester Institute of Technology for photographs illustrating several early forms of bookmaking technology, including cuneiform tablets and papyrus scroll fragments

The Cuneiform Digital Library Initiative (CDLI)
http://cdli.ucla.edu/
(accessed November 30, 2014)

The CDLI is a scholarly international effort by museum curators and historians to make available on the Web the content and analysis of early cuneiform tablets from leading cuneiform collections around the world.

Illuminated Manuscripts at the Getty Museum

http://www.getty.edu/art/

http://www.getty.edu/art/exhibitions/glory/

http://www.getty.edu/art/exhibitions/seeking/

(accessed November 30, 2014)

The J. Paul Getty museum has a leading collection of illuminated manuscripts dating from the ninth to the 16th centuries and representing many styles. Located in Los Angeles, California, the museum regularly features stunning public exhibitions from its illuminated manuscript collection. Many past exhibitions are also archived on their website.

Jefferson's Legacy: A Brief History of the Library of Congress

http://www.loc.gov/loc/legacy/toc.html

(accessed November 30, 2014)

This site is an illustrated Web version of the book by John Y. Cole (also available in print) that discusses the early years of our national library and Jefferson's key role in the collection's development.

Project Gutenberg

http://www.gutenberg.org/

(accessed November 30, 2014)

The volunteer staffed Project Gutenberg has been a pioneer in the distribution of full-text, public domain e-books since the early days of the Internet. More than 47,000 electronic-text titles (e-books) including many classics of English and European literature are available for free downloading.

Chapter 3

Types of Libraries and Library Careers

This chapter presents an overview of library job opportunities, together with a summary of the different organizational settings in which these career opportunities can be found. The entire landscape of libraries and information gathering is evolving with accelerating speed. Some question whether libraries will continue to exist as we knew them in past decades; others believe that the fundamental purpose of libraries—to organize and disseminate information—is needed now more than ever. It is difficult to determine with perfect clarity how this evolution will unfold for those beginning their careers now. Two observations, however, are very clear: those who see their role as keepers of books will be shelved themselves, and those who fulfill users' needs for information, imagination, and inspiration will always be in demand.

WHAT IS A LIBRARY?

There are hundreds of different kinds of libraries and library-like organizations. To the layperson, libraries seem the same, just as all library workers are the same. Even sophisticated library users generally do not understand the range of libraries that exist. Each library's clientele is different; therefore, each library's mission is different. Also, libraries' collections are different; therefore, their services must differ. What makes an organization a library? Traditionally, libraries have been defined as organizations that acquire, organize, and disseminate information. This is certainly true, but it does not differentiate libraries from many other entities. For example, newspapers are among the many other kinds of organizations that meet each of these criteria.

Libraries are generally divided into four major categories:

- Public libraries
- School library media centers
- Academic libraries
- Special libraries

Although these are the primary kinds of libraries, in practice libraries can be combinations of more than one type or subcategory. Each type of library has a distinct mission and a specific group of users to serve. This chapter also discusses missions of libraries that are sometimes similar to and in other ways distinctly different from each other, and how they are shaped by the needs of the clientele they serve.

HOW MANY LIBRARIES ARE IN THE UNITED STATES?

The American Library Association (ALA), the leading professional organization for the library field, estimates that there are just under 120,000 libraries of all types in the United States (see Table 3.1). These libraries range in size from those with small collections, a single part-time staff member, and limited operating hours, to the world's largest facility, the Library of Congress, with more than 160 million items and thousands of employees.[1]

Note: These statistics do not take into account the undoubtedly large number of libraries in churches and other nonprofit organizations that are staffed exclusively by volunteers.

LIBRARY EMPLOYMENT

In 2012, there were more than 166,000 professional librarians and more than 200,000 staff members working in the United States, as enumerated by the American Library Association in the following table.[2]

Note that these figures do not include individuals with library training and skills working for the following:

- Library networks and regional cooperatives that supply services to partner libraries
- Vendors, who develop and market products and services to libraries
- Consultants, freelance, outsourced, and temporary (usually grant-funded) library staff

TABLE 3.1 ALA Fact Sheet 1: Number of Libraries in the United States. http://www.ala.org/tools/libfactsheets/alalibraryfactsheet01. Used with permission from the American Library Association.

Public Libraries (administrative units)			**9,082**
	Central buildings*	8,895	
	Branch buildings	7,641	
	Total buildings	16,536	
Academic Libraries			**3,793**
	Less than four year	1,304	
	Four year and above	2,489	
School Libraries			**98,460**
	Public schools	81,200	
	Private schools	17,100	
	Bureau of Indian Affairs (BIA)	160	
Special Libraries*			**6,966**
Armed Forces Libraries			**252**
Government Libraries			**934**
Total			**119,487**

* The number of central buildings is different from the number of public libraries because some public library systems have no central building and some have more than one. Public Libraries in the United States Survey: Fiscal Year 2012 (December 2014) specifically explains in a footnote to Table 3: "Of the 9,041 public libraries in the 50 States and DC, 7,321 were single-outlet libraries and 1,720 were multiple-outlet libraries. Single-outlet libraries are a central library, bookmobile, or books-by-mail-only outlet. Multiple-outlet libraries have two or more direct service outlets, including some combination of one central library, branch(es), bookmobile(s), and/or books-by-mail-only outlets."

** Special libraries include corporate, medical, law, religious, and so forth.

Library Employment Outlook

What is the employment outlook for library positions? The lingering consequences of the Great Recession that began in 2007 are still evident. From 2007 through 2014, employment among all library workers decreased from 380,000 positions to 332,000.[3] However, according to the *Occupational Outlook Handbook*, employment of librarians is projected to grow at 7 percent between 2012–2022, while employment of paraprofessionals is projected to grow 15 percent through 2022, the latter faster than the average for all occupations.[4]

TABLE 3.2 ALA Fact Sheet 2: Number of Paid Library Staff in the United States. http://www.ala.org/tools/libfactsheets/alalibraryfactsheet02. Used with permission from the American Library Association.

	Librarians	Other Paid Staff	Total Paid Staff
Academic Libraries	26,606	59,145	85,751
Public Libraries	46,808	90,043	136,851
Public School Libraries	78,570	47,440	126,010
Private School Libraries	14,090	3,770	17,860
Bureau of Indian Education School Libraries	90	80	170
Total	166,164	200,478	366,642

Comparable figures for employment in special libraries (e.g., libraries serving businesses, scientific agencies, hospitals, law firms, and nonprofit organizations) are not available.

Library Worker Salaries and Hourly Rates

What are library workers paid? According to the Bureau of Labor Statistics, library worker pay in 2014 was as follows:

- Librarians employed by local governments earned a mean salary of $52,590 in 2014.
- Elementary and secondary school librarians earned a mean salary of $59,790 in 2014.
- Librarians in colleges, universities, and professional schools earned an average of $63,420.
- Library assistants employed by local governments earned a mean hourly wage of $15.46, those employed in elementary and secondary schools earned $15.02 per hour, and colleges and universities paid an average of $18.64 per hour.
- Library clerical assistants employed by local governments were paid an hourly mean wage of $12.04, elementary and secondary schools positions paid $12.86, and colleges and universities paid a mean hourly wage of $14.51.[5]

Library Staff Demographics

Who are library workers? In September of 2014, American Library Association members reported the following for the *Member Demographics Study*:

- 87.1 percent White
- 4.3 percent Black or African American

- 3.9 percent Hispanic or Latino
- 3.7 percent Other/Multiracial
- 3.5 percent Asian
- 1.1 percent American Indian or Alaska Native
- 0.3 percent Native Hawaiian or Other Pacific Islander[6]

Women have historically made up a majority of the library profession. In 1995, women were 83.9 percent of librarians; in 2003, women constituted 84.4 percent of librarians. Women represented 81 percent of graduates in Master's in Library Science (MLS) programs in 2012–2013. Black women constituted 3.5 percent of all MLS graduates, while Latina and Asian women accounted for 5 and 2.8 percent of the 2013 class, respectively.[7]

In terms of age, ALA membership as of September 2014 distributes as follows:

- 2.7 percent under the age of 25
- 20.9 percent ages 25–34
- 21.8 percent ages 35–44
- 20.7 percent 45–54
- 24.3 percent 55–64
- 8.4 percent 65–74
- 1.1 percent 75+[8]

PUBLIC LIBRARIES

The public library serves every citizen at every stage of life. The Declaration of Independence states that U.S. citizens possess the right to life, liberty, and pursuit of happiness, which is implicit in the mission statements of public libraries across the country. In addition to the traditional functions of providing reading materials for all ages, promoting literacy, and offering cultural events, public libraries increasingly provide access to information resources about employment, health, and other issues. Both today and in the past, public libraries have been a powerful force in the lives of immigrants, helping them learn how to become active and productive citizens.

Public libraries serve a wider range of needs and objectives than most other libraries. The public library has even been termed the *people's university*, providing access to knowledge in the library's treasure house of literary and cultural works and scientific and technical information. Because public libraries are so important, they exist in more than 16,000 locations in communities both large and small throughout the United States.

Public libraries have the broadest mission because they serve everyone. Children's and young adults' departments supplement local school libraries. In some communities, joint-use agreements have merged school and public libraries. Reference departments and periodical and nonfiction collections supplement local academic libraries. The business and adult services departments of public libraries may provide services to local users, businesses too small to maintain their own libraries, and larger companies that need information services outside their primary business focus. In addition, public libraries provide Internet access, which may be the only way some citizens are able to bridge the digital divide. As seen in Chapter 8, this relatively new service often places public libraries at the forefront of political disputes as the public's right to know collides with the need to protect children.

Library scholar and activist Kathleen de la Peña McCook describes the mission of the public library today as follows:

> The public library in cities and towns and rural areas across the United States is a community center for books and information. In any community, the local public library provides a sense of place, a refuge and a still point; it is a commons, a vital part of the public sphere and a laboratory of ideas. The public library supports family literacy, fosters lifelong learning, helps immigrants find a place, and gives a place to those for whom there is no other place to be. The public library provides a wide-open door to knowledge and information to people of all ages, abilities, ethnicities, and economic station.[9]

The service areas of public libraries are defined by a local geographic area with a specific tax base, usually a city or county. Some states are introducing statewide borrower cards that can be used in any public library in the state. In other areas, consortia of libraries of all types have reciprocal agreements to honor each other's users. Statewide or consortial licensing of databases is quite common, helping local libraries negotiate advantageous group pricing. These trends, combined with delivery via the World Wide Web, are redefining all library services, with public libraries often taking the lead.

Often a public library is part of a municipal or county government and often is its own department within the city or county government, with the library director reporting to the city manager, county executive, or similar authority. In other cases, the library is semi-autonomous, with a governing board appointed by the chief executive of the municipality. In this case, the chief librarian is responsible primarily to the library board and only secondarily responsible to the chief executive of the municipality. In yet other instances, a public library is its own autonomous unit of municipal government, with its own elected governing board and independent taxing authority. In this case, the chief librarian is responsible solely to the elected library board.

The mission of the public library is to meet the needs of its particular community. It may carry out that mission through a single facility or through a system of libraries with scores of service locations. Even within the same city or county, branches may require different hours of operation, collections of materials, and patterns of service to meet the needs of their clients. Factors, such as socioeconomic levels, ethnicity, languages spoken, and average age of the clientele served by a particular facility, usually drive the information needs of the community. A community of young families needs different services from a community made up primarily of retirees. A community with many recent immigrants has different needs from a place where most people are native-born English speakers.

The urban or rural nature of the community and the predominant economic activity of the region also have major impacts. In congested urban areas, libraries must be conveniently located near public transportation. In the suburbs, ample parking is essential. Rural areas may require that libraries come to their patrons in the form of a bookmobile that makes regular rounds to reach the dispersed population. Finally, the level of technology resources in the community will suggest the priority with which services must be delivered over the Web.

Public Library Objectives

As community needs have changed over the years, American public library objectives have changed to keep pace. Through much of the 19th century, education (adult education in particular) was the foremost objective of the public library. Late in that century and early in the 20th century, recreational reading and reference were added. Recreational reading was initially provided to promote literacy among laborers. Leisure reading gradually became a legitimate end in itself. The heightened social consciousness of the 1960s accelerated public library efforts to reach out to poor and undereducated people, a trend that is currently receiving new emphasis today.

In the 21st century, public libraries are mobilizing again to meet new community needs. The Web has fundamentally changed the way Americans view information, in turn causing librarians to re-examine whether the library is a place or a function. Should information be delivered to users any time and any place they want it? If so, what role does the library have in selecting and organizing the electronic information distributed? To what extent should digital social networking play in the library's efforts to meet community information, imagination, and inspiration needs? How can the public library provide access for those who do not have independent access to the information available on the Web? These questions pose great challenges to the libraries of the future and their staff members. The extent to which libraries address these challenges will determine the relevance of libraries to society in the future.

The biggest challenge for public libraries will be developing and delivering Web-based services while continuing to maintain current in-building services to those who are better served in the latter mode. Libraries are neither digital nor paper. They are both at the same time, and that is expensive in terms of resources, staff, and time.

Public Library Standards

In 1933, ALA published a two-page document as the first set of standards for U.S. public libraries. Ten years later, ALA's revised *Standards for Public Libraries* emphasized the need to provide free library service to community members. In 1956 and again in 1966, ALA updated and released new standards. The 1966 *Minimum Standards for Public Library Systems* stated that "service to all" was the primary mission of public libraries, placing new emphasis on users, particularly the one-third of the population who either had never used a library or had no access to free public library services. The

1966 standards also called for written collection development policies that governed regular acquisitions and weeding. Services and programs were to be developed to satisfy the needs of all individuals and groups. For specific user groups, such as children, young adults, and those with disabilities, separate standards were developed and published by the responsible divisions of the ALA.[10]

Although library systems are based on qualitative standards, librarians had long recognized the public relations value of stating these standards in quantitative terms. They found that government and community leaders could relate to standards that stipulated, for example, a certain amount of money per capita should be spent to support library services. Thus, the 1966 standards also included quantitative standards for such areas as services, materials, and staffing. These standards recommended that local community libraries be open at least six days a week and that bookmobile services be provided to areas without libraries; staff should include one-third professional and two-thirds support staff. Minimum numbers of staff were identified based on the population served. The number and types of materials to be provided were linked to the population served, and smaller branch library collections were backed up by a larger collection at the library headquarters.

These quantitative standards were not meant to be definitive, but were intended as guidelines that libraries should strive to meet. Although some libraries quickly and easily surpassed the standards, many libraries took five to ten years to reach them, and others still struggle to achieve them. As librarians were striving to meet these quantitative standards, they also began to recognize that libraries often had unique characteristics that sometimes did not fit a standard formula. The Public Library Association (PLA) assisted librarians in meeting this challenge by publishing *A Planning Process for Public Libraries* in 1980. This process stressed that an analysis of an individual library and its community, by community members, library board trustees, and library staff members, could be used to help identify library needs and set directions for library services.[11]

Although many librarians welcomed this emphasis on local community needs, they still felt a need to maintain some quantitative standards against which they could evaluate their library's level of services and materials. They recognized that many community leaders and governmental authorities were impressed by statistics such as the number of people who used the library and its materials and services. In 1982, PLA published *Output Measures for Public Libraries*, containing specific guidance for measuring library uses, such as the number of library visits or reference questions per capita. Use of the collection was measured in circulations per capita and the turnover rate (i.e., the number of total items in the collection divided by the items checked out). Even the availability of library materials was measured to determine how many material requests were filled and how long it took to fill them. These output measures could be used in conjunction with more traditional input measures (such as the number of items added to a collection) to quantify a library's services. Librarians could assess the effectiveness of their libraries with results from similar institutions.

PLA's current effort—the "Presidential Task Force on Performance Measurement"—was launched in 2013 to "develop standardized measures of effectiveness for widely offered public library programs and promote the train-ing for implementation and use of the measures across public libraries." Task force participants were invited from both geographically and operationally diverse public libraries. Using metrics such as these, many states provide aid to libraries to improve their standings in these measurements.[12]

Public Library Services

Once librarians determined the needs of their communities, they developed or expanded library collections, programs, and services to meet these needs. Perhaps the greatest differences between libraries were in the variety of library collections developed to fulfill specific roles. Books in other languages, as well as ethnic literature and resources reflecting local populations, were added. Libraries provided public-access computers and free wireless, while others provided materials supporting local school curricula, and still others supplied supplementary materials to their local schools for classroom use.

In addition, libraries also expanded their collections to include a wide vari-ety of formats. The traditional print materials of books, magazines, and news-papers were expanded to include large-print titles, college catalogs, business reports, and updated reference or financial services such as *Facts on File* and *Value Line*. Audiovisual materials were included in the mainstream of library collections, including movies, audiobooks, and art prints. Some libraries even produced their own radio and TV programs or ran their own cable TV channels to reach all segments of their populations.

Libraries gather information about community organizations, businesses, and governmental agencies to help residents find specific assistance. This information often is shared with other agencies, published in directories, or on the Web. Libraries work with social service, health, educational, business, governmental, and economic agencies and organizations to locate and provide information to help people resolve health, housing, family, job search, and legal problems.

In the midst of the recent Great Recession in 2008, ALA president James Rettig noted, "As the nation continues to experience a downturn in the econ-omy, libraries are providing the tools needed to help Americans get back on their feet. From free homework help to assisting with résumés and job searches, now more than ever libraries are proving they are valued and trusted resources."[13]

Age-Specific Services

In addition to developing diverse collections to satisfy multiple informa-tional demands, librarians established programs and services to meet the differing needs of target populations. For example, most public libraries pro-vide collections, programming, and staff for children's services. Collections in these library departments usually include picture books, multimedia kits, puppets, developmental toys, educational games, and animals (both live and stuffed). These materials are sometimes housed in separate, colorful, and engaging preschool corners or dedicated rooms, where children can climb on playscape equipment, recline on soft furniture, or enjoy reading books. They can listen to stories read aloud by their parents, watch mock puppet shows, or take part in a learning or craft activity without distracting other library patrons. Preschool story hours and puppet shows are presented to children at the library and at preschools and daycare centers. Specially trained "reading dogs" visit children's departments and listen as kids build confidence by reading aloud to the pets. Children's departments in public libraries often provide reading development and parenting skills workshops. As with the story hours themselves, some of these workshops may be conducted in languages other than English in order to connect with the community's specific needs.

The national nonprofit organization Family Place Libraries believes in attracting young children to U.S. public libraries even before they can read. Begun in 1996 at the Middle Country Public Library in Centereach, New York, the program now includes more than 435 libraries in 25 states. Their mission is to create "welcoming, developmentally appropriate early learning environments for very young children, their parents and caregivers."

> Family Place Libraries help transform parents into first teachers, and the program addresses the physical, social, emotional, and cognitive aspects of child development "to help build a foundation for learning during the critical first years of life."
>
> Family Place librarians collaborate with local service providers and early childhood educators to enhance the community environment for families with very young children and to reach new and/or underserved audiences. Thus, community agencies, educators, and family services providers also benefit from having a strong community partner able to reinforce or enhance their missions, share resources, and develop cooperative services.[14]

Public libraries provide in-house and outreach programs and services for school-age children, too. In many of these libraries, circulation of children's materials can be as much as one-third to one-half of the library's total circulation. To encourage such use, some libraries extend their summer reading clubs to year-round programs. They combine them with contests, such as Battle of the Books, which offer prizes and awards. Regular monthly programs often feature puppet shows, magic shows, animal acts, storytellers, or visiting performers. Outreach into the community may include children's services librarians presenting book talks or other literary presentations in local public or private school classrooms.

Another group of library patrons who use the library frequently after school is teenagers from age 12 to age 17. Activities for these young adults (YA) include makerspaces, where library users share supplies, skills, and ideas, working together on projects; homework clubs; reading groups; video gaming; robotics; and college entrance examination preparatory classes. Libraries also provide paperback collections containing multiple copies of best seller YA novels, series fiction, and nonfiction. Larger library systems hire dedicated YA librarians and establish young adult advisory councils or peer homework support groups. Afterschool activities and a welcoming environment at the neighborhood library can provide a safe, inviting space for youths.

Reference Services

Most public libraries emphasize reference service as one of their major roles. To support this service, libraries develop print and online collections that contain general reference encyclopedias, directories, dictionaries, yearbooks, handbooks, and atlases. Depending on their communities' needs and interests, libraries might also develop specialized subject reference collections. These could be business and finance collections, arts and humanities collections, regional history collections, English as a Second Language (ESL) materials, or special-interest collections, such as art history, genealogy, hunting and fishing, or home improvement and gardening. In addition to books, many collections have traditionally offered investment updating services, periodicals, municipal government codes and documents, and local history archives. To help their patrons use these materials more effectively, libraries provide both formal and informal instruction to individuals and groups about use of the library and its collections. Online instructional tutorials for mining these topical collections may also be developed for and used by motivated patrons.

Libraries also provide reference staff to help patrons locate specific information. Reference help includes on-site assistance in using the library's reference tools and database searching, and virtual reference service via chat, e-mail, or text. Telephone reference requests—once very popular—have greatly declined in favor of patron preference for virtual reference modalities. The range of services depends on the library's size, staffing, and funding resources. Large urban public libraries dedicate many staff members to reference services, with particular attention to the ability to locate materials in their special interest collections. Smaller libraries may depend on links to larger system libraries to answer to patrons' questions that are beyond the scope of local resources. Almost half of all library patrons use some form of these services.[15]

Public libraries large and small develop collections of current fiction, often including multiple copies of best sellers and genre books, such as science fiction, mysteries, and graphic novels. Library workers promote these materials with book lists, blog posts, social media recommendations, book discussion groups, author appearances, library displays, and face-out display shelving similar to that found in bookstores. In addition to books, other popular library collections include feature, documentary, and family-friendly films; CDs and DVDs; and tools supporting makerspace classes.

Adult programming topics are seemingly boundless, ranging from lectures, and film screenings, to art exhibits and craft demonstrations, to events featuring local historians and authors. Creative, educational, and entertaining programming is often delivered in partnership with the arts, business, and nonprofit sectors of the community. Public libraries also provide programs and services for populations with special needs, such as senior citizens, the homebound, and the disabled, including, audiobooks, Braille and large-print materials, and computers with accessibility features and devices. Especially in urban population centers, larger systems such as the Alameda County Library in California develop collections maintained inside jail facilities to serve the needs of the incarcerated.

Outreach Services

Many libraries further serve the independent learning needs of their adult patrons. Some librarians serve as examination proctors for distance-learning courses or make their meeting rooms available to local groups, such as gene-alogists or creative writing groups. In partnership with other educational institutions and community agencies, libraries help individual patrons study for credit courses or take high school equivalency tests, such as the General Education Degree (GED). Sometimes adult education classes are conducted at the library, or via video courses made available to library patrons. Also in support of adult independent learning, libraries reach beyond their traditional middle-class educated patrons to underserved populations. Libraries partici-pate in adult literacy programs by housing adult basic education materials and providing study rooms for literacy students and their volunteer tutors. Some libraries provide foreign-language collections and host classes in ESL. During economic downturns, libraries may promote job placement centers to help unemployed patrons.

In trying to meet the needs of their underserved populations, libraries also design outreach services for persons who cannot get to a main or branch library. Bookmobiles travel rural highways and city streets to deliver popular materials to all ages. In inner-city areas, bookmobiles are painted in bright, attractive designs and stocked with books, paperbacks, and magazines to help attract nonreaders. "Mediamobiles" tour inner-city areas to deliver library pro-grams to children and young adults on street corners.

The Read Rover is a bookmobile that was specifically designed with the day care community in mind. The Read Rover, with its brightly painted kangaroo on the outside, visits day care centers, home day care providers, and pre-kindergarten classes in Baltimore County, Maryland. The children come on board the truck to enjoy story time, and then the teachers or providers have a chance to select material to keep in their centers until Read Rover returns the following month.

As libraries reach out to serve these underserved patrons, many establish storefront branches or place materials collections in urban housing develop-ments and local ethnic or senior citizen centers. Prefabricated kiosk-type and pop-up libraries are erected in rural areas or urban shopping malls to provide quick and easy access to library materials. Local community members staff these facilities, and foreign-language-speaking librarians develop collections and services that meet the needs of the community's various ethnic popula-tions. In addition, libraries work with other agencies to provide voter registra-tion, notary publics, income tax forms, income-tax preparation assistance for low-income and senior residents, and health-testing programs.

Just as Redbox DVD outlets are a familiar feature in grocery stores, gas sta-tions, and mini-marts, many larger urban public libraries now provide vend-ing machines stocked with books and DVDs as an additional outreach effort. These automated book-dispensing machines are located in convenient spots within the library's service areas, including community youth centers, transit and rail centers, and shopping malls. Featuring current and popular books, these self-contained collections are open 24/7, allow cardholders to borrow library books and return them to the box when finished. The library vending machines can be easily relocated as physical space or community needs change. Much as the bookmobile concept extends service outside fixed public library building locations, so does the book vending machine with the added appeal of self-service.

Public Library Funding

Although many consider the public library to be an institution basic to civilization, public library collections and services are always affected by economic conditions. National and local economic recessions affect library services, as do the local community's political and social situations. As agencies that serve all persons from cradle to grave, public libraries sometimes try to be all things to all people. Public library staffs strive to provide equal service to patrons of all ages and interest groups in their communities. They factor in the ups and downs of library budgets, the availability of electronic technology, and the capabilities of networking with other libraries as they develop library programs and services to satisfy the needs of diverse patrons.

Beyond traditional tax revenue resources for libraries, legislation and grants have provided much needed funds. Three sources in particular—E-rate discounts via legislation, Bill and Melinda Gates Foundation grants, and Institute of Museum and Library Services (IMLS) grants—provide funds to make a difference in the quality of services offered by their public and school library partners.

Funding from Taxes

The growth and development of public library programs and services are vulnerable to economic changes in their communities. Public library revenues are controlled by the allocation of tax revenue—usually property taxes—by politicians. In some states and cities, the public library's ability to increase tax revenue is limited by legal or political considerations. In others, libraries must appeal directly to voters to increase their tax levies. To minimize their dependence on such sources, libraries have begun to explore additional sources of income and develop innovative sources to finance their services and programs.

Public libraries in growing communities have begun collecting a percentage of impact fees paid by real estate developers to help finance library services to new residents. Libraries have joined the Public Library Foundation or similar investment pools to increase the interest paid on their library funds. Many libraries have formed nonprofit Friends of the Library groups. Such organizations conduct used-book sales, library auctions, sales of library-related merchandise, and engage in fundraising. A few libraries have also launched profit-making ventures, such as retail shops or cafés operated by friends' groups within new or remodeled library buildings. Such activities also serve to raise the library's visibility in the community.

FIGURE 3.1 Friends' groups help to support a library through promotion, fundraising, and by increasing the level of community engagement. Reprinted by permission of Paula Zima.

Overdue fees, charged by a majority of public libraries, have been increased, and many libraries charge higher or additional processing fees for lost items. To help ease their economic plight, some libraries have initiated fees for formerly free services, such as reserving books or requesting interlibrary loans. Others also charge fees for expensive services, such as database searches, or the loan of premium materials, such as DVDs and current best sellers. These fees cause considerable debate within the library profession. Opponents of such fees claim that the income raised from them is not a sufficient reason to deny access to library materials and services to patrons who cannot afford them. In the final analysis, the revenues raised from all of these various methods account for only a small portion of the average public library's budget. Furthermore, libraries must be careful not to get involved with revenue schemes that can divert more staff time and energy from the direct provision of services than can be replaced in terms of additional revenue.

Cooperative library networks have had a positive effect on the ability of libraries to stretch their budgets and share their resources. By sharing the costs of technology, even small libraries can afford to join bibliographic cooperatives offering shared circulation, cataloging, and interlibrary loan capabilities. Regional and statewide resource networks facilitate sharing of materials and services with partner libraries via loan of physical books or digitized articles.

In addition to exchanging materials, libraries exchange their patrons, too. Reciprocal borrowing agreements among libraries enable patrons to visit and check out materials at other libraries throughout a regional system or state. Another benefit to cooperative agreements is that patrons can use computers, either in the library, in their homes, or on mobile devices, to see which libraries have specific materials they want. Through this cooperation, public libraries are able to expand the resources to which their users have access.

When providing library services, library administrators and their staffs take great care to ensure that everyone is treated equitably—whether the patron is a city council member, a library board trustee, or a young child. Library governing boards generally adopt the ALA "Library Bill of Rights" (see Appendix B) and ALA Video Round Table's "Freedom to View Statement."[16] Prudent libraries also institute written policies and procedures to protect the freedom of intellectual inquiry for their patrons. Such policies define free access to the library's collections by all users, stipulate protection of patron records from public inquiry, and provide a framework for challenges to library materials and services, as outlined in greater detail in Chapters 4 and 8.

Funding from States

Twenty states said there had been no change in the amount of state funding for public libraries in fiscal year 2014, and 14 said that funding had increased. In fiscal year 2013, 10 of 46 states had reported decreases in direct aid to public libraries; the following year, only two reported that direct support would decrease. For public libraries in states that increased funding, 11 states indicated that the level of state aid would increase by more than 10 percent. Montana's state librarian reported that direct aid for libraries quadrupled, and in Colorado, the state librarian reported an increase in state aid from zero to $2 million in fiscal year 2013–2014.

On the other side of the equation, two states have experienced funding decreases, and Louisiana's direct state aid for public libraries was eliminated entirely. Eleven states (not including Louisiana) have no direct aid to public libraries. "As with state aid for state libraries, most state librarians felt that funding would remain unchanged or that it was too soon to project the state of direct aid to public libraries," the 2014 ALA report noted. "Most states indicated . . . that the state library's ability to support public libraries is unchanged. Compared to FY2013, four more states indicated that the state has been impacted positively by state budget changes, and two fewer states indicated that the state library had been hindered by budget cuts."

Ten states reported public library closures, but of fewer than five libraries in each case. That figure is similar to the previous year's report, in which 11 states reported library closures. Twenty-two state librarians were aware of libraries in their state that reduced hours. More than half of the respondents were concerned about public libraries statewide lacking adequate Internet bandwidth to meet patrons' needs.[17]

E-Rate Program

The Schools and Libraries Universal Service Support Program, commonly known as the Educational-Rate Program, or E-rate, helps schools and libraries obtain affordable broadband access to the Internet. This funding source was established as part of the Telecommunications Act of 1996. Some of the corporate windfall profits realized from this legislative deregulation were redirected to the Federal Communications Commission (FCC) to provide discounts on Internet access to schools and libraries. In the first year of funding in 1998, more than 30,000 schools and libraries participated, with the deepest discounts going to schools and libraries in impoverished areas. It may seem hard to believe today, but in 1996, six out of seven public library systems had no Internet access, largely because of the ongoing cost of telecommunications charges.[18]

Funding requests from schools and libraries in fiscal year 2003 totaled $4.7 billion, but the program funding level remained at $2.25 billion. In addition to concerns about scope and funding levels for the program, E-rate has faced court challenges and legislative inquiries. The federal application process was so fraught that private consulting firms have found a new market helping schools apply.[19]

In December 2014, the Universal Service Administrative Company (USAC) of the FCC adopted the Second E-rate Modernization Order to adjust the E-rate spending cap, attempt to streamline the application process, and increase options for schools and libraries to acquire broadband connectivity at speeds that support new digital learning applications.[20] Access provided by E-rate subsidies is often the Internet option of only resort for those who have little or no Internet access at home, school, or work. The implementation of this transforming technology has led to one of the dominant public debates of recent times: to filter or not to filter public-access computers. This issue is discussed at greater length in Chapter 8.

Grant Funding

Funding from the Bill & Melinda Gates Foundation enhances E-rate discounts for libraries. Bill Gates, co-founder of Microsoft, and Melinda Gates, technologist and activist, established their foundation to coordinate their philanthropic interests in improving public health and reducing poverty worldwide, and expanding "educational opportunities and access to information technology" in the United States. Although funding to libraries and schools from the Gates Foundation does not approach the $2.25 billion generated by E-rate, it does provide goods and services that E-rate does not cover. The first grants, made in 1997 to approximately 1,000 U.S. public libraries "funded free Internet access . . . as a way to give all people ready access to information and the opportunities that come with digital skills and connectivity." Grants were used to provide new computers for library patrons and for staff technical training and support. First-year grants ranged from $4,000 for a small rural library requiring only one computer to $30,000 or more for larger library buildings that received 10 or more computers. Like E-rate, the Gates Foundation targets libraries in communities with the greatest unmet needs, using U.S. Census statistics and a study conducted by the ALA on public libraries and poverty to establish eligibility guidelines.

In 2002, the Gates Foundation expanded their library strategy into the Global Libraries program, working internationally in partnership with "governments and other public and private funders to expand technology access in public libraries, foster innovation in libraries, train library leaders, and advocate for policy changes that benefit public libraries."[21]

The Institute of Museum and Library Services (IMLS) is an independent agency of the United States federal government established in 1996. It is the main source of federal support for libraries and museums within the United States, working "at the national level and in coordination with state and local organizations to sustain heritage, culture, and knowledge; enhance learning and innovation; and support professional development."[22]

Public Library Use

How are public libraries used now and will they be needed in the future? Evidence is accumulating that public libraries are not just surviving; they are thriving in the 21st century in spite of—or because of—the Internet.

The Pew Research Center's Internet Project sheds light on both public library users and non-users. Their 2014 study on library engagement identified four basic types of patrons:

30 percent   **High Engagement**—strikingly positive view of public libraries; greatest library users; believe libraries are essential to individuals and communities

39 percent   **Medium Engagement**—information seekers; great technology users; reflect general U.S. population in demographics and opinions of libraries

17 percent   **Low Engagement**—previous users who have not used the library recently; somewhat negative feelings on library's importance individually, lower tech use

14 percent   **No Engagement**—others in household may use library; disconnected from neighbors and community in addition to libraries; lower income and education levels; only 45 percent believe libraries provide resources to help people succeed[23]

Satisfaction with public libraries has increased, according to Harris polls conducted in 2008 and 2014. The latter Harris Poll revealed that American adults are either "extremely" (24%) or "very" (42%) satisfied with their public libraries. This represents a 7 percent increase from 59 percent of Americans in 2008. An additional one in five is "somewhat" satisfied. Nine in ten Americans believe it is important for libraries to serve as a valuable educational resource, with 59 percent of adults specifying they feel this is very important. Meanwhile, just over three-fourths of adults consider it existing as a pillar of the community to be important. In addition, roughly seven in ten Americans agree that it is important for the library to be recognized as a community center (73%), a cultural center (70%), and a family destination (68%). Finally, 65 percent of American adults believe libraries serve as an entertainment resource.[24]

Continuing ALA studies show that the nation's "public libraries are engines of economic growth, contributing to local development through programming in early literacy, employment services and small-business development. Other studies show that libraries provide an excellent return on investment, have a measurable positive impact on the local economy and contribute to the stability, safety and quality of life of their neighborhoods."[25]

Public Library Staffing

As libraries develop new roles and goals of service, their staffing needs change. Computer literacy has become essential in every position. All staff should possess aptitude with basic productivity software, e-mail, and browsers, plus a working vocabulary that facilitates communication with non-technical users. Other positions require facility with social media sites and applications, blogging, podcasting, and website design. At managerial levels, computer literacy requires conceptual understanding of systems design, application programming, database management, query languages, and financial planning systems. Children's departments have been expanded to include specialists who are knowledgeable about the psychological and educational growth and development of their patrons. Across all staffing levels and within all divisions, excellent customer service skills are emphasized.

Filling these changing staff positions, however, is often difficult. The supply and demand of such specialties is not always well balanced. These library staffing needs vary greatly depending upon the size of a library and its location. Public libraries range from one- or two-person branches to main libraries with 50 to 100 staff members. Medium-to-large libraries usually have a large range of library positions at all levels filled with appropriately trained personnel. They might have many specialized librarians responsible for administration, reference and readers' advisory services, young adult services, collection development, and programming. Paraprofessional library technicians and clerical staff perform supportive tasks in such areas as access services, children's services, bookmobiles, outreach, and technical services.

Smaller libraries might have only one or two librarians to handle reference and children's services. In very small libraries, branches, or on bookmobiles, staff members tend to be generalists who perform all jobs, from checking out materials to helping people find books.

As libraries grow in size and complexity, staff members tend to become more specialized in their responsibilities and their job classifications more distinct. Many of these staff members have advanced education, although they might not have masters' degrees in library science. Their education and training may be in specialties other than library science. Accountants, graphic artists, information technologists and programmers, human resources staff, bilingual employees, and specialists in marketing or public relations are just a few of the varied types of personnel found in public libraries. There is also a very definite pattern of specialization among library personnel in larger library systems.

It is not unusual for library employees to work many years in one particular area of either public or technical services. For example, in the circulation department, one clerk may be responsible for reserves, one for overdue collections, one for stacks maintenance, and others for checking materials in and out. These clerks and library pages (shelvers) may be supervised by a library paraprofessional or by a librarian.

To deploy these staff members most effectively, public library administrators examine and evaluate their personnel policies and procedures. Library administrators often take the personal needs of their staff members into account as they design these policies. Nowhere is this need more evident than in scheduling staff for the public service desks. It is not unusual for a public library to be open seven days a week, and twelve hours a day on weekdays. Library administrators and supervisors find it challenging to schedule the 60- to 80-hour weeks that require one and one-half to two separate staffs working 40 hours each.

Public Libraries of the Future

In the immediate future, a disruptive challenge to public libraries may loom with the launch of commercial subscription services for e-books. Amazon launched Kindle Unlimited in the summer of 2014, giving users unlimited access to a Kindle-formatted selection of 600,000 e-books and 2,000 audiobooks for $10 per month. Scribd and Oyster were first to market an "all you can read" commercial e-book subscription platform, but Amazon's "financial resources, marketing clout, and massive base of Kindle users will doubtless raise consumer awareness of e-book subscription services while altering the competitive landscape for all providers of e-books, including libraries."[26]

Upon closer examination, however, these commercial services are not as appealing. At least 85 percent of the titles available on Kindle Unlimited were either self-published or already available in the public domain. Best sellers are generally not part of these programs. Given Amazon's heavy-handed tactics with major publishers on marketing and sales margins, it seems unlikely that the "big five" publishers—Penguin Random House, Simon & Schuster, HarperCollins, Macmillan, and Hachette Book Group—will be eager to participate.

One business writer, in "Public Libraries Disrupting the Likes of Amazon," sums up the case for public libraries neatly:

> There are obvious limitations to free services, such as availability, wait lists and time span for checked out materials. But for now, this is a terrific example of a public institution in the local community showing itself able to respond to disruptive forces, and provide viable resources to a wider audience with limited resources.[27]

Researchers forecasting the future of libraries constitute a large and lively part of the professional literature. Their prognostications are made within the context of societal trends and technology advances. These are the trends driving the future of libraries at present:

- Information will be everywhere
- Use of mobile and embedded technology will continue to increase
- Rise of "social knowledge," or using social media to identify, share, document, transfer, develop, use, or evaluate knowledge
- Longer life expectancy of users
- Integration of robotics in daily living[28]

SCHOOL LIBRARIES

A school library is an integral part of institutions educating students from kindergarten through the 12th grade (K-12). School libraries may be either private or public and may also be called library media centers or school library media centers. These libraries, as well as academic libraries in colleges and universities, are responsible for supporting the curriculum of the institutions to which they belong. Improving basic literacy is a key function of the library media center. In addition, school libraries also share with academic libraries the responsibility for promoting information literacy. Library staff members in schools and academic libraries teach students the process of how to find and evaluate the information they need, rather than merely locating the information for them. This process is essential for students to become lifelong learners and to function effectively as citizens in the economic and political arenas.

In many of today's schools, a well-run library may very well be the most active room in the entire school. Individual children go there to choose books, use computers, view DVDs, or listen to audio materials. Entire classes go to learn how to use media or to locate information for their reports. Groups of students may come for help in making PowerPoint presentations, designing Web pages, or producing videos for class projects. Professional librarians or media specialists, library media technicians, and clerks assist these students. These active learning centers have shown how effective they can be in a modern educational system. Yet it is surprising that such resource centers have taken so long to become basic parts of the educational institutions of this country.

Development of School Libraries

By the 1950s most secondary schools had libraries even if very small; in the 1970s many elementary school libraries were just getting started. What took the educational system so long to recognize that libraries are necessary components of the educational process? The answer lies in educational goals and methods of these decades. In the early centuries of our country's history, school consisted primarily of students memorizing information presented by a teacher. There were few textbooks, and students were not encouraged to become intellectually curious. The 19th century and the early part of the

20th century, stressed subject content taught from textbooks. In the 1920s and 1930s, emphasis shifted to the learner, and in the 1940s, to life adjustment and the education of youth for their future roles.[29]

During the space race of the 1950s and 1960s, U.S. education theories renewed focus on subject mastery to compete with education in the Soviet Union. The 1960s in particular emphasized the education of individual students according to their needs and abilities to prepare them for participation in American society. Unfortunately, economics often prevented schools and libraries from meeting these commendable goals. The situation became so grave that a 1983 U.S. National Commission on Excellence in Education report, *A Nation at Risk*, identified the United States as just that. This report determined that the United States had let its formal educational system deteriorate to a very dangerous level.[30] In response to this report, librarians drafted *Alliance for Excellence*, a statement that identified the important steps school libraries should take to reverse this deterioration.[31]

School Library Standards

At the turn of the 20th century, accreditation associations provided the major impetus for the development of centralized secondary or high school libraries. The purpose of these associations was to rate high schools so that colleges could compare graduates of one high school with graduates of another. Because libraries were included in the criteria listed by the associations, schools that wanted to become accredited had to develop libraries that met the standards of the accrediting associations.

In the 1920s, accrediting associations and the ALA began to develop standards for school libraries. However, these standards were not widely adopted. Instead, the major type of library service that schools provided, particularly below the high school level, consisted of traveling library collections from state agencies. In many cases, local public libraries provided school collections to classrooms and public librarians who visited the schools. Sometimes the public library was actually part of the school system or housed branches in the school buildings. These services seemed to be satisfactory for those school systems that still considered learning to be largely classroom oriented.

As educators in the 1940s began to recognize that students should be involved in the discovery of learning based on study and inquiry, they realized also that library services and materials were needed to support the expanded curriculum. To help identify needed library services and materials, ALA published standards for school library service in 1944, entitled *School Libraries for Today and Tomorrow*.[32] ALA also identified qualitative and quantitative standards for library resources and services that should be provided by a professional staff in a centralized library. Although these standards were applied in some high schools, very few elementary school libraries were established, and, on the whole, the concept of library services envisioned by the standards was seldom realized.

To encourage library development, ALA published a policy statement in 1956 that identified the important role the school library should play in a school's total instructional process. For the first time, the library was envisioned as a central school library that included all types of learning materials available to both students and teachers. The concepts of this statement were translated into new standards, *Standards for School Library Programs,* in 1960.[33] 'Adoption of these standards was greatly facilitated by national interest in improving U.S. education after the Russian satellite *Sputnik* was the first into space in 1957. In addition, the National Defense Education Act (NDEA) of 1958 provided funds for schools to buy print and non-print materials and equipment. By 1965, the Elementary and Secondary Education Act (ESEA) was signed into law; monies for purchasing school library books were among its provisions.

In combination, these events helped usher in a new era for library services. Educators began to recognize that libraries should be an integral part of the educational curriculum. Central libraries that contained all types of learning materials began to be developed in elementary, junior, and senior high schools. Librarians were recognized as teachers whose subject specialty enabled them to help students and teachers use such materials as books, audiotapes, records, films, filmstrips, transparencies, and programmed instruction. These materials were used in both the classroom and the library to help students learn. The concept of a school library changed to that of instructional materials center (IMC), where many learning activities took place simultaneously.

In an IMC, students and teachers could listen to or view the library's media, or they could produce their own. Students and teachers could also work in the library on group projects, hold meetings in its conference rooms, or study independently in the quiet areas. Library technical and clerical staff members were hired to provide instruction in the use of the library and its resources or to help students learn independently. Librarians were able to perform such professional tasks as offer in-service training to teachers in the use of audiovisual materials and equipment. They became active members of curriculum committees and teaching teams. In many school districts the modern school library finally arrived in the 1960s.

With IMCs well on their way to becoming part of many local school systems, new standards were proposed in 1969 by the American Association of School Librarians (AASL) and the Association of Educational Communications and Technology (AECT). These *Standards for School Media Centers* carried the IMC concept one step further.[34] They proposed that schools develop media programs and services that integrated all types of media into the curriculum based on their contributions to the educational program of the school, rather than on their formats. The standards also proposed replacing the terms *library, librarian, audiovisual center,* and *audiovisual specialist* with the newer terms *media center* and *media specialist* to better identify the integration of all forms of media. The 2013 school libraries study from the National Center for Education Statistics (NCES) found that more than 90 percent of traditional public schools have school libraries on-site, but only 49 percent of public charter schools do.[35]

From Library to Library Media Center

The concept of a media center caused great discussion in the educational and library worlds in the 1960s and '70s. Many school systems enthusiastically endorsed this concept and combined their library, audiovisual, video, and graphics operations and programs into one media department. Titles for such new departments varied from *media center* and *library media center* to *learning resource center, instructional media center, instructional resource center,* or *resource center.* Regardless of titles used, all endeavored to provide the media services recommended in the standards. Other librarians and audiovisual specialists had difficulty adjusting to this new concept, which required them to alter their thinking and their focus (a lesson in shifting paradigms that is still very relevant for librarians and library staff today). Often, they, as well as many educators, believed that the standards were utopian rather than practicable. To add to this confusion, the economic crisis of the 1970s virtually eliminated the federal monies that had been used to develop library services. To provide direction in this chaotic time, the AASL and AECT published new standards in 1975.

The 1975 standards, *Media Programs, District and School,* expanded the concept of media programs beyond the individual school to include services and facilities that could be provided at the district level.[36] The standards were based on the principle that media were a central part of the learning process and that if schools were to meet students' needs, they must provide quality media programs. These programs were a combination of district-wide and on-site services tailored to fit the educational goals and objectives of each individual school system. Although quantitative standards were included, the importance was on the qualitative aspect of the programs.

This emphasis was extended in 1988 with AASL's and AECT's publication of *Information Power: Guidelines for School Library Media Programs.* These groundbreaking standards responded to issues that had been raised in the U.S. National Commission on Excellence in Education's report, *A Nation at Risk,* and answered in librarians' *Alliance for Excellence* statement. In particular, *Alliance for Excellence* identified important steps that school library supporters should take to develop quality library services and resources for every school library. Libraries should incorporate their services and resource collections into their schools' curricula while providing access to materials and user instruction in information resources both within and outside the library. Each library should be well funded and staffed by well-educated and well-paid library media specialists. These library media professionals would actively collaborate with teachers and administrators on the most effective roles and activities for school libraries.

Information Power (1988) provided guidelines and directives to help library media personnel carry out these recommended steps. To identify and establish the best instructional programs, these guidelines emphasize the need for library media specialists to develop an active partnership with administrators and teachers.[37]

The guidelines also reinforced the role of the library media specialist as that of an information specialist, teacher, and instructional consultant working with teachers to fulfill curriculum needs. Access to information outside the library would be provided via interlibrary loans, multi-library networks, and electronic technologies. Intellectual freedom and intellectual access to diverse viewpoints was also encouraged. Finally, extensive guidelines were presented for the development of library media facilities designed specifically to serve individual school and curriculum needs.

The updated edition on these standards, *Empowering Learners: Guidelines for School Library Media Programs* (2009) recommends the following guidelines to achieve successful school libraries:

- Promote collaboration among members of the learning community and encourage learners to be independent, lifelong users and producers of ideas and information
- Promote reading as a foundational skill for learning, personal growth, and enjoyment
- Provide instruction that addresses multiple literacies, including information literacy, media literacy, visual literacy, and technology literacy
- Model an inquiry-based approach to learning and the information search process
- Conduct regular assessment of student learning to ensure the program is meeting its goals[38]

Initially, implementation of these guidelines was affected by both the educational and economic conditions. The majority of classroom teachers continued to rely on lecturing that did not require strong library media support. In addition, many administrators and teachers did not expect much involvement by library media specialists in the school's educational process. In such an educational climate, some school library media specialists felt uncomfortable adopting these new roles and becoming agents of change. The economic climate was also not conducive to the development of such comprehensive school library media programs. Although *A Nation at Risk* recognized the need for a strong educational program, local communities were often reluctant to finance such programs. To encourage these communities to implement strong school library media programs, most states adopted statewide school library media standards by 1990. Many of these states required local schools to meet these guidelines if they wanted to receive state or federal monies. Strong regional accreditation associations also encouraged the development of strong library media programs through their accreditation standards and local self-study requirements.

Although state and national guidelines have had some impact on the development of school library media programs, the largest influence is the philosophies, objectives, and economics of the individual school systems served. In many school systems, the library media programs not only stopped growing during the late 1980s and 90s, but also began to stagnate or shrink. In other school systems with excellent educational programs, outstanding library media programs were developed. These superior library media programs are no accident, however. The more successful and effective programs are based on stated philosophies and objectives carefully crafted by stakeholders. Library media center staff, administrators, teachers, students, and parents have worked together, sometimes in advisory committees, to develop library media programs and activities to meet the needs of individual students.

Current School Library Programs

School libraries today represent a major paradigm shift from the school libraries of the recent past. They operate as both virtual and physical spaces, with many resources available to patrons from anywhere they have access to the Internet. In addition to print books, magazines, newspapers, audio books and DVDs, many school libraries now offer 24/7 access to e-books, article and content databases, research guides, and technology help through their own websites. Databases can often be accessed with text-to-speech and may offer foreign language translations for students with a variety of special needs and skill levels. Providing mobile devices, such as e-readers (Kindle, Nook, etc.), laptops, tablets, and MP3 players, for student checkout is a growing trend. Some schools may offer these for students to take home overnight, or even for the entire school year. Most school libraries are now fully Internet/WiFi connected, providing computers for classes and individuals to use throughout the day, including extended open hours before and after school. Students and teachers are increasingly considering the library to be a place of learning and collaboration, and count on library staff to provide technology training and assistance. Library staff members need to be ready to assist students with a variety of needs, from traditional book recommendation and checkout, to project-based learning support using the latest computer programs, websites, and apps.

Major corporations as well as neighborhood businesses have become involved in local adopt-a-school programs to help schools and school libraries expand their programs. Some tech giants, such as Google, Apple, and Microsoft, offer educational discounts and programs. Other corporations such as CNN (Cable News Network) and Channel One broadcast news to schools without cost. Through these and other cooperative activities, school librarians find that they can stretch their budgets and expand the library media program's impact on the educational process.

School librarians, who take on the roles of teacher, information specialist, and instructional consultant, heighten this impact. As teachers and instructional consultants, they not only teach information literacy skills, but also work with teachers to integrate these skills into curriculum projects. Many of these librarians teach students, teachers, administrators, and parents how to use these new technology resources. Librarians work with teachers to develop such resources as independent learning programs or curriculum packages on specialized subjects using all types of media; they mentor students in youth created content and interactive presentations. To make library resources more readily available to students and teachers within the schools, library staff adopt flexible scheduling to accommodate both classes and individualized instruction. Library OPACs, content databases, and websites are accessible 24/7 to students on their mobile devices.

As information specialists, library media specialists also work with teachers to emphasize literature and the enjoyment of reading. Programs such as book clubs and contests are developed with teachers, administrators, and parents to reward students for increasing their reading; librarians also provide book talks in the classroom to stimulate interest in current genres and titles. To further encourage participation, media specialists market the entire library media program.

Many school systems with more than one school site have established library media programs at the district level to assist on-site library media center staff. By the 1990s, centralized district level operations such as materials ordering, cataloging, and processing, as well as circulation functions, were automated. Currently, district library media centers may also handle site licensing of e-books, subscription databases, and streaming video collections. The district library media staff members also help on-site library personnel develop programs to meet the educational goals of their individual schools.

The organization of school libraries depends upon the educational programs of the schools they serve. Most school libraries are centralized in one geographic area, whereas others have a central library media center supported by satellite subject resource centers. These centers may be adjacent to the central facility or adjacent to classes in their subject areas in other parts of the building. However, the program's ability to become fully integrated into the school's curriculum, rather than its organizational structure, that determines program effectiveness.

The school library itself continues to change. Mirroring the trend in collaborative learning areas found in academic libraries, spaces within school libraries for collaborative work among teachers, students, and library personnel are being created. Some libraries include small rooms for group study and collaboration as well as classrooms large enough for coordinated library-subject instruction.

School Library Funding

The ALA notes in the "State of America's Libraries Report 2014" that "school library spending on books and audiovisual materials decreased by an average of 10.5 percent ($760) from 2007–2008 ($7,260) to 2010–2011 ($6,500)." The report further notes, "School libraries continue to feel the combined pressures of recession-driven financial tightening and federal neglect, and school libraries in some districts and some states still face elimination or de-professionalization of their programs."[39]

The notable economic pressures on school library funding sources are perhaps even more severe than that of public libraries. The budget downturns continue to occur at the same time that new digital learning environments have increased the need for robust technology in school libraries. Funding from public and private granting agencies, in addition to the E-rate program to support ongoing broadband access, are described earlier in this chapter.

School Library Staffing

The development of quality library programs depends on the development of qualified library staff to manage these programs. Most states require that staff with teaching certification must be in charge whenever children are present. Thus, school librarians with teaching credentials should staff the majority of school libraries. These librarians have either a master's in library science or a master's in educational media, and some work under district library coordinators.

The success of the library program in each school often depends on the librarian's acceptance by the other teachers as an important member of the educational team. For a school librarian to be able to fulfill this role beyond the walls of the library, they need well-trained paraprofessionals and clerical staff who are capable of operating the library hour by hour or even day by day, freeing the librarian to work with teachers in their classrooms and other areas of the school beyond the physical library. Librarians plan services and coordinate programs with their staff and with teachers and administrators. When such a team is in place, students learn.

The NCES conducted a federal study on school libraries based on data gathered from schools during the 2011/2012 academic year. While some leaders in the library field find the results not representative of the true staffing picture on the ground, results from NCES survey included the following:

- About two-thirds (67%) of library media centers in traditional public schools had full-time, paid, state-certified library media center specialists.
- One-third (33%) of library media centers in public charter schools had full-time, paid, state-certified library media center specialists.
- Twenty percent of library media centers in traditional public schools had no state-certified library media center specialists (full or part time).
- Fifty-six percent of those in public charter schools had no state-certified library media center specialists (full or part time).
- Fifty-two percent of all public schools had paid, professional library media center staff with a master's degree in a library-related major field.
- Twenty-seven percent in public charter schools had paid and professional library media center staff with a master's degree.[40]

As school librarians become more successful in their educational role, they can turn the day-to-day operations of the library over to their support staff. Encouraged by national and state guidelines, many schools develop full-time library staff based on a ratio of one specialist to one technician and one clerk. At the building level, this means that library technicians often supervise clerks, students, and volunteers in checking materials in and out. Library media technicians also supervise building resource centers that are separate from the main library. In some smaller schools, library technicians operate individual school libraries under the direction of a system-wide librarian.

Effectiveness of School Libraries

Accountability in education is now emphasized, in part because of the *No Child Left Behind Act* of 2001, which links performance on standardized tests with rewards and/or penalties at the school level. Recent studies by NCES confirm that school library use increases test scores:

- Students in the lowest quartile of composite test scores make less focused use of library resources.
- Students in the middle and highest three quartiles of composite test scores reported higher use of library resources for assignments, in-school projects, and research papers.
- Seventy-nine percent of students reported library staff to be helpful or very helpful with finding research resources.
- Schools with fewer than 400 students were less likely to have state-certified librarians on staff. Catholic and other private schools were less likely than public schools to have state-certified librarians on staff. The Western United States, as a region, had the fewest state-certified librarians on staff.
- Sixty-two percent of school libraries had career and college databases.

Racial and ethnic differences in school library use also were apparent.[41]

A growing body of research reveals that school libraries have a positive impact on student performance, particularly on standardized tests. A 2005 study by Illinois School Library Media Association researchers confirmed that school library staff members with higher qualifications yielded significantly better student performance, stating, "The principal assets of a strong school library program are those who staff it—including both librarians and other staff." In this study, well-qualified library staff correlated to a 13 percent increase in reading performance for elementary, 8 percent for middle, and 7 percent for high school students. At elementary and middle school levels, the positive correlation between writing performance and school libraries staffed by professionally trained personnel is even stronger, with increases of more than 17 percent in students' scores. At the high school level, better-qualified staff in school libraries help to increase their schools' average ACT scores by almost 5 percent over those schools with libraries staffed by those with lesser training.[42]

Clearly, when library media center metrics, such as staffing, hours of service, information resources purchases, and technology availability, are maximized, reading scores improve. Studies from other states demonstrating similar findings about the power and efficacy of school libraries have been gathered at the website of Library Research Services.[43] While these results provide compelling evidence demonstrating the value of school libraries, the studies have yet to be translated into increased school library funding from legislators.

New Roles for School Librarians

Among the exciting new challenges for school library personnel is working with their districts on implementation of the Common Core State Standards (CCSS), a set of academic standards for mathematics and English language arts and literacy. Since its development in 2009, 43 states and the District of Columbia have adopted CCSS for K-12 use. These standards are designed to address and improve the academic progress of America's students by implementing a nationwide academic standards program, rather than the previous differing and piecemeal standards that varied from state to state. CCSS is meant to assist in reversing a current trend that finds many students still in need of remediation in their postsecondary work. Additionally, the new standards strive to prepare all students for future success in college, career, and life. Changes stemming from implementation of Common Core have drawn concern from parents and vocal critics. Thus, educators at K-12 levels need to be prepared to respond to basic questions about CCSS and help parents learn about the new standards program.

Common Core greatly affects school libraries and their staff. CCSS places a new focus on the use of primary sources and on increased reading of nonfiction materials especially in history and science, in addition to literature. Drawing on these resources, student content creation is emphasized across the curriculum. Thus, school library personnel now select, acquire, and provide access to Common Core-approved library resources and materials, often using district-wide licenses for productivity and collaborative software; electronic databases, and e-books; 3D printers and other technology that supports CCSS-compliant assignments and curriculum. In addition to purchasing these specific library materials, school library workers need to become very conversant in their use and application, so that they in turn can teach and mentor faculty and students on the use of these new tools and on content creation in project-based learning.

Leaders from the American Library Association, particularly recent ALA president Barbara Stripling, see new opportunities for school media centers and their workers in these standards. "On one hand, budget and testing pressures have led to decisions to eliminate or de-professionalize school libraries," noted Stripling. "On the other hand, the increased emphasis on college and career readiness, plus the integration of technology, has opened an unprecedented door to school librarian leadership."[44] To advance the goal that every U.S. school will have an effective school library program, Stripling and ALA developed a comprehensive advocacy campaign for school libraries in five critical areas:

- Literacy—Today's school librarians must be able to teach critical new literacy skills to enable young people to evaluate and make sense of text presented in all formats and to be producers and communicators of ideas, not just consumers of information.

- Inquiry—The mission of the school library is to ensure that students are equipped with essential critical-thinking and information skills, and school librarians must collaborate with classroom teachers to make inquiry an integral part of the school curriculum.

- Social and emotional growth—The school library must be a safe space for discovery and collaboration where young people develop self-confidence, learn perseverance, and acquire social skills like the ability to be part of a team and show respect for the perspectives of others.

- Creativity and imagination—School libraries must offer liberating experiences of imagination and creation. Students see characters in their minds as they listen to stories. Young people imagine their own stories or create expressions of their learning to share with others.

- Thoughtful use of technology—School librarians must teach students and teachers how to use the latest technology tools for personal and academic learning, communication, production, and collaboration.[45]

ACADEMIC LIBRARIES

Academic libraries are found in higher-education institutions, serving the twin goals of supporting the specific campus curricula while also serving the research needs of faculty, students, and the larger academic community. There are more than 3,600 academic libraries in the United States, in community colleges, private colleges, teaching and research universities, and technical institutions. Although novices to the field often refer to school libraries (serving K-12 students) as academic libraries, that is a misuse of the term as it is used by practitioners. Academic libraries are those serving college students and faculty; the missions and functions of these two categories of libraries are distinct and differ greatly. The mission of an academic library is to help its parent college or university to achieve the educational goals of its students and faculty.

The mission of community colleges is to teach undergraduate students in their first two years of college. The curriculum generally includes academic programs to prepare students to transfer to upper-division programs at four-year colleges as well as vocational training programs to prepare students for direct entry into the workforce. As junior colleges have evolved into colleges of the community and for the community, so the mission of the community college library has expanded from traditional curriculum support to include services for lifelong learners and community users. Distance learning courses continue to expand and challenge libraries to keep pace with the information needs of geographically remote students.

Libraries in institutions that support undergraduate and graduate programs differ from two-year college libraries. Funding levels and sources for four-year universities, as well as the scope and content of collections, contrast greatly with community college facilities. Large universities may provide separate subject-based libraries (e.g., business, life sciences, music, arts and humanities, special collections and archives, law, medicine) and may also have distinct library facilities serving undergraduates and graduates. These subject libraries often more closely resemble special libraries (discussed later in this chapter) than they do traditional academic libraries.

At the top of the academic library pyramid are the institutional members of the Association of Research Libraries (ARL), a nonprofit organization of 125 world-class research libraries in North America. Characterized by the depth, scope, and distinction of their collections, the librarians at ARL member institutions are leaders in strategic thinking in academic librarianship, providing a "forum for the exchange of ideas and [serving] as an agent for collective action."[46] ARL is perhaps best known to librarians as the creative impetus behind LibQUAL+, a suite of statistical services that libraries use to solicit library user feedback and implement change.

Academic libraries have moved from collection storehouses to learning and research centers, providing access to information in its varied forms. Previously, an academic library's volume count defined prestige. By the turn of this century, the leading academic library criterion had shifted to access to—rather than ownership of—information resources. Unique primary sources in special collections and archives enjoy new prominence and relevance as library administrators seek to distinguish their collections from those of other academic libraries.

Types of Academic Libraries

Over the past 45 years, the Carnegie Commission on Higher Education has created and refined a definitive classification, or taxonomy, of colleges and universities. The Carnegie Classification, together with the number and levels of degrees granted by an academic institution, inform the growth and development of academic libraries on individual campuses.

The 2010 Carnegie Classification list includes the following major categories:

- Doctoral/Research Universities
- Master's Colleges and Universities
- Baccalaureate Colleges
- Associate's Colleges
- Special Focus Institutions
  - Theological seminaries, Bible colleges, and other faith-related institutions
  - Medical schools and medical centers
  - Other health profession schools
  - Schools of engineering
  - Schools of business and management
  - Schools of art, music, and design
  - Schools of law
  - Other technology-related schools
  - Other special-focus institutions
- Tribal Colleges
- Not Classified (26 institutions)[47]

These classifications describe the breadth and depth of programs, with the caveat that some institutions straddle two or more classifications. This taxonomy also highlights different philosophies of library service. Different approaches taken by academic libraries are informed by the extent to which their parent institutions emphasize the creation of new knowledge.

All educational institutions are engaged in disseminating knowledge to their campus communities. The extent to which an institution focuses on this mission affects collection development and librarian skills sets in distinct ways. Supporting cutting-edge researchers in such disciplines as science, technology, engineering, and mathematics (STEM) requires specific (and expensive) collections and services. Researchers at ARL universities need unusual depth and scope in library collections, particularly archives and manuscripts as well as highly specialized information resources. Monograph collections of millions of volumes are therefore not uncommon. Professional journals, with rigorous standards for editing and publication, are a minimum requirement for knowledge bases of their fields.

Undergraduates, by contrast, are exploring varied disciplines and their related vocabularies and concepts. One of the misperceptions of academic librarianship is that if a library has a collection rich enough to support researchers, it must have more than enough resources to satisfy the needs of the undergraduates studying that same discipline. This is not the case. Undergraduates, by definition, are not generally prepared to understand and benefit from advanced discourse of specific disciplines. Smaller but tailored collections, measured in tens of thousands, are generally appropriate for lower-division undergraduates; a few hundred thousand appropriate volumes can support the needs of upper-division undergraduates. In any case, library support for the curricula taught in the classrooms is one vital measure of a good academic library.

As with faculty roles, librarian roles also differ within these institutions. Within the community colleges, faculty assignments are weighted almost exclusively toward classrooms and laboratories. Evaluation of instructors is centered on how well they help students learn—as are rewards, such as promotion and tenure. At most four-year universities, faculty members are expected not only to teach well in new learning environments, but also to publish scholarly research in their disciplines. The evaluation of faculty (which can include academic librarians) for retention, promotion, tenure, or termination is weighted on teaching (or librarian) effectiveness, scholarly publications, and campus and community service. In an undergraduate college focused on teaching and learning, librarians have educational backgrounds comparable to those of classroom faculty. The role each plays in helping students learn is also similar, so faculty status and resulting performance expectations for librarians reflect these demands.

A college library staff is generally much smaller than that of a university library. College libraries are likely to be staffed by five to ten professionals who are supported by paraprofessional, clerical, and student personnel. University libraries require many more, often highly specialized, staff members to acquire, process, and disseminate the information contained in much larger collections, which can range from several hundred thousand to millions of volumes. These larger libraries are correspondingly staffed with as many as several hundred professional, paraprofessional, technical, clerical, and student assistant personnel. Also, university libraries generally have large collections in almost every subject area, whereas college libraries tend to concentrate on the general arts and sciences with a strong emphasis on humanities, social sciences, and the physical and biological sciences.

Development of College and University Libraries

The majority of academic libraries began as mere adjuncts to the classroom, housed in small rooms and administered by part-time faculty members. As late as the 1920s, even the largest university libraries were no bigger than those of a modern-day medium-sized college. As published knowledge began to expand rapidly, academic libraries expanded their collections accordingly. During the mid-20th century, the collections of research university libraries doubled every 17 to 20 years. The large influx of students after World War II, largely funded by veterans' benefits, also placed a demand on libraries to provide materials in great quantities.

A typical academic library of the 1950s would have contained only print materials (books, serials, and pamphlets) housed in a single building. Universities sometimes kept collections in closed stack areas, to which only graduate students and faculty members were admitted. Undergraduates had to ask for books at a circulation desk and wait for the materials to be paged and delivered to them. Because research campuses were oriented to faculty and graduate student research, library objectives followed, rather than focusing primarily on the undergraduate support of classroom learning. Eventually, larger universities provided separate undergraduate libraries. The explosive growth of published information and professional literature made it clear that no library could meet all of the needs of their faculty and students, leading to increased cooperation with other libraries and the rise of interlibrary loans. By the 1960s, as academic libraries developed in new ways to support emerging educational disciplines and teaching styles, collections expanded beyond traditional print materials to include audio- and videotape, microforms, transparencies, and computer-assisted instruction.

Changes to academic library standards have led to the development of new assessment metrics. While previous academic standards had focused on traditional library materials and services, new standards emphasized quality learning resource programs and unfettered student access to library materials. Previously, the focus, particularly in university libraries, had been on serving faculty and graduate students. As the needs of undergraduate students gained importance, academic libraries focused on providing professional assistance on information resources to these students. Amassing large collections in anticipation of what someone might need in 20 years was no longer enough. Collections, though still important, are no longer an end in themselves. Rather, they are increasingly the means to the end of conveying information.

ALA's Association of College and Research Libraries (ACRL) develops guidelines, standards, and frameworks for academic libraries using the following principles:

- **Institutional effectiveness:** Libraries define, develop, and measure outcomes that contribute to institutional effectiveness and apply findings for purposes of continuous improvement.
- **Professional values:** Libraries advance professional values of intellectual freedom, intellectual property rights and values, user privacy and confidentiality, collaboration, and user-centered service.

- **Educational role:** Libraries partner in the educational mission of the institution to develop and support information-literate learners who can discover, access, and use information effectively for academic success, research, and lifelong learning.

- **Discovery:** Libraries enable users to discover information in all formats through effective use of technology and organization of knowledge.

- **Collections:** Libraries provide access to collections sufficient in quality, depth, diversity, format, and currency to support the research and teaching missions of the institution.

- **Space:** Libraries are the intellectual commons where users interact with ideas in both physical and virtual environments to expand learning and facilitate the creation of new knowledge.

- **Management/Administration:** Libraries engage in continuous planning and assessment to inform resource allocation and to meet their mission effectively and efficiently.

- **Personnel:** Libraries provide sufficient number and quality of personnel to ensure excellence and to function successfully in an environment of continuous change.

- **External relations:** Libraries engage the campus and broader community through multiple strategies in order to advocate, educate, and promote their value.[48]

The 2011 "ACRL Standards" represent new advances over the quantitative measures of the past. They parallel regional accrediting agencies in their emphasis on accountability in student learning outcomes and institutional effectiveness, shifting the focus from what is taught to what is learned—a subtle but profound change.

Technology

Academic libraries have also developed automated systems for library operations. Some libraries in universities were so successful in this development that they sold their products commercially under labels such as UTLAS (University of Toronto), BRS (Bibliographic Retrieval Services, State University of New York), and NOTIS (Northwestern University). As technology became more sophisticated, computer systems grew from single-purpose software for internal operations (e.g., circulation or cataloging) to integrated library systems, such as Illinois's Library Computer System (ILCS) including not only circulation and cataloging but also online public access catalogs (OPACs). Students and faculty from cooperating academic institutions can use the database as an online union catalog to locate and borrow materials via direct requests or interlibrary loan. Some systems include modules for serials control (Serials of Illinois Libraries or SILO), online search (BRS), and materials acquisitions that are also used for collection analysis and development.

In addition to providing automated services, academic libraries took the lead in intra-campus and inter-campus networking. In some cases, institution-wide computer centers and programs were added to the academic library's service roles. Computer labs were made available in libraries for students' homework use. Some schools, such as Carnegie-Mellon, made computers available in students' dormitory rooms. OPACs were made accessible to students and faculty in their dormitories, offices, or homes. Libraries promoted inter-campus networking using teleconferencing, plus audio- and video-based distance learning via satellite, TV, or the World Wide Web.

Libraries marketed their services to community business and economic leaders. Services such as consultation with professional librarians, library cards for local businesses, journal photocopying services, document delivery, and search services of expensive databases, such as *DIALOG* and *Lexis-Nexis*, were made available for a fee or in-kind donations. Many institutions made their resources available for a fee to local citizens.

Academic libraries also took the lead in developing resource-sharing networks with other libraries. Early recognition by these libraries that they must collaborate on resources, both bibliographically and physically, led to pilot resource-sharing programs. Such sharing originally began on an informal basis, with academic libraries in the same geographic area sharing materials or allowing reciprocal borrowing among their patrons. Academic institutions entered into consortial partnerships to share their educational resources and designate specific collecting areas by campus, reducing costly duplication of subject collections. The Center for Research Libraries provided cooperative storage facilities for significant but low-use materials for its members.

These developments placed renewed emphasis on teaching students specific ways to access information. In addition to conducting library orientation sessions, librarians developed computer and media programs highlighting specific departments or individual library resource tools. Librarians also are teaching credit and noncredit bibliographic instruction courses. In some cases, the courses were competency-based and a graduation requirement. Libraries also established programs to help first-generation college students gain greater understanding of the library as a learning tool. Academic librarians have reached out directly to undergraduates to promote library use. Indirect efforts of marketing library services through classroom faculty are even more successful.

Academic Institutions in the 21st Century

The fundamental academic library goals of collecting to support campus curricula and providing user services to the academic community have not changed, but the methods for accomplishing them have. These changes continue to manifest even as budget and funding pressures on academic collections and staffing linger because of the Great Recession that began in 2007. Therefore, the continuing importance of articulating and demonstrating the value of the academic library to upper-level campus administrators is a primary responsibility of academic library administrators. The ACRL is in the midst of a three-year project entitled "Assessment in Action: Academic Libraries and Student Success." This grant-funded project brings together librarians, faculty, and administrators to design and implement methods to strengthen the competencies of librarians in campus leadership and library advocacy, and examine the impact of the academic library on student learning outcomes.[49]

Trends

New ways of creating, acquiring, and using digital resources have led in tandem to new concepts and terms to describe how information is managed and shared, such as the following:

Knowledge Management (KM) is a "multidisciplinary approach to achieving institutional objectives by making the best use of knowledge. KM focuses on processes such as acquiring, creating, and sharing knowledge and the cultural and technical foundations that support them."[50] KM, established as a discipline in 1991, is now taught in business, information technology, and library and information science.

Digital Asset Management (DAM) is an umbrella term for the policies, procedures, and workflow needed for ingesting, annotating, cataloging, storing, and retrieving digital assets held in a variety of file formats, including text, audio, and visual files. DAM makes it possible for users to see full-text and images on demand over the Web. DAM professionals are proficient in spreadsheet, word processing, presentation, and collaboration software, plus project management skills, coding languages, and DAM systems, whether open-source or commercial.

Scholarly Communication is a "system through which research and other scholarly writings are created, evaluated for quality, disseminated to the scholarly community, and preserved for future use," as defined by the ARL.[51] The importance of creating alternative methods of scholarly communication arose in the mid-1980s, when library budgets were cut and the cost of journal subscriptions from commercial publishers rapidly began to escalate. This crisis in scholarly communication limited access to research for university students and, ironically, for the very academics who had published in these journals.

"Libraries and laboratories—crucial nodes of the World Wide Web—are buckling under economic pressure, and the information they diffuse is being diverted away from the public sphere, where it can do the most good," notes Robert Darnton. Information "comes filtered through expensive technologies and financed by powerful corporations." He writes:

> Consider the cost of scientific periodicals, most of which are published exclusively online. It has increased at four times the rate of inflation since 1986. The average price of a year's subscription to a chemistry journal is now $4,044. In 1970 it was $33. A subscription to the *Journal of Comparative Neurology* cost $30,860 in 2012—the equivalent of six hundred monographs. Three giant publishers—Reed Elsevier, Wiley-Blackwell, and Springer—publish 42 percent of all academic articles, and they make giant profits from them. In 2013 Elsevier turned a 39 percent profit on an income of £2.1 billion from its science, technical, and medical journals.[52]

Open Access refers to unrestricted online availability to peer-reviewed scholarly research, which has evolved largely in response to the crisis in scholarly communication. Even before the term *open access* was commonly used, librarians, academics, researchers, and funding agencies were using the power of World Wide Web to publish and deliver scholarly content. What began as a vehicle for delivering unfettered access to scholarly research has expanded to include such content as undergraduate capstone projects, graduate theses and dissertations, and even whole monographs.

Institutional Repositories (IRs) provide open-access methods for scholarly communication. IRs specifically address how a university, public library, or scholarly institution stores, preserves, and shares its intellectual capital with local users and an increasingly global community. As the need for institutional management of diffuse digital assets has grown, the technology and standards to create IRs are maturing to the point of acceptance and widespread adoption. By both establishing professional standards and taking leadership roles at university, academic libraries are using IRs to demonstrate value to their parent institutions.

In an influential 2002 paper, the Scholarly Publishing and Academic Resources Coalition (SPARC) defined academic institutional repositories as scholarly in content; cumulative and perpetual in access; defined by the institution; and providing open access to scholarly research according to professional standards.[53]

IR systems are generally either commercial, turnkey software used by libraries with little or no dedicated information technology support (i.e., Open-Text, Digital Commons) or open-source systems customized by on-staff library technologists, such as Dspace and Fedora.

According to ALA, "Academic libraries may become even more active participants in the knowledge creation cycle in their institution, and academic librarians are exploring ways to help campuses build infrastructures and service programs that will preserve their institutions' intellectual assets and make them available for use by others." These developments "highlight the need for research data services in colleges and universities, which is leading to a growing demand for library professionals with data management and analysis skills. While some academic libraries are already engaged in these activities, many others are examining ways they can best provide a range of research data services."[54] For a fuller discussion of the crisis in scholarly communication and the growth and development of institutional repositories, see Chapter 10.

Facilities

Librarians are changing the footprint of library interiors, using the space freed by the transition from print resources to digital information to create new collaborative learning environments. The impact of this shift is discussed fully in Chapters 7 and 10.

ALA has identified the following current trends in library building and renovation:

- Open-plan space, which provides flexibility and ensures that a building can easily be modified in the future.

- Semi-private space, which recognizes that open-plan space may not be appropriate for every activity or suit the taste of every user.

- Technology-rich space, which should permeate the library and enable users to be the best learners they can.[55]

"Furniture has emerged as a key factor in creating variety in the library experience . . . [because] it can easily be rearranged to change the look and feel of a space," states Les Watson, editor of *Better Library and Learning Spaces: Projects, Trends and Ideas.* Watson further believes that all libraries, and academic ones in particular, require "a variety of spaces that match the diversity of learners and their learning activities underpinned by capable staff, great technology, excellent resources, and timely and accurate understanding of user behavior and satisfaction."[56]

Helen Chu, director of Academic Technology at the University of Oregon, presents frequently on her experience implementing collaborative learning environments on academic libraries and campuses. Chu believes key elements in creating successful environments in which student and faculty learn together include peer (student) assistance, full-time expert staff, readily accessible tech books and journals, integrated technologies, furniture that facilitates conversation and collaboration, and a concierge to help navigate the resources and assistance available.[57] These elements must be more than a collection of expertly curated resources. Design of collaborative learning environments must be driven by content, new teaching methods, and supported by both the technology and the built environment.[58]

EDUCAUSE is a nonprofit association of influential information technology (IT), library, and educational leaders. This is the driving organization for the development of collaborative learning spaces known as *learning commons* or *information commons*. EDUCAUSE visualizes these repurposed library areas as "full-service learning, research, and project space," promoting group learning and digital and technological fluency for students and faculty alike.

> The modern commons is a meeting place, typically offering at least one area where students can rearrange furniture to accommodate impromptu planning sessions or secure a quiet place to work near a window. . . . The learning commons provides areas for group meetings, tools to support creative efforts, and on-staff specialists to provide help as needed. And yet the successful learning commons does not depend solely upon adaptable space configuration or the latest technological gear. Its strength lies in the relationships it supports, whether these are student-to-student, student-to-faculty, student-to-staff, student-to-equipment, or student-to-information. Learning commons are alive with the voices of students working together, establishing the kinds of connections that promote active, engaged learning.[59]

Resources

In the 21st century, academic libraries face the dilemma of keeping up with new electronic forms of information. Electronic products offer opportunities to provide library services in ways that were previously not possible—information can now be delivered anytime to any place. Continued growth in distance education course offerings (which in some cases have completely replaced on-site curriculum) also has a large impact on the strong demand for e-resources.

However, these services cannot be offered without funding for the infrastructure and the staff needed to support these innovations. ALA notes that

recent expenditure figures illustrate how librarians are "juggling their historical role in managing print materials and new demands for digital resources
and services, noting that most new funds for academic programs are in fact
coming from reallocation rather than new revenues."[60]

Studies by the Carnegie Foundation and other organizations suggest
that the metrics for academic libraries—and for colleges in general—must
be increasingly tied to undergraduate student success and educational outcomes. Regarding the newer model of collaborative teaching and learning,
one study found that "faculty influence library use in many ways including
through the classroom, through writing assignments that require library use,
or by simply interacting with undergraduates by working jointly on projects
or providing feedback on term papers." Additional findings from this study
that revealed undergraduates who wrote more term papers, attended college
full time, or devoted more time to studying, all spent more time engaged in
library use.[61]

As academic libraries become more integrated into the total learning experience, the concept of the library as something greater than a physical place
grows. The following information services can now be provided remotely:

- Electronic reserves
- E-books
- Full-text articles
- Online reservations for media, devices, and group study rooms
- Online information competency tutorials
- Online public access catalogs (OPACs)
- Full-text databases licensed for use remotely or in the library
- Digital archives and online exhibitions providing access to primary
  sources
- Virtual reference assistance
- Online interlibrary loan and reserve requests
- Student and faculty scholarship

Studies suggest that users are more likely to come to the library if they can
first check online to determine that relevant information and/or individual
assistance awaits them at the library. The shift to providing digital resources
at the convenience of the user, however, only underlines the importance of
transforming library buildings into welcoming and collaborative learning
spaces, as discussed earlier.

Academic Library Careers

An academic library director is often a dean of learning resources, who
reports to an academic vice president. The library dean is not only the administrator of a large facility, staff, and budget, but can also be active in the council
of deans and upper university administration. This expanded administrative

role strengthens and solidifies the library's place in academic institutions. As respected library leader and educator Richard De Gennaro observed in 1990, and which still resonates today, "the greatest challenge facing academic libraries is not funding or technology, but leadership and administrative ability."[62] Library leaders must be committed to making their libraries more accountable, innovative, and entrepreneurial. This is best accomplished by developing students who are fluent in the use of digital resources, integrating libraries into the academic curricula, and providing access to information for students and faculty needs regardless of location or format.

Academic libraries provided one-third of all jobs for new library school graduates in 2012, up from 26 percent in 2011, according to 2013 reports in *Library Journal.* "Academic libraries reported 85,752 full-time equivalent (FTE) staff working in 3,793 academic libraries during the fall of 2012, a decrease of 3.6 percent (3,191 positions) from 2010. The number of academic librarians decreased only 0.4 percent since 2010 to a total of 26,606 FTE positions. At the same time, FTE student enrollments have increased by 2.6 percent since 2010 to 24.2 million. Librarians accounted for 31 percent of the total number of FTE staff in academic libraries."

In addition to these statistics, the ALA 2014 report notes, "Data curation, digital resource management and preservation, assessment, scholarly communication, and improved services for graduate students are growth areas for academic libraries.[63] New job descriptions for librarians reflect these changes and include such titles as *digital scholarship services librarian, digital archivist, numeric and spatial data specialist, embedded librarian,* and *marketing and communication librarian.*

Increasingly, librarians working in a university or college are being freed from supervising in-house library operations. This shift allows librarians to reach out to teaching faculty and students beyond the walls of the library, play a demonstrable role in collaborative learning, and participate in campus governance. Librarians also now serve on higher education advisory committees at the consortial, regional, or state level.

Academic library support staff members are assuming new responsibility for supervision of day-to-day library activities, based on established service parameters, policies, and procedures. An associate's degree in library technology, including coursework in acquisitions, reference, and library computer systems, is usually a hiring requirement, along with the following abilities:

- Communication skills, to listen to and understand patrons' needs, provide clear answers to questions, and teach users how to find and use library resources

- Computer skills, to help students and faculty research topics, including using integrated library systems and newer discovery or "single search" services, such as Innovative Interfaces' Millennium or OCLC WorldShare

- Cataloging and processing skills, to ensure that library materials are correctly identified and retrievable on demand

- Interpersonal skills, to work effectively with other library employees, library users, student assistants, interns, and faculty

SPECIAL LIBRARIES AND INFORMATION CENTERS

As noted in Table 3.1 earlier in this chapter, there are some 7,000 different special libraries in the United States. The term *special library* is often used as an umbrella term to refer to any library that is not a public, school, or academic library. Most often, special libraries are devoted to specific subject areas, such as music or law; special formats, such as maps, archives, rare books, and manuscripts; or special clientele, such as hospital workers or prison inmates. Parent organizations or institutions, such as banks, insurance companies, churches and religious communities, and federal or state agencies often have special libraries. If there is an organization, corporation, institution, or group of people with a special need for library and information services, then a special library has probably been developed to address these needs. A few very different examples include the small Hearst Castle historical monument staff library, the Smithsonian Institution's research libraries, the comprehensive Coca-Cola corporate archives, and the voluminous LDS Family History Library in Utah.

With all this diversity, is there a unifying theme or common core that ties all of these libraries together? What could a large scientific library with thousands of volumes and many paid professionals have in common with a small local historical museum library with 1,000 books and a photograph collection cared for by volunteer staff members? What characteristics of these two libraries would enable one term to be used to define both?

First, special library services are very narrowly focused to support the activities of the library's parent organization. Second, their collection development is linked to very specialized subject areas. In both cases, these libraries develop their collections and design their services to directly support and further the objectives of a parent organization. Finally, these libraries are primarily concerned with actively seeking out and providing information to the organization's clients or patrons, rather than building broad collections for potential users. In other words, special libraries provide special and even individualized services for their patrons. These three characteristics are key elements of any special library or information center. Additionally, depending on the special library, their resources—on-site and virtual—may be accessible only to employees of their parent organization or may require permission to use.

The distinction between special libraries and other types of libraries is not always precise. Often, the subject-specific departmental libraries within large universities, public library systems, or government agencies function more like special libraries. The professional orientation of the staff is often focused on the subject matter. For example, music librarians often have their primary allegiance to the Music Library Association (MLA) rather than to the broad-based ALA, just as archivists are more aligned with the Society of American Archivists (SAA). Some special librarians have dual expertise and are actively involved in scholarship or practice of their libraries' subject disciplines as well as in librarianship.

Even within subdivisions of special libraries, there is unlimited variation in the types of libraries and the opportunities for employment. An example would a recent library-science class visit by law librarians from the following organizations:

- Large law firm in downtown Los Angeles
- Los Angeles County Law Library
- University of Southern California School of Law Library
- Ninth District Court of Appeals Library
- Outsourcing agency that specializes in placing temporary and permanent employees in law libraries

The librarian of the large firm and the court librarian serve only those within their own organizations. For the firm this is a competitive issue: it is in business to make money, and its information resources and the skills to retrieve them on demand are among its most valuable commodities. The firm does not want competitors to know what it is researching or to make it easy for those competitors to do similar research. In the case of the court library, confidentiality and privacy, more than competitiveness, are the driving forces. The entire clientele of the library comprise the judges and their immediate staffs. The judges need to be able to complete their research without being exposed to the prying eyes of others or the interruptions of chance encounters with parties to the litigation they are adjudicating.

At the opposite extreme, the Los Angeles County Law Library functions almost as a public library. Its collections make it the largest law library west of the Mississippi River. Although LA County's primary clientele are judges, lawyers, and their staffs, the general public constitutes more than 30 percent of its users.

Dress codes are another area in which law libraries differ greatly. The general rule seems to be that staff members dress slightly more conservatively than the typical clientele. One large law firm took the dress code one step further. It required all non-lawyers to wear a uniform. The firm was so large that not everyone knew the other employees who worked there. The lawyers felt the need to be able to walk into a room and immediately know who the members of their team were. Therefore, the company bought staff members blue blazers and gray skirts or slacks to wear on the job. Many of this firm's clients were bankers and others in the financial community who dress very conservatively.

Employees at other law libraries in Los Angeles dress less formally. Firms that specialize in entertainment law encourage their staff to dress more casually to blend in better with the customary attire of their clientele. Law school libraries where the primary clientele are college students and faculty also have more casual standards.

The growth and development of special libraries have varied widely. Yet for all of the variety in funding, type, subject, and clientele, special libraries and information centers continue to have more similarities than differences. Their financing, governance, resources, and services are strongly affected by their importance to the well-being of their parent organizations. Therefore, their fortunes can change quickly, as the fortunes of their parent organizations either flourish or falter.

Research Libraries

Research libraries are some of our most important special libraries. Because they have been developed to support the research needs of the world's scholars, they have traditionally been allied with academic libraries. Most are actually part of large universities, but many can be found outside academe. The New York Public Library (NYPL) has its own, mostly privately funded, research library as its central library; NYPL branches are tax-funded public libraries.

Other research libraries were originally established and endowed by wealthy benefactors. Often these research libraries are completely independent and without ties to a larger organization. They are governed by their own boards of directors, and manage their own collections, facilities, and endowments. Henry and Emily Folger, whose fortune came from Standard Oil, were discerning and avid collectors of works by and about William Shakespeare. Their personal library eventually became the renowned Folger Shakespeare Library in Washington, DC. Another example is New York's The Morgan Library & Museum, which began as the private library of financier Pierpont Morgan.

Yet other research libraries were founded to complement each other. The Newberry Library (humanities) and the John Crerar Library (physical and natural sciences) in Chicago built their collections to enhance each other and the Chicago Public Library (social sciences). Sometimes these libraries are no longer able to maintain their independence. The Crerar Library, for example, was absorbed into the University of Chicago in 1984. With the ability to digitize and share resources, independent research libraries are important—and often unique—links in the network of national information resources.

Federal Libraries

More than 1,500 federal libraries serve the various departments and agencies of the U.S. government. All federal libraries are considered special libraries because they serve the goals of their parent institutions and their users are usually staff members of these institutions. They include:

- National libraries—The Library of Congress (LC), National Library of Medicine, National Agricultural Library, National Library of Education (NLE).
- Cabinet-level libraries—Commerce, Defense, Energy, Justice, Labor, State, Treasury, and so forth.
- Agency libraries—National Aeronautics & Space Administration, National Science Foundation, National Archives and Records Administration, Supreme Court, Smithsonian Institution, so forth.
- Military and service academy libraries—Pentagon, Department of the Navy, U.S. Military Academy at West Point, so forth.

About 40 percent of these are scientific and technical (including health and medical) libraries that serve the special objectives of the agencies to which they belong. Another 40 percent are libraries at veterans' hospitals, federal prisons, and military installations. About 20 percent of all federal libraries serve the educational needs of active-duty personnel in U.S. armed forces, the military academies, and overseas schools for military dependents.

The importance of federal libraries to our national information resources is illustrated by their extensive research and subject collections. The most comprehensive federal collections are contained in the national libraries listed earlier. These four libraries not only provide extensive research collections in all forms of media, but also represent one-third of the total federal collections, one-half of all federal library expenditures, and two-fifths of all the personnel in federal libraries.

The nation's oldest federal cultural institution and the largest library in the world, the LC holds nearly 160 million items including books, recordings, photographs, maps and manuscripts in its collections and employs almost 5,000 people. Its name comes from its original mission to serve as the research arm of Congress, a purpose it still fulfills today. LC's formal mission is to "support the Congress in fulfilling its constitutional duties and to further the progress of knowledge and creativity for the benefit of the American people."[64]

Serving as a national library is still an unofficial function of the LC, although it has been steered in this direction by two important events. The first was Congress's purchase in 1815 of President Thomas Jefferson's personal library, then the largest private collection of books in the United States. Jefferson offered to sell his library to Congress as a replacement for the collection destroyed by the British during the War of 1812. "Although the broad scope of Jefferson's library was a cause for criticism of the purchase, Jefferson extolled the virtue of its broad sweep and established the principle of acquisition for the LC: 'There is in fact no subject to which a member of Congress may not have occasion to refer.' "[65]

The second event was the passage of the original U.S. Copyright Law in 1870, which required that two copies of every copyrighted work be submitted to LC. This national library function was further enhanced in the early 1900s, when the library began to sell its classification schedules and catalog cards to U.S. libraries. The *National Union Catalog* (NUC), the *Union List of Serials* (ULS), and the *National Union Catalog of Manuscript Collections* (NUCMC) enabled libraries to check the collections of the LC and the largest libraries in the United States. LC also became the designated national resource for creation of materials for users who are blind or physically disabled.

In addition to these major services to the nation, the primary purpose of LC is still to serve as a legislative library for Congress. Librarians of Congress have judiciously nurtured this relationship, and their skillful public relations have helped gain unparalleled financial support for the library and its programs, enabling LC and the other three national libraries to lead in the development of library automation programs. In the late 1950s, LC began exploring possibilities for automation of internal operations. By 1966, MAchine Readable Cataloging (MARC) was providing the framework and standards for computerizing cataloging data and has, with continual updating, become the standard worldwide. By the early 1990s, the LC catalog became available online to other libraries.

LC also leads in digitization initiatives, one of the earliest of which was *American Memory,* which "provides free and open access through the Internet to written and spoken words, sound recordings, still and moving images,

Blogs

Personal voices from the Library of Congress: compelling stories & fascinating facts.

Library of Congress Blog

Recent Posts

Celebrating Women: On Your Mark! Get Set! Mush!

Where Poetry Lives

Celebrating Women's History: Still Standing – The Story of Tammy Duckworth

Inside Adams: Science, Technology & Business

Recent Posts

Celebrating Librarian Extraordinaire Ruth S. Freitag

Carl Sagan, Imagination, Science, and Mentorship: An interview with David Grinspoon

Starting Points: Historical Statistics on African Americans

In The Muse: Performing Arts Blog

Recent Posts

Remembering Argos: Life and Loss in the Funeral Odes of Franz Liszt

Elias String Quartet Plays Haydn, Kurtág & Beethoven (March 7)

Gregory Porter Brings his Grammy-winning Jazz to the Coolidge

In Custodia Legis: Law Librarians of Congress

Recent Posts

The Sheinbein Saga and the Evolution of Israel's Extradition Law

Discovery: A Beginner's Guide

An interview with Jennifer Frazier, the Kentucky State Law Librarian

The Signal: Digital Preservation

Recent Posts

Nominations Now Open for the 2014 NDSA Innovation Awards

A Regional NDSA?

Things to Know About Personal Digital Archiving 2014

Teaching with the Library of Congress

Recent Posts

Creating Ripples of Change with Primary Sources from the Library of Congress

The Triangle Shirtwaist Factory Fire: Exploring Tragedy and Reform with Primary Sources

Visit us at Teaching and Learning and at ASCD!

Picture This: Library of Congress Prints & Photos

Recent Posts

St. Patrick's Day in the Army

Feast Your Eyes: Sold on Chocolate!

Caught Our Eyes: A Leaning Lighthouse

Copyright Matters: Digitization and Public Access

Recent Posts

Cumulative Motion Pictures and Dramas

Copyright digitization: Moving right along!

Getting ready for data capture: Sorting out the details in the catalog cards

From the Catbird Seat: Poetry & Literature at the Library of Congress

Recent Posts

Finding "Where Poetry Lives"

Kluge Center Spotlight: Arun Sood on Robert Burns

In Praise of Detective Peter, or How We Get By With a Little Help from Our Friends

Folklife Today

Recent Posts

Celebrating Women's History: Still Standing – The Story of Tammy Duckworth

The Aleutian Islands: WWII's Forgotten Campaign

Highlighting Ozark Collections for a Distinguished Guest

Voices of the Civil War

Recent Posts

"What shall men remember?"

"Those who struck at the nation's life, and those who struck to save it"

"Like a true yankee all ways escaped"

FIGURE 3.2 Several blogs from the Library of Congress website.
Courtesy Library of Congress, http://blogs.loc.gov/

prints, maps, and sheet music that document the American experience. It is a digital record of American history and creativity. More than 14 million public domain items are included from 90 historical collections." Similar archival digital collections have been launched at the state level.[66]

Reaching out to library users and the library profession, LC staff publishes blogs on 15 topics, including cinema, the Civil War, copyright and digitization, folklife, law, music, photographs, and teaching using resources from the vast collections at the LC.

The National Library of Medicine (NLM) (http://www.nlm.nih.gov/) developed *MEDLARS*, an online service that made 25 medical literature databases accessible to its 30,000 users by the early 1990s. The NLM's computerized cataloging information in the biomedical area was made available to medical libraries on *CATLINE*. Citations and indexes to articles were made available through *Index Medicus* or online through *MEDLINE* for the field of biomedicine. Because many of *MEDLARS*'s users were individuals, the NLM also provided *Grateful Med* software to allow health professionals access to more than 13 million references and abstracts via their personal computers. *PubMed* is now the access point for this content and much more, including 13 million abstracts, 14.2 million full-text articles, and selected content from 1809 to 1854. NLM also provides document delivery to medical libraries and health professionals and establishes regional medical libraries throughout the country to serve as resource centers. In-depth consumer health information is provided as well.[67]

The National Agriculture Library (NAL) (http://www.nal.usda.gov/) is a national leader in providing library and information services to the agricultural community. As early as 1970, the NAL made its computerized database, *AGRICOLA* (AGRICultural On Line Access), available to other libraries. The NAL is an active member of *AGLINET*, a voluntary association of 27 agricultural libraries, and U.S. Agriculture Information Network (*USAIN*), a national forum to discuss agricultural information issues. Because the success of any agricultural effort often depends on worldwide climate, the NAL also is an important part of the international agricultural information network, providing digital access to data, documents, and computer files throughout the world. Scientists, farmers, students, and laypeople use its information.

The NLE (http://ies.ed.gov/ncee/projects/nle/) was established in 1994, with materials dating from 1872. NLE's collections focus on education and related disciplines such as "law, public policy, economics, urban affairs, sociology, history, philosophy, and information science. The Library also serves as a depository under the Federal Depository Library Program of the U.S. Government Publishing Office, making available documents produced by various other federal government agencies. The Library offers information, statistical, and referral services to the Department of Education and other government agencies and institutions, and to the public."

Archives

Archives are the "non-current records of individuals, groups, institutions, and governments that contain information of enduring value. . . . Archives are located in federal, state, and local governments; schools, colleges, and universities; religious institutions; businesses; hospitals; museums; labor unions; and historical societies—wherever it is important to retain the records of people or organizations."[68]

Archivists acquire unique primary source materials, usually through donation, and provide mediated access and reference services on-site and remotely. These special collections contain many different formats, from traditional documents, photographs, handwritten manuscripts, and drawings, to newer media such as motion pictures, sound recordings, and *born-digital* files.

Because of the unique and often priceless nature of archival collections, archivists and special collections librarians must balance the competing needs of providing access to qualified researchers with storing and protecting original materials. Archives are contained in closed stacks, usually in a separate area of an institution. Researchers are not allowed into the stacks nor is interlibrary loan of archival materials permitted. Temperature, humidity, and lighting are carefully controlled to safeguard archives. Security measures, such as reading room and stack surveillance, identification and individual registration of researchers, limiting users to pencil and paper, and alarm and fire suppression systems, also protect archival materials from theft, vandalism, and disaster. Holdings in special collections, which differ in many ways from library materials, are usually:

- Original
- Unique
- Primary sources (created at the time of events described)
- Paper-based (manuscripts, documents, photographs, drawings) or digital
- Possess enduring value
- Accessed with finding aids

Archival arrangement and description is the counterpart to library cataloging. When archivists arrange and describe, or process, special collections for use by researchers, finding aids are produced. Encoded Archival Description (EAD) is the internationally accepted Extensible Markup Language (XML) standard for the exchange of finding aids online. Finding aids may vary somewhat because the collections they describe are unique, but EAD provides a uniform standard, much as MARC bibliographic records do in the library profession.

The National Archives and Records Administration (NARA) is an independent U.S. agency that preserves and provides access to government and historical records. Materials preserved in the National Archives must be necessary for government functioning, have enduring research worth, and/or provide citizens with information of value. NARA holds "approximately 10 billion pages of textual records; 12 million maps, charts, and architectural and engineering drawings; 25 million still photographs and graphics; 24 million aerial photographs; 300,000 reels of motion picture film; 400,000 video and sound recordings; and 133 terabytes of electronic data."[69] NARA has many facilities, including the original National Archives Building in downtown Washington, containing federal population censuses, land, pension, and military unit records; the larger National Archives facility at College Park, Maryland; 11 regional facilities across the country; and the National Personnel Records

Center in St. Louis (military archival records). NARA is also responsible for library facilities and collections for each president from Herbert Hoover to Barack Obama.

State archives exist in each of the 50 states as well. All house and provide access to state historical documents and visual materials, often in cooperation with state historical societies. State archives are often also charged with *records management* (RM) functions as a legally mandated responsibility. RM professionals are responsible for "controlling and governing what are considered to be the most important records of [the state] throughout the records life-cycle, which includes from the time such records are conceived through to their eventual disposal. This work includes identifying, classifying, prioritizing, storing, securing, archiving, preserving, retrieving, tracking and destroying of records. RM professionals are usually aligned with the Association of Records Managers and Administrators (now ARMA International) association and the Society of American Archivists.[70]

Professional archivists usually have master's degrees from ALA-accredited library schools, and frequently possess additional advanced degrees in the subjects (e.g., American literature, British history, Native American art, etc.) held in their archives. The Academy of Certified Archivists (ACA) offers a voluntary certification program, in cooperation with the leading national archival professional association, the Society of American Archivists. As with other special libraries, archives serve the major objectives of their parent organizations and institutions by providing both in-depth research and current information to their members as quickly and efficiently as possible. Paraprofessionals in archival settings generally possess undergraduate degrees, often in the humanities, and complete highly specialized training, such as the Western Archives Institute offered annually by the Society of California Archivists.

Corporate Libraries and Information Centers

Many large businesses and industries, including banks, insurance companies, public utilities, advertising agencies, newspapers, chemical companies, and aerospace corporations, have their own libraries. Though these companies' products may vary considerably, their libraries and information centers provide collections and services in support of their parent organizations. Access to special libraries is often limited to current employees of the organization, though depending on the agency, they may allow qualified outside researchers access as well.

The Los Angeles County Metropolitan Transportation Authority (Metro) is an interesting example of a special library that blends traditional on-site services and historical archives with a vibrant digital collection and a large virtual following. As a large quasi-governmental agency, this transportation library "documents the important and unique role of transportation in Southern California history and culture." Primary users include employees, other government agencies, and research institutions, but this special library also serves the general public and devotees of public transit and urban history.[71]

The San Diego Title Insurance and Trust Company maintained a remarkable corporate library and archives for more than three decades. Formally launched in 1946 with the enthusiastic support of Union Title Insurance and Trust Company founder John F. Forward Sr., the collection included original photographs and records of San Diego County land and property from 1870 to 1979, when a new corporate owner transferred more than 150,000 images to the San Diego Historical Society for professional care and organization.[72]

Because large corporations can be multifaceted, different corporate libraries are often found within the same organization. For example, Kaiser Permanente, a large health insurer, has medical libraries at each of its hospitals and a business library at its administrative center that focuses on management issues. Large businesses such as law firms, communications media, insurance companies, advertising agencies, and technology firms are dependent on trained staff in their libraries to support their business purposes. Law firms subscribe to expensive legal databases, such as *Lexis-Nexis* or *WestLaw* that make current court decisions instantaneously available upon release.

Some corporate libraries have morphed into information centers. The latter tend to also be responsible for internally generated information and records management, which are proprietary to the business. According to the Special Library Association (SLA): "An Information Professional ('IP') strategically uses information in his/her job to advance the mission of the organization . . . through the development, deployment, and management of information resources and services. The IP harnesses technology as a critical tool to accomplish goals. IPs include, but are not limited to, librarians, knowledge managers, chief information officers, web developers, information brokers, and consultants."

The following professional competencies are also defined by SLA:

- Managing information organizations
- Managing information resources
- Managing information services
- Applying information tools and technologies[73]

Information specialists develop collections that include resources in many formats from externally published materials, such as books, microforms, serials, patents, and conference reports; or of internally generated materials, such as research and technical reports, white papers, corporate and product indexes, and market surveys. The currency of information is of primary importance in special libraries and information centers. Arguably, the most important service any information center provides is rapid access to the parent organization's current and archival information, together with the latest business and topical information.

The information specialist saves corporate personnel valuable time and improves the competitiveness of the organization by providing individualized and specialized services. Conducting specialized research on demand for employees in proprietary technical, industry, science, or other topical databases is one common service. Advising personnel on automated current-awareness alerts and services within these same subscription databases is another. These automated alert services, which search current literature according to profiles customized for the specific research needs of individuals

FIGURE 3.3 Spencer Tracy and Katharine Hepburn clash over the computerization of a TV network's corporate library in the 1957 movie _Desk Set_. Courtesy Private Collection.

or groups, are an efficient method for keeping researchers abreast of new research developments in their fields. Some are available as a Really Simple Syndication (RSS) feed into a reader or aggregator, others are services such as table of contents searches specific to an electronic journal or collection.

Most corporate information centers circulate books; publish and maintain in-house wikis, bibliographies, and information updates; provide abstracting and translating services; set up RSS feeds; and produce copies of relevant articles or patents on demand.

Other Special Libraries

Special libraries are also found in museums, professional associations, and nonprofit organizations. Within these areas, many variations are based on the subject areas, organizations, or institutions that the library serves. For example, about 3,000 libraries are located in history, art, and science museums, in addition to those serving zoos, arboretums, historic houses, and national parks. These libraries vary in size and are funded by a mix of public agencies, endowments, and public–private partnerships. Many have small collections under 5,000 items and may be staffed by volunteers without library training. Museum libraries primarily serve the staff and researchers at their institutions, as well as qualified off-site scholars and researchers. Professional associations such as ALA, the American Dental Association, and the American Medical Association are well-established professional associations with libraries serving their members and executive staff.

State libraries have long been catalysts for public library cooperation, starting in 1890 when Massachusetts created a state Board of Library Commissioners charged to help communities establish and improve public libraries. Over the years, state library agencies played a major role in encouraging larger units of service to provide library resources. The Library Services Act (1956) and the Library Services and Construction Act (1964), which is now known as the Library Services and Technology Act, were milestones in the development of library service throughout the nation.

Many subject specialty libraries are connected with universities and colleges. These can be as numerous and varied as the university departments themselves. These include libraries dedicated to art, architecture, agriculture, astronomy, film archives, geography and maps, law, medicine, music, social science, sound archives, theater, and religious organizations.

Hospitals and medical centers often have two types of special libraries or one library that provides two distinct types of services. The first type is the patient library, which provides recreational, leisure, and enrichment reading for patients. These libraries usually have very flexible circulation routines, and services may be provided by volunteer staff rather than by paid staff who visit bedridden patients. The second type serves the research needs of the medical and other professional staff with access to the latest medical literature.

Among the other institutional libraries are prison libraries, which serve incarcerated populations. The goals of prison libraries have varied throughout the years as the philosophy of prison reform has changed. The first prison library collections contained moral and religious works to help prisoners see the error of their ways. Next, prison collections became important in supporting the educational system in the prison, and, finally, prison libraries became a part of the prisons' rehabilitative function. By the 1990s, literacy programs had become a major activity in many prison libraries. The biggest growth in prison libraries, though, has been in the area of legal information. Since the 1970s, federal courts have required that prisons provide adequate legal information that inmates can consult for drafting legal papers and briefs. As a result of this requirement, prisons have developed their own law libraries. In some states the department of corrections employs more library workers than any other state agency.

Management of Special Libraries

The administrator responsible for the special library or information center may not be a librarian, but a director or officer of a major department or division. Corporate librarians often report to directors of research and development or vice presidents of marketing. These administrators usually hire library and information staff members who support their own conceptions of library services. Thus, if a research and development (R&D) director considers library services important, then that person will provide a sufficient number of well-trained staff members to support the R&D function. Such a library might have a staff of information professionals supported by technicians and clerks. If another R&D director considers the materials more important than the services, the library staff might consist only of clerical workers, sometimes hired temporarily from an outsourcing agency. If either director were replaced, the services in that library or information center might be changed once again to fit the new director's viewpoint.

Personnel working in special libraries and information centers usually have more varied backgrounds than do staff in other types of libraries. The special librarian may have a degree in a subject specialty as well as in library science, and the staff may also include subject and language specialists. In fact, this subject expertise may be so important to companies and businesses that they may prefer a technician with subject specialization to a professional with a master's degree in library or information science. Large special libraries often include professional librarians or information scientists backed up by subject specialists, technicians, programmers, and clerks.

In other special libraries, someone who is a librarian or information specialist in name only may supervise several clerks and technicians. This manager may have a degree in the subject specialty of the parent corporation or institution, but may not have much knowledge of library or information science. In other cases, technicians may be offered a high wage to perform professional responsibilities for which they are not fully trained. At the opposite end of the spectrum, professional librarians or information specialists are often offered technician-level wages. Sometimes library services are outsourced (i.e., provided on a contract basis by an outside agency or vendor). Some organizations hire professional library consultants to set up a library that is then turned over to lower-paid personnel who are charged with carrying out daily operations.

The economic model on which the special library is based differs from that of other libraries. Because corporations exist to make a profit, the mission of the corporate library is to collect, organize, and provide information for the greatest effectiveness of the corporation. The profit-making motive may be one of the most influential factors in the makeup of a business or industrial library. In private sector corporations, libraries are sometimes operated as profit centers, rather than being treated as cost centers via general overhead.

Psychologically, this changes the entire equation. Such libraries must continually demonstrate their worth by generating a profit similar to other divisions of the organization. This is a foreign concept throughout much of the library world. Charge for library services? Although, intellectually, most library workers believe in the value of information, few of us expect to put this belief to the test in the marketplace.

The special library's users are on the company payroll. Therefore, corporate libraries are a direct cost to companies, no matter whether researchers gather their own information or have information center staff gather it for them. It is generally more cost-effective for information center staff to perform this activity because they are more skilled and it frees up time for other professionals to focus on business. Staff members in special libraries will go much further than other librarians not only to locate bibliographic citations, but also to obtain the documents, read, summarize, and analyze them, and write a report for the requesting department. In some corporations, information specialists join with department teams to work as researchers on corporate projects. Such active participation in a company's programs helps prove the library's worth to many corporate executives. Other types of businesses, particularly smaller businesses, might consider information services as peripheral to their profit goal and cut their libraries' staffing, materials, and funding when profits begin to sag. Thus, a corporate library must contribute to the parent corporation's bottom line to justify its continuing existence.

In the 1990s, some law and engineering firms began passing through, or billing the costs of such library and information services to the client. The librarian/researcher's time is tracked for the hours he or she works on a client's project. To this billable time is added a portion of the overhead costs associated with the research—collections, facilities, utilities, technology, supplies, subscriptions, support staff, and so forth. Therefore, billing rates in excess of $100 per hour are necessary to cover the costs of the services provided to the client. Often, these costs are billed directly to the client, along with the chargeable time of other professionals in the firm, such as lawyers, accountants, scientists, engineers, and consultants.

This constant financial focus has compelled staff members in special libraries and information centers to be entrepreneurial. Special librarians often charge back their services to the corporate department end user, such as the engineering or marketing departments. In addition, many special libraries and information centers began to provide fee-based services and consulting to external corporate or individual users who were not members of their own organization. Fees were charged for services such as online searches, reference service, and document delivery.

These fees have often enabled a library or information center to provide additional services for its primary clients. In contrast with public and academic libraries that have to face freedom-of-access concerns when charging similar fees, the special library or information center has to ensure that the benefits of providing such fee-based services do not reduce services to its primary clientele.

Librarians or information specialists may freelance as information brokers, providing services ranging from database searches, translations, market surveys, or writing white papers on specific topics. Clients often include corporations and individuals who do not have access to information centers or need specific information outside the realm of their collections. Information brokers' ability to specialize and produce results in a short span of time has made them invaluable resources for businesses and corporations.

Special libraries are the one area of the library industry where it appears the workforce has been shrinking since the beginning of the 21st century. Between 2002 and 2007 the number of paid staff in such libraries appears to have declined by about 7 percent.[74] Only time will tell if this is a continuing trend or if there is any correlation between staffing levels in special libraries and the services provided by independent information brokers.

SUMMARY

ALA calculates that there are just over 120,000 libraries of all types in the United States and 367,000 paid librarians and staff. Each type of library has a distinct mission and a specific group of users to serve.

American *public libraries* serve all citizens at every stage of life, whether they live in a large city or in the most remote rural area. Public libraries develop collections, programs, and services to fulfill their principle of service to all. Each library examines its community to identify, provide, and coordinate programs and services with other community agencies. In this process, a public library's success in meeting its community's needs is significantly affected by prevailing economic and political conditions at the local, state, and national levels.

School libraries play an important role in helping students learn. As librarians, they focus on information literacy for their students; they become more involved in curriculum development and when they are assisted in daily operations by well-trained support staff, research show a growth in student achievement levels. These studies provide evidence that good school libraries make a significant difference in learning outcomes.

Academic libraries in the United States have evolved to meet new educational objectives of their parent institutions that focus on student success and lifelong learning. Along with school libraries, they are placing increasing emphasis on building information literacy and digital literacy by teaching students how to find and evaluate information. Academic librarians are now active participants in the knowledge creation cycle on their campuses, building infrastructures and service programs that preserve their institutions' intellectual assets and make them available for use by others. Collections have been expanded to include all media, and library services have become more student-centered. Technology has expanded library resources and services while placing additional strain on budgets. Academic libraries have joined networks with other libraries to acquire, preserve, and share their resources. Academic librarians have embraced a more visible role in managing university intellectual capital, demonstrating their value to university administrators.

Special libraries and information centers provide services and build collections in defined subject areas and/or formats for a homogeneous clientele. They are more varied and distinct than any other type of library. Staff members often go further than other types of libraries to anticipate, locate, and synthesize the information needed by other members of the organization.

All libraries exist to meet the objectives of their parent institutions or their communities. Their fortunes mirror the economic health of those institutions and communities. Library budgets, staffing, and resources remain susceptible to economic downturns, as illustrated by the lingering Great Recession that began in 2007. The libraries that thrive are those that actively demonstrate their value, engage with their communities, and facilitate the goals of the larger body.

LIBRARY VISITS

Document your visits to at least four libraries. They should be libraries of the type that you think you might like to work in some day. At a minimum, collect the information needed to answer the following questions for each of the libraries you visit:

1. What is the library's complete name, address, telephone number, and website URL?

2. How easy is it to find the library?

3. How easy is it to find parking nearby?

4. How readily available is public transportation?

5. Define the library's primary clientele. What special information needs do the library's patrons have?

6. Is the library open to the public? If so, on what basis?

7. How many clients are eligible for library service?

8. How many clients are actually served or are registered users?

9. What is the annual budget of the library?

10. To which governing body, official, or administrator does the head of the library report?

11. What special services are offered to clientele?

12. What hours is the library building open?

13. Describe the nature, size, and scope of the library's collection.

14. What is the nature and size of the staff?

15. What staff did you observe? What impression did you get of the staff? Were they businesslike, casual, courteous, friendly?

16. Does the library have free WiFi access throughout the building? Is a password required to access WiFi? Is wireless printing available?

17. What is the size and adequacy of the library's physical facilities?

18. When you first enter the library, stop and look around. Is it obvious without consulting the staff where the following are located:

    - Circulation/reserve desk?
    - Reference/information desk?
    - Library catalog (OPAC)?
    - Public-access Internet terminals?
    - Hard copy periodicals?
    - Restrooms?
    - Printers, scanners, photocopiers?
    - Elevators and stairs?

19. How much and what type of furniture and seating are available for library users?

20. Does the library have an attractive and functional Web presence?

21. What library services can be accessed 24/7 over the Internet?

22. What new services has the Internet facilitated?

23. What social networking techniques been employed to interact with established or potential users?

24. Are there group study rooms and public meeting rooms?

25. Is there a makerspace room or area in the library? An art gallery or public art installation?

26. Into what cooperative arrangements with other libraries has this facility entered?

27. What public programming, educational offerings, and other outreach activities are offered?

28. What most impressed you about this library?

29. What most concerned you about this library?

30. Would you feel comfortable using this library in the future, both in person and online?

31. Do you think you would like to work here? List and discuss the pros and cons and come to a conclusion.

STUDY QUESTIONS

Public Libraries

1. Identify the major roles of public libraries.

2. Identify some of the major services libraries provide to fulfill these roles.

3. How have standards for public libraries changed?

4. Identify the levels of input and output measures recommended by the state library agency for the state in which you live.

5. Visit a public library that you have never visited before. Compare the library's objectives with those found in PLA documents. Are services of this library aligned with those discussed in the text? Also, compare the library's input and output measures in question number 4 with the staff, collections, and so forth.

6. If possible, visit both a neighborhood branch library as well as the central or main library site in the same system. How do they compare?

7. How are public libraries using the Internet to deliver traditional services to long-standing library users? How are they using technology to reach new or underserved audiences?

School Libraries

1. Identify the major objectives of school library programs.

2. Briefly describe school library's progression from the classroom library to the school library to the modern school library media center.

3. How has the Internet affected school library operations?

4. Compare your own state's standards with the guidelines presented in *Empowering Learners: Guidelines for School Library Media Programs.*

5. Identify the kinds of media that can be found in a school library media center.

6. Describe some services and programs provided in successful school library media programs.

7. Identify duties of the different levels of staff in the modern school library media center.

8. Visit a school library media center at a public school site and compare its objectives, staff, collection, and services with those described in this chapter. If possible, also visit a private school's library. How do they compare?

Academic Libraries

1. Define an academic library and describe some of the major types of academic libraries.

2. What are the main objectives of an academic library?

3. What are some of the new roles that academic librarians fulfill?

4. What are some of the major services academic libraries provide?

5. How has the Web changed opportunities in staff development for all levels of academic library employees?

6. List some examples of cooperative academic library resource-sharing and networking programs.

7. Visit a local academic institution and compare it with the objectives and services discussed in this chapter and the standards identified for that type of library.

8. Visit two types of academic institutions, such as a community college and a four-year college or university, to compare and contrast their libraries.

9. How are academic libraries serving the needs of distance education students who may never set foot inside the physical campus library?

10. What kind of information literacy activities are being offered in academic libraries?

Special Libraries

1. Identify the major objectives of special libraries and information centers.

2. Describe the relationship of a special library or information center to its parent institution.

3. Describe the scope and services of the four U.S. national libraries.

4. Describe the kinds of materials usually included in corporate libraries and information center collections.

5. List 10 examples of special libraries or information centers. How many of these have an online presence that is accessible to the public?

6. Make arrangements to visit two special libraries or information centers and compare their objectives, services, collections, and building security to those discussed in this chapter.

NOTES

1. American Library Association, "Number of Libraries in the United States," *ALA Fact Sheet 1*, accessed September 9, 2015, http://www.ala.org/tools/libfactsheets/alalibraryfactsheet01.

2. American Library Association, "Number of Paid Library Staff in the United States," *ALA Fact Sheet 2*, accessed September 9, 2015, http://www.ala.org/tools/libfactsheets/alalibraryfactsheet02.

3. AFL-CIO, Department for Professional Employees, "Library Workers: Facts & Figures," accessed September 7, 2015, http://dpeaflcio.org/programs-publications/issue-fact-sheets/library-workers-facts-figures/#_edn40.

4. U.S. Department of Labor, Bureau of Labor Statistics, "Librarians–Job Outlook," *Occupational Outlook Handbook, 2014–15 Edition*, accessed March 21, 2015, http://www.bls.gov/ooh/education-training-and-library/librarians.htm#tab-6; ibid., "Library Technicians and Assistants–Job Outlook," *Occupational Outlook Handbook, 2014–15 Edition*, accessed March 21, 2015, http://www.bls.gov/ooh/education-training-and-library/library-technicians-and-assistants.htm#tab-6.

5. U.S. Department of Labor, Bureau of Labor Statistics, *Occupational Outlook Handbook, 2014–15 Edition*, "Librarians–Pay," May 2014, accessed September 7, 2015, http://www.bls.gov/ooh/education-training-and-library/librarians.htm#tab-5; ibid., *Occupational Outlook Handbook, 2014–15 Edition*, "Library Assistants and Technicians–Pay," May 2014, accessed September 7, 2015, http://www.bls.gov/ooh/education-training-and-library/library-technicians-and-assistants.htm#tab-5.

6. American Library Association, Office for Research and Statistics, ALA Research Initiatives, "Member Demographics Study," September 2014, accessed September 7, 2015, http://www.ala.org/research/sites/ala.org.research/files/content/initiatives/membershipsurveys/September2014ALADemographics.pdf.

7. AFL-CIO, Department for Professional Employees, "Library Workers: Facts & Figures," accessed September 7, 2015, http://dpeaflcio.org/programs-publications/issue-fact-sheets/library-workers-facts-figures/#_edn40.

8. American Library Association, Office for Research and Statistics, ALA Research Initiatives, "Member Demographics Study," September 2014, accessed September 7, 2015, http://www.ala.org/research/sites/ala.org.research/files/content/initiatives/membershipsurveys/September2014ALADemographics.pdf.

9. Kathleen de la Peña McCook, *Introduction to Public Librarianship*, 1st ed. (New York: Neal-Schuman, 2004), 1.

10. Guy A. Marco, *The American Public Library Handbook* (Santa Barbara, CA: Libraries Unlimited, 2011), 152.

11. Vernon E. Palmour, Marcia C. Bellassai, and Nancy V. DeWath, *A Planning Process for Public Libraries* (Chicago: American Library Association, 1980).

12. Douglas L. Zweizig and E. J. Rodger, *Output Measures for Public Libraries: A Manual for Standardized Procedures,* 2nd ed. (Chicago: ALA Editions, 1982) and Public Library Association, "Presidential Task Force on Performance Measurement," accessed March 25, 2015, http://www.ala.org/pla/performancemeasurement.

13. American Library Association, "New National Poll Shows Library Card Registration Reaches Historic High," *ALA Public Information Office* [press release], September 23, 2008, accessed March 19, 2015, http://www.ala.org/news/news/pressreleases2008/September2008/ORSharris.

14. Family Place Libraries, "What Makes a Family Place Library?," accessed March 19, 2015, http://www.familyplacelibraries.org/whatMakes.html.

15. American Library Association, "Public Library Use," *ALA Library Fact Sheet 6,* accessed March 19, 2015, http://www.ala.org/tools/libfactsheets/alalibraryfactsheet06.

16. American Library Association Video Round Table, "Freedom to View Statement," accessed March 19, 2015, http://www.ala.org/vrt/professionalresources/vrtresources/freedomtoview.

17. All statistics and quoted material in this section from American Library Association, "State of America's Libraries Report 2014: Public Libraries," accessed March 19, 2015, http://www.ala.org/news/state-americas-libraries-report-2014/public-libraries.

18. Universal Service Administrative Company, "SLC Issues the First Wave of Funding Commitment Decision Letters," [press release], November 23, 1998, http://www.sl.universalservice.org/whatsnew/1998/111998.asp; American Library Association, "Public Internet Access At Nation's Library Systems Increases Sharply; Library Branches Lag," *American Library Association Washington Office Electronic Newsline* (*ALAWON*), accessed March 20, 2015, http://www.ala.org/cfapps/archive.cfm?path=washoff/alawon/alwn6100.html.

19. Angela A. Gilroy, "Telecommunications Discounts for Schools and Libraries: The 'E-Rate' Program and Controversies," *Congressional Research Service,* (2003: IB98040) accessed March 19, 2015, http://digital.library.unt.edu/ark:/67531/metacrs5526/m1/1/high_res_d/IB98040_2003Jun27.pdf.

20. Federal Communications Commission, "E-rate Modernization Order," July 11, 2014, accessed March 19, 2015, http://www.fcc.gov/document/fcc-releases-e-rate-modernization-order; ibid., "Second E-rate Modernization Order," December 11, 2014, accessed March 19, 2015, http://www.fcc.gov/document/fcc-continues-e-rate-reboot-meet-nations-digital-learning-needs; ibid., "Summary of the Second E-Rate Modernization Order," December 11, 2014, accessed March 19, 2015, http://www.fcc.gov/page/summary-second-e-rate-modernization-order.

21. Bill and Melinda Gates Foundation, "What We Do: Global Libraries Strategic Overview," accessed March 19, 2015, http://www.gatesfoundation.org/What-We-Do/Global-Development/Global-Libraries.

22. Institute of Museum and Library Services, "Connecting People to Information and Ideas," accessed March 18, 2015, http://www.imls.gov/assets/1/AssetManager/IMLS_Identity.pdf.

23. Lee Rainie, "Who Uses Libraries and Who Doesn't: A Special Typology" (conference presentation, American Library Association's Annual Conference, Las Vegas, NV, June 30, 2014), *Pew Research Center for Internet, Science and Tech,* accessed March 18, 2015, http://www.pewinternet.org/2014/06/30/who-uses-libraries-and-who-doesnt-a-special-typology/.

24. Hannah Pollack, "Satisfaction with Public Libraries Has Increased Since 2008," *Harris Poll #89*, September 24, 2014, accessed March 19, 2015, http://www.harrisinteractive.com/NewsRoom/HarrisPolls/tabid/447/mid/1508/articleId/1501/ctl/ReadCustom%20Default/Default.aspx.

25. American Library Association, "Public Libraries Are Engines of Economic Growth, Studies Show," April 14, 2008, Public Information Office press release summarizing the "State of America's Libraries Report 2008," accessed March 20, 2015, http://www.ala.org/news/news/pressreleases2008/april2008/2008statereport.

26. Matt Enis, "Librarians, Media React to Launch of Kindle Unlimited," *The Digital Shift*, July 25, 2014, accessed March 20, 2015, http://www.thedigitalshift.com/2014/07/ebooks/librarians-media-react-launch-kindle-unlimited/.

27. "Public Libraries Disrupting the Likes of Amazon," *Inside Finance,* August 14, 2014, accessed March 20, 2015, http://insidefinance.org/public-libraries-disrupting-the-likes-of-amazon/.

28. Joseph Janes, ed., "The Librarian in 2020 | Reinventing Libraries," *Library Journal,* October 20, 2013, accessed March 20, 2015, http://lj.libraryjournal.com/2013/10/future-of-libraries/the-librarian-in-2020-reinventing-libraries/# excerpted from Stacey A. Aldrich and Jarrid P. Keller, "IV: Place," in *The Library 2020: Today's Leading Visionaries Describe Tomorrow's Library,* ed. Joseph Janes (Lanham, MD: The Scarecrow Press, Inc., 2013).

29. Jean Key Gates, *Introduction to Librarianship* (New York: McGraw-Hill, 1968), 220–221.

30. United States National Commission on Excellence in Education, *A Nation at Risk: The Imperative for Educational Reform: A Report to the Nation and the Secretary of Education,* United States Department of Education (Washington, DC: The Commission, 1983), accessed March 20, 2015, https://www2.ed.gov/pubs/NatAtRisk/risk.html.

31. *Alliance for Excellence: Librarians Respond to "A Nation at Risk:" Recommendations and Strategies from Libraries and the Learning Society* (Washington, DC: U.S. Department of Education, Office of Educational Research and Improvement, Center for Libraries and Education Improvement, 1984).

32. Committee on Postwar Planning of the American Library Association, *School Libraries for Today and Tomorrow,* (Chicago: American Library Association, 1944).

33. Association of School Librarians, *Standards for School Library Programs* (Chicago: American Library Association, 1960).

34. Joint Committee of the American Association of School Librarians and the Department of Audiovisual Instruction of the National Education Association, *Standards for School and Media Programs* (Chicago: American Library Association, 1969).

35. Amy Bitterman, Lucinda Gray, and Rebecca Goldring, *Characteristics of Public Elementary and Secondary School Library Media Centers in the United States: Results From the 2011–12 Schools and Staffing Survey First Look,* NCES 2013-315 (Washington, DC: U.S. National Center for Education Statistics, 2013), accessed March 20, 2015, http://nces.ed.gov/pubs2013/2013315.pdf.

36. American Association of School Librarians, *Media Programs: District and School* (Chicago: American Library Association, 1975).

37. American Association of School Librarians and Association for Educational Communications and Technology, *Information Power: Guidelines for School Library Media Programs* (Chicago: American Library Association, 1988); American Association of School Librarians, *Empowering Learners: Guidelines for School Library Media Programs* (Chicago: American Association of School Librarians, 2009).

38. *Empowering Learners: Guidelines for School Library Media Programs* (Chicago: American Association of School Librarians, 2009), 19.

39. American Library Association, "State of America's Libraries Report 2014: Executive Summary," accessed March 19, 2015, http://www.ala.org/news/state-americas-libraries-report-2014/public-libraries.

40. Amy Bitterman, Lucinda Gray, and Rebecca Goldring, *Characteristics of Public Elementary and Secondary School Library Media Centers in the United States: Results from the 2011–12 Schools and Staffing Survey First Look*, NCES 2013-315 (Washington, DC: U.S. National Center for Education Statistics, 2013), accessed March 20, 2015, http://nces.ed.gov/pubs2013/2013315.pdf.

41. American Library Association, "National Center for Education Statistics Study Confirms Library Use Increases Test Scores," Public Information Office press release, February 10, 2005, accessed March 19, 2015, http://www.ala.org/news/news/pressreleases2005/february2005/ncesstudyonlibraryuse extracted from Leslie Scott, *School Library Media Centers: Selected Results from the Education Longitudinal Study of 2002 (ELS:2002)*, NCES 2005-302 (Washington, DC: National Center for Education Statistics, 2005), accessed March 20, 2015, http://nces.ed.gov/pubs2005/2005302.pdf.

42. Keith Curry Lance, Marcia J. Rodney, and Christine Hamilton-Pennell, *Powerful Libraries Make Powerful Learners: The Illinois Study* (Canton, IL: Illinois School Library Media Association, 2005), accessed March 20, 2015, http://www.islma.org/pdf/ILStudy2.pdf.

43. Library Research Services, "School Libraries Impact Studies," accessed March 20, 2015, http://www.lrs.org/data-tools/school-libraries/impact-studies/.

44. American Library Association, "State of America's Libraries Report 2014: School Libraries," accessed March 20, 2015, http://www.ala.org/news/state-americas-libraries-report-2014/school-libraries.

45. Barbara K. Stripling, "Advocating for School Librarians: The Peril and Promise of School Libraries," *American Libraries*, January 8, 2014, accessed March 20, 2015, http://www.americanlibrariesmagazine.org/article/advocating-school-librarians.

46. Association of Research Libraries, "Membership," accessed March 20, 2015, http://www.arl.org/membership. The European-based counterpart of ARL, LIBER, is the main research libraries network in Europe. Founded in 1971 as a non-governmental organization of research libraries under the auspices of the Council of Europe, LIBER encompasses more than 420 national, university, and other libraries in 46 countries. http://sparceurope.org/related-organizations/.

47. In 2015, the Carnegie Classification of Institutions of Higher Education was transferred to Indiana University Bloomington's Center for Postsecondary Research. The Classification retains the same title and Carnegie name. "Carnegie Classification of Institutions of Higher Education," accessed March 20, 2015, http://carnegieclassifications.iu.edu.

48. Association of College and Research Libraries, "Standards for Libraries in Higher Education" (October 2011), accessed March 20, 2015, http://www.ala.org/acrl/standards/standardslibraries.

49. Association of College and Research Libraries, "Assessment in Action: Academic Libraries and Student Success," accessed March 20, 2015, http://www.ala.org/acrl/AiA.

50. University of North Carolina at Chapel Hill, "Introduction to Knowledge Management," March 19, 2007, accessed March 21, 2015, http://web.archive.org/web/20070319233812/http://www.unc.edu/~sunnyliu/inls258/Introduction_to_Knowledge_Management.html.

51. Association of Research Libraries, "Scholarly Communication," accessed March 21, 2015, http://www.arl.org/focus-areas/scholarly-communication. And Ray English, "Scholarly Communication and the Academy: The Importance of the ACRL Initiative" *Portal: Libraries and the Academy* 3, no. 2 (2003): 337-340, accessed March 21, 2015, https://muse.jhu.edu/login?auth=0&type=summary&url=/journals/portal_libraries_and_the_academy/v003/3.2english.pdf.

52. Robert Darnton, "A World Digital Library Is Coming True!" *New York Review of Books,* May 22, 2014, accessed March 21, 2015, http://www.nybooks.com/articles/archives/2014/may/22/world-digital-library-coming-true.

53. Raym Crow, "The Case for Institutional Repositories: A SPARC Position Paper," *ARL Bimonthly Report* 223 (2002), accessed March 21, 2015, http://works.bepress.com/ir_research/7.

54. American Library Association, "State of America's Libraries Report 2014: Academic Libraries," accessed March 21, 2015, http://www.ala.org/news/state-americas-libraries-report-2014/academic-libraries.

55. American Library Association, "State of America's Libraries Report 2014: Library Construction," accessed March 21, 2015, http://www.ala.org/news/state-americas-libraries-report-2014/library-construction.

56. Les Watson, ed., *Better Library and Learning Spaces: Projects, Trends and Ideas* (London: Facet Publishing, 2013).

57. Helen Y. Chu and Andre Chinn, "On the Cutting Edge: Innovative Services That Blend Technology with Purpose" (presentation and paper, EDUCAUSE West Southwest Regional Conference, Austin, TX, February 2013), accessed March 18, 2015, http://works.bepress.com/helen_chu/8.

58. Helen Y. Chu, "UO Libraries Shape the Student Academic Experience" (presentation, University of Oregon Libraries Advancement Council, Eugene, OR, May 2015), accessed May 18, 2015, http://works.bepress.com/helen_chu/9/.

59. EDUCAUSE, "7 *Things You Should Know About: The Modern Learning Commons," EDUCAUSE Learning Initiative,* April 11, 2011, accessed March 21, 2015, https://net.educause.edu/ir/library/pdf/ELI7071.pdf.

60. Scott Jaschik, "Pressure on the Provosts: 2014 Survey of Chief Academic Officers," *Inside Higher Ed,* January 23, 2014, accessed March 21, 2015, https://www.insidehighered.com/news/survey/pressure-provosts-2014-survey-chief-academic-officers.

61. Ethelene Whitmire, "Academic Library Performance Measures and Undergraduates' Library Use and Educational Outcomes" *Library & Information Science Research* 24 (2002): 107–128, accessed March 21, 2015, http://polaris.gseis.ucla.edu/ewhitmir/lisr2002.pdf.

62. Richard De Gennaro in Allen B. Veaner, *Academic Librarianship in a Transformational Age: Programs, Politics and Personnel* (Boston: G. K. Hall, 1990), xiii.

63. American Library Association, "State of America's Libraries Report 2014: Academic Libraries," accessed March 21, 2015, http://www.ala.org/news/state-americas-libraries-report-2014/academic-libraries.

64. Library of Congress, "About the Library," accessed March 21, 2015, http://www.loc.gov/about.

65. Congress purchased Jefferson's library for $23,950. A second fire on Christmas Eve of 1851, destroyed nearly two-thirds of the 6,487 volumes Congress had purchased from Jefferson. Through a generous grant from Jerry and Gene Jones, the Library of Congress is attempting to reassemble Jefferson's library as it was sold to Congress. Library of Congress, "Thomas Jefferson: Jefferson's Library," accessed March 21, 2015, http://www.loc.gov/exhibits/jefferson/jefflib.html.

66. Library of Congress, "American Memory," http://memory.loc.gov/ammem/index.html and "State Digital Resources: Memory Projects, Online Encyclopedias, Historical & Cultural Materials Collections," both accessed March 11, 2015, http://www.loc.gov/rr/program/bib/statememory/#Multi.

67. U.S. National Library of Medicine, National Institutes of Health, "PubMed," *Home-PubMed-NCBI,* accessed March 21, 2015, http://www.ncbi.nlm.nih.gov/pubmed.

68. Society of American Archivists, "So You Want to Be an Archivist: An Overview of the Archives Profession," accessed March 10, 2015, http://www2.archivists.org/profession.

69. National Archives and Records Administration, "About the National Archives of the United States General Information Leaflet, Number 1," accessed April 7, 2015, http://www.archives.gov/publications/general-info-leaflets/1-about-archives.html.

70. ARMA International, *Glossary of Records and Information Management Terms,* 4th ed. (Overland Park, KS: ARMA International, 2012).

71. Los Angeles County Metropolitan Transportation Authority (Metro), "Dorothy Peyton Gray Transportation Library," accessed March 21, 2015, http://www.metro.net/about/library/.

72. San Diego History Center, "Title Insurance Photograph Collection, 1870–1979," *Guide to the Photograph Collections,* accessed March 21, 2015, http://www.sandiegohistory.org/photocollect/clist1.htm#3.

73. Special Libraries Association, "Competencies," accessed March 21, 2015, https://www.sla.org/about-sla/competencies/.

74. José-Marie Griffiths and Donald King, "The Future of Librarians in the Workforce: Status of Special Libraries" (presentation, Special Libraries Association Annual Conference, Seattle, WA, June 16, 2008), http://sils.unc.edu/sites/default/files/general/research/presentations/2008SLAFFinal1.pdf.

RESOURCES

Library Careers and Standards

Books

Greer, Roger C., Robert Grover, and Susan G. Fowler. *Introduction to the Library and Information Profession.* 2nd ed. Santa Barbara, CA: Libraries Unlimited, 2013.

Hunt, Deborah and David Grossman. *The Librarian's Skillbook: 51 Essential Career Skills for Information Professionals.* San Leandro, CA: Information Edge, 2013.

Shontz, Priscilla K. and Richard A. Murray. *What Do Employers Want? A Guide for Library Science Students.* Santa Barbara, CA: Libraries Unlimited, 2012.

Websites

American Library Association—About the ALA. http://www.ala.org/tools/about-ala-library.

American Library Association—Making a Living Making a Difference: An Initiative of the American Library Association. http://librarycareers.drupalgardens.com.

American Library Association—Standards and Guidelines. http://www.ala.org/tools/guidelines/standardsguidelines.

Occupational Outlook Handbook—Archivists, Curators, and Museum Workers. http://www.bls.gov/ooh/education-training-and-library/curators-museum-technicians-and-conservators.htm.

Occupational Outlook Handbook—Audio-Visual and Multimedia Collections Specialists. http://www.bls.gov/oes/current/oes259011.htm.

Occupational Outlook Handbook—Librarians. http://www.bls.gov/ooh/education-training-and-library/librarians.htm

Occupational Outlook Handbook—Library Technicians and Assistants. http://www.bls.gov/ooh/education-training-and-library/library-technicians-and-assistants.htm.

Society of American Archivists—So You Want to Be an Archivist: An Overview of the Archives Profession. http://www2.archivists.org/profession.

Society of American Archivists—Standards Portal. http://www2.archivists.org/standards.

Special Libraries Association—Manage Your Career. https://www.sla.org/career-center.

Public Libraries

Books

Griffiths, José-Marie and Donald R. King. *A Strong Future for the Public Library Use and Employment.* Chicago: American Library Association, 2011. Excerpt at: http://www.alastore.ala.org/pdf/9780838935880_excerpt.pdf

Marco, Guy A. *The American Public Library Handbook.* Santa Barbara, CA: Libraries Unlimited, 2011.

McClure, Charles R. and Paul T Jaeger. *Public Libraries and Internet Service Roles: Measuring and Maximizing Internet Services.* Chicago: ALA Editions, 2009.

McCook, Kathleen de la Peña. *Introduction to Public Librarianship.* 2nd rev. ed. New York: Neal-Schuman, 2011.

Nelson, Sandra S., Ellen Altman, and Diane Mayo. *Managing for Results: Effective Resource Allocation for Public Libraries.* Chicago: American Library Association, 2000.

Shuman, Bruce A. *Beyond the Library of the Future: More Alternative Futures for the Public Library.* Englewood, CO: Libraries Unlimited, 1997.

Van Horn, Nancy, et al. *Output Measures for Public Libraries: A Manual for Standardized Procedures.* 2nd ed. Chicago: American Library Association, 1987.

Webb, T. D. *Public Library Organization and Structure.* Jefferson, NC: McFarland, 1989.

Websites

American Library Association—Public Library Use. http://www.ala.org/tools/libfactsheets/alalibraryfactsheet06.

American Library Association, Public Library Association—About the Public Library Association. http://www.ala.org/pla/.

American Library Association, Public Library Association, and Institute for Museum and Library Services—Connect to the World. http://digitallearn.org/.

Bill & Melinda Gates Foundation—Libraries: Changing Lives, Transforming Communities, 2012. http://www.youtube.com/watch?v=7cwsrgMOcLA.
Bill & Melinda Gates Foundation—Libraries: Linking Seniors in a Digital World, 2012. http://www.youtube.com/watch?v=HhOZpcqQtgQ.

School Libraries

Books

American Association of School Librarians. *Empowering Learners: Guidelines for School Library Media Programs.* Chicago: American Library Association, 2009.
American Association of School Librarians and Association for Educational Communications and Technology. *Information Power: Guidelines for School Library Media Programs.* Chicago: American Library Association, 1988.
Harada, Violet H. and Sharon Coatney, eds. *Inquiry and the Common Core: Librarians and Teachers Designing Teaching for Learning.* Santa Barbara, CA: Libraries Unlimited, 2013.
Haycock, Ken, ed. *Foundations for Effective School Library Media Programs.* Englewood, CO: Libraries Unlimited, 1999.
Lance, Keith Curry, Marcia J. Rodney, and Christine Hamilton-Pennell, *Powerful Libraries Make Powerful Learners: The Illinois Study.* Canton, IL: Illinois School Library Media Association, 2005. Also at: http://www.islma.org/pdf/ILStudy2.pdf.
Rosenfeld, Esther and David V. Loertscher. *Toward a 21st-Century School Library Media Program.* Metuchen, NJ: Scarecrow Press, 2007.
School Libraries Work! 3rd ed. New York: Scholastic Publishing, 2008. Also at: http://www2.scholastic.com/content/collateral_resources/pdf/s/slw3_2008.pdf.
Woolls, Blanche, Ann C. Weeks, and Sharon Coatney. *The School Library Manager.* 5th ed. Santa Barbara, CA: Libraries Unlimited, 2013.

Websites

International Association of School Librarianship.http://iasl-online.mlanet.org.
Library Research Services—School Libraries Impact Studies. http://www.lrs.org/data-tools/school-libraries/impact-studies/.

Academic Libraries

Books

Cohen, Laura B., *Library 2.0 Initiatives in Academic Libraries.* Chicago: Association of College and Research Libraries, 2007.
Courtney, Nancy. *Academic Library Outreach: Beyond the Campus Walls.* Westport, CT: Libraries Unlimited, 2008.
Diamond, Tom. *Middle Management in Academic and Public Libraries.* Santa Barbara, CA: Libraries Unlimited, 2012.
Dowell, David R. and Gerard B. McCabe, eds. *It's All about Student Learning: Managing Community and Other College Libraries in the 21st Century.* Westport, CT: Libraries Unlimited, 2006.

Snavely, Loanne, ed. *Student Engagement and the Academic Library*. Santa Barbara, CA: Libraries Unlimited, 2012.

Wikoff, Karin, *Electronic Resources Management in the Academic Library: A Professional Guide*. Santa Barbara, CA: Libraries Unlimited, 2011.

Welburn, William C., Janice Welburn, and Beth McNeil, eds. *Advocacy, Outreach and the Nation's Academic Libraries: A Call for Action*. Chicago: ACRL, 2010.

Papers/Articles/Presentations

Chew, Katherine, James Stemper, Caroline Lilyard, and Mary Schoenborn. "User-Defined Valued Metrics for Electronic Journals." Paper and presentation at Library Assessment Conference, Charlottesville, VA, October 29–31, 2012. http://purl.umn.edu/144461.

Chu, Helen Y. "Creating a Shared Vision: Learning Space Design for a Distributed Campus." Paper and presentation at APRU Video Conference on Learning Spaces, March 2, 2011, http://works.bepress.com/helen_chu/6/.

Chu, Helen Y. and Andre Chinn. "On the Cutting Edge: Innovative Services That Blend Technology with Purpose." Paper and presentation at EDUCAUSE West Southwest Regional Conference, Austin, TX, February 2013, http://works.bepress.com/helen_chu/8.

Jain, Priti. "New Trends and Future Applications/Directions of Institutional Repositories in Academic Institutions." *Library Review* 60 no. 2, (2011): 125–141. http://50.17.193.184/omeka/files/original/a2f02e36f4c5a0bacf6a43dc88dfa340.pdf.

Lynch, Clifford A. "Institutional Repositories: Essential Infrastructure for Scholarship in the Digital Age." *ARL Bimonthly Report* 226, (February 2003), 1–7. http://www.cni.org/publications/cliffs-pubs/institutional-repositories-infrastructure-for-scholarship/.

Websites

Association of College and Research Libraries—Academic Library Building Design. http://www.ala.org/acrl/academic-library-building-design-resources-planning.

Association of College and Research Libraries—Information Literacy Resources. http://www.ala.org/acrl/issues/infolit.

Association of College and Research Libraries—Marketing @ Your Library. http://www.ala.org/acrl/issues/marketing.

Association of College and Research Libraries—Scholarly Communication. http://www.ala.org/acrl/issues/scholcomm.

Coalition for Networked Information. http://www.cni.org/.

Special Libraries

Books

Benedetti, Joan M., ed. *Art Museum Libraries and Librarianship*. [Ottawa]: Scarecrow Press and Art Libraries Society of North America, 2007.

Matarazzo, James M. and Toby Pearlstein. *Special Libraries: A Survival Guide*. Santa Barbara, CA: Libraries Unlimited, 2013.

Matthews, Joseph R. *The Bottom Line: Determining and Communicating the Value of the Special Libraries.* Westport, CT: Libraries Unlimited, 2002.

Porter, Cathy A., et al. *Special Libraries: A Guide for Management.* 4th ed. Washington, DC: Special Libraries Association, 1997.

Russell, Keith W. and Maria G. Piza, eds. "Agricultural Libraries and Information." *Library Trends* 38, no. 3 (1990): 327–338.

Websites

American Association for State and Local History, Presidential Sites & Library Conference. http://about.aaslh.org/2014-psl-conference/.

ARMA International. http://www.arma.org/

Art Libraries Society of North America. https://www.arlisna.org/about/about-the-society.

Medical Library Association. https://www.mlanet.org/.

Medical Library Association—Journal of the Medical Library Association. https://www.mlanet.org/publications/jmla.

Society of American Archivists—About SAA. http://www2.archivists.org.

Society of American Archivists—Associated Organizations & Associations. http://www2.archivists.org/assoc-orgs.

Special Libraries Association. https://www.sla.org/.

Western Association of Map Libraries—Map Librarians' Toolbox. http://www.waml.org/maptools.html.

Chapter 4

Collections

When it comes to assessing the quality and resources of a library or information center, one of the major aspects to consider is the agency's collection of materials. Today, that no longer means just what a library physically owns, but, increasingly, what it provides access to, regardless of the format. Collections now consist of books, magazines, newspapers, CDs, and DVDs housed in physical buildings along with free and subscription-based e-books, documents, periodicals, images, streaming video, and multimedia that are available electronically to patrons of that library. New formats of information packaging are emerging regularly to add to the list.

Regardless of delivery formats, library collections are selected, acquired, cataloged, processed, and supplied to customers based on well-thought-out collection development policies, user profiles, organizational principles, and price considerations. This often comes as a surprise to patrons. Unlike the highly visible services of the reference and circulation departments, the selection, purchasing, cataloging, and processing of items usually do not involve the public directly but rather take place behind the scenes. Typically, the division where these activities take place is called the *technical services department.*

It is probably fair to say that the development of library collections is one of the least understood aspects of library work to outsiders. When one of the authors worked in an urban public library, a patron was quite upset when she discovered that a particular new fiction title was not in the collection. "Why don't you have it?" she complained. "I thought publishers sent libraries free samples of all the new books." False! On the contrary, the close relationship between libraries and publishers is that of buyer and seller, respectively.

DETERMINING USER NEEDS

Every library has its own distinct set of user needs that influence the development of its collection. As the staff endeavor to make a collection as responsive as possible to those information needs, they turn to direct patron input (e.g., user surveys, patron suggestions, and item requests), demographics of their client base, staff observations, and usage and circulation patterns. Publishing trends, new product releases, and current events are also factors to be considered as library staff members attempt to respond to ongoing needs, anticipate future demands, and build an overall collection that retains a measure of lasting value.

Collecting priorities should be driven by the demographics of the library's user groups. Depending on the type of library, this might mean reviewing current enrollment data, student reading levels, and languages spoken at home for K-12 school libraries. Public libraries may rely on the U.S. population census and local municipal data that analyzes their service area to inform their collection building. Academic libraries study enrollment demographics, as well as curriculum and degree offerings at their institution. Special libraries' collections are driven by their parent company's mission, products, niche markets, and other research focus. And, of course, each of these user profiles and data describing them need to be revisited regularly and library collecting strategies revised as the client groups change or morph.

Patron-driven acquisition, also referred to as usage-driven acquisition, is a newer concept in collection building that has become very popular in the last decade and is expected to continue to grow. This is where a library, partnering with a vendor, "purchases" an electronic resource such as an e-book, once a predetermined number of patrons have chosen it, clicked on it, or previewed it. Thus, patron interest can be set up to trigger a purchase-on-demand of the chosen title to add to the library's e-book holdings. There are many variations of the patron-driven acquisition model now evolving, including some that also trigger purchase of a print copy once the e-book version has proved to be in demand.[1] Statistics of use—database searches, e-book accesses, website visits, circulation of physical books, periodicals, DVDs, and other tangible resources—are all metrics that need to be measured and evaluated to factor in to collection building priorities.

Advisory committees or library boards may also contribute their input on collections, especially if they represent a geographic sector of the library's service area. Of course, the library or information center's budgetary resources also greatly impact overall purchasing decisions. Many state university or college systems and other academic library cooperatives are able to form a buying consortium and negotiate a group rate with a particular vendor or vendors. This qualifies all of their member libraries to special pricing from these producers of key products, such as subscription databases. And this arrangement simplifies the billing and other paperwork for the vendors since they do not have to bill each member library separately.

The end result is that no individual library or information center collection is alike. And their primary users wouldn't want them to be. For example, academic library collections typically reflect the curriculum offered in their educational institutions. Thus, a polytechnic university with large science, engineering, and architecture departments can be expected to have significant library holdings in those areas, as well as a broad-based collection to support lower division, general education classes. A local public library will provide recreational reading and offer a wide range of popular materials on business topics, consumer information, regional history, and local government issues suited to its users' demographics. An art museum research library can be expected to collect overview information on art history and material on the museum's specific art holdings, periods, and artists, as well as data on inter-pretation, preservation, curatorial techniques, and fundraising.

Donations

Many libraries small and large will have individuals or groups approach them with the offer of a large donation of materials. The proposed donation could be the collection of a deceased family member or it could be the personal library of a subject expert who is downsizing his or her household. There is no single formula for making a decision on accepting such a proposed gift; each donation needs to be carefully reviewed and possibly professionally appraised depending on the extent, subject matter, and condition of materials. A library's mission statement, selection policy (see next section), and collection prior-ities will help inform the decision about the appropriateness of accepting a donation of materials for that particular library's permanent collection. Other donations to libraries may come in the form of an endowment fund or a one-time bequest. These might be solicited through the advancement department or could be a surprise gift from a longtime library supporter. Such funds may be earmarked for special collecting areas or designated for specific formats (e.g., multicultural children's books, foreign language materials, genre films, technology, etc.) based on the interests of the donor and terms of the gift. Most librarians especially appreciate an unrestricted gift of funds that can be put to use where it is most needed.

Libraries and the Role of Social Networking

An aspect of the Internet that is influencing library collection building is the use of social networking tools to gather and share patron reading preferences and to promote a feeling of community among all stakeholders of a library. The phenomenon known as social networking began in 2002, and emphasizes the power of the Web to build community—among strangers as well as friends, family, and colleagues. Early sites promoting social networking included Friendster and MySpace. While those have faded from the scene, Facebook, Flickr, Twitter, Instagram, LinkedIn and many others have become household names and incredibly popular among all age groups. Blog (short for "Weblog") hosting is often a part of social network sites. Much like instant messaging (IM) and the earlier chat rooms, social media represent not only a fresh, immedi-ate, visual, and convenient way to connect and to maintain relationships, but another venue where people elect to spend their time, both recreationally and professionally. For those hooked on sites such as Facebook, checking one's personal site multiple times per day for posts from family, friends, coworkers, businesses and other feeds is as much a part of the daily routine as checking traditional e-mail or brushing one's teeth.

The library world has had much discussion as to how social media can be best integrated into library services and how they can be successfully used as tools to build community and to further a participatory culture among library patrons. Other key goals of utilizing social media are to increase overall awareness of the library program, highlight collections and services, gather patron input, and cultivate a sense of a library's value to its service area.

The expansive New York Public Library system makes maximum use of the full range of social media with its own e-mail newsletters, blogs, videos, and podcasts, and by posting a steady stream of engaging content including vintage library photos, recommended reading lists, news of author appearances, snow closures, and more. Denver Public Library's website promotes its digital collections and features a variety of active blogs promoting its own resources from local history, to music, to young adult (YA) literature with blog text links to an open public access catalog (OPAC) record of the item in its system's holdings.

For large public and university libraries, successful use of social networking means hiring dedicated in-house staff who are responsible for sophisticated planning, design, maintenance, and evaluation of marketing media. For smaller libraries, the challenge here is how to skillfully use key social media on a more limited basis, but to do so effectively with fewer resources and by integrating duties into existing staff positions.

Another innovative social networking service that is growing in use among libraries is online book clubs. This is where a commercial company, such as DearReader.com sends regular e-mail snippets of text from newly released books to subscribed library patrons, who then share their comments about their reading experiences and their favorite titles with others in the club. The online reading club promotes the sharing of good reads, builds friendships, and also encourages library use, circulation of materials, overall readership, and provides patron input for selection staff. Since its content is provided by an outsourced business, it is not as labor intensive for library staff as populating and maintaining in-house social networking sites.

Social media, skillfully and thoughtfully managed/implemented, makes use of current and popular technology to accomplish many strategic goals for libraries: encouraging community engagement, building public relations, and promoting library services. While some employees may feel skeptical about the use of social media on a personal basis, managers and employers now assume this to be a core skill in their staff to be utilized to promote the library, archives, or museum's brand.

A Flood of Information

For years we have been hearing of the information explosion that surrounds us, and there is no sign of it letting up any time soon. Although computer technology has made great inroads in the storage and retrieval of massive quantities of information, there does not seem to be any reduction in the volume of data, but, rather, the contrary. Trying to estimate the size of the entire Web is rather difficult due to its highly dynamic nature. As of mid-2015, a survey by the British company Netcraft counted some 850 million websites (each of which include many individual pages). Expectations are that the 1 billion sites mark will be achieved by 2016.[2] Any way you try to measure it, the exponential growth of the World Wide Web only adds to the information deluge that already engulfs us.

At the same time, U.S. book production hit a record-setting total of over 190,000 new titles and editions by the end of 2011 according to the yearly industry analysis provided in the *Bowker Annual.*[3] It does seem rather over-whelming. How will a researcher ever find the website, book, article, or item of data that he or she needs? How will an information specialist know which quality products to select, purchase, and add to his or her information center?

SELECTION TOOLS

Although there are no comprehensive magic lists, librarians rely on industry tools, along with direct user input and their own professional judgment, to make selection and purchasing decisions. These may include reviewing media, core collection lists or bibliographies, lists of award-winning titles, and industry listservs.

Review Media

Critical or evaluative reviews of books, as well as those of magazines, DVDs, audio books, CDs, e-book, and computer software, are published by many sources for the retail trade and for the library business. Such reviews help library professionals decide on relevance and quality before making a purchase. Because it would be impossible to preview, read, or listen to each individual item under consideration, perusing reputable review media is a time-saver. Bear in mind that there are many items in print and multimedia that are never reviewed. Whether an item garners a favorable review, poor review, or no review, the decision to acquire it is still up to the library's selector.

Listed next are some of the established reviewing sources for books and other media commonly in use by library collections staff and retail booksellers:

Major reviewing media for adult titles

Booklist

Choice

Kirkus Reviews

Library Journal

New York Times Book Review

Publishers Weekly

Science Books & Films

Major reviewing media for children's titles

Booklist

Horn Book Magazine

Kirkus Reviews

School Library Connection

School Library Journal

Besides being well respected, these publications devote the bulk of every issue to reviews, each covering thousands of releases annually. Many other specialized and nontraditional periodicals with critical reviews exist as well, although the numbers of reviews included in each of these are much smaller. For most aforementioned titles, the current trend is for full access to all reviews to be available only by paid subscription both in the print periodical version and the online digital version. Most of the websites offer many free features, such as best book lists, author interview or video clips, or current articles as teasers or samples of the full online version; many offer free 30-day trials of their online sites.

Some weekly newspapers, such as the *New York Times*, offer Web access to a searchable archive of book reviews (in the case of the *New York Times*, since 1981). Many newspapers offer their weekly book reviews or author and books news on a free Really Simple Syndication (RSS) feed so that readers can easily receive them as regular updates accessible via a news feed reader or aggregator. This is a convenient method to receive ongoing current Web content without having to remember to check each site manually or having an e-mail inbox swamped with individually sent articles. No doubt policies and access will continue to change as electronic distribution and subscription models evolve. In addition, many online booksellers post in-house editorial comments, excerpts from published critical reviews, and reader/customer opinions free of charge on their websites.

Core Collection Lists

Jobbers, library trade associations, and publishers produce core collection lists or bibliographies. These serve as a starting point for establishing an opening-day library collection or for updating an existing one. Such lists may or may not be annotated or contain reviews. However, inclusion in such a list is usually an implied recommendation. The following are just a few representative core lists—there are many more available. Full citations are listed in the resources section near the end of this chapter; most of these now have an online updating component.

Periodicals

Magazines for Libraries

Reference collections

Recommended Reference Books for Small and Medium-Sized Libraries and Media Centers

Children's collections

Best Books for Children: Preschool Through Grade 6

Best Books for Middle School and Junior High Readers Grades 6–9

Best Books for High School Readers Grades 9–12

Medical libraries

Doody's Core Titles

Academic libraries

Choice's Outstanding Academic Titles

Best Seller Lists

While the term *best seller* is often used very loosely in publicity, ads, and on dust jackets to encourage sales and promote authors, inclusion on best seller lists can still be a valuable indicator for those building library collections.

Probably the most prestigious and best-known ranking is the *New York Times* weekly best seller list, which is actually comprised of multiple categories (hardcover fiction/nonfiction, trade paperback fiction/nonfiction, mass-market fiction, e-books, children's picture books, etc.). Many other large national daily newspapers as well as library/publishing industry trade periodicals, such as *Publishers Weekly* also compile regular lists of current sales.

Trying to uncover what sales data each publication bases its rankings on can be challenging. Lists reporting current titles based on high library circulation are included in each issue of *Library Journal* thus providing a different measure of popularity: high borrowing rates instead of sales figures.

It's a wise idea to become familiar with best seller lists, especially if working in a public library or K-12 school setting. Perusing various best seller lists gives one an idea of which titles are being strongly marketed, which ones are getting attention and "buzz" and of current trends in publishing/reading. It is a good method for staying aware of author names in the news and of movie tie-ins with published works; inclusion on best seller lists is often a strong indication that your library will want to consider a specific title for purchase.

Of course, there are many, many worthwhile titles produced (either by traditional publishing houses or self-published) that never make it on any best seller or awards lists. This is another reason to look at critical reviews in various trade publications and in newspaper sections featuring "Books," as well as to browse social media sites with reader input like Goodreads.com. Though, with mega bookseller Amazon now owning Goodreads.com, the issues of potential conflict of interest and a lack of neutrality on the site arise. Similar leading social media websites—Library Thing and Shelfari—also focusing on book discovery and sharing are owned, at least in part, by Amazon as well.

Many publications such as major national daily newspapers and library/publishing industry trade periodicals also come up with an end-of-year "best titles list" or "recommended reading list." For example, see the *Washington Post's* "Best Books of 2014" *or Library Journal's* "Best 100 References Books." These compilations can also be useful checklists for collection development.

Award-Winning Titles

Many literary awards are given out each year in various categories, such as children's literature, YA literature, adult works, science titles, and so on. Some of the most prestigious awards include the Newbery Medal for the most out-standing contribution to children's literature, the Caldecott Medal for the most distinguished picture book, and the Coretta Scott King Book Award for works by African American authors/illustrators for children's and teen levels. Representative adult awards include the Pulitzer Prize and the National Book Awards, both of which recognize several categories of fiction, nonfiction, and drama.

In terms of collection development, award-winning titles and even runner-up titles automatically garner a lot of media attention, and for libraries this translates into patron curiosity and demand. Such award winners are often "must buys" for libraries, or are at least favorably considered for purchase as they relate to the collection development criteria for each particular library or information center collection. Start-up collections for newly opened school libraries or for new public library branches routinely include backlists of prestigious award-winning titles, since the receipt of a literary prize is seen as an indicator of high quality literature and likely of enduring value. See the Resources section at the end of the chapter to locate lists of current and backlist award recipients.

Industry Blogs and E-Mail Lists

Online discussion groups such as blogs, listservs, and other electronic mailing lists that focus on a particular type of library or information center can be helpful because they often include book, e-book, or film reviews by members of the group. These are best used as an augmentation to perusing the major reviewing media because the quantity of items covered on blogs and mailing lists may be very limited. These reviews can be a good source for discovering publications by small publishers, specialty items, or items written by colleagues in the field.

WHO SELECTS?

Responsibility for the selection process varies considerably depending on the size of a library or information center and the number of professional librarians on staff. Large university and research libraries with collections numbering in the millions of items will have many subject specialists, resource coordinators, or bibliographers who are experts in their field. Each librarian specialist has responsibility for the selection of materials within his or her area of expertise; for example, French language and literature, environmental sciences, architecture and city planning, American literature, and so forth.

For smaller libraries, areas of responsibility are usually delineated among librarian positions. In a medium-sized public library, selection assignments might be divided up as follows: children's materials, YA resources, current fiction, general reference, business reference, medical reference, local history, art and architecture, and so on. Sometimes selection assignments are based on classification system divisions (e.g., 000s, 100s, etc., for collections using the

Dewey Decimal scheme). Branch librarians may have direct responsibility for building their own collections, or they may work with a centralized system-wide selection team.

For the solo librarian or technician operating a small special library independently, selection is just one of the many tasks to be juggled. School librarians or technicians may work independently in selecting materials or in close conjunction with district level staff.

SELECTION POLICIES

Most well-run libraries and information centers have a written statement that articulates their vision and policies for developing their collection. Two terms in frequent use for this document are *collection development policy* and *materials selection policy*. Although sometimes used interchangeably, they are different. Former Oregon State University Acquisitions Librarian, Richard Brumley, put it succinctly:

> A materials selection policy is much more limited: [It discusses] what criteria are used in purchasing (or accepting gift) books, journals, CDs, videos, etc., for a library. A collection development policy is much broader: in addition to criteria for selecting materials, it will include such things as collection assessment, weeding criteria, preservation and conservation, balance of monographs to serials, switching formats (print to CD to Web), liaison to academic departments, serials cancellation projects, etc. One is more apt to use the term *collection development policy* in academic libraries or large research libraries, while the term *materials selection policy* has a greater public library connotation.[4]

Written Selection Policies

Why do we need material selection or collection development policies in our libraries and information centers? Having a written selection policy has many advantages, including the following:

It formalizes a plan for selecting materials. By drafting a document, library staff members are forced to plan ahead and to think critically about their selection procedure. What are the library's collection goals? What does the library intend to acquire? By making the policy statement formal, the staff is guided in making selection decisions and discouraged from making frivolous purchases. A written policy is taken more seriously than an informal, verbal one. It also gives the agency a starting point for continuous review and revision. As with any effective policy, periodic updating is needed.

It provides a chance to draft a new mission statement for the library or revisit an existing one. In the past, many library agencies placed most of their efforts into the routines of day-to-day operations, such as assisting patrons, stocking and restocking materials, essentially keeping the "store" open. Long-term planning efforts were minimal or overlooked. A written document forces staff to identify, review, or revitalize a mission statement, which is a vital first step in the planning process.

Whether beginning the design of a new facility or updating a policy for an existing library, a mission statement provides a focal point for ensuing discussion and reflection. To begin with, review of the parent agency's mission statement is necessary. From that, the library's own mission statement evolves. This can be a thought-provoking exercise that leads staff to discuss the purpose of the organization, its clientele, objectives, core values, and other visionary and organizational concepts.

It prioritizes areas for purchase. As discussed previously, both materials selection and collection development policies describe priority areas for purchase as well as delineate limitations or types of material not collected. For example, public libraries may indicate that they do not collect comic books, textbooks, or workbooks, considering these consumable items best purchased by patrons for their individual use. Smaller college libraries may indicate that they only purchase materials related to class offerings. A corporate information center may decline to purchase fiction or popular best sellers, focusing instead on technical, work-related materials.

It establishes responsibility. A written policy usually spells out which library positions are charged with selection and also who has the final responsibility for what is on the library's shelves, network, or website. For schools and other publicly accessible libraries, the policy should also delineate who has the authority to approve or deny removal of a challenged title.

It becomes official policy. A formal policy document may need to be reviewed by a governing board or council. This process allows for input and review from other employees and from the library's constituents. In the best case, this process helps build support and understanding of the library's role at all levels.

It protects library and staff in cases of complaint or controversy. When a complaint arises and a citizen, parent, or patron questions the appropriateness of an item in the collection, a written policy gives the library or information center credibility. With an approved plan in hand, staff can respond that the purchase meets the selection criteria, is an award-winning book or resource, has received positive reviews, is age appropriate, and so on. A thorough policy should set out specific requirements for the process of challenging an item for removal from the collection.

Criteria for Selection

As part of their written selection policy document, many libraries will delineate specific criteria that they look for when considering materials for purchase. These criteria should also be applied to donations that are accepted for the collection, as well as to items culled during discarding. Some commonly used criteria include the following:

1. Topic: Is this a subject area that the library collection focuses on?

2. Reading level: Is the level appropriate for the library's clientele?

3. Currency: Is the information up to date and timely?

4. Demand: Is much demand anticipated for the topic or for the author; is it tied in with other media?

5. Cost: How does the price compare with other similar items? *The Library and Book Trade Almanac* tracks average annual pricing in many categories.

6. Author's credentials: Does the author seem to be credible and knowledgeable on the topic?

7. Publisher or producer's reputation: Is the publisher a small, specialty, or vanity press or a major publishing house; what other titles have they produced? Is this a self-published title?

8. Features: Does the item have desirable features or extras? For a print source: an index, bibliographies, special appendices, maps, graphics, a CD, or a companion website? For an online e-book source: dynamic content, regular updating, and multiple user access?

9. Resource sharing: Will other local libraries purchase it?

10. Available in other media: Which version is the most appropriate: print, multimedia, or digital?

CENSORSHIP

No discussion of collection building for libraries and information centers in the United States would be complete without considering censorship and the concept of the freedom to read. Guaranteed by the First Amendment of the Constitution, the right to free speech and expression has been broadly supported by library trade associations, the publishing industry, retail booksellers, and by many individual librarians. For library employees this has meant discouraging censorship, advocating patrons' freedom to read or view materials, stocking a diversity of information from different viewpoints, refraining from limiting library materials because of personal beliefs, and remaining neutral when providing access to information. Some of the ethics concerning the topic of censorship is discussed in more detail in Chapter 8.

The American Library Association (ALA) first devised its "Library Bill of Rights" (see Appendix B) in 1948 to interpret library services in light of the First Amendment. Within ALA, its high profile Office for Intellectual Freedom (OIF) is charged with educating librarians and the public about the importance of freedom of expression. The OIF website is an excellent source of information on the office's activities and on the promotion of free access to libraries and library materials. Other groups also advocate an individual's right to view or read; for example, the American Film and Video Association's "Freedom to View" statement supports the access rights of minors and adults to multimedia materials. Such statements share the belief that it is the right of each individual to make his or her own decision regarding what to read or view. In the case of minors, these policies explicitly state that it is the responsibility of a parent to supervise and monitor children's choices. Many library agencies and information centers have incorporated these concepts into their own formal selection and service policies.

In practice, academic and research libraries and corporate information centers are more realistically able to support full access and to take an uncompromising anti-censorship stance because their clientele is adult. Those in public and school libraries regulate access to controversial materials and have long been creative in their strategies, from locking book cases, to requiring parental permission slips for access, to avoiding the purchase of controversial books or videos. In some school libraries, sensitive materials may be housed as special reading and require a counselor's or teacher's referral for access.

What Is Censorship?

What, then, is censorship? A broad definition of censorship is *the practice of suppressing or deleting material considered to be objectionable.* As it most often applies to public or school libraries, censorship is the act of removing titles from the library collection. Typically, books are challenged because they have been selected as required school reading for a certain class or grade level. Parents or other interested parties will often protest a choice as objectionable and seek to have it removed from the reading list, and, perhaps, also from the library shelves.

Classics, dictionaries, contemporary novels, nonfiction works, picture books (the familiar as well as the lesser known) all show up on the list of titles banned, removed, or challenged. Steinbeck's *Of Mice and Men,* Maya Angelou's autobiographical *I Know Why the Caged Bird Sings,* many of Judy Blume's preteen titles, the popular Harry Potter novels by J. K. Rowling, the *American Heritage Dictionary,* and Mark Twain's *Adventures of Huckleberry Finn* are perennial targets for removal. See *Banned in the U.S.A.* by Herbert Foerstel (listed in the Resources section) for a detailed historical treatment of this heated topic, and see also Chapter 8 (Ethics in the Information Age) for further discussion.

Challenged books generate a hotbed of controversy and media coverage for public and school libraries, with much debate ensuing on both sides of the issue. Ironically, challenging a book also stirs up much interest and curiosity about the item in question, which frequently results in increased readership of a controversial title. In the challenge process, library staff members are called upon to support their criteria for having purchased the title, and this often translates into submitting their selection policy document to public scrutiny. Most savvy library and school administrators will have in place a detailed process to be followed in consideration of the withdrawal of a title. Based on a Supreme Court ruling, one of the elements of the formula for determining obscenity is to measure an item against the community standards of each specific locality. In other words, each local area sets its own standard for considering items objectionable or appropriate based on the collective opinion of the citizens of the community. This can be a rather imprecise measure for settling a challenge case.

Another twist on censorship that doesn't draw media attention but is all too familiar to library staff is the stealthy actions of individual patrons to censor materials they deem offensive. Some library customers take it upon themselves to remove these materials by ripping out the offending pages, mutilating pictures, or stealing the items in question.

Censorship Versus Selection

Naturally, the question arises: How does the selection philosophy and process that take place in libraries differ from censorship? As discussed previously in this chapter, the selection process is based ideally on articulated criteria for purchasing the highest quality and most appropriate material for a given collection and is not used as a means to ban information.

Librarians and information managers have a professional responsibility to be inclusive, not exclusive, in their collection development, and to refrain from withholding topics because of their own personal beliefs. At the other end of the acquisitions continuum, weeding also should not be seen as a means for removing controversial items. Ideally, libraries and information centers, as nonpartisan suppliers of information, should support in their holdings a wide range of ideas and viewpoints for their customers to access, leaving each reader to draw their own conclusions.

Selection policies might include prioritized categories for purchase or, conversely, areas to be omitted in the collection process. Although some might argue that this is censorship, the intent is to prioritize purchases based on established local needs, because few libraries can afford to buy everything.

The following quotation from longtime American library school educator and scholar on intellectual freedom issues, Lester Asheim, is over half a century ago old now, yet it still rings true in trying to define the ideal spirit of professional library staff as they approach this sensitive responsibility.

Liberty or Control?

Selection, then, begins with a presumption in favor of liberty of thought; censorship, with a presumption in favor of thought control. Selection's approach to the book is positive, seeking, its values in the book as a book, and in the book as a whole. Censorship's approach is negative, seeking for vulnerable characteristics wherever they can be found-anywhere within the book, or even outside it. Selection seeks to protect the right of the reader to read; censorship seeks to protect-not the right-but the reader himself from the fancied effects of his reading. The selector has faith in the intelligence of the reader; the censor has faith only in his own.[5]

What About the Internet?

The rationale described above was originally devised to clarify the difference between selection and censorship when referring to individual items. But with the Internet, librarians are challenged in applying and testing the freedom-of-access philosophy. The quandary is that the old laws don't apply. The concept of selecting quality materials based on local criteria doesn't apply because, unless effective filters are in place, web-based resources are not acquired piecemeal. It's mostly an all or nothing acquisition. Official government sites, open access science journals, Facebook, online retail shopping, gambling sites, personal home pages, and more abound, all with text, colorful images, photographs, sound, music, and video. It just happens that this same environment works equally well for distributing offensive or pornographic material as it does for federal tax forms. So as the Internet has vastly expanded the research sources available to patrons, it also introduces new challenges with respect to computers in use in a public venue, such as a library or open computer lab. And beyond the library environment, it also has brought about challenges for all employers in terms of offering instant access to potentially recreational and "time-wasting" activities during the work day: Some companies or agencies block social media sites from all employer-provided computers while in the workplace.

The Internet knows no geographical boundaries per se, so the established rule of relying on community standards to determine what is offensive material cannot be applied here. The federal government has been unable to successfully place limits on pornographic content on the Internet through the so-called decency acts and other similarly intentioned bills.

Librarians are coping by implementing policies that discourage viewing of potentially offensive or pornographic material, such as placing terminals in full view of staff, installing privacy shields on computer monitors, requiring parental signatures on consent forms, implementing limits on computer access time per patron, and posting acceptable use policies. School librarians may be required to use filtering software in an effort to restrict access to predetermined age-inappropriate, pornographic, or other sites, and also to block searches using offensive keywords. The reality is that this doesn't ensure no student will find inappropriate material accidentally or because students have learned ways around such efforts. In contrast, many public libraries fall back on their support of the freedom to read and view policies, cautioning all adult patrons that it is up to them to screen and monitor their children's use of the Internet just as they would with DVDs, CDs, books, and other materials.

As library staff would be the first to admit, this is straddling a difficult line, promoting access to information while dealing with concerns about viewing pornography in a public place. But there is something very different about a patron peering at a full-color screen of pornographic images or video in plain view of children and others, as opposed to a solitary reader perusing an art book of nude figures while tucked away in a corner cubicle. The freedom to read and view has become an even more complex issue, with no easy answers.

COLLECTION MAINTENANCE AND WEEDING

Mention weeding to most library staff and they will either groan or reply virtuously that they never have enough time to get to it. Although it is often a least favorite task, weeding or deselecting is an essential aspect of maintaining a relevant, appealing, and timely collection of materials.

Weeding is defined as evaluating existing library holdings for possible replacement, repair, updating, or discarding. It is often carried out in conjunction with an inventory project, a facility remodel, a move into new quarters, installation of bar coding, conversion to a new automated system, or repurposing of library space.

It's doubtful that any other library can rival the collecting scope of the Library of Congress, whose "collections comprise the world's most comprehensive record of human creativity and knowledge."[6] Nonetheless, even that venerable institution, with its more than 160 million items, does not maintain everything. Although many large research, academic, and special libraries do maintain serious, scholarly, historical collections of great breadth, all collections still need periodic, and often regular, weeding. Thoughtful deselecting of obsolete, damaged, superseded, or otherwise inappropriate materials complements the care given to the selection of new materials at the beginning of the collection development process.

Another driving force behind the need to cull collections is shelving or storage limits. Floor and stack space are often at a premium; thus, it's not efficient to clutter costly space with unneeded or unused materials. One of many advantages of the digital revolution in publishing is the savings in physical storage or display space that online editions bring. However, this potential is achieved only with careful planning and hard work.

As an example, we can look at a local community college library to illustrate the typical decisions facing librarians as they review, renew, replace, or discard familiar sources each year. A major space alteration coupled with the conversion to a new integrated library system (ILS) system prompted the decision to discard all VHS tapes in the college's collection. A modest budget had been made available to upgrade high-use titles to DVD or streaming video formats. The process has involved several steps and care has been taken to closely involve campus faculty in the project.

Since most of the films had been curriculum related and shown in a classroom session or served as supplementary viewing material for students, current instructors were notified several times by all-campus e-mail of the pending removal of the VHS tapes. Meanwhile, librarians set about reviewing all of the tapes for content currency, recent usage, and circulation statistics. For those films relevant and in current use by faculty, library staff determined whether each title existed in a DVD or streaming format that could be purchased by the institution as a replacement for the outmoded VHS. While some instructors thought that the college could just "record the tape onto a DVD," copyright considerations prevented that for almost all items.

Where titles were available in both formats, DVDs and three-year streaming licenses, preferences varied considerably among instructors. In addition to faculty preferences ("I only show streaming in my classroom" or "I prefer the DVD") other issues needed consideration. Where courses were offered as distance education the streaming format was required. For face-to-face courses, some campus classrooms in older buildings did not yet have the broadband width to reliably support streaming film, so DVD would be needed there for the time being. When there was no match for an exact title in a digital format, efforts were made to locate a product that closely resembled the original content and treatment. And as the streaming licenses next come up for renewal, the review and decision process will need to be repeated again, likely with new options to consider.

Other aspects of collection maintenance include shelf reading on a periodic basis to assure correct placement of physical items on library shelves and inventorying extent items—often done annually or during building holiday closures—against a holdings list to identify lost, missing, stolen, or misplaced items. The regular culling of multiple copies of a title that is now past its peak demand period is another needed housekeeping task. From time to time, specific collections (e.g., children's multi-media kits or books, YA titles, oversize volumes, DVDs, audio CDs) may need to be consolidated, shifted, or moved to new locations. This might entail removal of existing bolted and braced stacks or replacement of existing furniture with new or different-sized shelving. Transfer of resources deemed historic, unique, or in fragile physical condition from open stacks to a more protected environment such as a secured local history room or an archives is another example of routine collection maintenance.

In the management of corporate or governmental collections, there may be very specific retention schedules in place by the organization that dictate how long to keep certain records before de-accessioning or destroying them. In this case, being sure to follow retention and removal procedures at specified intervals is a key element of collection maintenance.

For collections of e-books, which often come "bundled" from the vendor which means sold as a package or set of many titles and with the publication dates of items ranging over a decade or more, the option for an individual library to remove specific titles that seem outdated is not an easy proposition at this time; this may change in the future as e-book vendors offer more customized collecting options.[7]

As with selection, the issues to consider in weeding are many. Cost, currency, physical or electronic storage space, ease of use, currency of format, and customer preference are all critical considerations. Many industry jobbers such as Follett, which caters to K-12 school libraries, offer collection evaluation and mapping services that can pinpoint aging and superseded titles and overall subject gaps in the library's collection. Taking advantage of this type of analysis can be extremely helpful in implementing a weeding and replacement effort.

CHANGING FORMATS OF INFORMATION

In the Information Age, librarians and information specialists can be sure of one thing: information will continue to be repackaged, often at a rapid and overwhelming pace. Other current trends include the continuing merger of large national and international publishers, an emphasis on converting print reference titles to Web-based products, and reliance on the Web for subscriptions to full-text periodical databases. Electronic publishing of textbooks and original book-length works (e-books) continues to grow, but the lack of a standard delivery platform remains an issue even while the medium's popular acceptance by students and readers has placed this format in the forefront of publishing growth. Publishers will continue to produce new works and to repackage old ones—sometimes those already owned by a library. Each must be critically evaluated before library funds to purchase or subscribe are committed.

The huge, collaborative, high profile Google Books Library Project (formerly called Google Book Search) by search engine giant and innovator Google began amid much controversy in 2004 with its plans to digitize the world's books (estimated at some 130 million titles) and make them available online.[8]

Including partnerships with over 40 major academic and research libraries (Harvard, Princeton, University of California, Oxford, and others), the
project has generated lots of attention with its revolutionary results, as well
as controversy among publishers and authors who do not want their copyrights violated. Over a decade into the effort and with massive digitizing still
ongoing, the reality is that this collaborative collection development has a
huge impact on library practitioners, library collections, and library users.[9]
Having 24/7 access and search capabilities to items that may have been
tucked away in library stacks or relegated to off-site storage buildings provides an amazing extended collection to all. While researchers were formerly
dependent on physical visits for access, digitization of the full-text or limited pages (as the copyright terms for each work allows) through the Google
Books database now brings an "extended collection" to users as they discover these resources on their own or are referred to them by a reference
librarian.

As publishing formats continue to morph, a problem faced by many librarians attempting to maintain in-depth research or historical back files is the
inevitable gap between leasing temporary access and permanent ownership.
Renting electronic access means that libraries no longer possess their own
copies of books, periodicals, or other works. Rather, they are at the mercy
of publishers who may or may not change their access policies or begin
charging additional fees for access to archives. For serious research and
larger libraries, this uncertainty often means maintaining dual subscriptions, both print and electronic, to ensure access to the complete run of a
periodical or reference title. Thus, collecting a comprehensive collection can
be expensive.

Once touted as the cost-saving answer to the problem of mushrooming
materials costs for libraries, electronic publishing clearly provides significant added value over print equivalents with its instant delivery, 24/7 remote
access, convenience, and many sophisticated searching enhancements. Who
can imagine turning the clock back and going without such access? But electronic reference products and services rarely provide cost savings over print
versions. And the unspoken reality is that traditional allocations for book budgets keep shrinking as funds are used to pay for electronic editions.

In an era of changing information formats that is at once both exciting and
challenging, perhaps the touchstone for collection managers is to adhere to
the old adage of knowing their collections, both hard copy and virtual, while
continuing to seek out the customers' changing needs.

STUDY QUESTIONS

1. Find a copy of the mission statement for your college or university
   library. Where did you find it published (e.g., on the library's website,
   in the college catalog, elsewhere)? Do you agree with the mission as
   stated? Why or why not?

2. Study the selection policy for a library of your choice. Is it up to
   date? Does it specify guidelines for weeding as well as collecting new

materials? Discuss the similarities and differences between these two processes. Does the policy document include the process for handling challenges or requests for removal of materials?

3. Some libraries are posting their selection policies on their websites. What are the pros and cons of publishing these documents on the Web?

4. What is Banned Books Week? Who sponsors it and what is its purpose?

5. Are you aware of any recent attempt to challenge a book or other resource at your local public library? Describe the circumstances and the outcome.

6. Does your local public library use social media (e.g., Facebook, Twitter, Goodreads.com) as community-building tools? Try following one networking site for your public library; is their social media stream engaging for library users? Does the library consider it to be a successful outreach effort? Are you able to submit your ideas on new purchases for the collection?

7. How do critical reviews for a book or e-book published in library trade periodicals such as *Kirkus Reviews* differ from user-generated comments found on Amazon and Goodreads.com? What value does each offer to library staff responsible for selecting materials?

NOTES

1. Karin J. Fulton, "The Rise of Patron-Driven Acquisitions: A Literature Review," *Georgia Library Quarterly* 51, no. 3, article 10 (2014): 1–3, http://digital commons.kennesaw.edu/glq/vol51/iss3/10.
2. "April 2015 Web Server Survey," *Netcraft*, http://news.netcraft.com/archives/category/web-server-survey/ (accessed May 5, 2015).
3. Dave Bogart, ed., *Library and Book Trade Almanac*, 58th ed. (Medford, NJ: Information Today, 2013), 435.
4. Richard Brumley, e-mail to author, January 27, 1999.
5. Lester Asheim, "Not Censorship But Selection," *Wilson Library Bulletin* 28 (September 1953): 67.
6. "Frequently Asked Questions," *Library of Congress*, http://www.loc.gov/about/frequently-asked-questions/#what_lc (accessed April 27, 2015).
7. Jeanette Larson, *CREW: A Weeding Manual for Modern Libraries, Addendum on e-books*, (Austin, TX: Texas State Library and Archives Commission, 2012), 4–5, https://www.tsl.texas.gov/sites/default/files/public/tslac/ld/ld/pubs/crew/crewebooksaddendum12.pdf.
8. Leonid Taycher, "Books of the World, Stand Up and Be Counted! All 129,864,880 of You." *Google Book Search* (blog), August 5, 2010 (8:26 a.m.), http://book search.blogspot.com/2010/08/books-of-world-stand-up-and-be-counted.html.
9. Terence K. Huwe, "Building Digital Libraries. Collaborative Collection Development Comes of Age," *Computers in Libraries* 35, no. 3 (2015): 25–27, http://pqasb.pqarchiver.com/infotoday/doc/1680527012.html.

RESOURCES

Books

Barr, Catherine. *Best Books for High School Readers Grades 9–12*. 3rd ed. Santa Barbara, CA: Libraries Unlimited, 2013.

Barr, Catherine. *Best Books for Middle School and Junior High Readers Grades 6–9*. 3rd ed. Santa Barbara, CA: Libraries Unlimited, 2013.

Barr, Catherine and Jamie Campbell Naidoo. *Best Books for Children: Preschool Through Grade 6*. 10th ed. Santa Barbara, CA: Libraries Unlimited, 2014.

Bartlett, Rebecca Ann, ed. *Choice's Outstanding Academic Titles, 2007–2011*. Chicago: American Library Association, 2012. (And see each January issue of *Choice* for annual lists of print and electronic sources selected as Outstanding Academic Titles.)

Doyle, Robert P. *Banned Books: Challenging Our Freedom to Read, 2014 Edition*. Chicago: American Library Association, 2014.

Foerstel, Herbert N. *Banned in the U.S.A.: A Reference Guide to Book Censorship in Schools and Public Libraries*. 2nd ed. Westport, CT: Greenwood Press, 2002.

Hysell, Shannon Graff, ed. *Recommended Reference Books for Small and Medium-Sized Libraries and Media Centers*. 2015 ed. Santa Barbara, CA: Libraries Unlimited, 2015.

Laguardia, Cheryl, ed. *Magazines for Libraries: For the General Reader and School, Junior College, College, University, and Public Libraries*. 23rd ed. Ann Arbor, MI: Proquest, 2014. (And see the free resource *Magazines for Libraries Update* at http://bit.ly/1CEOGvI and http://www.proquest.com/blog/pqblog/2014/Meet-Cheryl-LaGuardia-MFL.html.)

Websites

ALA Youth Media Awards
http://www.ala.org/yalsa/reads4teens/book-lists-and-awards
http://www.ala.org/yalsa/bookawards/booklists/members
(accessed May 5, 2015)
Provides overview information on the many annual awards presented by the American Library Association (ALA) honoring books, videos, and other high quality materials for children and teenagers. Names and describes the major awards, including the Newbery, Caldecott, Coretta Scott King, Michael L. Printz, Margaret A. Edwards, and several others. The site also has links to news of current award winners and backlists of all winners through the years.

Bulletin of the Center for Children's Books
http://www.press.jhu.edu/journals/bulletin_of_the_center_for_childrens_books/
(accessed May 5, 2015)
Founded in 1945, this is a leading children's book review periodical very useful for school and public librarians. Compiled by the Graduate School of Library and Information Science, University of Illinois at Urbana-Champaign and published by Johns Hopkins University Press.

Collection Development on LibraryJournal.com
http://reviews.libraryjournal.com/category/collection-development/
(accessed May 5, 2015)

Part of the industry-leading periodical *Library Journal*'s website, this interactive feature carries a variety of recent best seller rankings, other recommended lists, and archived reviews.

CREW: A Weeding Manual for Modern Libraries

https://www.tsl.texas.gov/ld/pubs/crew/index.html

(accessed May 15, 2015)

Published by the Texas State Library and Archives Commission, librarian Jeanette Larson provides an overview and best practices for evaluating and weeding library collections. Includes addendum on weeding as it applies to e-books.

Doody's Core Titles

http://www.doody.com/dct/Content/DCTHistory.asp

(accessed May 5, 2015)

This collection development tool for essential purchases in the medical field is updated annually by content specialists and librarians. As of 2004, it replaced the previous standard by Alfred N. Brandon and Dorothy R. Hill *Selected List of Books and Journals for the Small Medical Library.*

Goodreads.com

http://www.goodreads.com/

(accessed May 5, 2015)

Among the various social media sites focusing on current books, publishing, author promotion, and sharing of reader comments, Goodreads.com is the most visible. Founded in 2007 by Otis Chandler, software engineer and descendant of the founders of the *Los Angeles Times,* the site was sold to the mega-retailer Amazon.com in 2013. Helpful source for trends, reader input especially for current YA and adult fiction.

National Book Foundation

http://www.nationalbook.org/

(accessed May 5, 2015)

Since 1950, this foundation has presented its prestigious annual awards to "enhance the public's awareness of exceptional books written by fellow Americans, and to increase the popularity of reading in general." View press releases on current awards and lists of past prizewinners.

New York Times

http://www.nytimes.com/pages/books/

(accessed May 5, 2015)

Searchable, online archive of book reviews from the respected *New York Times* daily and Sunday sections.

Office of Intellectual Freedom

http://www.ala.org/offices/oif

(accessed May 5, 2015)

From ALA's Office of Intellectual Freedom. An extensive resource of updates, policies, and interpretations on the freedom to view and read as it affects libraries, librarians, and patrons.

Chapter 5

Preparing Materials for Use

The careful selection of library items described in the preceding chapter is just the first of multiple stages in the preparation of materials for use by customers. Further steps include acquisition, cataloging, classification, and, for hard copy formats, physical processing of each requested item. Although every library develops its own routine for handling these operations, there are many shared activities and functions common to both the largest and smallest of collections.

ACQUISITION

Selection is the systematic process of choosing materials relevant to a library or information center, whereas acquisition is the nuts and bolts of procuring titles and paying the companies that produce or supply the items. As with selection, acquisition is usually under the umbrella of technical services in a library and takes place out of the public eye.

According to the *Library and Book Trade Almanac* (formerly known as the *Bowker Annual: Library and Book Trade Almanac*), more than 190,000 book titles were produced in the United States in 2011.[1] These were the products of about 3,100 American book publishers.[2] The relationship of buyer and seller closely binds libraries and publishers together.

Numerous types and sizes of publishers now offer multimedia and electronic works in addition to the more traditional print titles. Most libraries and information centers select books and other publications from a variety of publishers in order to fill their collection needs. Publishers may include large corporate publishers owned by powerful media outlets; university presses, which produce more scholarly and esoteric titles of limited appeal; regional publishers specializing in a geographic area; children's publishing houses; and small or alternative presses, which produce limited print runs on a variety of material, including poetry, literature, health, religion, and other topics. Self-published titles have grown in diversity and quality and may also be selected by librarians for purchase. Some publishers narrowly limit the subject areas in which they produce titles, or focus on a particular age group, foreign language, or other demographic.

Reference book publishers closely target the library market and may include library professionals as editorial consultants to develop relevant and timely products. Trade publishers direct their products at a particular professional or industry group. Seasoned librarians develop name recognition of and an appreciation for many specific publishers as they purchase their materials over the years. This is helpful in the selection process because a publisher's reputation can influence a decision of whether or not to buy an item.

As in the rest of the corporate world, mergers are continuing to occur in the publishing industry, both nationally and internationally. This trend tends to make library professionals, booksellers, and others worry about the resulting tight control of what gets published and the quandary of having too few outlets to allow for varied voices and points of view. One recent example was the merger of two large, leading publishing houses, Penguin and Random House. An additional concern is the consolidation of multiple media under one roof—for example, bookselling and book social media, as exemplified by giant retailer Amazon's purchase of the formerly independently owned Goodreads.com, the flourishing book/reading focused social networking site. Such mergers further narrow the information sources to which the public is exposed.

To gain an overview of the North American publishing industry, browse the annual reference work *Literary Market Place (LMP)*. This publication is produced both in hard copy and as a subscription online database. A comprehensive directory of the region's publishing industry, *LMP* is essential for locating and identifying information about publishers and ancillary services, such as jobbers, bookbinders, electronic publishing services, and so forth, and includes a classified index to publishing houses by specialty. Some publishing companies depend in part on regional sales personnel to market and sell their products. The sales representatives may call on libraries in their territory to promote and vend their title list. Many other publishers work either directly with libraries and retail outlets or through middlemen known as *jobbers* to sell their products.

The Services of a Jobber

Librarians and technicians in libraries, media, and information centers most commonly use jobbers or wholesalers to acquire materials for their collections. Jobbers and wholesalers are industry middlemen who supply books, e-books, CDs, DVDs, and other materials to retail stores and libraries from hundreds of individual publishers. Familiar industry names include Brodart, Baker and Taylor, Ingram, BWI, Blackwell, Mackin, Mook and Blanchard, and many more. For library science students and novices to the world of libraries, conferences and industry trade shows also provide good opportunities to visit jobbers' booths and find out about their many specialized services.

Jobbers pass on to libraries a discount from the publisher on the suggested retail or list price of an item. Typically, discounts range from a low of 5 percent to a high of 40 percent. Other services offered by wholesalers include customized processing and cataloging of materials, special heavy-duty bindings, MARC records, foreign language titles, bar codes, standing orders, opening-day collections, and other customized collection management options.

Although the majority of library purchases are handled through jobbers for convenience, efficiency, and cost savings, some small presses, self-published titles, print-on-demand books, and other specialty producers may require that an order be placed directly with them, thus bypassing jobbers. For libraries purchasing thousands of titles each year, relying on jobbers for the bulk of acquisitions is a necessity. Because *direct orders*—that is, placing an order directly with the specific publishing house—are more time-consuming for a library staff to handle and track, these are typically kept to a minimum.

Most libraries work with a number of different wholesalers to acquire the variety of materials their collection demands. Just as there are general and specialty publishing firms, there are jobbers that handle mainstream current releases of e-books, audio books, and print titles and those that deal exclusively with medical or legal resources, foreign-language publications, or only with periodical subscriptions. Thus, most libraries have accounts with multiple wholesalers to procure all the materials they need. And even with various jobbers to choose from, many librarians in libraries and information centers make some purchases from their community or online bookseller because of immediate need, exclusive distribution, or other considerations. The growth and success of online booksellers have also contributed to the trend of libraries buying slightly used copies (in good condition) of books through these sites rather than paying a higher price for a brand new copy even with the jobber price breaks.

Order Plans

Many jobbers and individual publishers offer an acquisitions service known as an *approval plan.* When subscribing to an approval plan, a library submits a detailed profile of its selection criteria to the jobber, who then automatically ships materials matching the profile to the library. Items are still subject to approval by the acquisitions librarian or other designated staff. After on-site review, undesirable items are returned without penalty. The objectives are to save staff time in the selection and ordering processes for certain predictable subject areas, to be able to select with the book in hand rather than relying solely on a review, and to expedite the receipt of materials. Generally, approval plans work best for very large libraries, which are likely to purchase the majority of titles released by designated publishers anyway. If much more than 5 percent of the titles received on approval are being returned, the library's profile needs to be adjusted. Some jobbers also offer smaller, more targeted selection plans for specific collections such as new young adult (YA) literature or current best seller fiction rather than a broad-based approval plan including all subject areas.

Standing orders or *continuation plans* are another time-saver for libraries and good business for publishers or wholesalers. With a standing order contract, a library indicates that it will automatically purchase each new edition of a title; there is no need to be on the watch for an upcoming edition. Upon release, the publication is immediately supplied and the library is billed. Standing order status is most likely to be applied to standard reference works and sets, where a library is confident it wants each new edition of a must-have title.

Another service offered by some companies is book rental, as opposed to outright purchase. For example, the McNaughton Books service by Brodart, which allows libraries to lease a certain quantity of new releases, is a popular choice, particularly among public libraries. The staff preselects titles from a monthly catalog of forthcoming titles. This provides a steady infusion of new, in-demand titles that can either be returned when their popularity has waned or, if needed, purchased to add to the permanent library collection.

This service provides an effective solution for meeting the rush of interest that often accompanies the release of highly promoted titles and popular best sellers. Multiple copies of such a title can be rented at a savings, and, because the service provides the books as shelf-ready, staff processing time is saved as well. Rental plans can improve customer satisfaction while saving the staff time and money. Some libraries pass on the cost of such a program to patrons, charging daily rental fees for these books; others choose to absorb the cost and circulate them free of charge.

Many jobbers and vendors employ professional librarians to enhance their customer service and provide innovative ideas for products. As a job seeker, you may want to explore employment opportunities among the many industry wholesalers, product vendors, and supply companies.

Although a company may sometimes function both as a wholesaler of materials and a seller of library-specific supplies, there are many firms that vend only the unique equipment, furnishings, shelving, housing, security devices, and other supplies targeted for the library industry. A few examples of library supply and equipment companies are Demco, Gaylord, Highsmith, Library Bureau, and Metal Edge. There are many others.

Leasing

Many business, financial, and marketing publications, such as telephone company crisscross directories and corporate directories, have long been available to library collections not through outright purchase but rather through lease agreements. This keeps older, used copies from being retained or resold, thus allowing the publishers tighter control over the use of their valuable data and final published products.

Licensing

As libraries' reliance on electronic sources of information, or e-collections, grows, so does the importance of negotiating the licensing agreement with the publisher, now a standard part of the acquisitions process. Commonplace with the purchase of computer software, then with CD-ROM products, and now with Web-delivered sources, licensing is a growing area of library responsibility. The procurement of online sources may be handled directly with the company that produces the database, e-books, streaming video, or other information product, or the resources may be procured through a library purchasing consortia.

In some cases, when library consortia such as academic library systems have negotiated group purchase deals, an intermediary agency may serve as a bursar or third party in implementing the leases. This third-party arrangement gives libraries more leverage in bargaining with large corporations. A license will specify the terms of access that the library or information center is agreeing to with their purchase; this may vary from annual pricing for just one year's access to the more expensive ongoing access with retrospective access rights.

Licenses are arranged for specific periods of time—typically on an annual basis, though it is sometimes possible to negotiate multiple-year agreements. Access to the e-collection, once the license period is over, varies depending on the terms of the agreement. In some cases, if the contract is not renewed or paid, access to the e-collection vanishes overnight, with nothing to show for the library's past investments. Thus, the licensing concept is a very significant one for libraries, with access rather than ownership as a core issue.

Publishers use licensing as a legal means of controlling the use of their products. Thus, licensing agreements are legal contracts that bear scrutiny by the acquiring party, in this case, the library (licensee). Generally, the seller (or licensor) prepares the contract with the terms of the agreement. In many cases, individual libraries do not have a level negotiating position in dealing with large content providers. In this situation, libraries run the risk of giving up certain rights that they and their patrons would have enjoyed if the rights had been defined by copyright laws that allow for fair use, particularly in educational settings. Care should be taken to make sure that library personnel understand what they are being asked to agree to when they negotiate a license.

Fees are usually determined by the approximate number of users allowed access—for example, the number of employees in a corporation, the size of a school's student body, the current enrollment of a university, or the population served by a public library. A site license may include access for multiple offices, branches, or campuses affiliated with the main library agency, or the agreement may require additional site licenses to provide access to these other physical locations. In some agreements, a password allows users remote access from off-site, such as from home or from another location. In other cases, access is restricted to on-site computers only, based on a range of authenticated Internet Protocol (IP) addresses that uniquely identify the computers in the licensee's library. Although providing value-added service and an ever-increasing number of convenient options, typical licensed electronic products, such as indexing and abstracting services and full-text databases of journals, are not cheaper than their print equivalents. In fact, they often cost substantially more. In some cases, the publisher imposes restrictions or conditions along with the electronic access, such as requiring the licensee to maintain simultaneous print subscriptions to its products, although this practice appears to be waning.

Consortia Efforts

As statewide and regional library consortia in the United States mature, a high priority for them is to seek site licenses to make selected electronic resources available to their entire membership. These consortia may include libraries of similar size and type, such as an academic library group, or may be a regional, multi-type network with everything from prison libraries to school libraries to museum research facilities and more. An example of an academic library group is the Community College Library Consortium. This cooperative buying group represents the largest system of higher education in the United States, the 113 public community colleges in California, and actively negotiates consortium pricing and licensing agreements for online database subscriptions, streaming video, and e-book collections. In Britain and other European countries, national site licensing is being piloted for all the university and polytechnic libraries of an entire country. This means that all current students and all faculty members within a particular country have access to certain products in electronic form.[3] For all such library groups or consortia, negotiated contract rates for library regions, university systems, or other memberships can often provide significant price breaks.

Library Concerns

Besides the expense of electronic subscriptions and the slippery issue of perpetual access, there are other challenges to e-collections. Especially noticeable with periodical databases is that, to appeal to the widest possible range of potential library clients, publishers often mix scholarly and popular titles into one product. The result can be an unfocused mishmash—something that did not occur with previous customized, individual print subscriptions. And the library cannot narrowly refine its collection within an e-journal product as it could with individual hard copy subscriptions; an electronic subscription is a package deal.

Some vendors are now talking about allowing individual libraries to tailor the list of titles they want to include in the index along with the full-text offered to patrons. It remains to be seen if this trial option will be judged as commercially viable. It is much more labor intensive, both for the vendor and for the library. It is easier to try to make one size fit all. However, from the researcher's point of view, it might be best to have an index to all electronic and print holdings for which full text is immediately available—whether online or on-site. Why tantalize customers with citations if the documents are not readily available? Another development due to transform the researcher's experience is the promise of "single search" tools, which integrate a library's print holdings listed in an online public access catalog (OPAC) with its online tools, to result in one universal search for resources, rather than multiple searches within separate databases and catalog.

Other concerns include licensing restrictions on what librarians consider standard library services and practices, such as providing interlibrary loans for periodical articles from an electronic resource. Also, there is no guarantee that the particular titles found in an e-collection today will, in fact, be there tomorrow. The arrangements between the actual periodical publishers and the producers of the e-product are subject to change and revision, resulting in the addition and deletion of titles without notice to subscribers.

Some good guidelines and active discussions of the issues surrounding e-collections can be found by visiting the websites of the leading trade associations and by joining listservs that focus on licensing issues. The licensing of electronic resources is very much an evolving area where the old rules don't apply. Library staff responsible for acquiring these resources and for negotiating licenses will want to keep up-to-date on the issues and should be encouraged to actively lobby publishers to make their collection needs known.

Finally, never accept publishers' definition of what *copyright* or *fair use* means. This is one of the few issues on which publishers and librarians have divergent viewpoints and conflicting interests. Many publishers use license agreements in an attempt to get librarians to give up rights inherent under the fair use clause of the copyright law. On the other hand, many publishers are very generous in granting libraries, particularly those in educational institutions, rights to use their materials in ways that may well go beyond what copyright laws mandate.

Electronic Ordering Systems

Compared to the neighborhood book dealer, the chain store at the mall, or your favorite online bookseller, the local library has always been plagued with an abysmally slow turnaround time in making hard copy materials available for patrons. Many of the services offered by jobbers focus on speeding up delivery and outsourcing processing and cataloging tasks. The end result should mean faster provision of materials to library customers.

The advent of Web-based order placement has delivered on the promise of speed at that starting point in the acquisitions process. Established customers can quickly place an order by accessing the Internet, and, with the click of a mouse, instantly submit their order to the jobber. The old, tedious task of generating paper order cards, then filing and tracking them, has been left behind.

At the heart of today's ordering systems is the International Standard Book Number (ISBN). A unique number assigned before publication to a book or specific edition of a book, the ISBN identifies the work's national, geographic, language, or other group, and its publisher, title, edition, and volume number. ISBNs are critical when ordering a specific title and are the key identifier for electronic acquisitions systems both in libraries and in the retail world.

Originally a 10-digit number when it was first adopted in 1969, the ISBN was expanded to a 13-digit sequence in 2007 to accommodate the future need for more numbers. Today, the two sequences are being referred to as ISBN-10 and ISBN-13 to differentiate between them. The revision of the ISBN has impacted publishers, distributors, booksellers large and small, libraries, and vendors, as they have had to adjust their workflow to deal with the new, longer numbers.

To take full advantage of doing business in a Web-based ordering environment, library staff may be required to use a bank credit card for payment. Many e-businesses are set up to accept credit cards only. Parent institutions may need to be educated about the advantages of allowing library staff to commit funds in this manner, which appears to bypass some of the fiscal safeguards that are typical in the workplace. As an added incentive to customers using Web-based ordering, some vendors may offer discounts when a credit card is used because this method frees them from complicated billing procedures.

In addition to the advantages of paperless orders and swift submission of those orders, Web-based acquisition consolidates what were once several separate, time-consuming clerical tasks. Most bibliographic verification can now be accomplished through browsing publishers' or retailers' websites. By toggling back and forth between a bibliographic utility, the library's automated system, and the jobber's website, order requests can be checked quickly against current holdings, then the verified order submitted. Accounting records are generated easily, and the MARC record for an on-order item can be added immediately to the library catalog, giving patrons a status report on the title that is being acquired.

The standardization of Web technology is an improvement over earlier, automated ordering systems, which relied on software and hardware that was specific to each vendor. With a Web interface, the process is familiar, easy, and doesn't require disks or CDs. The speed, ease of use, and consolidation of tasks that have resulted from Web-based ordering frees up staff time for learning new technologies, computer maintenance and troubleshooting, special projects, and other tasks.

Out-of-Print Materials

Books, DVDs, individual periodical issues, and other materials in demand by researchers and needed as replacement copies for library collections often may be out of print. This means that the publisher is no longer producing the item, and no new copies are available for order. Out-of-print status may be temporary or permanent. Either way, a library in need of an out-of-print title may contact a search service or query an out-of-print dealer to attempt to procure a copy. Out-of-print and second-hand book dealers abound online now, and, of course, there are the traditional "brick-and-mortar" dealers as well. Surcharges added by dealers vary considerably.

CATALOGING AND CLASSIFICATION

As shipments of new items arrive in the technical services area, they are unpacked, checked against packing slips, and examined for defects. If there are no problems with the order, the items are ready for the cataloging staff to handle. The purpose of cataloging materials is twofold: (1) to provide a shelf address or location for each book, CD, DVD, e-book, or other item, and (2) to provide specific information for the library holdings database. After technical services staff assign classification numbers (more commonly referred to as call numbers), determine subject headings, and provide descriptive information on an item, all is entered into the library's database, known as an OPAC. This database of information provides a master inventory of holdings and allows patrons to search the automated catalog, from on-site or off-site. It answers the following questions, among others: "What books or resources does the library carry on my topic?" "Does the library have a specific book or resource?" "Where is it located?" "Is it available now?" "Is it a hard copy book I can check out; or is it an e-book that I link to?"

The two most common classification methods in use in North American libraries are the Library of Congress (LC) and Dewey Decimal systems. LC evolved from the original organizing scheme that U.S. president Thomas Jefferson used for his own book collection before selling it to the new national library. An alpha–numeric system, LC is in use mostly in larger libraries, such as academic and research facilities. Melvil Dewey's decimal-based scheme was introduced in 1876 and remains the standard among American public and school libraries. It has been translated into many languages and is commonly used outside of the United States as well. An example of a more specialized classification is the Superintendent of Documents (SuDocs) system, used for large government document collections. SuDocs divides a collection into subgroups of documents based on the agency that issued or produced them.

One influential thinker and librarian outside of the United States was the Indian scholar Shiyali Ramamrita Ranganathan (1892–1972), whose major contributions to library science centered around classification and indexing theory. Ranganathan's Colon Classification (CC) system was developed as an attempt to improve on the Dewey Decimal system. Its name comes from the use of colons to separate facets in class numbers.

In addition, Ranganathan's 1931 treatise *The Five Laws of Library Science* is considered a classic in the field; it is still referred to and has been re-examined to explore how it applies to ideals of library service in today's Information Age. For example, Ranganathan's First Law, "Books Are For Use," can still inspire a spirited debate on a blog or in a face-to-face discussion about contemporary access and copyright issues.

The automation of library bibliographic records began with the invention of the MARC record. MARC records have long been a standard way of recording and sharing information about a bibliographic item. By using three types of content designators—tags, subfield codes, and indicators—the information is stored electronically and can be retrieved and interpreted by any other computer in the world that is programmed to read MARC records. For example, anyone reading a MARC record can assume that information found in the 245 field is information about the title and author, listed exactly in the form as it is shown on the title page of the book. Variant title information, such as the spine title, would be in the 246 field. The records can contain all the information displayed in OPACs as well as additional information that is useful to librarians. It is beyond the purpose of this text to fully explain the intricacies of the actual MARC coding. Readers who seek a deeper level of understanding should refer to the resources section at the end of this chapter for a referral to a tutorial.

Once one library has cataloged a book or another real or virtual bibliographic item and has coded the resulting cataloging data into MARC format, that data can be passed on to other libraries and read by their cataloging software without human intervention. This allows libraries to acquire cataloging data from the LC and other libraries with respected cataloging standards without repeating the labor-intensive effort of original cataloging. The receiving library has only to verify that the MARC record actually describes the item in hand and not some other edition or variant.

MARC format was originally developed by the LC in the 1960s, but quickly evolved into a decades-long, international standard for exchanging bibliographic data. For example, the Diet Library in Tokyo serves many of the functions of the national library of Japan. Japanese books are cataloged there and coded into MARC format. The resulting MARC records are used by libraries the world over who want to have Japanese vernacular records for the Japanese books in their collections. As the Internet has raised the bar with sophisticated natural language searching and metadata tagging common to today's powerful search engines, a heated debate within the library field has been whether MARC is still viable. As a response to this concern and to the changing standards for accessing information, by 2006 LC developed a framework for working with MARC data in an Extensible Markup Language (XML) environment called the MARC21 XML Schema. Today, LC is spearheading the preparation for gradually phasing out the MARC record and replacing it with a new standard for bibliographic description called BIBFRAME. Transition to BIBFRAME will provide the library community a foundation for the future with linked bibliographic description, Web functionality, and a broader linked data environment. BIBFRAME will also dovetail with Resource Description and Access (RDA), the new descriptive cataloging standard intended to replace the long-standing Anglo-American Cataloguing Rules (AACR2) for formulating bibliographic data. Designed for the digital era, RDA focuses on metadata for all types of content and media to enhance resource discovery and data sharing across the Web. RDA has undergone several years of testing by LC and other large libraries before implementation. Leading the way with the rollout are LC, the British Library, National Library of Australia, University of Chicago, and other major research facilities.

Together, BIBFRAME and RDA will position library cataloging standards for the semantic web. As with all conversions from existing standards to newly developed ones, costs, training, and time are key issues for full implementation.

Current focus in RDA implementation for the average library is to train staff and to draft new policies as to what blend of AACR2 and RDA will be used during this time of transition. Larger libraries with more in-house cataloging librarians are sharing training documentation and policies that they create. Batch record changes are happening on the consortium level for resource-sharing library systems. For smaller or independent library players, access to shared cataloging is cost effective and helps to facilitate change in a positive way. For all sizes and types of libraries, making sure the new records display in ways that are useful for patrons is a key focus.[4]

As major vendors such as Online Computer Library Center (OCLC) are creating RDA records for all new materials, the majority of library systems are then receiving those records and accepting them, so this use of sharing cataloging data facilitates RDA implementation. Meanwhile, producers of databases and other discovery systems are eagerly implementing RDA standards, so that search fields are more intuitive for users. See the *RDA Toolkit* site listed at the end of this chapter for a variety of tutorial methods, updating videos,

and blogs. Instructional materials have also been translated into other languages, so it is hoped that RDA can be more easily applied internationally by
libraries, archives, museums, and other cultural institutions.

Descriptive Versus Subject Cataloging

Two types of cataloging take place for each item in a collection, descriptive cataloging and subject cataloging. *Descriptive cataloging* delineates the
physical characteristics of a book, film, data file, e-book, or other material.
Depending on the format, this may include data such as size and physical
dimensions, number of pages, length of running time, accompanying leaflets
or CDs, URL for access, and so forth. *Subject cataloging* focuses on content
by identifying the primary subject or subjects of an item and then assigning
the best subject headings and classification number to reflect this. The goal is
to allow researchers to search an OPAC by keyword, author, title, subject, or
other access point to discover and locate an item of potential interest based on
the carefully assigned headings and call numbers.

At one time, most cataloging was done on a one-by-one basis, with each individual item scrutinized and cataloged from scratch. This was a labor-intensive
activity and resulted in massive duplication of effort. With the invention of
many timesaving solutions, such as the catalog card distribution program at
LC, the ability to purchase digital cataloging data from jobbers, and today's
cooperative catalogs and worldwide bibliographic utilities, there has been a
sizeable reduction in the amount of original cataloging required by library staff.
Instead, copy cataloging has become commonplace for a large majority of items.

By searching a large, reliable database of completed bibliographic records,
such as those on OCLC, a library cataloging technician can locate the data
for a specific item, then download or copy that information to use in local
records. The customary placement of Cataloging-in-Publication (CIP) data in
new releases, a joint effort since 1971 by LC and publishers to standardize
cataloging data, is another helpful tool to expedite cataloging. Check the verso
page (i.e., the reverse side of the title page, which will be a left-hand page) to
find CIP data in many books.

Cooperative databases, such as the substantial OCLC holdings referred to
previously, are built from records submitted by LC and supplemented by member libraries, museums, and other research agencies. According to its website
(http://www.oclc.org) as of 2015, OCLC's WorldCat record count exceeded
2 billion, and that database grows by nearly one new record every 10 seconds.[5]
E-book, video, DVD, and nonprint titles are increasingly represented on this
database. Thus, the need for labor-intensive, original cataloging still exists,
but on a decreasing basis.

A significant amount of original cataloging does take place in larger academic and research libraries with collections that include government documents, first editions, manuscript and archival materials, foreign language
titles, scholarly serials, and scientific proceedings. In these facilities, there are
often multiple language specialists among the technical services staff whose
responsibility is to catalog all items in their area (e.g., Romance languages,
Arabic languages, Slavic languages, Asian languages).

Along with the decrease in the need for original cataloging, the automation of most libraries' card files has also meant the elimination of many of the tedious, repetitive tasks of old such as updating and filing of cards in the physical catalog drawers and in the accompanying shelf list. And the catalog bureaus themselves have a new life and purpose: A search of eBay or other stores selling vintage furniture will find lots of discarded library catalog models for sale, coveted both by interior and home decorators for quality woodwork and for their nostalgic appeal.

Cataloging operations have changed dramatically over the last 45 years (and are continuing to evolve in exciting new directions). The authors have observed that most libraries now provide original cataloging for less than 10 percent of their acquisitions, and many smaller libraries can find acceptable cataloging copy for all but 1 or 2 percent of new materials. These exceptions in need of original cataloging might include items such as local government documents, local history items, self-published titles, and the occasional output from a small publisher. Rather than reinventing the wheel at each library around the world, the cataloging process has become much more streamlined

FIGURE 5.1 Jewel Mazique checks the correct filing of catalog cards at the Library of Congress, 1942. Courtesy Library of Congress, Prints and Photographs Division, LC-DIG-fsa-8d02860.

that has also impacted the need for employees whose jobs are solely devoted to cataloging tasks. Instead, technical services staff may now be found dividing their time between cataloging responsibilities and duties such as the upgrading and maintenance of OPACs, coordination of electronic resources accounts, and digitalization projects.

Processing

The last step in the chain of events before stocking the shelves for customer use is to physically process each item. Although many aspects of technical services are highly automated, the processing that must take place before a tangible item is shelf-ready remains a low-tech operation. Stamping materials with library ownership stamps, adhering call number labels and label protectors, installing magnetic security tapes, applying protective book jacket covers, and other tasks are necessary to protect materials from theft and to make them accessible on the shelves.

Larger libraries have separate acquisitions and cataloging divisions within the *technical services department*, where head librarians oversee each operation and the library technicians, clerks, student assistants, and volunteers. Many library employees who have a preference for limited public contact find their niche in the predictable workflow of acquisitions and cataloging. They also take much satisfaction in the ongoing stocking of the library, previewing new materials, and knowing that they are providing patrons with a steady incoming flow of the resources they need.

Physical processing requires an exacting attention to detail and an ability to follow through on lengthy, complex tasks where accuracy is critical. In larger research libraries, knowledge of a foreign language is often required, as is an understanding of the subdivisions of fields of knowledge. In these facilities, the processing of monographs may be an entirely separate operation from the processing of serials and periodicals, with different departments maintained to acquire, catalog, and physically prepare each category for researchers' use. In the largest *technical services departments*, workflow may be assigned based on the language or subject of the material being processed. In contrast, one person does it all in the smallest of branch libraries or information centers from routine tasks to the more intellectually challenging projects.

SPECIAL MATERIALS

Certain types of information formats that libraries collect don't conform to the standard acquisitions, cataloging, and processing model described previously. In fact, within research, university, and larger public libraries, it is typical to find separate departments organized around formats such as periodicals, manuscripts, rare books, institutional archives, local history, microforms, and government documents. Each of these materials has unique housing, display, and access needs that may warrant the organization of its own discrete department.

Periodical Collections

Any discussion of *periodical collections* must take into account the definitions of the terms *periodical* and *serial*. Based on the authors' experiences and conversations with colleagues, there is considerable ambiguity as to the precise meanings of the terms. Added to that, there are many localized variations of use in the workplace that are often dependent on the size of the library's collection.

Arlene Taylor uses the following definitions in her classic textbook *Introduction to Cataloging and Classification*:[6]

Serial: A publication issued in successive parts at regular or irregular intervals and intended to continue indefinitely. Included are periodicals, newspapers, proceedings, reports, memoirs, annuals, and numbered monographic series.

Periodical: A publication with a distinctive title, which appears in successive numbers or parts at stated or regular intervals and which is intended to continue indefinitely. Usually each issue contains articles by several contributors. Newspapers and memoirs, proceedings, journals, etc., of corporate bodies primarily related to their internal affairs are not included in this definition.

As is apparent from the definitions, *serial* is a much broader term than *periodical,* and in very large research and academic libraries with sizeable holdings of scientific proceedings, annuals, and so on, the distinction will have significance. For purposes of general discussion, this book will use the more common term *periodical.*

Periodicals account for a critical part of any library, media, or information center's research collection. In many disciplines, particularly scientific and technical, periodicals form the primary and almost exclusive means of communicating new knowledge. Published with predictable frequency, which may be weekly, monthly, quarterly, or at other intervals, periodicals provide a continual flow of fresh information into the library collection.

Periodical publications differ in concept and coverage from books. Also known as monographs, books are single works, although they may come out in multiple parts or volumes, are not intended to continue indefinitely, and tend to treat a topic in more depth than a periodical article. The term *monograph* also has a narrower, technical meaning, but in this work the term will be used in its generic sense. Periodical issues are numbered consecutively with sequential volume and issue numbers to differentiate between each unique part and to reflect their publishing order. Frequent fluctuations in the publishing of periodicals, such as title changes, title splits, mergers, acquisitions, cessations, and other events, require special cataloging expertise to properly compile and revise holdings records for them.

In addition, most periodicals now maintain companion websites that differ in many ways from their corresponding hard copy formats. Access to both current and retrospective content on these companion websites varies greatly. Access to the full contents of the current issue may be free to all, while only paid subscribers can read previous or archival issues. Other periodical sites offer all readers free, unrestricted access to current and back issues. Yet others make available the immediate purchase of downloads of a single issue or single article for non-subscribers, while allowing subscribers access with a login. Most periodical companion websites share a common trait in that they are updated much more frequently than their print versions and may display unique or additional content not found in the printed issue.

Categories of Periodicals

Periodicals are typically divided into several categories based on their targeted audience and technical level. *Magazines* tend to be written for the layperson, use vocabulary easily understood by the average reader, and are glossy, full-color publications replete with advertisements and photographs. Think of the familiar publications found in supermarket newsstands and in doctors' waiting rooms—those are magazines.

In contrast, *journals* are written for a particular academic or professional audience. Scholars and professors in the field are the major contributors. Articles and studies may be reviewed or juried by an editorial board of highly respected peers before being accepted for publication in a particular journal. Journals assume that their readers have specialized vocabulary and knowledge, often at a highly technical level. Expect journal articles to be signed—that is, the author or authors are given an obvious byline with their professional credentials noted. At the end of the journal article, there is usually an extensive bibliography, list of works cited, or other documentation for further reference.

In terms of physical appearance, journals are not as eye-catching as magazines because they do not try to appeal to the general public. Often, they have few ads and few illustrations. Graphs or charts that are included often require some technical knowledge on the part of the reader.

Trade periodicals fall in between the two previous categories. These tend to be written for a specific professional or industry group, such as nurses, librarians, electricians, network managers, and so forth. Their content is narrowly focused on the given field, but the reading and vocabulary level is usually discernible to the layperson.

Then there is the *newspaper*—perhaps the publication most familiar to the reading public. Newspapers range from prestigious national dailies to weekly rural papers. Their content focuses on breaking news, current events, weather, and sports, among other topics. Note that according to the definitions cited above, a newspaper is technically a serial rather than a periodical. In practical usage in the workplace, newspapers are treated, processed, and housed much like the periodicals described previously.

It is important to note that with the continued rapid growth of periodical publishing on the Internet, the distinctions between categories so obvious in the hard copy counterparts are becoming blurred. And for many of today's students for whom online sources are their point of reference, asking them to evaluate the differences between periodical types can be a challenging task.

Hard Copy Needs

Because of their ongoing publication, relatively small size, and often time-sensitive value, hard copy periodicals require much labor-intensive handling before they make it onto the library's shelves for patron access. In large library facilities, tracking the receipt of each issue, individual labeling, security tattle-taping, shelving, and eventual binding can employ many library technicians and student assistants.

Some of the processing needs that often require a separate periodicals department include the following:

- The currency of contents requires a very short turnaround time in making the periodicals available to customers.
- The slim size makes periodicals vulnerable to theft, so care must be taken in attaching security targets (tattletapes) to each issue.
- The high use, vulnerability to vandalism or theft may require a closed stack or reserve collection, which increase both space and staffing needs.
- The ongoing publication requires the claiming of lost or missing replacement issues to maintain a complete title run.
- The wear and tear on the paper copies may necessitate binding into annual volumes for durability and long-term or archival retention.
- The temporary housing of current, high-interest issues in display shelving, rather than stacks, for customer convenience and browsing increases overall handling requirements.

In summary, periodicals add a vital element of timely material covering an incredible diversity of subject areas to any library collection. In hard copy, they require labor-intensive processing and a high level of maintenance to ensure access and complete back files.

Even though today's libraries rely increasingly on electronic access to periodical indexes and full-text article databases for their current subscriptions, the majority maintains a mix of paper copies and electronic versions. In some cases, this translates into purchasing simultaneous subscriptions to the same title to ensure access to periodical archives or back runs. In other cases, publishers require a paper subscription before they will grant access to an e-subscription. The model varies, but hard copy periodicals are still a key component of library collections.

New Models for Periodical Search and Access

In recent years, the movement known as Open Access (OA) has flourished in opposition to the traditional print publishing business of scholarly journals, especially the academic, peer-reviewed ones. OA advocates for unrestricted Web access to these scientific journals as well as unrestricted reuse (so, instead of copyright restrictions on reusing, use relies on the terms outlined by the Creative Commons Attribution-Only license [CC-BY]).[7]

Oftentimes resource access is free to all users via a Web publisher adhering to the OA concept. Robust examples of the OA publication model include the oft-cited and respected *Public Library of Science (PLOS)* family of journals and blogs (http://www.plos.org/) and *BioMed Central* (http://www.biomedcentral .com), both focusing on the biomedical science disciplines. Another aspect of the OA model is very speedy delivery of scholarly research via the Web, as opposed to the typically slower commercial publication schedules and embargoes of the subscription-only print or proprietary database models.

An ongoing debate ensues between traditional publishers and the newer open access movement as to the viability, economics, and philosophy of both means of scholarly research dissemination. And this vibrant exchange is not limited to just commercial publishers and academic writers; librarians, educational administrators, government officials, funding agencies, journal editorial staff and research society publishers, in addition to general users/readers, all have a stake in the discussion. According to an oft-cited study conducted on the access to scholarly articles published during 2008, about 20 percent were found to be freely available for that year.[8] And even the OA leader *PLOS* remarks on its website that "even today, only a small percentage of the scientific, technical, and medical (STM) literature is available via OA."[9]

Another popular and heavily used access point for periodical literature, both peer-reviewed journals as well as magazines, is Google Scholar. This freely accessible Web search engine returns a variety of results, across all disciplines, including both free articles and those requiring payment to download or a paid subscription password to view. Additionally, Google Scholar indexes books, abstracts and other resources, some of which are free to access, while others offer various options for purchasing access.

Yet another resource, which offers access to an ever-growing database of periodical titles, is JSTOR, which began in 1995. While most access is via a subscription account purchased by an academic library for use by students and faculty, JSTOR does offer some earlier journal content available for free to anyone. Presently, the database's content focuses on the arts, humanities, and sciences with a mix of current scholarly journals, historical journal titles, and some books. Many different bundling options are available for purchase.

Staffing

Larger libraries of all types may employ professionals whose primary responsibility is overseeing the periodicals collection. A periodicals, or serials, librarian typically coordinates the selection, acquisition, processing, organization, and management of the library's periodicals collection. In large research libraries, which receive many print subscriptions, several serials assistants are employed in the check in, claiming, and cataloging of periodicals to get them to the public as near to the time of arrival as possible. Increasingly, periodicals librarians and their staff devote less of their time to the handling of individual physical titles as the emphasis of their work shifts to the negotiating and tracking of licensing agreements for electronic periodical sources such as the JSTOR digital archives, and ever-growing databases such as Proquest, EBSCOhost, Lexis-Nexis, and other large commercial services.

New products, publishing trends, title changes, and emerging patron preferences in this rapidly changing area make such a job more dynamic and challenging than it was in the past, when emphasis was often centered on balancing tight budgets with collection needs as subscription prices spiraled upward. That fiscal challenge has not disappeared. Rather, it has morphed into the question of how to maintain existing collections with budget dollars split between hard copy titles and electronic subscriptions, and then, in addition, possibly adding new subscriptions to electronic periodical resources—all set against the backdrop of static funding levels.

Special Collections

Collections of original manuscripts, photographs, architectural drawings, diaries, first editions, realia, institutional archives, and other unique materials usually with an historical focus are often centered in a section of the library known as the *special collections department.* Such a department focuses on the acquisition, management, storage, preservation, and user access of these special holdings, just as a general library unit operates its general book and multimedia collection. In the very biggest of libraries there may be multiple special collections departments (e.g., archives, manuscripts, rare books, fine press, and local history). How these collections are differentiated depends on local needs. Typically, *archives* refer to documents generated by the organization itself in the daily course of doing business (e.g., by the college or municipality or corporation of which the library is a subordinate unit). Similar documents originating from outside the organization might be housed in an entirely separate unit called *manuscripts.* Care and organization of these materials are very similar. Rare books and local history departments are less distinct divisions and tend to blend many of the characteristics from general collections with those of special collections.

Even the largest of libraries severely limit the scope of the manuscripts they collect. For example, the library at the University of Illinois–Urbana is the third largest university research library in the United States; its Rare Book & Manuscript Library has nearly 500,000 books and more than 9,000 linear feet of manuscript materials; however, there are only a handful of topics for which it attempts to collect any scrap of information, regardless of the format. Among those topics earmarked for comprehensive collecting are materials by and about President Abraham Lincoln and Pulitzer winning author/poet Carl Sandburg, both famous residents of the state. This is an example of the general practice of collecting policy being determined by the curriculum or research focus of the parent institution.

Sources for Acquiring Materials

Because of the unusual nature of the materials in special collections, the acquisition, processing, and cataloging aspects of these items are handled very differently from more traditional library materials. In terms of acquisitions, an institutional archive will receive selected noncurrent records from other departments within its agency. For example, older publications, photographs, architectural plans, and transcripts of presidential speeches (for a college or corporation), or mayoral speeches (for a municipality) will be transferred to the institution's archival repository. In addition, retired faculty or staff often make donations of materials after leaving their positions with the agency.

The institutions that have substantial acquisitions budgets for manuscripts are usually limited to large, scholarly research and academic libraries. Materials may be purchased from manuscript vendors who work in the subject areas in which the department collects (e.g., Californiana, New Jerseyana, Civil War, John Steinbeck, women authors, American children's literature). Often, dealers very familiar with a collection's focus suggest relevant items of interest from their inventory to special collections staff for possible purchase.

Materials also frequently come from private sources, often as donations. As a result, the cultivation of potential donors plays an important role in the ongoing collection development efforts of a special collections department. Careful record keeping in the form of deeds of gift, appraisals, and correspondence follows each donation of materials. A deed of gift documents the legal transfer of ownership, specifies any restrictions on use or reproduction, conveys literary and other rights, and verifies the provenance or origin of a collection.

Materials may be acquired as large collections, in small lots, or singly. The special collections department at Cal Poly University, San Luis Obispo, recently received the personal and business papers of a locally prominent, pioneering mercantile family. Before processing, the donation comprised some 100 cartons along with hundreds of loose ledgers, maps, drawings, and other oversized items. In contrast, the same department just purchased a slim, handwritten 1849 Gold Rush-era diary from a rare book and manuscript dealer.

MARC Format, Encoded Archival Description, and Finding Aids

Another distinction of special collections is found in the accessing and cataloging of materials. Unlike book materials, each item is not individually indexed in an OPAC. For example, a manuscript or archival collection consisting of correspondence, historical photographs, and ephemera might contain 5,000 individual pieces; rather than devising a cataloging record for each scrap of paper or image, the bibliographic record describes the collection as a unit. A distinct MARC record protocol for Archival and Manuscript Control (MARC-AMC) was devised for cataloging archives and manuscripts, but it has since been superseded by MARC 21. All prior separate formats, such as the AMC bibliographic format, have been fully integrated into MARC 21. The ability of MARC format to handle archival and manuscript materials has meant that collection-level bibliographic records for these collections can be added to a library's OPAC. Compiling such a record may be a joint effort between special collections personnel and cataloging staff. In the largest libraries, there may be staff whose sole job is to catalog rare books or manuscript materials. As mentioned earlier, BIBFRAME is currently being developed as a successor to MARC, so watch for future changes.

In addition to the MARC record, special collections are accessed in much more detail through an archival tool known as a *finding aid* or *descriptive guide.* A finding aid or guide describes and provides an inventory of materials (manuscripts, papers, photographs, multimedia, etc.) within a collection.

Typically, this includes some narrative material describing the history and significance of the collection and its creator(s), biographical notes on the creator(s), and the physical arrangement, size, and formats of materials. A brief inventory or container list of the holdings follows. In terms of physical and intellectual organization, each collection is broken down hierarchically into series, subseries, boxes, and folders. The organizational framework for each individual collection within the department reflects the unique contents of that collection, and, wherever possible, is based on the provenance or origin of the materials. Today, many libraries routinely publish their finding aids online to assist researchers in preparing for an on-site visit to their special collections. This may take the form of html Web pages or PDF files on a library's website, or as an XML encoded finding aid hosted by a regional archival cooperative, such as the OAC, Online Archive of California (http://www.oac.cdlib.org/).

Encoded Archival Description (EAD) using *Extensible Markup Language (XML)* is the current standard for use with archival finding aids. Like other markup languages, XML prepares documents for publishing on the Web, with varied display and search options. Preparation of an online finding aid can be completed in-house with the help of an authoring program or by contracting with a mark-up vendor.

Traditional book classification systems, such as LC or Dewey are not generally applied to special collections materials. Because of their varying shapes, sizes, and often fragile condition, materials found in special collections are also housed differently than books, CDs, DVDs, or other physical packages of information that can literally stand on their own. Manuscripts, photographs, and the like are placed inside special acid-free storage boxes, folders, and sleeves of varying sizes, which house them and also contribute to their preservation and stabilization. The original condition of each historical item is closely guarded; no library ownership stamps, sticky call labels, Post-it® notes, or colored dots are allowed on the materials. It is likely that the staff of the special collections department handle all processing for these materials.

Emphasis on Preservation

Special collections departments take seriously their preservation mission. Controlling the environment within the department, much like a museum does, is an important element of ensuring long-term access to unique, historical materials. Temperature and humidity extremes are to be avoided because they can advance decay or deterioration of materials. Sophisticated air control systems or heating ventilation and air-conditioning (HVAC), treated windowpanes, dehumidifiers, humidifiers, and meters that measure temperature and humidity, called *thermohygrometers,* are all used to monitor the environment. The use of acid-free storage containers and file folders, Mylar® sleeves, and other stable protective housing is standard procedure.

Research etiquette also emphasizes preservation. Special collections departments are closed stack areas where materials are paged or retrieved by staff for on-site review and study by researchers, one box or folder at a time. Patrons are often required to wear white, cotton gloves when handling original items. This prevents the transfer of oil from the hands to the historical materials. Writing implements are restricted to pencils only, again to protect the special materials from any permanent damage or defacing. Materials are noncirculating, and there may be photocopying or photography limitations to minimize handling of fragile, original items or because of deed restrictions.

Because of the unique nature of the materials and their potential value on the retail market, special collections items are especially vulnerable to theft, so greater security precautions and restricted user access are the norm. Photo identification, research credentials, or other documentation may be required of patrons prior to accessing materials. For some large, scholarly, independent institutions such as California's Huntington Library or the Folger Shakespeare Library in Washington, DC, letters of recommendation and an application may be required of potential researchers before access privileges are granted. Building or reading rooms are equipped with security systems to control and monitor access.

FIGURE 5.2 Researchers in special collections or archives departments may be required to wear cotton gloves when viewing manuscripts or other fragile materials. Reprinted by permission of Special Collections and Archives, California Polytechnic State University.

Conservation Efforts

At times, conservation techniques must also be applied in an attempt to reverse water or smoke damage, to stabilize deterioration as with high-acid content in paper, or to mitigate other problems with documents. Some very large research and university libraries have their own conservation labs on-site such as LC, Los Angeles's Getty Museum, and Yale University. The majority of libraries send their conservation work to outside specialists because of the highly skilled and labor-intensive nature of such work.

It is tempting to think that the expensive and time-consuming effort of preserving original documents can be abandoned now that information can be digitized so easily. However, every storage medium has a different shelf life, and, in many cases, these are not known until some time has passed. Although today we herald the wonders of computers, it remains to be seen what the life span of digital storage will be. On the other hand, high-quality "permanent paper" buffered and with low-acid content still remains the most durable and reliable medium, with a life span of approximately 500 years.

In addition to the breakdown of the storage medium itself, the obsolescence of the playback equipment (e.g., microfilm reader, computer programs, discs, and drives) can also prevent access to information and necessitate its transfer from one medium to another. After all, how many libraries still have film loop readers? As storage technology changes, so does the playback hardware. Equipment for reading data stored on the early 8" and 5-1/4" floppy disks is difficult to find, and accessing 3-1/2" diskette and zip disks presumes library ownership of operational older model computers. When considering the transfer of information from its original format (e.g., paper, photograph, 16mm film, floppy disk, zip drive) to a newer medium, archivists are also aware that, for some scholars, the container is as much a focus for research as is the information within.

Institutional Repositories

As the Web continues to mature, an application that is growing in widespread acceptance and popularity is that of the *institutional repository.* Often this type of effort originates in the library of an institution, or it might also be a project assigned to a library department such as a special collections unit. What is an institutional repository? The earliest applications were in large universities where they aspired to capture and make available the scholarly publishing (lectures, periodical articles, conference papers, theses, dissertations, data sets, etc.) of their faculties via the Web. Model programs include the University of California's California Digital Library (http://www.cdlib.org/), University of Rochester's UR Research (https://urresearch.rochester.edu/), and Purdue University Libraries' E-Scholar (http://e-scholar.lib.purdue.edu/).

In addition to publicizing and making scholarship electronically accessible, such repositories, also called digital repositories, serve a valuable role by promoting the institution as a whole, as they provide free, publicly available information to the public at large, to students, to staff and faculty, and to alumni and potential donors. Preservation of material is another major motivation behind most institutional repositories, as library managers look to this as a method for preserving and enhancing access to local history materials, photographic and other visual media, manuscript and archival collections.

Some of the key issues involved in the start-up and maintenance of institutional repositories are winning "buy-in" to the project from faculty and other potential contributors, setting policy standards for content submission, dealing with copyright and licensing issues, finding appropriate software to manage such collections (e.g., CONTENTdm, DSpace, Fedora, Embark, and others), and, of course, securing overall funding and ongoing support.

Staffing

Staff who work in special collections may be called librarians and library technicians; digital archivists and digital technicians; archivists and archival technicians as well as other varying job titles. Thus, professional training requirements vary accordingly. It is fair to say that a degree in history, or at least an affinity for history, is an important requirement for those considering a career in this area. A national certification program for archivists was implemented in 1989. The independent, not-for-profit Academy of Certified Archivists provides standardized certification through an examination or petition process. For those interested in further exploring these specialties, the Society of American Archivists' website is listed in the Resources section at the end of this chapter.

Although some would argue that librarians and archivists are entirely different breeds, the authors (both of whom have worked in special collections settings) choose to differ with that point of view. The careful selection of materials according to a plan, preparation of items for researchers' use, and access and reference services are all required in both arenas. Emphasis on electronic access to information, especially digital imaging and institutional repositories, is very timely and is greatly transforming special collections, just as it is impacting other areas of library services.

Microforms

Microforms have come in many different sizes and variations since their initial use in libraries during the 1930s. Microfilm and microfiche remain the two types most commonly found in libraries, archives, and research centers today. Microfilm editions are photographs of each page of an original periodical, newspaper, thesis, or other document. The images are produced on rolls of film, typically 35 millimeters in size. To read the miniaturized document, which is not legible to the naked eye, the film reel must be loaded into a microfilm reader, which enlarges the tiny, reduced-size print to legible size. Microfiche editions are cards of 16-millimeter film. Common sizes include 3 inch by 5 inch, 4 inch by 6 inch, and 3 inch by 7 inch. These are all significantly reduced and must be placed in a microfiche reader machine to magnify the text. Most modern readers also produce photocopies of the document page. Other types of microforms in use over the years have included aperture cards, microcards, ultrafiche, and other variations of microphotography.

For more than half of the 20th century, microforms were a major storage medium in libraries and information centers of all sizes.[10] Advantages to this miniaturized format included the preservation of hard copy data, reduction in shelving and space needs, and, in its high-quality form, stability and a long life span as a reliable storage medium. Archival quality microfilm (also called silver halide microfilm) will last for approximately 200 years.[11] Microfilm has been particularly well suited to interlibrary loan because its compact size makes it easy to ship, and playback machines have been standard worldwide, thus eliminating concerns about incompatibility between libraries.

Making Microforms Accessible

For approximately 50 years, libraries building retrospective collections purchased mainstream periodical and newspaper titles in microfilm from special microform vendors who worked exclusively with that medium. For in-house or smaller local publications, libraries have contracted with other companies to produce microfilm records of these unique titles.

Once received by the library, the film requires special, labor-intensive processing before it is shelf-ready. This includes inserting stoppers at the end of each reel and labeling the film leaders and storage boxes. Special storage cabinets are used for both microfilm and fiche; they are rarely shelved on regular-sized book stacks.

As for user access, the library must provide patrons with readers or printers and keep them in good working order. Staff assistance in the use of the machines is also required. In large microfilm reading rooms, such as those found in the National Archives' regional branches, trained volunteers are available to help with equipment use and problems. And, of course, all of this requires dedicated library floor space.

National cataloging standards call for separate cataloging records to be made for different formats of a title. So, in theory, where microform holdings form archives or backups of hard copy titles, they require additional work from a cataloging perspective. (In practice, many libraries cut corners on this standard by adding holdings data in different formats to the main bibliographic record.)

Patron Resistance

Although accepted among seasoned staff, microforms have never been a favorite among patrons. For researchers, eyestrain and repetitive use syndrome are physical discomforts that result from long hours in front of a reader. Another source of frustration (to the library staff as well as to patrons) is the breakage of microform reader parts, which occurs with frequent use. Also, poor quality film can be blurry and illegible. Anyone who has done genealogical research and has accessed early 19th-century newspapers and census records on microfilm will empathize.

Most students today are totally unfamiliar with microforms, not having been exposed to the medium in junior or senior high school. If they have an occasion to refer to a microform resource, say, for historical information, it would be the equivalent experience of placing an LP on a stereo turntable.

Status of Microforms

Today, microfilm and microfiche collections of archival materials such as long runs of periodical back files, and other historical materials are still found in libraries. Prior to the advent of electronic information storage, microforms were hailed as the solution to the never-ending library-space dilemma. But the Internet has significantly impacted the previously longstanding practice of storing noncurrent periodicals and newspapers on microfilm, and, less frequently, on microfiche. As Web-based periodical archives and databases began to reach back more than a decade or two, most libraries canceled their ongoing microfilm subscriptions and began relying solely on their online holdings.

Additionally, retrospective microfilm holdings are now being completely deaccessioned and discarded in many smaller public and academic libraries—something that 15 years ago would have been seen as rash. Instead, librarians are turning to the growing availability of access to large digital back files of mainstream magazines, journals, and newspapers. One familiar example is the ProQuest Historical Newspaper product that began with full-image access to the major papers *The New York Times* and *The Los Angeles Times* dating back to the mid-1800s. ProQuest continues to offer access to other titles, including major regional U.S. and international English language newspapers. These products are purchased as annual or multi-year subscriptions by libraries.

Although perpetual access (that is, the guaranteed, continued access to retrospective holdings online) remains an unsettled issue, it is likely that microform publishing will continue to decrease significantly. It is not uncommon to see frequent posts offering discarded microform collections and readers on library listservs these days.

An exception is found with holdings such as small local or regional newspapers from the 19th and 20th centuries. These are unique historical resources of great value to that specific local community, but the research value is too limited to warrant digitization by a major vendor. Funds for retrospective digitization of large runs of microforms may be difficult to find within the budget of a single library agency. On the other hand, that type of conversion project is currently one that granting agencies such as National Endowment of the Humanities, National Historical Publications and Records Commission, or Institute of Museum and Library Services are supporting. With the continued emphasis by these lead agencies on preservation of and enhanced modern access to materials in paper or microform, seeking grant funding for a digital conversion could be just the ticket.

During its first decade or so, the distinct emphasis of the Web was the provision of current materials. But new trends are emerging with the digital conversion of some large, key microform historical collections: the National Archives and the Church of Jesus Christ of Latter-Day Saints' (Mormons) vast family history facility in Salt Lake City have both been almost exclusively microform-based collections for decades. Between the two, they house a major percentage of the world's genealogical and historical resources and are used extensively by professional and lay researchers daily.

Enhanced digital access to these popular collections is under continual development. For example, leading for-profit genealogical publisher, Ancestry.

com, has digitized the heavily used U.S. Population Censuses held by the National Archives, taking some 10 years to complete the conversion process. The huge (and amazing) searchable database is now available to paid subscribers as part of Ancestry's ever-growing digital family history collection. (The censuses on microfilm are still available for free perusal to researchers at National Archives branches.) An ongoing digitization effort by the LDS is their Family History Archive at the Harold B. Lee Library, Brigham Young University, which when completed will make available some 100,000 family histories on the library's website.

Similarly, the ProQuest publishing group has digitized over a century's worth of Sanborn Insurance Fire Maps as well as the leading U.S. national daily newspapers mentioned earlier. While the search interfaces and the display options for some of these digitized collections leaves room for improvement, they remain attractive products. These digitization efforts are all very labor intensive and require up-front capital, and the product pricing of these subscription databases reflects that start-up investment, which is most often made by private sector companies.

Although not inexpensive, another alternative for enhanced viewing of microfilmed documents exists. Special digital microfilm scanners can digitize film or fiche images for distribution over computer networks to desktop and mobile computers, allowing for electronic distribution or viewing. This conversion process combines photographic and electronic imaging technologies. Adopters of this conversion technology have been corporate libraries and their record management centers.

It remains to be seen whether the further retrospective conversion of microfilm holdings into online formats and databases will be lucrative enough for commercial publishers to pursue fully. Even if the demand is there and the numbers play out, it is likely that the oldest and most obscure titles will remain in library collections on their microfilm rolls and fiche cards. Historians, genealogists, and other researchers, as well as library staffers, will continue to encounter microfilm when accessing some retrospective titles.

Meanwhile, for family historians who are serious about genealogical and historical research, the Latter Day Saints still has an enormous microforms collection in their repository in Salt Lake City, Utah. Accessible to church members and the general public alike, this collection may be the first introduction to the use of microfilm reels and microfiche sheets for many patrons; however, the large cadre of LSD members staff each floor of the library and enthusiastically aid visitors in their use of the microfilm readers, and printers.

Government Documents

Although they represent an enormous wealth of data on almost any subject imaginable, government documents tend to be overlooked by the average researcher as sources of information. "Gov docs," as they are nicknamed by library staff, are those publications produced by or for a government agency; this includes foreign, international, federal, provincial, state, county, parish, city, or other jurisdictions. In the United States, the Government Publishing Office

(GPO) is the agency charged with producing, distributing, selling, protecting, and preserving documents for all three branches of the federal government.

As such, the GPO is one of the world's largest publishers. According to its website, it has some 380,000 government documents publically available, free of charge on the GPO site Federal Digital System ("FDsys") at http://www .fdsys.gov. In addition, its online U.S. Government Bookstore unit sells a variety of high-interest titles to both consumers and libraries. Formats for purchase include hard copy, microfiche, e-books, datafiles, magazines, and more.

Compared to commercially published books that often have attractive, attention-getting packaging and professionally designed covers and illustrations, government publications are often plain and more drab in appearance. However, the lack of frills also keeps the price down, and, as a whole, government publications are very reasonably priced; sometimes they are even free. The variety of topics covered and the diverse audiences for which these publications are written are wide ranging. A short pamphlet on good parenting skills, a checklist of resident bird species at a national park, a technical report from the Surgeon General on secondhand tobacco effects, or the multi-volume, annual *U.S. Budget* are all examples of documents produced by our national government agencies. Government publications are often key sources for detailed statistics on many aspects of life, from the population census to motor vehicle fatalities, to the number of fish netted, to precise rainfall tallies.

GPO Website

Creative and efficient dissemination of information has always been a point of pride and a mandate for the GPO. Over the years, this has meant using new technologies to package and distribute documents from federal agencies. The GPO was an early adopter of producing publications in CD-ROM format and, also, when the Web was young in 1994, was quick to launch an information-rich website for the public called GPO Access. That early Web presence focused on providing online access to federal documents that had originated in a print format. Today, the GPO (which was recently renamed from Government Printing Office to Government Publishing Office) continues to review and study its mission, and to improve and enhance information dissemination through its website including access to authenticated content from born-digital sources.[12]

The GPO Web portal provides links to many services, including its *Catalog of U.S. Government Publications (CGP)*. *CGP* is the finding tool for electronic and print publications from the legislative, executive, and judicial branches of the federal government. The database includes descriptive records (including assigned SuDocs classification numbers) for historical and current publications as well as containing direct Web links to those documents that are available online. Another feature is the askGPO virtual help desk to answer questions about its publications, products, library accounts, and to provide support for depository library staff as well. For in-depth instruction in drilling down into the Federal Digital System (FDsys) a variety of topical video tutorials and webinars are available on the site—tailored for specific research needs such as locating presidential papers, congressional bills and hearings.

The robust site also features historical information on the agency including archival photographs, narratives and videos depicting the development of the GPO since 1861. Users can follow links to social media sites that help promote and publicize recent and historically relevant GPO documents to libraries, researchers, and students.

Federal Depository Library Program

Since 1813, the federal government has designated depository libraries to ensure consumers access to many of its core publications in the effort to maintain an informed citizenry. Today, the Federal Depository Library Program (FDLP) consists of some 1,200 participating libraries throughout the nation. These libraries are officially designated at one of two levels for the regular receipt of information in print, multimedia, and electronic formats: (1) regional, and (2) selective. Materials are sent to the library at no cost. In return, the depository libraries provide organization, space, housing, and professional reference assistance, available to all citizens who want access. Although many documents and publications from these federal agencies are now readily available electronically, depository libraries continue to receive core documents in print or tangible form. The handy locator map feature on their website makes finding a depository library in a given state or region very easy. Larger depository facilities and other major research and academic libraries may also maintain historical collections of government documents

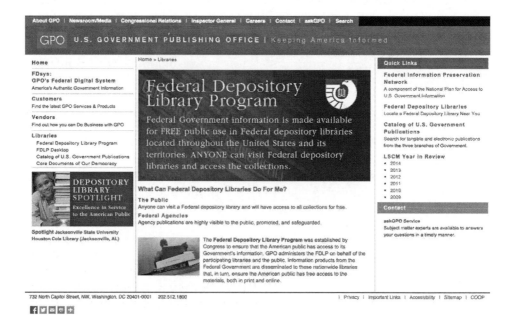

FIGURE 5.3 The U.S. Government Publishing Office (GPO) website provides access to the agency's many services of interest to libraries, information centers, and researchers. Courtesy U.S. Government Publishing Office.

in print, microforms, or other formats for those researchers needing to study pre-Internet era materials.

Tangible publications received as part of the official federal depository arrangement may have mandatory retention schedules, and they cannot be weeded in the usual fashion. Instead, they must be discarded according to the program's designated withdrawal policies. This may prove challenging for participating libraries today as they actively emphasize "increasing access to electronic collections and reducing the size of the print footprint."[13] Through the depository libraries, the federal government disseminates key information to the public at large. Many state governments also have depository arrangements with libraries to provide convenient access to their documents for citizens.

A separate website for ordering free and very inexpensive federal government books, pamphlets, and other resources can be found at Publications. USA.gov. Operated by the Federal Citizen Information Center (FCIC), its focus is on providing access, either print or digital downloads, to federal government publications of interest to consumers and citizens.

Diversity of Formats to Process

A hallmark of government documents (especially those from the federal government) has been the diverse formats in which they are produced. Printed materials include monographs, technical reports, periodicals, booklets, pamphlets, brochures, maps, microforms; multimedia ranges from e-books to CD-ROMs to DVDs. The online publishing of government information dramatically increased in the 1990s with the growth of the Web and today electronic distribution is the primary dissemination channel for much of the government data in the United States, at national, state, and local levels.

For the FDLP members or other libraries who choose to maintain print or hard copy collections of government documents, from a processing point of view, the diversity of formats of these materials can be a bit problematic. Irregular sizes, spiral bindings without spines for labeling, and the constantly changing formats for a single title require additional staff time and special handling before they are shelf-ready. In addition, there are depository status labeling requirements and retention mandates to which depository libraries must adhere.

The steady flow of depository products can mean a serious space commitment for the library, and the diverse formats need various styles and sizes of shelving to accommodate them all. Many government publications are new editions of standard titles that replace older versions, and, thus, constant weeding of superseded items is required.

Although publishing of the bulk of government documents on the Web is a major convenience in access, distribution, and space-savings, it presents a new question in terms of long-term, archival access. Currently, policy planning for preserving or capturing digital documents—which can be very ephemeral in nature—is underway. The goal of the agency is to progress from merely Web dissemination of documents to becoming a trusted digital repository and leader in the preservation of federal electronic content.[14] Just as the federal depository library system has provided a system for preserving public access to publications in print, microfilm, and other formats, a policy needs to be implemented to ensure permanent access for digital documents.[15]

Housing Government Documents: To Separate or Integrate?

Where physical collections of government documents exist, circulation policies are established by each library itself. Librarians also may decide how best to house the materials—for example, they may separate the government documents from the rest of their collection or they may integrate them into their main stacks.

In many larger library or research facilities, government documents may be housed separately from the main collection. There are a variety of issues that play into this decision. A significant one is that federal documents have their own distinct classification system called SuDocs, which is often used in place of the more common Dewey Decimal or LC codes. When the SuDocs classification is applied, a separate shelving sequence is required. If the collection of documents is large, then this requires a sizeable commitment of floor space and shelving, both commodities much in demand for other library uses.

Large university libraries like UC Berkeley or Yale that own extensive historical collections of federal, state, and even colonial government documents often utilize closed stacks areas or off-site remote storage facilities to house older, low-use items, especially those in microform. Thus, researchers desiring access to more vintage holdings may need to place a request in advance for retrieval of historical documents. For the library staff, remote storage of government documents means the need to maintain an accurate inventory of these holdings, as well as additional staff (often student assistants or interns) for the physical retrieval of requested items. Additionally, conditions of off-site facilities need to be safe and secure for those staff assigned to page the materials and to implement any housekeeping or weeding chores there. Access to older government documents may depend on special indexes produced commercially, by the government or by the library itself; this contrasts with the relative ease of online access to more contemporary publications.

Cataloging issues also often argue for providing a separate reading room or department for government publications. Because they originate from hundreds of different agencies, there is no standardized format for producing government documents. And with each new presidential administration, there is often reorganization or renaming of federal agencies, which further confuses the collection of publications. As a result, government documents are notorious for their lack of basic bibliographic data so critical for compiling library cataloging records; often, no author is cited, there may be several variant titles on the work, a publication date may be lacking, and so forth.

Federal documents are in the public domain; thus, no dated copyright statement is required on the work. (Copyrighting of state-produced materials varies for each state.) Hence, performing full MARC cataloging and adding each record to the library's OPAC is an expensive and labor-intensive task. In fact, government documents are often relegated to the last priority by the cataloging staff because of this. It is not unusual to have government publications in a sort of cataloging limbo, where they are put out on the shelves for public access and use but are not included in the OPAC. Although government publications may be inventoried in a departmental index, this practice obviously limits full access for researchers who believe that the library catalog is comprehensive.

Commercial cataloging vendors specific to government publications have developed to assist libraries and agencies with various cataloging, processing, and conversion tasks. One such firm is Marcive. Drawing from a library's designated profile of government documents received, the company supplies the cataloging record and accompanying labels and processing data. The ability to rely more on this type of outsourcing service could make a great difference in reducing the traditional cataloging backlog of government document departments.

Another reason for maintaining a separate room for government documents is that it allows for specialization among staff. By focusing primarily on the complexities of the documents collection, professional and support staff are able to hone their expertise and provide high-quality service to customers using these specialized materials.

Proponents for integrating government documents into the main library collection argue that keeping them separate only contributes to their being overlooked. And the use of yet another mysterious classification system only further intimidates and confuses researchers, presenting one more obstacle to overall access. There is no argument that maintaining a separate department and another service desk is an added expense in the library's budget. Except in the cases of very large and retrospective documents collections and those FDLS members, for most libraries today relying on electronic access to current government documents is the much-preferred approach. The commitment to provide access to governmental resources for an informed citizenry must be balanced with the need to utilize limited library resources (such as personnel, shelving, and library floor space) to meet a broad range of priorities.

Acquisition Choices

Collections librarians have several approaches to obtaining federal documents. As with books and other more familiar library materials, there are jobbers who specialize in providing government publications, such as the long-time documents wholesaler Bernan. Participation in the federal depository library program, as previously described, is another option.

In recent years, the GPO has phased out its network of 20 retail bookstores in major cities that used to sell popular hard copy titles and has replaced them with the all-online U.S. Government Bookstore site as mentioned earlier. The Bookstore also offers standing order arrangements for purchase and shipment of key reoccurring titles and series.

Another acquisitions approach is to use the *CGP*, the finding tool for federal publications. It includes descriptive records for historical and current publications as well as direct links to those that are available online or held by a designated depository library. This replaces the old standby *Monthly Catalog of U.S. Government Publications*, which over the years had morphed from unwieldy print and microform versions to online ordering. SuDocs classification numbers are also provided for each title in the *CGP*.

At the regional and local government levels, library staff often acquire materials directly from the issuing agencies by being placed on a mailing list or by direct query. Although this approach may be necessary for local publications, any library with a significant collection of government documents will try to maximize the use of jobbers for acquisitions because it would be prohibitively labor-intensive to contact all levels of government agencies in this manner.

With any of these methods for gaining awareness of and eventually ordering government publications, there is very little reliance on reviewing media. Only a few periodicals cover the release and review of government documents and government websites for librarians. A current cross-disciplinary title is the *Government Information Quarterly,* a periodical published by Elsevier Inc. to which major academic libraries with large document collections subscribe.

For an historical perspective on the sweeping changes brought to the world of government documents by the evolution of the Web, the terrorist attacks of 9/11, and the USA PATRIOT Act, see the *Changing Face of Government Information: Providing Access,* edited by Suhasini L. Kumar.[16]

DIVERSE JOB OPPORTUNITIES

The library activities, such as acquisitions, licensing, cataloging, and processing, that take place behind the doors of technical services offer many interesting career paths, at both the technician and professional levels for those who excel in detailed work, possess strong computer skills, and prefer limited public interface.

Certain library materials, such as periodicals, special collections, microforms, and government documents, require customized skills to properly handle the special needs and services that these formats bring with them. Such departments also afford diverse career opportunities—many of which are overshadowed by the higher profile public service jobs in reference, circulation, and outreach. Those who enjoy variety in their daily work life—a blend of selection and acquisition, processing, interacting with vendors, digitizing, and reference service to users—are encouraged to investigate these areas of specialization. And, of course, working for the library industry support companies, jobbers, and vendors is another career track.

Associations such as the ALA have professional sections devoted to technical services areas, such as acquisitions, collection management, metadata management, and serials/continuing resources, along with round table groups for government documents, federal government librarianship, and students. The Society of American Archivists (SAA) supports member sections focusing on such issues as electronic records, visual materials, preservation, and reference/access/outreach, as well as sections for students, college and university archives, business archives, and more. Connecting with working professionals as mentors is an effective way to explore an area of specialization within the field.

STUDY QUESTIONS

1. Check sources such as the current edition of the *Library and Book Trade Almanac* or a trade periodical such as *Publishers Weekly* to locate recent figures on the number of hard copy books being published today. Is it increasing or declining? What current trends in the publishing industry do you think are affecting the production of hard copy titles?

2. Outline the stages that a book passes through to get onto the shelves of your college library. What is the typical turnaround time from the placement of the initial order to receipt by the library? Then how long does it take to be ready for public use? How does a CD or DVD compare?

3. Find out the names of five jobbers active in the library trade. How are they different in the services they offer? How are they similar?

4. Select a popular magazine title of your choice. Find out in what formats it is currently available (e.g., hard copy, full digital Web version, limited Web version, etc.). What is the annual subscription price for each format? Are there options for bundling a print subscription with full access to the digital magazine? What about access to the digital archives or back issues of the magazine? How does the annual library or institutional subscription price vary from an individual's subscription price?

5. Visit a special collections department, such as a university archives, a manuscript department, a local history room, or a museum library. Describe some of their major holdings. What security precautions are in place when you visit them in person? What types of digital images or digitized manuscripts from their collection do they offer access to online?

6. Do you have access to the JSTOR digital library through your college or public library? How do you find it compares with Google Scholar for locating journal articles in your field of interest?

7. Go to a U.S. government portal site like http://www.usa.gov/ or http://www.gpoaccess.gov. Browse the site and then visit five federal agency websites. Did you discover any agencies that you had no knowledge of before?

NOTES

1. *Library and Book Trade Almanac*, 58th ed. (Medford, NJ: Information Today, 2012), 435.
2. *ProQuest Statistical Abstract of the United States: 2013* (Lanham, MD: Bernan Press, 2012), 732.

3. *E-collections* listserv, e-mail to author, April 3, 2000, and Xiaohua Zhu, "The National Site Licensing of Electronic Resources: An Institutional Perspective," *Journal of Library and Information Studies* 9, no.1 (June 2011): 51–76, accessed April 20, 2015, http://jlis.lis.ntu.edu.tw/article/v9-1-3.pdf.

4. Carina Love, e-mail message to authors, May 4, 2015.

5. OCLC, "WorldCat: A Global Library Resource," *OCLC Online Computer Library Center*, April 21, 2014, http://www.oclc.org/en-US/worldcat/catalog.

6. Arlene Taylor, *Introduction to Cataloging and Classification*, 10th ed. (Westport, CT: Libraries Unlimited, 2006), 541, 544.

7. Creative Commons, "CC Attribution 4.0 International License (CC BY 4.0)," *Creative Commons*, July 25, 2014, http://creativecommons.org/licenses/by/4.0/.

8. Bo-Christer Björk, Patrik Welling, Mikael Laakso, Peter Majlender, Turid Hedlund, and Guðni Guðnason, "Open Access to the Scientific Journal Literature: Situation 2009," *PLOS.org*, June 23, 2010, http://www.plosone.org/article/info%3Adoi%2F10.1371%2Fjournal.pone.0011273.

9. "Get Involved," *PLOS.org*, accessed April 20, 2015, http://www.plos.org/get-involved/.

10. Allen B. Veaner, "Microforms," in *Encyclopedia of Library History*, Wayne A. Wiegand and Donald G. Davis, eds. (New York: Garland Publishing, 1994), 435.

11. Karen Kaplan, "The Culture's Immortal, But Not the Disk," *Los Angeles Times*, February 16, 1998.

12. George Barnum and Gil Baldwin, "Digital Preservation at the U.S. Government Printing Office: White Paper, Version 2.0," *U.S. Government Printing Office*, July 9, 2008, accessed April 6, 2015, http://www.gpo.gov/pdfs/fdsys-info/documents/preservation-white-paper_20080709.pdf.

13. Steven L. Sowell, Michael H. Boock, Lawrence A. Landis, and Jennifer E. Nutefall, "Between a Rock and a Hard Place: Managing Government Document Collections in a Digital World," *Collection Management* 37, no. 2 (2012): 98–109, accessed April 6, 2015, http://dx.doi.org/10.1080/01462679.2012.656554.

14. "FY 2013, Library Services & Content Management (LSCM): Year in Review," *U.S. Government Printing Office*, 2014, accessed April 13, 2015, http://www.gpo.gov/pdfs/LSCM_2013_Year_in_Review.pdf.

15. "Science Information in Peril," *Los Angeles Times*, March 1, 2000. And Nikki Swartz, "NARA Taps Lockheed for Archives Project," *Information Management Journal*, November/December 2005, 7.

16. Suhasini L. Kumar, ed., *Changing Face of Government Information: Providing Access in the Twenty-First Century* (Binghamton, NY: The Haworth Press, 2006).

RESOURCES

Books and Articles

Bahde, Anne, Heather Smedberg, and Mattie Taormina, eds. *Using Primary Sources: Hands-On Instructional Exercises*. Santa Barbara, CA: Libraries Unlimited, 2014.

Carmicheal, David W. *Organizing Archival Records: A Practical Method of Arrangement and Description for Small Archives*. 3rd ed. Lanham, MD: AltaMira Press, 2012.

Evans, G. Edward and Margaret Zarnosky Saponaro. *Collection Management Basics*, (previous editions entitled *Developing Library and Information Center Collections*). 6th ed. Santa Barbara, CA: Libraries Unlimited, 2012.

Forte, Eric J., Cassandra J. Hartnett, and Andrea L. Sevetson. *Fundamentals of Government Information: Mining, Finding, Evaluating, and Using Government Resources.* New York: Neal-Schuman, 2011.

Gao, Fang Huang, Heather Tennison, and Janet A. Weber. *Demystifying Serials Cataloging: A Book of Examples.* Santa Barbara, CA: Libraries Unlimited, 2012.

Haynes, Elizabeth, Joanna F. Fountain, and Michele Zwierski. *Unlocking the Mysteries of Cataloging: A Workbook of Examples.* 2nd ed. Santa Barbara, CA: Libraries Unlimited, 2015.

Intner, Sheila S. and Jean Weihs. *Standard Cataloging for School and Public Libraries.* 5th ed. Santa Barbara, CA: Libraries Unlimited, 2015.

Joudrey, Daniel N., Arlene G. Taylor, and David P. Miller. *Introduction to Cataloging and Classification.* 11th ed. Santa Barbara, CA: Libraries Unlimited, 2015.

Leibowitz, Faye. "Serial Joy and Serial Sorrow: The Experience of the Paraprofessional Serials Manager." *Serials Review* 38, no. 4 (2012): 254–257.

Mering, Margaret, ed. *RDA Workbook: Learning the Basics of Resource Description and Access.* Santa Barbara, CA: Libraries Unlimited, 2015.

Monson, Jane D. *Jump-Start Your Career as a Digital Librarian: A LITA Guide.* Chicago: ALA Neal-Schuman, 2012.

Mukherjee, Bhaskar. *Scholarly Communication in Library and Information Services: The Impacts of Open Access Journals and E-Journals on a Changing Scenario.* Oxford, UK: Chandos Publishing, 2010.

O'Toole, James M. and Richard J. Cox. *Understanding Archives and Manuscripts.* (Archival Fundamentals Series II). Chicago: Society of American Archivists, 2006.

Taylor, Arlene G. and Daniel N. Joudrey. *The Organization of Information.* 3rd ed. Santa Barbara, CA: Libraries Unlimited, 2008.

Wagner, Dora and Kent Gerber. "Building a Shared Digital Collection: The Experience of the Cooperating Libraries in Consortium." *College & Undergraduate Libraries* 38, no. 2/3 (2011): 272–290.

Weber, Mary Beth, ed. *Rethinking Library Technical Services: Redefining Our Profession for the Future.* Lanham, MD: Rowman & Littlefield Publishers, 2015.

Websites

Bancroft Library, University of California, Berkeley
http://bancroft.berkeley.edu/
(accessed April 1, 2015)
One of the West Coast's leading primary source repositories has an extensive website and provides electronic access to finding aids for many of its special collections as part of the Online Archive of California.

Cal Poly University Archives/Special Collections
http://lib.calpoly.edu/find-and-borrow/collections-and-archives/
(accessed April 1, 2015)
An example of a university special collections department website. The department posts its hours, contact information, mission statement, reading room guidelines, reference services provided, and reproduction rules. A list of manuscript collections with electronic finding aids is provided along with digitized images, collections, and exhibits.

Call Numbers 101
http://www.youtube.com/watch?v=AXHOMMvQkQU
(accessed April 1, 2015)

Short but clear YouTube video by University of California Riverside Libraries on the use of the LC call number system.

Five Laws of Library Science http://arizona.openrepository.com/arizona/handle/10150/105454

(accessed April 1, 2015)

Contains the full text of each chapter of the classic work *The Five Laws of Library Science* by the Indian scholar S. R. Ranganathan (1892–1972). First published in 1931, but still holds much relevance.

Getty Conservation Institute

http://www.getty.edu/conservation/

(accessed April 1, 2015)

Part of the renowned J. Paul Getty Center in Los Angeles, the Getty Conservation Institute's extensive website features project videos, a newsletter, many free publications, and relevant links on conservation issues.

How to Read Call Numbers

http://www.library.arizona.edu/help/tutorials/callnumbers

(accessed April 1, 2015)

University of Arizona Libraries developed this brief visual with the basics about locating and deciphering Library of Congress system call numbers. Useful for new hires and for library patrons.

Introduction to the Dewey Decimal Classification

http://www.oclc.org/content/dam/oclc/dewey/versions/print/intro.pdf

(accessed April 1, 2015)

OCLC, which publishes the Dewey Classification volumes, provides a detailed overview of the Dewey Decimal system, summaries of the tables, many helpful examples, and information on ordering Dewey publications. For library staff new to cataloging and classification principles.

Library of Congress: Preservation Division

http://www.loc.gov/preservation/

(accessed April 1, 2015)

Highlights our national library's Preservation Division, which has been a world leader in developing many modern conservation practices. Information for library and archival professionals as well as for the general patron includes: care and storage for special collections, case studies on conservation projects, and preservation FAQs.

Northeast Document Conservation Center

http://www.nedcc.org/

(accessed April 1, 2015)

This highly regarded, nonprofit regional conservation center specializes in preservation of paper-based materials. They assist libraries, archives, historical organizations, museums, and other repositories without their own facilities in conservation efforts. In addition, they are a leader in the preservation and conservation fields.

RDA Toolkit: Resource Description & Access

http://www.rdatoolkit.org/

(accessed April 1, 2015)

With RDA as the new standard for resource description and access, librarians, staff, and students will want to learn more about it and how to use it effectively when cataloging materials to this new model. The Toolkit is an integrated, browser-based, online subscription product that lets users interact with cataloging-related documents and helpful resources including a blog and videos, and to connect with an active community of cataloguers. Spanish language version also available.

Society of American Archivists
http://www.archivists.org/
>   (accessed April 1, 2015)
>   The leading national archival professional association, SAA, provides a site
>   that includes membership information, continuing education opportunities,
>   best practices, employment links, glossary of archival terms, and more.
Understanding Call Numbers
http://www.lib.lsu.edu/instruction/callnumbers/callnum01.html
>   (accessed April 1, 2015)
>   Louisiana State University Libraries' very detailed overview, explanation, and
>   comparison of the three major classification systems in use in the U.S.: Dew-
>   ey, LC, and SuDocs. This tutorial is geared for staff.
Understanding MARC Bibliographic
http://www.loc.gov/marc/umb/umbhome.html
>   (accessed April 1, 2015)
>   Authoritative tutorial written by Betty Furrie and reviewed and edited by the
>   Network Development and MARC Standards Office, Library of Congress. For
>   those wanting more thorough knowledge of the MARC record.
U.S. Government Publishing Office (GPO)
http://www.gpo.gov/
>   (accessed April 1, 2015)
>   Formerly known as the Government Printing Office, this robust website pro-
>   vides electronic access to a wealth of important information produced by all
>   three branches of the Federal Government. The department's mission is to
>   "keep America informed in the Digital Age" through its responsibility to pub-
>   lish and store government information in various formats, including digital
>   and print. Find lists of bestselling GPO publications, place orders for federal
>   documents, locate a Federal Depository Library, set up library standing or-
>   ders of important federal documents.

Chapter 6

Circulation

Just as in a retail establishment, efficient inventory control, supplying desired products, and good customer service are important elements in managing a successful library. Each individual book, e-book, CD, DVD, map, course reserve reading, e-reader, laptop, tablet device, or other material needs to be tracked as it *circulates* or is accessed, whether digitally, within a reading room, in and out of a department, or is physically removed from the library for use elsewhere. In addition to offering products that clients need and want, friendly and professional assistance is also critical in generating satisfied repeat customers. It does not matter how well other areas of the library function; if the connection to the customer is not made successfully, the library has not served its purpose. Both inventory control and customer service fail or succeed largely based on the effectiveness of the circulation department.

The most visible sign of a library's inventory control or circulation efforts is the service counter, where the official charging and discharging of tangible library materials take place as well as where much of the official registration of would-be library patrons is processed. A central circulation desk is, most often, a hub of activity. Besides the obvious checkout transactions, many other activities go on at a circulation service counter, including referral to other departments, answering directional questions, fines collection, processing initial library membership, and updating a member's account status as needed. As with the location of cashier stations in retail stores, the careful positioning of a circulation desk is a critical part of the inventory control operation. Strategic placement helps deter theft, provides the ability to count and view inbound and outbound traffic, and offers convenience to customers as they enter and exit the facility.

For many customers, regardless of the type of library, frontline circulation desk employees are often the first and only staff with whom they come in contact as they visit the library. (Although, with self-check out stations often an option today, it is possible for some patrons to bypass staff interaction altogether.) Thus, the public relations value of all interactions at the circulation counter should never be underestimated. And first impressions—positive or negative—leave a customer with lasting memories. As the old adage says, "You never get a second chance to make a first impression."

Most customers and novice staff see the circulation department as being synonymous with only those operations that take place at the service counter. But, in fact, there are other circulation-related responsibilities that take place away from the physical space of the service desk. These operations may include reshelving, management of reserve collections, document delivery and interlibrary loan (ILL) services, collection inventory and maintenance, library security, and overall management of the building's use.

In small libraries, branch outlets, or other facilities staffed by a solo librarian or technician, the circulation desk also doubles as a reference counter or all-in-one service point. Larger libraries have a separate service counter dedicated just to circulation functions and typically positioned adjacent to the main entrance/exit. Departmental collections, such as government documents, local history, children's room, archives, and others, may handle their own circulation, and thus a very large library may have several checkout counters on different floors or locations in various departments.

ACCESS TO LIBRARY MATERIALS

The designation *circulation department* is a familiar one, but such a department may also be named borrowers' services, loan services, or access services, particularly in larger university, public, or research facilities. These latter names clearly reflect the department's emphasis on making library resources available to borrowers in any modality. Traditionally, that has meant physically loaning out materials to qualified borrowers so that they can take them home, to school, to the office, to work, to an adjacent building, and use them off-site.

As electronic access to resources continues to grow dramatically, the actual loaning out of a tangible item is only one type of access. Increasingly, libraries provide remote access to holdings data along with the actual full-text documents themselves for their qualifying clientele. Typically, this includes e-books and electronic reserve collections (e-reserves), sophisticated databases, indexes, full-text periodicals, as well as digitized images, maps, historical photographs and more, as copyright ownership and licensing agreements allow. In some cases, access is free to all interested users; in others, access is limited to qualified borrowers who receive a password, user ID, PIN, subscription number, or other unique code that lets them log on to the library's electronic holdings.

Circulation Terminology

When discussing the loaning out of library materials, there are several commonly used terms that tend to confuse library users. These terms define the circulation status of the book, DVD, government document, e-reader, or other physical item. Materials that do not leave the premises of the library or information center include those designated as reference, rare books, archival materials, and other specially identified items that, because of age, condition, demand, or value, may call for restricted use. Available for in-house use only, *reference* materials tend to be multi-volume sets, handbooks, dictionaries, indexes, and other works that can be consulted briefly for facts or overview information. They may also be expensive, or frequently used, or both; the implication being that patrons can study them on-site and photocopy or photograph the needed pages, whereas the volumes themselves remain in the library at all times to maximize their use by the greatest number of individuals.

In contrast to the restrictions of the reference status, materials designated as *circulating* may be checked out to registered borrowers. In the majority of libraries and information centers that stress full service and maximum access to materials, it is typical for the bulk of the collection to circulate. However, in the case of specialized materials, such as those discussed in Chapter 5 (e.g., microforms, special collections, archives, current hard copy periodicals, maps, fine press books, and other unique items), circulation may be very limited, or the entire collection may be for reference use only.

Reserve status is normally found in school and academic library environments. Reserve materials are high-use items required for study by classes during a semester or school term; the number of copies is less than the number of students, so shared use must be closely enforced. Examples of reserve materials include copies of required textbooks, supplementary course readings, homework solutions, sample tests and assignments, or other curriculum-linked items. The materials may be part of the permanent library collection that has been transferred temporarily to reserve status, or they may be the property of an instructor who has loaned them to the library for the duration of the course. Public and special libraries will also, on occasion, classify materials as reserve to meet the requirements of seasonal school assignments or in-house training needs.

The electronic provision of reserve collections is growing, especially in academic libraries. *E-reserves* provide Web access to course-related readings and other materials selected by a professor; documents are accessible only to students currently enrolled in the class. Newer releases of online public access catalogs (OPACs) feature an e-reserve module for seamless delivery of required readings, book chapters, lecture notes, sample quizzes, and so forth to authorized users (e.g., enrolled students). Copyright permission must be obtained whether from the professor—in the case of quizzes, notes, and study packs—or from the commercial publishers of texts, books, and other educational resources.

Deciding on Loan Periods and Circulation Status

Library access policies today are a far cry from the chained books and closed stacks of earlier times. Although total anytime/anywhere access is not yet a reality for most researchers, the current emphasis on maximizing availability can be seen in patron-centered services such as extended staffing and building hours, extensive remote access to OPACS and databases, e-book collections, online renewals, electronic course reserves, and e-mail or chat reference assistance. However, there are legitimate reasons why the circulation of certain physical materials may need to be regulated or denied. Some items that typically have limited circulation status include but aren't restricted to the following:

- One-of-a-kind items (e.g., the only copy of an out-of-print item)
- High-demand items (e.g., class-required items)
- Reference materials (e.g., items not designed for reading cover to cover that can be briefly referred to or sections photocopied or photographed)
- Sets or series (e.g., multi-volume print encyclopedias, print series, bound volumes of print periodicals, or print periodical indexes where a missing volume lessens the value of the set as a whole)
- Fragile or rare items (e.g., original manuscripts, drawings, maps, or photographs that could be damaged by extra handling)
- Expensive items (e.g., items that are costly to replace or of high value)
- Items with a record of being stolen (e.g., there are certain topics in every library that are considered "hot"; anything dealing with these topics is prone to theft)
- Items with copyright and security issues (e.g., lending software may violate copyright laws and can also spread viruses)
- Items that require special playback equipment (e.g., microfilm)

Once a collection or an item has been reviewed, if it warrants checkout but with limitations, there are other options for limiting its status in addition to the basic reference and reserve categories discussed previously. The library's standard loan period (e.g., two days, two weeks, one month, etc.) can be modified so that material is returned earlier and is available sooner for other users. Limiting the renewal of materials is another option. For example, policies for certain materials may be that no renewals are allowed or that only one renewal is possible. Renewals also may be dependent on whether another patron has placed a request or hold on that exact item. All of these options and many more can be attached to the record of a specific item in a library's integrated library system (ILS).

Restriction by user type is another standard circulation policy. For example, in an academic environment it is not unusual to limit the borrowing of DVDs to instructors only or to restrict the checkout of reserve course-related items to currently registered and enrolled students. Also, in a college or university library, alumni or community cardholders may have only partial borrowing privileges, whereas current students, faculty, and staff enjoy full privileges. Loan periods may also differ by user type. In a corporate setting, permanent employees may have longer borrowing periods for materials or even no due dates, whereas temporary or contract employees may only access materials for short intervals. College professors are often able to borrow materials for an entire term, whereas their students are limited to a two- or three-week loan period. In an elementary school setting, students in the lower primary grades often are more limited in the number of library materials they can check out than older, more mature students in the upper grade levels. Loan periods for elementary students may also vary by age group, with shorter time for the youngest pupils, which, in turn, encourages them to return more frequently for fresh materials. Some school librarians allow check-out of books over the summer vacation to help alleviate loss of reading skills.

Correctional institutions have their own unique issues and constituent concerns regarding inmate access to print library materials and whether there is any access at all to the Internet. Public libraries may offer limited temporary or vacation accounts of several months' duration for seasonal residents (e.g., snowbirds, vacation home owners, or military dependents) to their community. Some public libraries also offer *universal borrowing,* extending their direct loan privileges to eligible borrowers of other public libraries in the state, county, or otherwise defined region.

Unfortunately, circulation restrictions according to a user's age may be in place in school libraries or in public libraries. Although a broad reading of the First Amendment, as is advocated by the ALA's "Access to Library Resources and Services for Minors: An Interpretation of the Library Bill of Rights,"[1] (formerly entitled "Free Access to Libraries for Minors") argues against such age restrictions, they are, in fact, common. Local public library systems in particular may limit the checkout of CDs, DVDs, games, or software to those 18 years old and over; the rationale for this type of policy may be based on content, on the need for special care of multimedia materials, or because of an item's replacement cost. Minors initiating a library account will usually be required to obtain the signature of an accompanying parent or guardian.

Though not frequently advertised, many libraries and information centers will modify loan status of an item at the discretion of the librarian on duty. Such loans tend to be allowed only on a case-by-case basis and usually consist of waiving the standard circulation status or extending the loan period of an item based on special circumstances.

With all of these circulation policy options, balancing the individual's access needs with those of the library's clientele as a whole is a key concern. Additionally, the security of library materials is a consideration in decision making. As with all policies, circulation rules need to be revisited and revised on a regular basis—especially as new formats or services come along—to keep them current with borrowers' needs and usage patterns. So, a healthy dose of common sense along with some flexibility helps keep policies reasonable.

As the online renewal of books by patrons becomes more commonplace, many libraries are revising their standing renewal policies to work in this newer environment. In some cases, telephone renewal is being augmented or replaced by the online option, with an eye toward eventually eliminating phone-in renewals. Online renewal offers convenience to users, and, once implemented, reduces the overall amount of staff time spent on renewals. However, a negative issue is that users do not always notice when an online renewal attempt has been denied. Denial of a renewal might occur because of a recall or hold on the title, outstanding patron fines on library materials, or other reasons. The result is that the patron keeps the book, CD, or DVD for an additional loan period, erroneously thinking that he or she is acting legally. Instead, the item accrues overdue fines, and, upon return by the patron, an unpleasant situation could arise.

E-book and audiobook collection vendors often have a different method of restricting circulation, or, more precisely, electronic access to titles. Depending on the licensing level that the library has purchased from the vendor, there may be concurrent user limits. In other words, the number of library users that can electronically access or download a given title concurrently may be limited. In some cases, that means only one subscriber at a time may open an e-book to view or download its contents; in other cases, it could be 10 users at once. There may also be a time limit for viewing or check-out (e.g., 24 hours or some other time period). Once the allotted time is up, the item is automatically returned and it becomes available for other subscribers to view. There are many different models and they may change each time the library agency renews its subscription to the digital resource package.

Overdue Fines

For public and academic libraries, a familiar practice is to charge borrowers a fee for the late return of materials. Although this may seem like an annoying penalty for the tardy customer, the rationale behind these fees is to gather tangible materials back so that they are available to the rest of the user population. In other words, assuring timely access for all is the motivation behind the fines. Contrary to popular opinion, few libraries get rich off their overdue fines. While enforcing a policy of overdue fines has traditionally been the status quo, there are librarians who have revisited this model, instead emphasizing the positive public relations value of eliminating late fees. One inspiration to rethink this has been the example of the very successful Netflix subscription film service, which famously threw out any late fees (or even due dates) for members using its DVD mail-out service.

Overdue fine policies and fee schedules usually must be approved by the parent organization of a library, such as a school board, city council, board of supervisors, advisory board, or other governing body. Once approved, it is good customer service to clearly post and publicize these fee rates both on websites and at circulation counters. As first-time borrowers are registered in person at a library, the overdue policies and fees should be explained, along with the borrowers' new access privileges.

The collection of overdue fines is a time-consuming task. When a library or information center is able to link outstanding overdue fines to their parent organization's operations, the process becomes more efficient. University and college libraries track outstanding fines as part of a student's overall account at the institution. When fines remain unpaid, other key services, such as registration for courses, retrieval of grades, or transcript requests, are blocked, often quickly resulting in timely payment of library fines. Although they seldom charge overdue fines, school librarians and technicians often contact parents directly about overdue or lost material, meanwhile limiting library privileges and postponing the release of student report cards.

An increasing number of library systems hire collection agencies to follow up on delinquent or long overdue accounts. This get-tough stance represents a more efficient method than previous in-house efforts because collection agencies have access to customer data and credit records and are in the business of delinquent accounts collection.

At the other end of the policy spectrum, some libraries choose to waive overdue fees altogether. After calculating the cost of tracking, processing, and collecting overdue fines on their own or through a collection agent, they decide to discontinue the practice. Rather, they emphasize the safe return of materials and charge only replacement costs if the item is lost or damaged. The positive public relations value of a no-fines policy is another consideration that may convince some in libraries and information centers to take that route. There is no one model for assessing late fees in special libraries. Especially, in a corporate information center environment, it is likely to prove counter-productive to penalize employees or even departments with monetary fines as they are, after all, all part of the company supported team.

Amnesty weeks or fine-free weeks have been popular, especially with public libraries. These are often timed to coincide with National Library Week in late April or with an individual library's anniversary, remodel, new branch opening, or other special event. With no questions asked, no fees assessed, it can be another positive public relations approach. Just bring them back!

Other Fines

Although library overdue fines get the most attention, there are other fines commonly assessed to borrowers. When patrons lose or damage library materials, they may either be charged the actual replacement value of the item (or, if out of print, the cost of something comparable), or the library may have set a flat fee for various categories (e.g., adult hardback book, $30; children's hardback book, $20; multi-volume DVD set, $100). Many libraries add a processing fee to the replacement charge as a revenue recovery method for processing time and supplies. These fees typically can be as little as $5 or more than $30, with academic libraries on the high end. This type of charge is similar in concept to a restocking fee charged by some retail stores for returned merchandise.

Although the hard and fast rules surrounding library fines have been the butt of countless jokes and newspaper cartoons, in fact, many agencies employ alternative methods of accepting payment for those who cannot pay in cash. Volunteer time in the library or the donation of like material plus a processing fee may sometimes be accepted in lieu of outright cash payment.

Whether or not overdue fines and lost/damaged fees are recovered from patrons, all libraries need to build into their budgets regular, ongoing funds for replacement and repair of materials. To not do so is to be in a state of denial about operating costs.

Patron Registration

Patron registration is the opening of a new account for a qualified library customer. It is a process very similar to walking into a department store, such as Macy's, Kohl's or Nordstrom's, and signing up for a store credit card. In this case, the library card takes the place of the store charge card. Libraries vary greatly in the way they handle the registration process. Public libraries tend to have the most stringent procedures for registering new patrons and verifying their identification and address. This makes sense, because their patron base is large, ever changing, mobile, and not intimately known to them. Many public libraries utilize online patron registration forms that allow customers to fill out the required information and instantly submit the completed form to the library. This may qualify them for immediate temporary access to resources. Library staff members then process the form and wait for the patron to appear in person with the appropriate photo identification before finalizing the new permanent library card or account.

Academic libraries may rely on official campus identification cards and draw from current enrollment databases for patron verification. Special libraries may vary from not requiring registration at all, on the one hand, to a very formal process involving security clearance, on the other.

Depending upon the type of circulation system, school librarians consult class databases supplied by teachers or the administrative office at the beginning of the academic term to open student accounts for a given school year. If a school district issues identification cards to students, this will be what they use to take resources from the library.

In the case of some private research facilities or university libraries, community members with no affiliation to the institution may be able to purchase access privileges. In this case, the registration process involves payment of a fee in addition to the collection of name, address, e-mail, and other identifying account information.

Why Register Patrons?

Librarians have many valid reasons to register patrons. Some of the major reasons include the following:

- To verify that a person qualifies to use the specific library
- To determine the patron's level of borrowing privileges, once qualified
- To establish a record of who borrowed what items
- To have contact information to locate patrons with overdue materials
- To have contact information to notify patrons about the status of holds, ILLs, or other requested materials
- To verify a patron's account for authentication when accessing resources remotely
- To verify a patron's account for use of self-help services such as self-checkout, placing holds, and paying fines
- To collect demographic information on the customer base for planning purposes
- To collect statistical information on the circulation of all materials for planning purposes

- To recall from a patron items needed for reserve or other special use
- To include patrons on the library's e-mail and postal mailing lists to receive marketing, programming news, and other library information (if this option is approved by the patron)

Privacy of Patron Records

Once patron data have been gathered and become part of the library's database of customer information, it is very important for staff to realize that this personal data is private. Industry ethics and laws in some states advocate that such confidential information be afforded both internal and external privacy protection. This means that neither personal data collected nor an individual's circulation records are to be shared with outside agencies; nor are these records accessible to library staff (or other agency personnel) other than those who are assigned to work with them. So access to the data is limited to those who must use it in the performance of their duties. This issue and others relating to workplace ethics are discussed more fully in another section of this book in Chapter 8, "Ethics in the Information Age."

Stacks Maintenance

Physical maintenance of the library's tangible collections is crucial to an efficient operation. In most libraries, such collection maintenance tasks are managed by the circulation department as an extension of their primary mission to provide access to and track the loan of materials. Admittedly, these are housekeeping tasks and tend to be somewhat tedious chores that must be done to maintain quality library service.

Some of the key maintenance tasks include shelving and shelf reading; cleaning, repairing and rebinding items; relocating collections; and inventorying items. Although the accurate and rapid reshelving of all materials is an ongoing, daily activity in any library, the other tasks take place on a more periodic basis. Many library facilities that are closed to students for holiday or summer breaks select that time to conduct a hands-on inventory of their collections. For those libraries and information centers that do not close for extended periods of time, collection inventorying or shifting of collections in the stacks may be done in phases, with parts of the collection temporarily unavailable while the process is underway.

Management of the building as a whole also often falls under the purview of the circulation staff. This might include monitoring of study rooms, classrooms, or labs; daily closing and opening of the library building; responsibility for clearing the building of all persons in the case of a fire alarm or other emergency alert.

LIBRARY CIRCULATION SYSTEMS

Today most libraries, information centers, and school media centers have an automated circulation system in place, usually as part of an ILS. These integrated systems consist of *relational databases* containing information about library collections, services, and users. Databases are relational when the information can be accessed and/or combined in many different ways on demand. Usually ILSs have two graphical interfaces to access these databases: one used by library staff behind the scenes and another graphical interface for the public.

When librarians first began to automate, they linked their databases of bibliographic records with databases of patron circulation records to form integrated OPACs. ILSs have now advanced to the point that library vendors create and sell *enterprise-level software,* or systems specifically designed for libraries and their different functions or services. ILS vendors now offer modules for these specific areas, including acquisitions, cataloging, circulation, serials, and, of course, OPACs.

Most of today's systems provide a module that is accessible on the Web, allowing anytime/anywhere searching by patrons and staff. In addition, those OPAC systems that are fully *Z 39.50* compatible allow a user to simultaneously search catalogs from two or more different libraries, even if each catalog is running software from different vendors. Z 39.50 is a protocol by which one OPAC transfers a search inquiry or other data to another OPAC, without the user being required to reenter the information, using the precise search keys of the second OPAC. Since the Z 39.50 protocol predates Web technology, there are various efforts underway to modify it to better mesh with the modern Web-based environment.

For many larger academic and public libraries, their current system may be a fifth- or sixth-generation system. Early use of computerized library circulation systems began in the 1960s at large, academic facilities. Many of these libraries had been experimenting in the prior decade with key punch cards to tabulate circulation.[2] Before the advent of commercial software packages, some of these libraries developed their own homegrown automated circulation systems, usually in concert with campus or municipal computer departments. In the early 1970s, CL Systems, Inc. (later to become known as CLSI) was one of the first commercial vendors to begin selling turnkey library circulation systems. They were soon followed by many other companies offering software solutions for basic library circulation tasks.[3]

These early automated systems were limited to circulation control functions—check-in and check-out transactions, calculation of fines, printing of overdue notices, and placing of items on hold—all of which are time-consuming, laborious, and repetitive, but necessary tasks for accurate inventory control and library operation. Typically, these early turnkey and homegrown systems were not integrated to include bibliographic look-up functions for the public. Thus, the wooden card catalog, with its numerous drawers filled with index cards, remained the tool for patron access to a library's holdings. Maintenance of the card catalog required an ongoing effort of detailed, repetitive, painstaking work by cataloging department staff.

The first OPACs, which married the patron records with a detailed database of the library's holdings and were geared for public use, arrived on the scene in the early 1980s.[4] As OPACs matured and became commonplace in the next 15 years or so, that longtime staple of libraries, the card catalog, was superseded by a computer screen. Across the nation and around the world, libraries began closing their card catalogs. Even the venerable *New Yorker* magazine noted with mixed emotions this passing of a cultural icon. In 1994, an article much read and discussed at the time, by staff writer Nicholson Baker caused quite a stir in the library world as he mourned the closing of Harvard's card catalog and questioned the need for installation of its automated system, HOLLIS.[5]

Although there have certainly been growing pains associated with the initial transfer to OPACs (and these adjustments continue with migrations to each new generational system), library staff will overwhelmingly attest to the major benefits and operational efficiency that automation has brought both to patrons and to employees. For customers, this has meant improved, decentralized access and convenience, many user-centered features, and the demystification of library processes. OPACs, by providing precise title location and availability data, have also allowed customers to play a more active role and enabled patron-initiated placement of holds. For library staff, integrated computer systems have automated many tedious, repetitive tasks associated with circulation's record-keeping functions and technical services' cataloging operations.

Some patrons still lament the conversion to computer access and feel at a loss. An older, longtime library user recently said to one of the authors, "I feel like I have lost the college library since the installation of computers. Without the card catalog, I don't even want to come into the library." A renewed effort to assist and train seniors and other reluctant computer users is one approach to mitigating this discomfort, but realistically, there will always be some researchers who resist any change from the familiar.

Since the early OPACs of the 1980s, there have been many advances and improvements in the product, parallel to developments in computer hardware and software technology overall. Currently, Web interfaces are the state of the art for automated library systems. These contemporary card catalogs are remotely accessible 24/7 and offer to the general public value-added features, such as online renewal, personal account information, viewing of digital resources, Google Books Previews of materials, mobile-ready interfaces, and collated holdings information for nearby libraries and beyond.

Automation of library systems comes with a hefty price tag. Installation of a new system is regarded by library agencies as a major capital expenditure, and often costs in the six-figure price range. For most public sector library agencies, a competitive bid process is required with vendors submitting complex responses to library-generated requests for proposals, or RFPs.

OPACs in Common Use

At the beginning of the new millennium, OPACs were in common use across the United States. Exact statistics for all types of libraries are not available, especially for schools and for special libraries for which data gathering tends to be difficult, but trends are visible to practitioners in the field. One such observation by Dick Boss, a respected library automation consultant, estimated that nearly 100 percent of the nation's 2,000 largest libraries were automated by 1999.[6]

Libraries and archives make major investments when purchasing automation products, both during the initial implementation stage and in ongoing annual renewal fees paid to vendors for support, software maintenance, and system upgrades. ILS systems are the backbone for the efficient management of any library's daily operations as well as the key to providing discovery and access to their collections and services.

Those libraries that are still relying on a manual system for their circulation and other operations tend to be smaller, rural, poorly funded, and not members of any type of library network or consortium. These typically include smaller special libraries, such as those found in churches, museums, historical societies and archives, nonprofit organizations, minor government agencies, or on Native American reservations.[7] School libraries in smaller private or parochial schools, as well as those located in isolated and rural public school districts, are other examples of libraries that may lack automated systems. Because these libraries are without partners, are minimally funded, are often staffed by volunteers or temporary help, have limited telecommunications infrastructures, and have done little to convert existing paper records to machine-readable formats, the roadblocks to installation of an OPAC are many.

Grant funding from private sources and membership in state-funded, multitype library networks are helping isolated libraries and information centers progress toward automation. Although no single grant will provide a ready-to-use OPAC on a silver platter, specific grants can assist a library in laying the groundwork needed before conversion from a manual to an automated system can take place. Various state and national telecommunications measures provide infrastructure funding for needy schools and libraries, and grants from the private Gates Foundation provide updated hardware, software, and staff training. (See Chapter 3 for further discussion on this.) By partnering with state-funded, multi-type library consortia, a once-isolated library can gain much needed expertise, access to consultants, and reduced pricing as part of a larger group.

For certain targeted underserved groups, there is the possibility of dedicated federal grant funding through the Institute of Museum and Library Services (IMLS). They support initiatives that focus on establishing new or enhancing existing library services and technology for Native American, Hawaiian, and Alaskan tribal collections. Basic library infrastructure, such as an automated circulation system and ILS are often included in these grants.[8]

Early Circulation Methods

Ledgers were the earliest method used in libraries for tracking information on library users and the items they borrowed. For the system to function well, multiple ledgers were required. Each transaction for a business day was noted in chronological order in a daybook. Later, data from the daybook was copied into separate ledgers, which provided access by patron name and book title.

The ledger that contained the borrowing record of each patron was arranged alphabetically by the borrower's last name and several pages were allowed to record ongoing entries. The third ledger listed each book in the collection and several pages were reserved to record successive borrowers and their respective due dates. Between them, the three logs provided three different access points to circulation data. The daybook provided a daily transaction log, but to verify a patron's account, the alphabetical patron ledger needed to be consulted. To ascertain the whereabouts of a particular book, the book ledger needed to be viewed. Ledgers were in common use in American libraries until about the time of the American Civil War.[9]

An earlier variant method, which eliminated the need for multiple ledgers, was the so-called dummy system. Wood dummies—that is, blocks with lined paper attached to them—were used to represent each book; as a patron checked out a book, his or her name and the book's due date were noted on the side of the book dummy. The dummy was then placed in the empty shelf space to indicate that the book was charged out. A variation of this was to have a dummy wooden block represent each patron. The correct block was then placed on the shelf as the book was removed; book title and due date were then written on the wooden dummy.[10] An obvious limitation of this version was that each patron was limited to borrowing one book at a time.

These early tracking systems worked successfully only when small numbers of both borrowers and circulating items were involved. Once the number of patrons, the volume of use, and the collection size increased, these methods quickly became cumbersome and inefficient.

Improvements on the ledger method of tracking circulation led to various systems that used paper slips. These transaction slips functioned like receipts and were inserted into a book pocket attached to the inside of each tome. Further improvements on the slip system led to the two-card method. One pre-prepared card held key bibliographic information about a book, such as author, title, call number, and copy number, and was tucked inside the book pocket. The second card contained borrower identification and was kept at the charging desk for a borrower's signature at checkout. Both cards were stamped with the due date when an item was checked out.

The Newark System, named after its first use at the Newark, New Jersey, Public Library in 1896, was a popular example of the two-card system and was in widespread use for several decades. Approximately 30 years later, a refinement of the two-card system, known as the Detroit Self-Charging System, raised efficiency with the use of preprinted due date cards and library identification cards.[11]

Although these systems seem archaic today, during electrical outages or computer malfunctions, library staff may need to revert to variations on these manual systems to try to maintain some order over circulation. A library technician intern in a local school district encountered just such a situation recently. Besides her own unfamiliarity with the manual system, she found that not all of the elementary school children were able to sign their names, which presented further complications during the outage period.

In the latter half of the 20th century, many systems for printing due date cards, book cards, charge cards, and borrowers' identification cards were developed to replace the earlier manual tasks of typing, stamping, and signing. Borrower identification cards ranged from paper to embossed plastic to the now common ID cards with optically readable barcodes.

The Library Card as a Symbol of Opportunity

Though the details surrounding the first borrower's card issued to a customer are lost to history, the concept of possessing one's own library card remains a symbol of opportunity and lifelong learning. A library card is the key to the free public library services that are a right for all citizens in the United States.

For residents, families, retirees, and immigrants new to a community, the initial trip to the public library to sign up for a user's card is a first step in accessing local programs and services. It is a fact well known to public library staff that for newly released prisoners and others returning to mainstream society, signing up for a library card in their new town is a recommended early step in their rehabilitation. A library identification card is equated with attaining literacy; the pursuit of pleasure reading; exploration of resources for study, research, and job search; Internet access; cultural enrichment programs; a sense of belonging to a community and more.

For young readers, a first library card is a proud possession that encourages them to grow their reading skills. The American Library Association (ALA) promotes National Library Card Sign-Up Month each September with news releases reminding parents "that a library card is the most important school supply of all" and it is usually free. Such a campaign emphasizes the important and multifaceted community resource that a library is to its customers and the vital role it plays in the education and development of children as well as offering lifelong learning opportunities for adults.

Characteristics of an Automated Circulation System

Upon examination, the key characteristics of a modern automated circulation system are not too different from the basic inventory control needs of the 19th-century manual systems described previously. Accuracy and detail are important aspects of efficient inventory control, and thus are of primary importance in a library circulation system.

At minimum, a circulation system needs to record and track four key elements relating to library circulation: (1) who borrowed the item, (2) the exact item borrowed, (3) when the item was borrowed, and (4) when it is due back. Advanced systems should also track whether items are overdue; lost; missing; loaned to another library; withdrawn for repair, binding, display, or digitization; or on the shelf and available for use. Most newer systems also indicate the status of books or other materials that have been ordered or are undergoing in-house library processing.

Another important function is to track the status of all registered borrowers, either active or inactive, and especially those with overdue items, outstanding fines, blocks, or other problems with their accounts. Modern systems are also able to match requests for holds with incoming items. Upon patron or staff request, the system must be able to flag the record of an item that is charged out and then acknowledge that the requestor is next in line to receive the desired title when it is returned.

Another essential function of a circulation system is to provide detailed statistics relating to the circulation of items. Key statistics include, at a minimum, the number of times a particular item has been checked out; overall circulation by week, month, or other period; circulation by individual library outlet, branch, department, or entire system; and circulation by call number.

Increasing Internet use by patrons makes it essential that modern, integrated circulation systems offer a Web-based interface in its OPAC module. OPACs with Web access for patrons are very effective, using the same platform upon which other key library services and research tools are available to users. Usability is a key factor, however. Just because library staff think that a system is easy to use does not mean that the public will find the interface equally convenient and intuitive. When well-designed, such an interface provides customers with the convenience of easily toggling between a library OPAC and other Web resources. Anytime/anywhere access, patron authentication, patron-initiated holds, ILL requests, and account tracking, are all features that library users have increasingly come to expect.

A rule of thumb for all library automation systems is that library administration direct a comprehensive review of the library's ILS at least every seven years, including a survey of vendors and their current products and features, with replacement of the extant system a likely goal. In the interim period, updates and upgrades (e.g., new software releases) to the system are provided by the vendor every year or two, delivering new features and capabilities.

Automation Resources

Although reviewing and deciding on an automation vendor is a daunting task, there are currently many reputable sources to help a library manager or other staff with the selection of a new vendor and new products. Marshall Breeding, a leading analyst and writer in the field of the library technology industry, publishes an annual analysis of the library automation marketplace related to the automation of North American libraries and also includes international trends.[12] The trade periodicals *Computers in Libraries* and *Information Today* regularly include articles analyzing major ILS companies and comparing their features, as well as presenting strategies to help in selecting the appropriate product for your library's environment and needs.

Library Technology Reports, a periodical published by the ALA, is another authoritative source for information on library systems and technology products. "Library Systems Landscape," an annual feature of *Library Journal* examines the developments and news in the marketplace of library automation including, "the impact of recent mergers, the continued adoption of next-generation library services platforms, the emergence of mobile-optimized staff clients, and new partnerships and feature development in the open source arena."[13]

Professional conferences aimed for the library generalist, as well as those that specifically target technical staff, also prove extremely valuable for data gathering, both from the automation vendors themselves and from library and information center colleagues in attendance. Examples include, but are by no means limited to, Internet Librarian, annual meetings of state and regional library associations, the annual and midwinter sessions of the ALA, and yearly conferences of the Canadian Library Association and the Special Libraries Association. Typically, at the exhibit hall of the conference, the major automation vendors host booths staffed by sales and technical representatives who are there to answer questions and demonstrate their software products.

User groups of a particular automation platform (e.g., OCLC WorldShare, Voyager, Millennium, SIRSI, etc.) help provide a different perspective to balance the vendor's point of view. These groups are comprised of professional librarians and staff who communicate through a listserv or blog and often hold periodic regional workshops. Querying user groups before making a purchase decision or when drafting the specifications for an RFP can be a valuable way to evaluate products and customer satisfaction. Once a system has been chosen, participation in a user group provides support, shared expertise, and strength in numbers when lobbying the vendor for improvements. With Web access to most OPACs a given feature, another means of testing the performance of a potential system is to use it anonymously just as a patron would. In addition, in-person visits to library sites provide a unique chance to watch multiple users at work on a system and to consult with technical services staff.

With the great strides gained in computerized systems over the past four decades, library routines have become increasingly streamlined with each new generation of automated systems, especially in the area of circulation functions. The once standard tasks of manually date-stamping books or calculating overdue fines by hand are now seen as quaint and old-fashioned routines that only appear in classic movies. The trend of personalizing one's Web account, so popular on retail websites like Amazon.com and with college campus portals (MyCalPoly, MyCuesta, etc.), is also becoming commonplace with the newer releases of OPAC software. Such customization may allow patrons to save past OPAC searches, submit, track, and cancel ILL requests, suggest titles for library acquisition, get e-mail alerts or RSS alerts, and take advantage of other time-saving and convenient functions.

LIBRARY SECURITY

Thieves in an archive? Violence in a library? Yes, sadly, it is true. There are many patrons, members of the general public, and even novice staff members who cherish the concept of a library as a safe haven from the woes of the outside world. Unfortunately, libraries, archives, and information centers are prone to purposeful theft, vandalism, and other crimes. Just as there seems to be more news media coverage of violent events in general, libraries have their share of shootings, seemingly senseless attacks, and other crimes that make the daily news.

Because the circulation or loan services department is responsible for a large part of the library facility, the broader issues of library security and crime also tend to fall under its jurisdiction. Generally, there are two categories of security issues. The first category is offenses involving library property. This includes the theft of library materials or equipment, mutilation or intentional damage to library materials or equipment, and vandalism to the building or furnishings. The second category is offenses against people—staff or patrons—that take place inside the library building. Examples of such offenses include abusive conduct, assault, and indecent exposure.

Security in libraries is not a new concern. During the Roman Empire, it was the custom for a conquering army to pillage library buildings as they swept through a city, taking library books as spoils of war. In more modern times, a notorious library thief, Stephen Blumberg, was convicted in the 1990s and served a prison term for the theft of approximately 24,000 volumes from libraries in 45 states.[14]

Theft

The most common incidents of crime are theft or mutilation of library materials. The perpetrator may be a student with no money for the photocopy machine, a kleptomaniac, a self-appointed censor, or a professional thief out to make a profit. It could also be a library employee or a passionate collector who is tempted to steal public property and add it to their home shelves. Inadvertent removal of library or archives materials can also take place.

Electronic theft detection systems were first installed in libraries in the 1960s. By the 1980s, all but the smallest libraries and information centers were using some type of security system to deter theft. Once the library market was saturated, vendors targeted retail stores to find additional customers for their security products. Known in the industry as *materials control systems* or *theft detection systems* the most commonly used systems are found in libraries, supermarkets, and retail stores. Although not foolproof, they do lower losses through the concept of deterrence. Many would-be thieves, seeing a security gate or locking turnstile at an exit point, are discouraged from attempting to steal an item. Setting off an alarm and being confronted with possession of an unauthorized item in a public place is embarrassing at the least.

Such systems in and of themselves are by no means infallible. But when combined with vigilant staff monitoring, good lighting, and clear visual corridors, security systems have generally reduced pilferage by about 80 percent over that experienced by a library with no security devices in place, according to 3M, a major vendor of such systems.[15]

Library, archives, and information center personnel may choose from various models of materials control systems; some work on radio frequency, others on electromagnetism. Typically, a screen or gate detects sensitized items. Each item—such as a book, magazine, map, DVD case—carries a hidden or disguised target. When properly checked out, the item is desensitized and the target turned off, and the patron passes through the security gate uneventfully. When an item has not been checked out properly and has not been desensitized, passing it through the gate triggers an alarm and locks the gate or turnstile. Options to the turnstile include the addition of flashing red lights or loud, recorded messages to increase the visibility of an unauthorized exit. Larger library facilities may place security gates on every floor or at all reading room exits. When in use, these detection system turnstiles and gates must

FIGURE 6.1 Security equipment positioned at checkout counters and building exits can help discourage library theft. Reprinted by permission of 3M Library Systems.

comply with the Americans with Disabilities Act (ADA) so as not to present a physical barrier to access for those in wheelchairs or scooters.

Pass-around systems are another variation on security arrangements. This alternative, which is used in video stores and retail chains, is most likely to be used in small library settings where patrons are unlikely to bring items back into the building until they are ready to relinquish them. In such a system, the item is never desensitized. Instead, it is passed around the security gate by a staff member, after being checked out, and handed to the customer who is standing outside the security zone.

Preventive Measures

Attention to overall facility security increases the effectiveness of theft detection systems. A good place to begin is with a survey of the library's security. Conduct the survey with security or police personnel to gain their expert input. Assess vulnerable areas, such as unsecured windows and unalarmed delivery or staff entrances that allow one to circumvent the secured entrances. Control all exits with gates, alarms, locks, cameras, electronic keypads, or guards to minimize such security gaps.

Internal library procedures should also be considered. For example, how long do new materials lie around in the technical services area before a security or tattletape target is applied to them? Who has access to the new, unprocessed materials? Don't overlook library, custodial, or other building staff, or outside delivery people. Does the technical services area need to be a locked, secured space? Taking active measures, such as locking down computers and peripherals, TV monitors, DVD players, and other property can help prevent equipment loss.

When building a new library from scratch, staff has the advantage of taking security issues into consideration with the architect and designing a facility from the ground up to deter theft and crime. Attention to preserving visual corridors in reading rooms and stack areas that allow for surveillance by personnel from service counters can increase the security of collections, staff, and patrons. Minimizing poorly lit stack areas and dark, remote corners in the library facility is also very important. Similar safety and design concerns apply to the library building itself and to adjacent parking areas. Although not often discussed in the literature on library security issues, the safety of these adjacent areas is an important issue. If unsafe, it can provide a barrier to patron access to the library and its services.

Within existing library structures, there are various methods for augmenting security, such as increased lighting, video surveillance cameras, a library security guard to patrol the building, staff visibility at all service points, and enhanced materials controls systems. Attempting to offer reasonable loan periods on library materials is another consideration that could impact theft and mutilation. For example, if an item can be checked out for only two days and patrons need the material for a longer period, they may think that stealing it is the best answer to satisfy their needs.

Realistic Policies

As with most security systems, a determined or practiced thief will find a way around them. So the bottom line for library staff is that losses to the collection will occur. Therefore, realistic administrators need to allow for some shrinkage in the collection and to budget funds for the replacement of stolen or damaged items. Also, setting aside funds to periodically repair, upgrade, or replace security systems is a necessary planning strategy. To be cost-effective, the overall cost of the security measures should not exceed the amount saved by having those procedures in place.

Having a policy in place with the library's parent organization for penalizing a perpetrator is a necessary step. Typically, in an academic library, students can be fined, placed on probation, or at least sent to the dean's office for a warning when caught stealing or vandalizing library property. In K-12 school settings, disciplinary action can be taken and parents notified. Public libraries will want to have good working relations with their local police departments to provide them needed support with security issues. Library staff should not attempt to physically restrain suspected thieves or perpetrators, but should summon the assistance of police or trained security personnel. Consider the addition of installing silent "panic" buttons behind each public service desk throughout the library, archives, or museum facility. When pressed, these buttons will alert local security, police, or emergency services of a situation and summon their assistance.

As with many other elements of a library or information center (relevancy of collections, helpfulness of staff, public hours, availability of parking or public transit, and so on) the library's reputation for safety will be known in the community and will affect patron satisfaction and usage levels.

Mutilation

The purposeful act of mutilation may involve cutting out a section of a book or magazine with the intent of taking just those pages needed by the irresponsible patron. Or it may involve destroying pages or tearing whole volumes from their spines in an effort to eliminate offensive photographs or text. Because mutilation typically occurs inside the reading room or library building, security systems are of little help in catching perpetrators in the act. If a security target remains attached to the pages that were removed and the perpetrator attempts to pass through the exit security gate with those targeted pages, they can be caught at that time and dealt with. Sadly, however, the damage to materials is already done. Sometimes the purpose of the mutilation is simply a prank to defeat the security system.

In a school or academic setting where much usage is linked to topical course assignments, informing faculty of the problem can help catch a potential mutilator. Some libraries periodically mount displays of damaged and mutilated materials in an attempt to educate patrons and perhaps deter would-be mutilators.

Problem Patrons

Those libraries that are open to use by the general public are the most apt to encounter problem patrons. Because these facilities are open for long hours (often including evenings and weekends), and provide warm, comfortable shelter, they are inviting places for homeless and other needy people. No identification is required to enter, and there is an abundance of free resources, entertainment, and information available, comfortable seating and tables, along with restrooms and hot, running water.

Most problem patron behavior can be characterized as falling into the following categories: nuisance behavior (e.g., lonely or elderly people who monopolize reference personnel or carry on long-winded monologues); criminal behavior (e.g., theft, vandalizing or defacing materials or property, performing sexually lewd acts); unattended children (often their parents think they can use a library as a "safe" and free place in lieu of appropriate child care); and various types of behavior that are often bizarre, unpredictable, and threatening and exhibited by mentally disturbed patrons.

Many libraries provide special staff training conducted by outside experts, social service workers, or local law enforcement personnel in dealing with problematic individuals. Such training usually includes conflict resolution, safety issues, defusing difficult situations, and other techniques. Dealing with problem patrons in the course of a workday is a genuine issue for staff at all levels in many libraries, and they deserve access to this training to best prepare them for handling such interactions.

Formal, written library policies (approved by the governing board, city council, library administration, or other appropriate authority) can be helpful in addressing commonly encountered issues such as unattended minors with no parents or guardians present; standards of behavior expected for library visitors including noise levels, good personal hygiene, overly offensive smells, and so forth. Such policies are often crafted after long experience with these matters and give the library agency a framework for taking action when needed. Failure to comply with these standards may result in the loss of library privileges for an offending patron or even banning them from the premises. The overall purpose of such policies is to ensure a safe space and a high-quality library experience for all users.

Balancing access to services for all with the need to regulate inappropriate or questionable behavior that may interfere with another person's ability to use and enjoy the facility has always been a challenge in those libraries that are available to the public at large. Collaborative relationships with city or campus police, local homeless shelters, and other area social services agencies are key to maintaining a secure library environment. Urban and larger libraries often employ and train their own on-site security personnel.

Some proactive solutions for dealing with some of these issues include holding after school homework help sessions staffed by library personnel and trained community volunteers. Teen volunteer programs and reading clubs for kids offer other enrichment activities for minors in the library during the afternoon hours. A few metropolitan public libraries are experimenting with adding in-house social workers or peer counselors to their team specifically to assist impoverished patrons. Often grant funding can be found to support these community endeavors based in the library.

Disaster Preparedness

Another aspect of library security is disaster preparedness and recovery. Also referred to as emergency preparedness, this is a related but much larger security issue that focuses on making a library facility and its staff ready in the event of a natural disaster, such as flood, fire, earthquake, tornado, or the like. Dealing with situations perpetrated by criminals, terrorists, or disturbed individuals such as bombings, arson, taking hostages, and active shooters are also included in emergency preparedness training. Just as with theft, libraries do not have a special immunity from disasters.

To have a viable written disaster plan, much advance footwork, preparation, and coordination is needed. An up-to-date, written library disaster plan is probably part of a larger campus, school district, corporate, city, or inter-agency's overall plan. Typically, a disaster plan should specify the chain of command for decision making, and include data such as current contact information for those in the command chain, maps and building floor plans, evacuation routes, and procedures. Highest priority collections for removal or safeguarding should be indicated. Computer data backups, especially all OPAC files, should be housed at an alternate, remote location in case on-site files are unrecoverable.

Disaster preparedness planning also includes a recovery phase, where library staff access, assess, salvage, and, if possible, restore collections and resources harmed during a disaster. Some library staff may receive additional specialized training in disaster preparedness; these staff in turn can then train coworkers.

A thorough discussion of disaster preparedness and recovery is beyond the scope of this textbook. Many comprehensive books have been written about this topic, and certain library industry websites provide helpful emergency checklists. The ALA website features a Disaster Preparedness and Recovery section developed in collaboration with Heritage Preservation, a nonprofit institute assisting cultural heritage agencies on various aspects of conservation. See: http://www.ala.org/advocacy/govinfo/disasterpreparedness. Features include a template for the creation of a comprehensive disaster plan, actual disaster plans submitted by other libraries and archives, and lessons learned by Gulf Coast libraries from the devastating hurricanes in 2005.

Whether the responsibility of a library director managing a multi-branch system or the solo librarian operating a small, special library, disaster preparedness policy, procedures, and training are to be taken seriously. Staff should be well prepared to take care of emergency situations.

INTERLIBRARY LOAN SERVICES

Interlibrary loan is an important service whereby individual libraries agree to share their collections and to supply materials to one another for patron use. Upon the receipt of a patron's request, the borrowing library asks another facility to supply a needed book, DVD, or copy of a periodical article for a minimal fee (typically $10 to $20), or sometimes free of charge (in which case the library is absorbing costs in lieu of passing these on to its patrons). Often, agreements are drawn up among member libraries belonging to regional networks or consortia that formalize this cooperation. But, typically, those libraries that receive public funds, such as state colleges and universities and public systems will automatically accept requests from other libraries without a formal cooperating agreement, though they may impose fees for or restrictions on the transaction. In contrast, special libraries that are part of private corporations or institutions, such as those in law firms and businesses, and that do not belong to any networks, are under no obligation to loan out their resources. In fact, for reasons of competitive intelligence, they may not want to do so because it might assist a rival business and takes time away from their own internal workflow.

In state-funded library networks, all libraries that want to receive services must provide some level of access to their own collections as a prerequisite to membership. This may take the form of providing on-site use, ILL services, access to specialized reference services, or even direct borrowing to qualifying customers affiliated with the network.

Often, ILL services are under the umbrella of a circulation or loan access department because each external loan, though it requires special handling and attention, is just another type of borrowing transaction. The net result of this resource sharing is better service for library customers. Specifically, patrons have access to a much-expanded resource base. Even in the information-rich age of the 21st century, no single library can have it all. Through the use of ILL, the boundaries of a single library's collection, or even a system's, are extended far beyond its own hard copy and electronic holdings. It can be an especially useful tool in locating technical and historical periodical articles or a book that may have been published locally by a small press or a title that has long been out of print.

The "Interlibrary Loan Code for the United States," a document compiled by the Reference and User Services division of the ALA, serves as a guideline for libraries in general and for any systems or networks that want to develop their own ILL policies. As the "Explanatory Supplement to the Code" states:

> Interlibrary loan (ILL) is intended to complement local collections and is not a substitute for good library collections intended to meet the routine needs of users. ILL is based on a tradition of sharing resources between various types and sizes of libraries and rests on the belief that no library, no matter how large or well supported, is self-sufficient in today's world. It is also evident that some libraries are net borrowers (borrow more than they lend) and others are net lenders (lend more than they borrow), but the system of interlibrary loan still rests on the belief that all libraries should be willing to lend if they are willing to borrow.[16]

Regarding the involvement and reciprocity implied in such a nationwide effort, the Code notes:

> The effectiveness of the national interlibrary loan system depends upon participation of libraries of all types and sizes.[17]

Implied by the code and as discussed in the supplement is the premise that libraries of all types and sizes should be willing to share their resources liberally so that a relatively small group of resource-rich libraries is not overburdened.

For researchers in the know, ILL has been one of the best-kept secrets of libraries. There are rarely big, bright signs offering this extended service, though mention of it can commonly be located by drilling down through a library website or scanning their FAQs. Rather, it has typically been sug-gested to patrons on a case-by-case basis as the reference interview pro-gresses or when the request for information cannot be filled locally. Today, that is changing. With discovery and one search systems in more common use in library OPACs, a library patron may stumble upon the ILL option once logged into the search interface or they may be automatically prompted to place an ILL request when searching for a desired item that is not held locally.

Retail shopping has a model similar to ILL that is perhaps more familiar to most consumers. Think about shopping in a bricks and mortar retail store and finding that the exact sweater (size, color, style) you want is not available in that store's on-site inventory. When you inquire how you can get the desired item, an employee then checks his or her system's computerized inventory that includes other store locations and company warehouses. After viewing the inventory status for that item, he or she suggests you can order the exact sweater directly through their website and have it shipped to your home address. Shipping may or may not be offered free of charge to the consumer, just as can be the case with ILL.

The first formal mention of ILL in America was in a letter to the editor in *Library Journal's* premier issue in 1876. ILL became common in the 1920s, although cooperative loaning between libraries had already been taking place for some time prior to that.[18] With the adoption of the first ALA "Interlibrary Loan Code" in 1919 and the growing number of union or shared catalogs of library holdings, ILL became firmly established.[19] Standardized paper forms were developed mid-century and were in common usage until the advent of OCLC's ILL model, when faxing and then e-mail in the 1990s rendered the multipart paper forms obsolete. Today, expect to find ILL request forms posted on most individual libraries' websites or, once a user has logged in to a search interface and been authenticated, found there as an option. Paper ILL forms can still be found in use by some of very smallest libraries or by rural, independent libraries that are not yet affiliated with any regional network or consortia.

Common Guidelines on ILL Requests

Certain types of library materials may not be available for ILL because of their physical size, shape or condition, copyright restrictions, or local demand. Typically, these materials include, but are not limited to, computer software; rare, very old, fragile, or valuable books; most newly released books; the hard copy issue of a journal in its entirety; many audiovisual materials; and items classified as reference books. Each library sets its own limitations on what materials it will and will not loan out, with periodic review as to these categories. In addition, copyright law officially restricts the number of articles that can be photocopied or scanned from the same journal issue without incurring royalty fees.

An important concept of ILL is that the service is designed to locate and obtain a specific book or article citation; thus, ILL is not a subject search for materials but a search for a supplying library that owns a precise title not available at the local level. The ILL service is considered to be a supplement and enhancement to the on-site collection. On the other hand, ILL should not be mistaken as a substitute for collection development in individual libraries. If an item is repeatedly requested through ILL, it is an indication that there is a justified local need for that item, and purchase for the permanent collection should be seriously considered. Repeat requests for ILL may also provide data for cooperative collection development efforts among libraries.

When requesting an item through ILL, there is a direct correlation between the accuracy and completeness of the book, DVD, or journal article citation provided and the likelihood of the material being located. Staff from the borrowing library search large databases such as OCLC's WorldCat to locate an item that matches the citation provided by the customer. So when a patron submits a citation with the author's name misspelled or omitted, incomplete publishing data, or other inaccuracies, the chances of locating the material are diminished.

A library worker at the borrowing library queries several different libraries that own the requested item to see if it is available for loan. Multiple queries are usually required because the requested resource may be already checked out, withdrawn temporarily for repair, or a high-demand item the potential lender cannot spare. If it is an older item, the loan may be refused because it is too fragile and/or scarce to be released to another library, or in a format (e.g., microfilm) that is prohibited from loan. Delays in ILL may be caused by items located in remote storage facilities that require retrieval and longer delivery time, items that are requested from foreign countries, or even just backlogs created by staffing shortages or library schedules. Diligent ILL library staff and technicians often will search until they find a free supplier so they can save the patron from having to pay a service charge.

Patrons frequently ask, "How long before my ILL request will come in?" The reality of ILL is that the turnaround time for receiving the desired material varies with each specific request. For researchers and students using this inexpensive but sometimes slow service, the caveat is "submit your request as early as possible" before a project deadline. Anecdotal evidence and the disclaimers on many library websites indicate that, for libraries using modern methods of ILL processing, the bulk of requests arrive within a two-week period. But on a case-by-case basis, the turnaround time can be unpredictable. And, certainly, international loan requests may take considerably longer to fill. Increasingly, ILL requests may be fulfilled using digitized resources, which can speed up the turnaround time for a request.

In some geographical regions of the United States, resource-rich libraries have organized their own sharing systems as a means of providing affordable, timely resource delivery for their patrons. Link+ is one such example. A resource sharing system in the West, membership is open to any library in California, Oregon, Nevada, or Arizona. Major academic libraries and larger public libraries comprise the membership. Each library pays to belong to the resource sharing network; most agencies then absorb the operating costs and pass on the premium loan service to their qualifying library patrons free of charge. Hallmarks of the Link+ service include patron-initiated loan requests from an OPAC, speedy fulfillment, and status tracking. Ohio also has a similar resource sharing group called OhioLINK that draws from the holdings of numerous major academic and research libraries within the state.

Limitations on the ILL Service

No discussion of the benefits of interlibrary sharing would be complete without mention of the potential abuses and imbalances that can arise. Many libraries have limits on the number of active ILL requests that a patron can have at any one time. One of the authors remembers an eager nursing student at a community college who, during a single library visit, submitted requests for 25 articles from specialized health periodicals. From that time on, that small college library instituted a limit of 10 ILL items at once, per patron, which is still generous. Some libraries may have a limit on active requests in any stage of the process; so, perhaps, three active requests at any one time. This would mean, once a loan request has been fulfilled and turned back in it would no longer be considered active and the patron would be eligible to submit another new request. Other agencies, especially public libraries, may place a limit on repeat ILL requests for the exact same title by the exact same person within a calendar year or other defined time frame. Note that some libraries will not lend or borrow internationally. Magazine or journal articles that are now commonly delivered as links to electronic holdings (if not as PDF attachments to e-mail), may only be accessible for a couple of weeks after initial patron e-mail notification, at which point the access then times out.

Staff time is a consideration when setting reasonable limits on ILLs, as is the estimated cost of each ILL transaction. One estimate conducted at a metropolitan public library put the minimum cost in staff time for processing an ILL request to borrow an item at an average of $10 per unit.[20] Calculating the cost of an ILL transaction can provide a basis for determining a fee schedule in an effort to recover the costs of the service. One source for suggestions on computing costs is the *Interlibrary Loan Practices Handbook*.[21]

Another consideration is that completed ILL requests often lie on the hold shelf of the requesting library, never to be picked up by the patron. The reasons that library patrons neglect to pick up these items vary, but it might be that they found another supplier, refused to pay any ILL charges, simply forgot, or lost interest in the material that was once so urgently needed. Placing a limit on the number of simultaneous ILL requests per patron helps balance the needs of borrowing and supplying libraries. Remember that in the case of a borrowed tangible item such as a book or DVD, when it is sent out on loan, that title remains unavailable to researchers at the home library for three to four weeks.

Because of their vast resources and the breadth of their collections, large university and research libraries were traditionally deluged with requests for technical, medical, and other materials not available in small, generalized library collections. This created quite an imbalance, with large facilities constantly being asked for material and small libraries rarely receiving loan requests. For this reason, early ILL codes recommended that "the requesting library should avoid sending the burden of its requests to a few libraries. Major resource libraries should be used as a last resort."[22] The current code stays well away from such a recommendation, but it remains a common sense guideline among practicing ILL library technicians.

As a means of remedying this transaction imbalance, some states have set up a system of ILL reimbursement within their boundaries. This means that a public library receives a set dollar amount as reimbursement for supplying an ILL requested for a library patron from outside its jurisdiction. According to a study in January 2000 by Himmel and Wilson (library consultants on such reimbursement programs), of the 45 states responding to the survey,

22 received some type of state reimbursement for ILL, whereas the same number did not. (One state did not respond to the question.)[23]

The widespread use of automated library catalogs, especially union catalogs such as the ubiquitous OCLC WorldCat that delineate holdings of libraries worldwide, along with other advances in technology in the past decades, have greatly enhanced the process of identifying potential ILL suppliers. Locating those libraries that hold a desired title is now much faster and easier overall. Plus, the ability to identify various libraries—small or large, well known or lesser known, in state or out of state, helps to spread the resource sharing more equitably.

OCLC's WorldShare offers library management applications and platform services built on an open, cloud-based platform. Because of its integration with other libraries, WorldShare ILL facilitates library user access to electronically delivered resources and print materials, both in local collections and the collections of other member libraries. Integration with the WorldCat OPAC promises to reduce turnaround time on article requests from days to hours, saving staff time and improving ILL user satisfaction. WorldShare also identifies freely available, open-access resources to help conserve ILL budgets.

How It Works

Here is an illustration of how the service typically works. While investigating her family history, one of the authors found a reference to a Canadian local history book, *The History of the County of Guysborough, Nova Scotia*, originally compiled in 1877. While the content of the book is available for online searching or viewing through a scanning project, the requestor's preference was to obtain the entire physical book. The request was placed with the Cuesta College Library's loan services department, using its Web-based ILL form. The request form (see Figures 6.2 and 6.3 for examples) is part of the library's website and is accessible to campus students, staff, and faculty (http://library .cuesta.cc.ca.us/illoan.htm). Because the college is a paid subscriber to the bibliographic utility OCLC, its expansive international database of members' holdings was then searched for this title. More than 15 potential supplying libraries were identified. Several libraries were queried unsuccessfully before the University of Windsor in Ontario, Canada, agreed to supply the physical title. A hard copy volume was shipped fourth-class library rate to the borrowing library, along with an invoice of $10. This patron was allowed to check the book out for two weeks and promptly paid the fee directly to the loaning library. Another option often used with international borrowing transactions is the use of IFLA coupons for payment, thus eliminating the issue of varying currencies across country borders.[24]

Compared to the expense of trying to obtain a copy of this out-of-print title, or, even more costly, having to journey cross-country to read the book in a Canadian library, the small fee was well worth the convenience of having the book shipped to the customer's library.

Interlibrary Loan Request

Find A Book
  WebCat
  eBooks
  Other Library Catalogs

Find An Article
  Journal
  Magazine
  Newspaper
  Database List
  PHL

Search The Internet
  Search Engines
  Websites by Subject

Research Assistance
  Research by Subject
  Citation Guides
  Library Tutorial
  Evaluating Sources
  Research Skills Class

English 201A Workbook
  Updates & Corrections
  Questions 45-54

Library/Information
Technology Program
  Program Home
  Registration Calendar
  Course Offerings

Library Services
  Interlibrary Loan
  Course Reserves
  Cal Poly Library
  Columbia Students
  For Faculty
  Friends of the Library

About The Library
  Hours | Policies
  Staff | FAQs
  Open Computer Lab
  Library Map | Blog
  Directions | Parking
  Suggestions

  Other Catalogs >>>

Materials unavailable at the Cuesta College Libraries may be obtained from other libraries. All Cuesta faculty, staff, and students may use this service. For additional information, please see the information desk librarian or contact the Interlibrary Loan Department (805)546-3100 ext. 2469.

Fields followed by a * are required fields and must be filled out in order for your request to be processed.

Processing time for most requests is 7-10 days.

Borrower Identification

Name: _____ * 	Date of Request: _____ * (mm/dd/yy)

Library or Student body card #: _____ 	Need before: _____ * (mm/dd/yy)

Phone: _____ * (i.e. 805-123-1234) 	E-mail: _____

Willing to pay:* ○ Yes ○ No 	If yes:* ○ $1-5 ○ $6-10 ○ over $10

Please indicate who are you? * 	Where would you like to pick up the item? *
○ Cuesta College Employee 	○ San Luis Obispo Campus
○ Cuesta College Student 	○ North County Campus
○ SLO County Community User

Book Request

Author: _____ 	Title: _____

Publisher: _____ 	Edition: _____ (if any)

Date: _____ 	Series: _____ (if any)

Magazine or Journal Article

Journal Title: _____

Volume #: _____ Issue #: _____ Month: _____

Year: _____ Pages: _____

Author of article: _____

Title of article: _____

Briefly describe where you located the item you are requesting:

FIGURE 6.2 Many college, university, and public libraries provide online interlibrary loan forms as a convenience for patrons. Reprinted by permission of Cuesta College Library, San Luis Obispo, California.

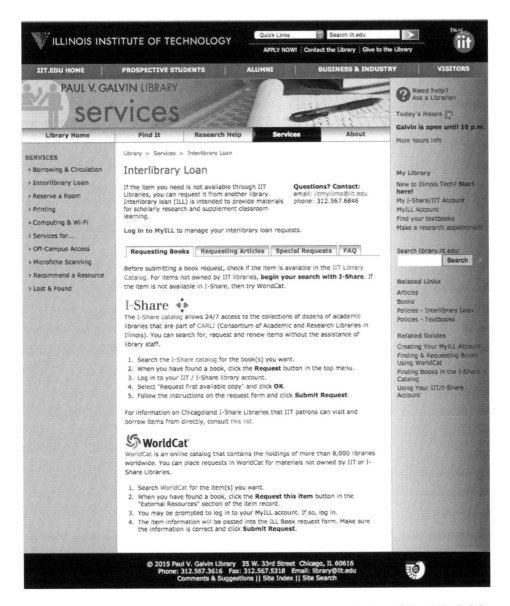

FIGURE 6.3 Interlibrary loan form. Reprinted by permission of Paul V. Galvin Library, Illinois Institute of Technology.

Initiating an ILL Request

For many patrons, an ILL request is prompted by a visit to their library. Often such a request begins at the circulation desk when a patron realizes that a desired item is not held locally. Frequently, it may also develop as the final step of a reference interview, as local resources are explored and found to be inadequate. For patrons who search a library's OPAC remotely and are familiar with the ILL service, a request might be submitted via e-mail. Increasingly, many libraries now have complete ILL forms available on their websites or within their OPACs. Again, each library will determine how it accepts an ILL request. Often, ILL services are limited to current, valid, qualifying patrons, so that whatever form the request takes—an e-mail inquiry, a completed ILL form submitted from a website or an OPAC, or an in-person request—some verification of the patron's account is performed.

Historically, an important aspect of ILL is that the transaction is library-to-library. It is true that changes are now on the horizon that will make online, customer-initiated ILL requests more commonplace within official library networks, but patrons will still need to be members in good standing at one of the participating libraries. Authentication of their status will be part of the log-on interface. At the current time at the majority of libraries in the United States, patrons cannot initiate a request on their own, independent of a home library affiliation. The borrowing library, whether placing the request or authenticating a subscriber to place a request themselves, in effect, vouches for the patron's careful use of a supplied item. Affiliation with a home library also helps to ensure the prompt return of borrowed items to the lending library and the collection of any service fees charged. In many cases, the loaned item, once delivered, does not leave the borrowing library. For example, loaned microfilm must be used on-site in the requesting patron's library. Often, unique or older books, such as local history titles or reference books, are loaned with the understanding that the customer must read them on-site in his or her home library.

Direct Borrowing

Direct borrowing (and its companion term *direct loaning*) is a variation on the ILL services described previously and one that many seasoned library users have yet to experience. Rather than the model found in traditional ILL services where the lending takes place from library-to-library, with direct borrowing the book or other item is lent directly to a qualifying borrower. In library consortia where direct borrowing is an agreed-upon service, patrons from one participating library can walk into any other member library and check-out items. The computer system of the lending library verifies that patrons are in good standing with their home library before authorizing the transactions. The home library generally is responsible for enforcing loan periods. In some arrangements, the patron must return borrowed items to the lending library. In others, the items can be returned to any participating library.

A colleague had the opportunity to use direct borrowing when he worked at an engineering university in Chicago, the Illinois Institute of Technology (IIT). That university participated in a consortium with more than 30 other academic libraries in Illinois. Because his personal research interests were centered in the social sciences, the library resources that met his needs were more likely to be found in the collections of other consortium members than they were on the shelves of the library at his own institution.

The OPAC of IIT was linked with those of the other libraries in the consortium. Therefore, the researcher could easily check to determine which members of the group held the desired titles. Because the circulation systems were also linked, it was possible to determine if any of those book titles were missing, already checked out, or restricted from circulation by virtue of being categorized as rare, reference, or reserve materials. Generally, the author found titles of interest to be available at the libraries of two comprehensive universities that were both along his daily commuting path. With this as the case, he had three options:

1. Stop at a holding (lending) library on his route home, hoping that no one had checked out the book in the meantime.

2. Request that the item be pulled from the shelf and immediately charged out to him and held at the lending library until he could pick it up.

3. Request that the item be charged out to him and delivered to his home library by means of a state-funded delivery service if he could wait a few days for the item.

Although direct borrowing has never been nearly as commonplace as the library-to-library loan method, the current growth in distance education courses may see both of these services become staples for the far-flung, off-campus student who needs anywhere/anytime access to course-required materials or supplemental resources.

Document Delivery Services

A variety of sources provide what is referred to as *document delivery,* a service similar in concept to ILL. Here again, the full citation for the item required must be supplied to the document delivery firm. Most of these are commercial firms, although many larger university libraries also offer such a service to regional professionals or to the general public on a fee basis. Document delivery differs fundamentally from traditional ILL in several ways:

- The service is not restricted to library card holders; any individual or business with a valid credit card can patronize a document delivery firm.
- The service uses a broader array of suppliers, including regional, national, and foreign libraries; private firms and contractors; national and foreign government agencies; individuals; publishers; and others to procure the desired content or item.
- The emphasis is on rapid, convenient delivery, copyright compliance, and confidentiality in procuring the requested item.
- The status of requests is available using an order number provided to the customer.
- The service can be more costly when compared to the subsidized low or free costs of interlibrary loan.

Document delivery firms are often located in communities with large academic, technical, or research libraries, and they may employ regular as well as contract employees in their effort to quickly locate, retrieve, photocopy, scan, and deliver on-demand access to materials. While more and more of these firms draw solely from digital content that they aggregate or have access to, there are also companies that will provide more customized services that might include scanning from microfilm or locating hard copy materials. Examples of a few large, established document delivery vendors include Ingenta (http://www.ingentaconnect.com/), the U.S. Department of Commerce National Technical Information Service (http://www.ntis.gov/), and Documents Delivered (http://www.documentsdelivered.com/).

Document delivery firms are often active members of and advertise with the professional associations from which they draw their clientele such as the Special Libraries Association, the American Association of Law Libraries, or the Medical Library Association. For those looking for a reputable document delivery provider, checking with such an industry trade association could be helpful in getting a referral.

Like many other vendors in the library and information industry, document delivery companies may be specialized. Some may supply only medical sources, others may specialize in patent data, and other firms may provide access to a wide range of subject area materials, ranging from newspaper and periodical articles, to monographs, scientific proceedings, and foreign language materials.

Special libraries and information centers, such as those in law firms, corporations, and medical facilities where competitive intelligence and other time-sensitive business decisions often influence rush information requests have traditionally been frequent users of document delivery vendors. In these scenarios, whenever possible, the cost of document delivery transactions is billed to a client or charged back to a specific department within the organization. For these information centers that do not necessarily need ongoing subscriptions to dozens of academic and technical databases (unlike an academic library would), the appeal of utilizing a document delivery firm is that they do not have to commit to annual contracts or licenses. Instead, they order documents as needed on a pay-per-use basis. Typically, for established customers there are many options for payment including credit cards, deposit accounts, and regular account billing.

Well-funded academic libraries often have accounts with commercial document delivery firms and pay all or part of the fees to supply items to their faculty, staff, and currently enrolled students. In this case, the end user cannot distinguish between an item acquired through the traditional ILL process and one procured through a commercial firm. The cost and means are transparent to the satisfied patron. In fact, many large academic libraries will avoid using the potentially confusing term *interlibrary loan* and just refer to the provision of all materials not readily available in their own library as *document delivery*.

Easier Access to ILL

Although the ILL service to date has been primarily used by serious researchers, faculty, authors, genealogists, and seasoned library patrons, there are many indications that the service is undergoing a renaissance. As a result of recent technical innovations such as the widespread use of discovery and one search capability in library OPACs, authenticated patrons are seamlessly offered an option to request from another facility a resource that does not show up in their local library's holdings. Use of confusing library jargon such as ILL is often being replaced on library websites, in search tools, and databases with more straightforward wording such as request, deliver, or find. With the reality of faster fulfillment due to improved delivery standards and the convenience of providing electronically delivered documents, libraries themselves are less wary of promoting ILLs. Electronic journal providers are becoming more inclined to allow direct delivery of PDF files or timed access through a Web link, eliminating the need for ILL staff to go through labor intensive, multiple conversions between paper and electronic formats. In general, library resource sharing practices, attitudes, and policies have moved to being more consumer-centered.

ILL is being discovered by new groups of students and researchers. Distance education, where students, regardless of geographical location, use the Web to access course materials online and never meet in any physical classroom or visit a bricks-and-mortar library, is projected to be a continued growth industry for colleges and universities. These academic institutions must make required and supplementary materials available to their far-flung students in a convenient manner. This often means providing them with full ILL services and subsidizing all or part of any costs. Requested books or DVDs might be physically delivered to a student's home or office; access to library-purchased streaming video can be granted for the duration of the academic term; articles and readings may be delivered via e-mail or viewed on the Web with password access. Commercial document delivery firms may also be used to provide materials to students in a speedy manner, with the cost absorbed, or at least subsidized, by the university. In turn, these commercial document delivery providers benefit from technological advances and from a general increased awareness of their services.

The increase in multi-type library consortiums with shared holdings lists such as found in the OCLC WorldShare product will also encourage ILL activity by making holdings data more transparent and readily available to patrons. After checking a holdings list display, qualified researchers then click through to an ILL request form that is also online. Quickly, conveniently, and at the point-of-need, the patron can then submit a timely request for a needed item.

The nonstop growth in digitalization and electronic resource sharing also provides a handy supplement to the ILL process for the patron and for the librarian or library technician. With the huge Google Books initiative as well as many larger institutions scanning unique and historic titles and providing their contents free for accessing online, it is always worth a try to first attempt to locate a work online, either for a preview or snippet (partial) view, or in its entirety. The venerable Library of Congress began a pilot effort in 2001 to scan certain short, fragile tangible works from its collection that are in the public domain as a way of expanding ILL access. After filling these ILL requests with limited digital viewing access for the requesting patron, the scans were then made available to all for viewing in their permanent digital collections. So, in this case, the initial ILL query led to a scan-on-demand response, which in turn opened up access to that document to the public at large.[25] Overall, ILL has entered a new and improved phase with increased efficiency and more rapid fulfillment speed that benefits both the requesting researcher and the library staff managing the transactions.

STUDY QUESTIONS

1. In your college library, what is the name of the department that handles circulation? Which department processes interlibrary loans (ILLs)? How many people are employed in each department, and at what job levels are they employed (e.g., student assistants, pages, library technicians, librarians, managers)?

2. What is the distinction between the designations *reference* and *reserve* for library materials?

3. Does your college library offer e-reserves as an alternative to physical copies of required course texts and materials?

4. What are some of the considerations that must be balanced when setting circulation policies for the loan of a library or information center's tangible materials?

5. Do circulation or access policies apply to remotely accessed e-books or e-reserves?

6. What is your opinion about limiting access to library materials (especially DVDs or streaming video) according to a patron's age? In a public library? In a school library?

7. Are overdue fines a necessary evil in the management of a library's collection? Explain why or why not.

8. Name the key functions of a modern automated circulation system. What are some other features that provide added value and that library customers have come to expect?

9. Why are libraries, archives, and information centers vulnerable to theft? Name some basic preventive measures that can be taken to mitigate the theft of tangible materials.

10. What are some strategies to best prepare library staff for encounters with patrons in need of social services (homeless, unattended minors, etc.)?

11. Have you placed an ILL request in the past year? If so, were you satisfied with the materials obtained and the overall service? Explain why or why not.

12. How do ILL and document delivery services differ? How are they alike?

NOTES

1. American Library Association, "Free Access to Libraries for Minors: An Interpretation of the Library Bill of Rights," 2004, accessed August 1, 2015, http://www.ala.org/Template.cfm?Section=interpretations&Template=/ContentManagement/ContentDisplay.cfm&ContentID=8639.
2. Wayne A. Wiegand and Donald G. Davis, Jr., eds., *Encyclopedia of Library History* (New York: Garland Publishing, 1994), 143.
3. Ernest Muro, *Automation Services for Libraries: A Resource Handbook* (Annandale, NJ: Vendor Relations Press, 1991), 5, 6, 14, 24, 25.
4. Ibid., 25, 26.
5. Nicholson Baker, "Discards," *New Yorker*, April 4, 1994.
6. Dick Boss, e-mail to the author, March 15, 1999.
7. Arlene G. Taylor, *Organization of Information* (Englewood, CO: Libraries Unlimited, 1999), 24.
8. Sandy Tharp Thee, "Library Programs Tailored for a Tribal Community," *Champions of Change to the White House*, June 17, 2013, accessed August 1, 2015, https://www.whitehouse.gov/blog/2013/06/17/library-programs-tailored-tribal-community.
9. Nevada Wallis Thompson, *Circulation Systems for School Library Media Centers: Manual to Microcomputer* (Littleton, CO: Libraries Unlimited, 1985), 4–12.
10. Wayne A. Wiegand and Donald G. Davis, Jr., eds., *Encyclopedia of Library History* (New York: Garland Publishing, 1994), 142–43.
11. Ibid.
12. Marshall Breeding, "Library Systems Report 2015: Operationalizing Innovation," *American Libraries*, May 1, 2015, accessed August 1, 2015, http://librarytechnology.org/repository/item.pl?id=20535.
13. Matt Enis, "Managing Multiplicity: Library Systems Landscape 2015," *The Digital Shift* (blog) *Library Journal*, April 7, 2015, accessed August 24, 2015, http://www.thedigitalshift.com/tag/lsp/.
14. Laurie Becklund, "Man Writes Novel Chapter in Annals of Library Thefts," *Los Angeles Times*, Home Edition, April 28, 1991.
15. "3M Quality Guaran*three*," 3M Library Systems, 2007, accessed August 1, 2015, https://multimedia.3m.com/mws/media/135785O/3m-quality-guaranthree-2007.pdf
16. Reference and User Services Association (RUSA), Interlibrary Loan Committee, "Interlibrary Loan Code for the United States, Explanatory Supplement," *American Library Association*, 1994, last revised 2008, accessed July 30, 2015, http://www.ala.org/rusa/resources/guidelines/interlibraryloancode.
17. Ibid, "Interlibrary Loan Code for the United States," http://www.ala.org/rusa/resources/guidelines/interlibrary.
18. Arthur Curley and Dorothy Broderick, *Building Library Collections*, 6th ed. (Metuchen, NJ: Scarecrow Press, 1985), 174.
19. Wayne A. Wiegand and Donald G. Davis, Jr., eds., *Encyclopedia of Library History* (New York: Garland Publishing, 1994), 285–86.
20. Nancy O'Neill, Santa Monica Public Library, e-mail to author, September 28, 2000.
21. Cherie Weible and Karen Janke, eds., *Interlibrary Loan Practices Handbook*, 3rd ed. (Chicago: American Library Association, 2011).
22. Virginia Boucher, *Interlibrary Loan Practices Handbook*, 2nd ed. (Chicago: American Library Association, 1997), 152.

23. *Supporting Interlibrary Loan and Direct Loan Services in California's Multi-Type Library Environment* (Milton, WI: Himmel and Wilson Library Consultants, 2000), 7.
24. International Federation of Library Associations and Institutions (IFLA), "IFLA Voucher Scheme," May 2014, accessed August 17, 2015, http://www.ifla.org/voucher-scheme. International Federation of Library Associations and Institutions (IFLA) is the leading international organization representing the interests of library and information services and their users on a global basis.
25. RUSA MOUSS, Interlibrary Loan Committee, "Library of Congress Liaison Report, ALA Midwinter 2002," *American Library Association*, January 2002, accessed August 1, 2015, http://www.ala.org/rusa/sections/stars/section/illcom/lcmidwinter2002.

RESOURCES

Articles

Conrad, Suzanna. "Collection Development and Circulation Policies in Prison Libraries: An Exploratory Survey of Librarians in US Correctional Institutions." *The Library Quarterly: Information, Community, Policy* 82, no. 4 (October 2012): 407–427. http://www.jstor.org/stable/10.1086/667435.

Cowan, Alison Leigh. "Guilty Plea in Theft from Drew Archive." *New York Times*, Late Edition (East Coast), January 7, 2011: A.17. http://www.nytimes.com/2011/01/07/nyregion/07drew.html?_r=0.

Evans, Donna. "At the Central Library, a Litany of Lewd Acts." *Los Angeles Downtown News*, November 22, 2013. http://www.ladowntownnews.com/news/at-the-central-library-a-litany-of-lewd-acts/article_0f211f94-5311-11e3-8c1f-001a4bcf887a.html.

Harris-Keith, Colleen. "Evaluating the Staffing of an Interlibrary Loan Unit." *Journal of Access Services* 11, no. 3 (July 2014): 150–158. doi:10.1080/15367967.2014.914425.

Jessop, Lauren and Terra Plato. "To Fine or Not to Fine?" *Feliciter* (Canadian Library Association) 57, no. 2 (2011): 71–73.

Kaaland, Christie. "The School Library's Role During Critical Times." *School Library Monthly*, February 2015. http://www.schoollibrarymonthly.com/articles/Kaaland2015-v31n4p32.html.

Linderfelt, K. A. "Charging Systems." *Library Journal*, June 1881, 178–82.

Mehrens, Elizabeth. "Alleged Thefts Disquieting for Libraries: A Noted Researcher Is Charged with Stealing $900,000 in Rare Maps from a Yale Collection." *Los Angeles Times*, September 10, 2005: A.12. http://articles.latimes.com/2005/sep/10/nation/na-maps10.

Moreillon, Judi. "Policy Challenge: Food in the Library." *School Library Monthly*, April 2013: 26–27. http://www.schoollibrarymonthly.com/ARTICLES/pdf/QRv29n7p26.pdf.

Nieves, Evelyn. "Public Libraries: The New Homeless Shelters. They're Hiring Social Workers, Nurses and Other Outreach Workers to Serve Their Neediest Visitors." *Salon*, March 7, 2013. Originally appeared on *AlterNet*. http://www.salon.com/2013/03/07/public_libraries_the_new_homeless_shelters_partner/.

Plummer, Mary W. "Loan Systems." *Library Journal*, July 1893: 242–47.

Books

Albrecht, Steve. *Library Security: Better Communication, Safer Facilities*. Chicago: American Library Association, 2015.

Graham, Warren. *The Black Belt Librarian: Real World Safety & Security*. Chicago: American Library Association, 2012.

Halsted, Deborah D., Shari C. Clifton, and Daniel T. Wilson. *Library as Safe Haven: Disaster Planning, Response, and Recovery: A How-To-Do-It Manual for Librarians*. Chicago: ALA Neal-Schuman, 2014.

Higher Education Interlibrary Loan Management Benchmarks, 2014 Edition. New York: Primary Research Group, Inc., 2013.

Kahn, Miriam B. *Disaster Response and Planning for Libraries*. 3rd ed. Chicago: American Library Association, 2012.

Kahn, Miriam B. *The Library Security and Safety Guide to Prevention, Planning, and Response*. Chicago: American Library Association, 2009.

Mosley, Shelley E, Dennis C. Tucker, and Sandra Van Winkle. *Crash Course in Dealing with Difficult Library Customers*. Santa Barbara, CA: Libraries Unlimited, 2013.

Rubin, Rhea J. *Defusing the Angry Patron: A How-to-Do-It Manual for Librarians*. 2nd ed. New York: Neal-Schuman Publishers, Inc., 2011.

Sander, Janelle, Lori S. Mestre, and Eric Kurt. *Going Beyond Loaning Books to Loaning Technologies: A Practical Guide for Librarians*. The Practical Guides for Librarians Series, Book 13. Lanham, MD: Rowman & Littlefield Publishers, 2015.

Weible, Cherie and Karen Janke, eds. *Interlibrary Loan Practices Handbook*. 3rd ed. Chicago: American Library Association, 2011.

Websites

Access Services Conference
http://www.accessservicesconference.org/
(accessed July 28, 2015)
An annual national conference focusing on current issues relating to all areas of access services in academic libraries (e.g., customer service, ILL innovations, managing course textbooks and e-reserves, loaning technology, campus outreach, library safety issues, etc.) For both professional and technician levels.

Disaster Information Management Research Center
http://disasterinfo.nlm.nih.gov/dimrc/emerpreplibraries.html
(accessed July 28, 2015)
An innovative initiative sponsored by the National Library of Medicine to promote the role of librarians and information specialists in the provision of disaster-related information resources to their communities. A variety of resources include a listserv discussing current disaster-related resources, workshops on community preparedness and disaster awareness events, temporary free access to full text articles from major biomedicine titles to healthcare professionals, librarians, and the public affected by disasters.

Disaster Preparedness Clearinghouse
http://www.ala.org/alcts/resources/preserv/disasterclear
"Developed by the Association for Library Collections & Technical Services, a division of the American Library Association, this site is a selective resource

for libraries of all sizes and types. It contains resources, links to the disaster preparedness sites of agencies whose primary role is emergency response or conservation, and information on available training."

The Rethinking Resource Sharing Initiative
http://rethinkingresourcesharing.org
(accessed July 28, 2015)

Encourages and recognizes innovative thinking on contemporary resource sharing models for public and academic libraries. Dedicated to developing and integrating new solutions for use in discovery and integrated library systems, as well as for delivery of both physical and virtual materials. International members include library practitioners, archivists, vendors, and publishers.

Chapter 7

Reference Service

What is reference service? The centerpiece of reference service is an individual reference transaction. The transaction occurs when highly trained staff members provide walk-in, telephone, e-mail, or live interactive chat consultation with library customers. The consultation is generally one on one, and therefore, can be specifically targeted to resolve the information or research needs of individual patrons. Thus, the primary activity of a reference unit is to directly aid specific customers in their quests for information and in the effective use of resources. Although all divisions of a library or information center ultimately serve the customer, reference service is one of the more direct and visible efforts regardless of the type of library environment.

A September 2013 survey of public library usage conducted by the Pew Research Center entitled *How Americans Value Public Libraries in Their Communities* found: "Some 61% of Americans ages 16 and older say they have a library card for a public library."[1] Also in 2013, a separate Pew national survey, *Library Services in the Digital Age*, explored the public library attitudes of Americans 16 years and above; the results reported that "80% say reference librarians are a 'very important' service of libraries."[2]

Reference continues to be a well-used service.

A reference service counter may also be called Research Services, the Information Desk, the Help Desk, or other similar names, all connoting the provision of assistance. In most libraries these terms are used interchangeably. Popular terms for virtual reference services—which are also referred to as digital or electronic reference—are *Ask the Librarian, E-Reference, Ask-Now*, and other phrases implying real time interaction or at least a speedy response time.

In very large libraries there may be multiple service desks, each with a very specific function. For example, in such a library, the Information Desk may be found in a very visible and readily accessible location, such as a first floor or entrance area, where general and directional referring occurs. More specialized problem-solving would then take place in subject-oriented locales (e.g., the Fine Arts section or the Science and Technology section), often as a result of a referral from the Information Desk. Roving reference librarians, equipped with a smart phone or tablet, can also be found in larger libraries, serving as a mobile service resource.

In such arrangements, the rationale is for the Information Desk staff to screen patron requests, answer the routine questions, and refer the more complex ones to more highly trained and often subject-specialist librarians. In some ways this would be similar to nurses screening patients and referring the more serious problems to doctors while handling routine matters themselves. However, in most libraries, all reference activities take place at one service point.

Each community of information seekers has its own distinct set of needs. Whether that community is an affluent suburban population, attorneys in a legal firm, middle school students, or university students or professors, they will interact uniquely with the reference department serving them by requesting different information. Because of the ongoing interaction between reference staff and patrons, this department often has a pulse on those local information needs, at least those that are articulated and expressed to the staff.

In addition to providing research guidance, a secondary goal of reference service in many libraries is to teach users how to conduct searches and to use resources in an effort to become self-sufficient in their investigations. Reference staff spend much of their time instructing customers on how to navigate their way through the ever-growing virtual sea of information. This may be achieved through face-to-face, one-on-one tutoring, with self-paced online tutorials, or by more formalized classroom-like education.

The goal of helping customers become self-sufficient is both a necessity and a mission for most libraries. Academic and school libraries, like their parent institutions, have a teaching mission. Information literacy, as well as literacy in traditional reading, writing, and arithmetic, is critical to students' success in all aspects of their lives. In addition, libraries are not generally staffed at levels that allow reference staff the luxury of actually doing the research for each customer, even if it would be faster and more enjoyable for all concerned. The needs of other customers must also be met. Also, once customers have learned one information skill, they may be able to perform it unaided the next time they need similar data. They will then return to the reference staff with more complex and more interesting challenges, having been able to solve the more mundane problems on their own.

In contrast with academic, school, and public-serving library settings, within many special libraries the goal of teaching patrons some self-sufficiency in their searching does not apply. In this setting, the primary customers are highly specialized and highly paid professionals within the organization. It is more cost-effective for the library staff to collect and synthesize the information than it is to train the specialists to do their own research. For example, in a law firm library, the library staff time spent on a particular case may be billed directly to the client instead of just being absorbed as overhead. Even if the client is being billed $70 to $100 per hour for library research, this is considerably less than the hourly billing rate for attorneys in the firm. In addition, the library staff can probably find the information more efficiently than the attorneys can. Thus, the clients save money and perhaps get better service as well.

A question that often comes up in today's Information Age is: "With so much information available on the Internet, why would anyone need to use a Reference Librarian?" In 2006, a study from the University of Michigan's Comprehensive Cancer Center reported that cancer patients looking for medical information about their particular disease found more information by seeking assistance from a reference librarian than by searching on their own.[3] Overall career experience, as well as the daily frequency of searching and access to subscription databases not available to the general public were all factors in making librarian-mediated searches more productive. Perhaps the answer to the continued value placed on library reference services since then, is that, just like so many other ventures, they continue to evolve in order to answer the current needs of their customers and to reflect changed ways of doing business (in this case, locating, evaluating, accessing and manipulating information).

For example, specialized patient-support health libraries sponsored by hospitals and medical centers such as the Stanford Health Library and the Hearst Cancer Resource Center, both in California, or the Massachusetts General Hospital's Blum Patient and Family Learning Center, reach out to patients by providing them access to free expert medical reference searching and information retrieval. The rise of such agency information centers (different from their own internal medical libraries serving hospital staff) attests to the recognition of the ongoing needs of consumers and patients for mediated assistance in locating critical and specific health data. So while anyone can use their favorite search engine to retrieve tons of medical information on the Web, individuals value assistance from health services librarians or medical library staff as they guide families and patients in mining newer technologies such as a digital *Physicians' Desk Reference*, the extensive *PubMed* resources, or the acclaimed *Public Library of Science (PLOS)* databases.

Another recent example of the evolution of reference services related to health and wellness is the seen in the Institute of Museum and Library Services' (IMLS) initiative "Health Happens at Libraries." This effort funds specialized training for reference staff in public libraries to keep them abreast of current resources and best practices as they respond to their community's need for reliable access to health information. With the rollout of the national Affordable Care Act in the United States, health information literacy for library staff and for patrons was determined to be a high priority and this project aims to address that.

THE EVOLUTION OF REFERENCE SERVICE

Up until the last decade of the 20th century, the mark of a superior reference librarian was a comprehensive, working familiarity with sources such as standard titles, their publishers, contents, scope, frequency of publication, and their counterparts on various free and fee-based databases. With the phenomenon of the World Wide Web and the continuing proliferation of electronic sources, this ability to "know it all" has changed significantly. Because of its very nature, the contents of the Web are limitless, highly dynamic, and defy memorization. Some reference books may have online editions similar to or the same as their print versions; some have interactive, continuously updated versions online; and some refuse to have a Web presence, remaining available in print form only. Information publishing has changed dramatically and will continue to move in new directions that may be beyond conventional wisdom.

The Modern Reference Desk

Despite an active industry watch against negative and demeaning stereotypes of librarians, the image of a stern, white, middle-aged, single female with glasses and dowdy clothing is a perennial one in the media. (One humorous rejoinder to that stereotype has been the popularity of The Librarian Action Figure plastic doll, which depicts a middle-aged librarian and is found on many a library reference countertop. While production is now discontinued, eager shoppers can find them at online auction sites!) In reality, library reference workers are a diverse, technologically savvy, and very people-oriented group.

Reference technicians and librarians typically staff a service desk where the tools of the trade consist of several formats. A dual monitor computer workstation with a Web-based library catalog and periodical databases, full Internet access, chat software, a fax or data modem, color printer, scanner, and e-mail, all networked to the local area network, is the centerpiece of the reference desk. Swivel-screen monitors allow for shared viewing of a search with patrons. A telephone, either desktop or mobile, remains an essential resource. Also, key ready reference print resources are often very close at hand with access to a larger reference collection of print materials in an adjacent area.

Surrounded by an ever-changing array of resources, reference librarians or technicians spend their workdays adeptly toggling back and forth between electronic tools and physically moving from computer workstations to patron's mobile devices to print resources or even historic runs of microforms as each question demands. Today's reference worker is equally at ease in the worlds of electronic and print information.

An ongoing challenge for the modern reference librarian is knowing which is more important in a given search, an Internet-based resource or a print source. An important factor is whether the library relies only on free online resources or has been able to purchase or subscribe to additional electronic resources beyond the free Web. Another variable is the issue of whether to purchase electronic versions of print resources; generally, electronic versions that are more sophisticated and with value-added search capabilities tend to be more expensive than their print counterparts. The majority of libraries are currently looking closely at past preferences for purchasing print versions of books based on cost savings. The enhanced value of electronic versions, the growth in distance education courses, and the increased demand by the public for 24/7 remotely-accessible, online library sources all are strong driving forces behind the re-evaluation of maintaining hard-copy editions of many former classic reference books.

One reference librarian, Tina Lau, recommends: "Sometimes, the Internet resource is all you have in a subject area unless you work at a very large library. The same criteria of authority, accuracy, objectivity, coverage, and timeliness apply to an Internet resource as to a print resource. One set of guidelines for evaluating webpages can be found at http://www.lib.berkeley.edu/Teaching Lib/Guides/Internet/Evaluate.html."

Although the reliance on electronic tools increases as we speak, computers do crash occasionally, and there are those days when power outages mean that library staff must rely solely on print sources in the library. Also, for those patrons still reluctant to use computer-based resources because of their age, disabilities, reticence, cultural reasons, or learning style preference, print tools may be their preferred medium.

No Question Too Trivial

Seasoned reference librarians and technicians attest that a major stimulus of the job is the wide spectrum of reference questions they encounter each day. During the course of one week in the authors' county, the following questions were asked at the local reference desks of public, academic, and special libraries:

I want to start a muffin company. Can you help me research the market for such a venture?

Do you have CliffsNotes for *Hamlet*?

Do you have a repair manual for a 1976 Ford Mustang?

My child is doing a report on Kwanzaa. What do you have?

I'm trying to find the original street names in our city's historic downtown area.

Where do I find current census data for the tri-counties, especially breakdowns by ethnicity?

I'm doing a stock market report and need the beta for Pepsi.

My term paper is on the history of sewers and water management systems on campus and in town. Where do I start?

Although an unusual or difficult request may be memorable because of the challenge it poses or because of its novelty, within each type of library or information center there are well-defined patterns to the reference questions asked; and some degree of predictability or recurrence can be expected for a certain percentage of the queries. For reference staff, it is this mix of the familiar and the exotic that keeps them on their toes.

Job Skills for Reference Service

What are the job skills needed to effectively perform reference services in a library, school media center, or information center? The following combination of communication skills, personal attributes, and technical competency are highly recommended for reference staff:

Interpersonal skills. With a high level of customer interaction in reference, it is essential to have strong people skills, enjoy public contact, and be approachable and patient.

Knowledge of information sources. Keeping current with print and electronic resources and keeping pace with their many rapidly changing formats and contents is critical. Staying aware of current events and breaking news, as well as trending topics relevant to your particular clientele is a must.

Perseverance. Searches often require sustained effort and creative thinking in the hunt for information.

Sense of curiosity. It may seem low tech, but a good reference librarian should enjoy playing detective and be motivated by the hunt for information, regardless of the specific query or subject or information format.

Ability to work as a team player. As one member of the library's reference team, most staff will likely work independently as well as with other staff. Collegiality in sharing information and search techniques, referring patrons, or in training reference desk assistants makes the job go more smoothly.

Training skills. Providing on-demand instruction for customers in the use of various print or technology-based tools is an important and ongoing task. The ability to do this in multiple mediums, in person or via e-mail or live chat, is now becoming a required skill for reference staff.

Verbal and written communication skills. Many patrons are researching sensitive topics and may be hesitant or unable to articulate their information requests clearly. An ability to deal sensitively with customers while ferreting out their needs is a must. This applies to in-person reference service as well as virtual interactions. An additional skill for the virtual medium is fast and accurate keyboarding.

Technologically adept. For today's library customers, receiving reference assistance in locating their desired information is often not the end of the transaction. Many may also need help manipulating, storing, printing, saving, or repackaging the source found. For reference staff, that means being adept with printers, smartphones, scanners, commonly used software/applications, and so on.

Evaluating Information

Along with instructing library customers and helping them locate data and manipulate it, reference librarians and technicians also assist them in evaluating the credibility and relevance of what they have found. This role is becoming increasingly more visible in the era of instantaneous electronic information and the easy access to self-publishing present via the Internet. Many industry leaders see this as the librarian's most significant role in the future. As with the old saying, "Just because it's in print, don't believe it," even more scrutiny must be applied to digital sources. Many of the traditional elements relied upon for evaluating a book—for example, a publisher's name and location or an author's credentials—may not be present on a website. The very act of publishing on the Web is accessible to anyone with no editing or review process required at all.

Wikipedia

Wiki software (derived from the Hawaiian word *wiki*, to hurry) allows the content on a website to be easily and quickly contributed and edited by any reader with editorial clearance, unlike pages marked-up with traditional html or xhtml. A well-known example of a wiki is found at the free "people's" encyclopedia Wikipedia, operated by the nonprofit Wikimedia Foundation. Founded in 2001, Wikipedia is free to access, multi-lingual and is now ubiquitous. Wikis have many uses, especially for collaborative writing, but in the case of Wikipedia it is often considered controversial as a reference tool or reliable academic resource because the content written is not necessarily submitted by expert sources.

Many reference librarians and professors have mixed feelings about using Wikipedia because of this lack of credibility and/or knowledge about the contributor; one commonsense approach is to avoid using it as a stand-alone source, instead using it in conjunction with another more traditionally edited, quality-controlled source. As Wikipedia has expanded, it also has placed more emphasis on attributing its encyclopedia entries with reference citations to document the data and provide readers with links to supporting sources. Among librarians and high school and college instructors you will often hear Wikipedia recommended as a "pre-search" or "pre-research" tool—that is, a place to begin your search to ascertain key information like the spelling of a term, geographical data, and other basic overview facts. Then, with that data in hand, proceed on to well-vetted sources in full-text newspaper and periodical databases; primary resources; sources with more transparency as to the authors, their credentials, expertise, etc.

Another interesting point about Wikipedia is that there have been many "locked" entries (submission or editing of content is blocked) due to purposeful submissions of false or inflammatory content. Entries for current political figures, celebrities, and controversial issues often become hot button topics and wiki editing may be disabled for a while until the debate subsides.

Primary and Secondary Sources

Another important distinction in assisting researchers to locate or evaluate information is whether the material is a primary or secondary source. Secondary source materials are probably most familiar to novice researchers and students. Compilations and summaries of information, such as encyclopedias, fact books, almanacs, and textbooks, are considered secondary sources. This is because the information is a generation or more removed from the original source; it may have been abridged, paraphrased, abstracted, critiqued, translated, or otherwise interpreted by various authors and editors. To those unfamiliar with a subject area, secondary sources can be easier to understand because another person has tried to place the material within a meaningful context.

In contrast, looking at a primary source enables researchers to study firsthand accounts and to draw their own conclusions from these original documents. Primary materials include original letters, diaries, maps, scientific studies, datasets, speeches, and photographs and are especially favored by historians, other scholars, and professional writers for study or perusal. Consider the difference between browsing George Washington's actual words and thoughts as conveyed in his personal letters compared with reading a summary of his point of view in a biographical account; studying an original, hand-drawn town site map versus reading a textual description of the location of an ancestor's property; consulting the actual data table in a scientific study versus reading a newspaper account or hearing a TV news sound bite summarizing it. Therefore, primary sources carry greater credibility than do secondary sources because people have not filtered their content.

Whether with print, multimedia, or electronic sources, or whether the sources are primary or secondary, reference staff guides users through the evaluation process. Questions to ask when evaluating information include the following:

Credibility:

Is it clear who is responsible for creation of the document? Is an author's name, a group name, or another sponsor credited on the document?

Can the credentials or authority of the author or publisher be clearly identified?

Is current contact information for the author or publisher provided?

Is the author affiliated with an established publisher, business, university, or other organization?

Does the URL of a website provide any clues as to the sponsoring group?

Is there a print or Web counterpart to the information at hand?

Is the information supported with a bibliography, works cited page, or footnotes?

Bias:

Can any political, philosophical, religious, or other bias to the information presented be detected?

Are all points of view presented on the topic, or only a single view?

Is the source trying to sell a product, idea, or service?

Currency:

Does the document have a date on it? Can one locate when it was published, posted, last updated, or created?

Does it seem that the information is updated regularly?

Appropriateness:

Does the information meet the customer's need?

Is the reading level appropriate for the customer?

Is the level of technical information appropriate?

Is the coverage or length adequate?

The Best Source for the Job at Hand

With the prevalence of personal computers and, especially, mobile devices at home, work, school, and in the library, many users (especially younger patrons) think that the Internet is the only tool available or the only source needed for all possible research. Patrons may also assume that the first computer they walk up to houses all the programs and tools that the library has to offer. This may or may not be the case.

These common scenarios reinforce the importance of another advisory role of the reference librarian: recommending the best tool for the research need at hand. The Web's wonderful explosion of access to information can also translate into a confusing welter of options for a library customer. Until recently, patrons frequently have asked: "Do I check the Web, the electronic card catalog, the library portal, the subscription databases, or just use Google?" As an information advisor, the reference librarian or technician is well equipped to direct a user to the best tool, which means time saved and a less frustrating research experience for the customer. With use of the more sophisticated "one search" and discovery tools becoming more commonplace with ILS and OPAC upgrades, libraries are finding less initial clarification needed by customers as they begin a search. But library patrons will still need guidance in interpreting the distinction between various types of resources as they are returned in one larger aggregated results list.

REFERENCE INTERVIEW

Step back for a moment and think of the all-too-common frustration level that you feel when you come away empty-handed or unsatisfied from a visit to a retail store, a municipal agency, a physician's office, or another service venue. With your information quest unsatisfied or perhaps only partially filled, you go away thinking, "They didn't give me any answers. That was a waste of time. I still don't have what I need." This can be the case for people who patronize a library or information center.

Reference librarians are not psychics. Thus, before they can advise customers on the best source or guide them in the use of tools, a crucial exchange must take place: the reference interview. This interview is a unique interaction between the reference librarian or technician and the library user. In many cases, the successful outcome of the user's visit to the library will be based on a careful reference interview. Often, this conversation determines not only where the answer can be found, but also what the specific question or need is. Respected library educator and author William Katz defined this interaction as a dialog "between the librarian with expert knowledge and the layperson in need of information."[4] Ideally, this dialog takes place before beginning a search, thus providing the librarian with key data for interpreting the question in terms of library resources.

Reference Interview Steps

The following outline delineates the typical sequence of a reference interview. This is not always a linear model; it may be necessary to return to the second step if no appropriate source is located. The model applies to walk-in and telephone reference requests as well as to virtual reference interactions.

1. *Initial question*: Customer poses query to reference librarian or staff.

2. *Clarification of the question*: Staff initiates a dialog to attempt to clarify the actual needs of the customer and to try to elicit more information, such as the level or format required, the amount of data needed, an applicable deadline, and so forth. This conversation between reference staff and the customer may be brief or it may continue throughout the search itself.

3. *Translating the question into potential library sources*: Library staff takes the lead by suggesting potential sources and finding out what has already been consulted before formulating a search strategy.

4. *The search*: The reference librarian or technician guides the patron through the search of appropriate sources. Simultaneously, they implement point-of-use instruction with each tool consulted so that the patron gains some knowledge for future independent searching.

5. *Follow up*: This is an important closing element that is often overlooked, but that is essential from a customer service point of view. As the search progresses, the librarian should query the patron, "Is this what you needed?" to be sure that the search is on track. As patrons are left to evaluate the located material on their own, reference staff should offer, "Let me know if you need more help." This leaves the door open for a renewed search or other additional help.

Categories of Reference Questions

When is a reference interview necessary? To answer this, it is first helpful to consider the types of questions reference librarians typically encounter. Although there are many methods for analyzing queries, the following all-purpose division devised by William Katz is logical.[5] This scheme classifies queries into four general categories: *directional, ready reference, specific search,* and *research*. With the ever-increasing dependence on computer use for delivery and access of information, a fifth category has since emerged that we will add to Katz's list and call *technical assistance*. Of course, as with any attempt to categorize things, not all reference questions will fit neatly into one of these five divisions, but may be hybrids of one or more categories. Additionally, there are the types of queries known as *readers' advisory service*—more common in public and K-12 libraries. It is sometimes considered another category of reference question, though it often has its own distinct interview.

Directional Category

These are straightforward questions that deal with location or existence of a service or resource. Typically, it is not necessary to spend time delving further than what is asked for. Staff knowledge of the building, services, and policies are sufficient to answer these queries. Examples of directional questions include the following:

"Where is the photocopy machine?"

"Do you have wireless Internet access here?"

"Where is the children's department?"

"Where do I get a library card?"

"Where is the printer for this computer?"

Ready Reference Category

Quick, single-fact queries, ready reference requests are reminiscent of questions from Trivial Pursuit® board games or TV quiz shows. They often deal with isolated statistics or facts that require verification and fact finding. To answer these queries, turn to online and print sources such as encyclopedias, almanacs, statistical compendiums, directories, dictionaries, as well as quick Web searches using regular or meta search engines. Google's definitions search, phone book search, and other features are very useful for many basic ready reference questions such as spelling look-ups, personal names, business names, phone numbers, and address listings. Some ready reference queries may require a reference interview for clarification. Examples of ready reference questions include the following:

"Which U.S. president was never married?"

"I need the Web address for the National Archives."

"I need the birth and death dates of Elvis Presley."

"How do you say good morning in Spanish?"

An example of a ready reference question in a reference interview is as follows:

Patron: I need the current population of New Jersey.
Staff: How current does the population figure need to be?
Patron: The most current available.
Staff: Do you need a total population, or breakdowns by county, sex, or ethnicity?

Specific Search Category

This is a more involved and time-consuming level of inquiry than the isolated fact finding required of ready reference questions. Gathering overview or background information may be the first step, followed by further delving into the subject. A patron may want to browse materials and read about a topic to become familiar with it, and then eventually refine the search further. Specific search queries require a reference interview to elicit facts and identify a direction for the search. Sources used may range widely from online or print encyclopedias at the start, to books, periodicals, government documents, and websites as the search progresses. Examples of specific search questions are as follows:

"What do you have on swimming pools?"

"I'm doing a term paper on Julia Morgan, the architect. Do you have information on her?"

"Do you have information about the history of the Ebola epidemic?"

"We need cultural guidelines for business travelers to Indonesia."

"I need everything there is on our competitor's new CEO."

Examples of specific search questions in a reference interview are as follows:

Patron: I need information on becoming a ranger.
Staff: What kind of information do you need? Do you need a job description or perhaps a job exam study book?
Patron: Hmm. Maybe both.
Staff: What type of ranger? Park ranger, forest ranger, Texas Ranger, or something else?

Research Category

Although the word *research* is often used quite loosely (e.g., "I want to research the phone number for this company"), it is used here to convey a sophisticated level of inquiry that implies in-depth study of a topic or issue. Research queries may require ongoing investigation, with multiple trips to the reference desk. They will probably entail using a variety of primary and secondary sources and may use interlibrary loan or document delivery services. Accessing very technical and fee-based databases may be appropriate. After in-house sources have been exhausted, referrals to other libraries, information centers, museums, or agencies will be needed. The research level of investigation is characterized by the synthesis and analysis of information, not merely the copying of it. A reference interview at this level could be fairly lengthy because the librarian will need to ascertain the topic, determine what previous research has been completed or sources consulted, figure out the technical level of information needed, and so on. Examples of research questions include the following:

"I'm studying the effects of sun exposure on skin cancer and need recent scientific studies about it."

"What are the latest theories on the disappearance of Amelia Earhart?"

"I'm writing a journal article on the medical uses of aromatherapy in the United States and in Europe."

Technical Assistance Category

This is a relatively new and ever-growing category of reference questions. The complexity or simplicity of answering or resolving such questions varies greatly. As with all other reference queries, technical assistance questions come from both patrons inside the library reading room and virtual patrons querying reference staff by telephone, e-mail, or e-reference. In some cases, a librarian might refer the more complicated technical questions to an on-site or remote Help Desk that is staffed specifically to deal with technical support. Examples are:

"How can I log on to the library databases from home?"

"Is there a mobile app for your library catalog?"

"How do I log on to Moodle?"

"I forgot my password; how do I get a new one?"

"How do I use your online interlibrary loan request form?"

"How do I print from this computer?"

"Can I use my flash drive in the library's computer?"

"How do I use the 3D printer?"

"How do I connect my laptop computer to your WiFi access?"

"Will my e-reader access the library's e-books?"

Readers' Advisory Service

Readers' advisory service is a term used mostly in relation to public libraries. This is where librarians or library staff respond to a patron's request such as, "I really enjoyed this mystery series. How can I find more good murder mysteries like this?"

By understanding publishing and reading trends, being familiar with their own library's collection, and utilizing the many reference books, online lists, and social media reader groups, the librarian will attempt to recommend in a nonjudgmental manner likely candidate titles and authors with similar appeal. A reader might be seeking recommendations within a genre (romance, mystery, westerns, graphic novels, Christian fiction, etc.) or for a particular age level (picture books, juvenile, young adult), or other niches. Much like asking the bookseller in a retail context for a recommendation, readers' advisory seeks to make a suitable match between reader and book. While it might refer to any category of book (or film), readers' advisory often centers on helping a customer discover fiction titles.

Today there are many sophisticated tools for aiding in book discovery such as the recommendation algorithm featured in websites such as Amazon.com, Netflix, and Goodreads. Based on a user's previous interactions on that site (purchases, viewings, posts, etc.) these sites offer suggestions of "top picks" or "best guesses" for that reader's next selection.

Many workshops, webinars, and textbooks are available for honing staff's readers' advisory skills; and outreach efforts for disseminating reader recommendations and book discovery are many. They include preparing and promoting lists or bibliographies of "like" readings for patrons; in-library displays featuring authors with similar appeal; structuring library-sponsored book discussions around a theme; using the library's Facebook page or Goodreads page to distribute customized lists for members.

Reference Interview Techniques

Practitioners can employ several straightforward techniques to help carry out successful reference interviews with customers. The following is a brief overview of these techniques. For more in-depth coverage, refer to works listed in the Resources section at the end of this chapter.

Open-Ended Questions

Whenever possible, ask an open-ended question to allow for more than a staccato yes or no answer. When you engage a customer in a dialogue, clues about their information needs should emerge to help carry out the search.

Patron: I want something for a paper on Shakespeare.
Staff: What kind of project are you working on?
Patron: It's a term paper on Hamlet.
Staff: How long does your paper need to be?
Patron: Ten pages with fifteen sources cited.
Staff: Where have you looked so far?

Asking the two-part question can be also helpful. For example:

Patron: I need something on Amelia Earhart.
Staff: Are you interested in her life story or in a particular flying record?

Active Listening

Whether on the job or in our personal lives, the art of listening is a skill that we often take for granted. Active listening takes a conscious effort, and, when used effectively, is a technique that can be vital to anyone staffing a service desk or involved with customer interaction. Active listening means paying close attention to a speaker's comments and hearing the speaker out, rather than jumping in or cutting the person off. In the interest of saving time, it is easy to feel compelled to second-guess a need and quickly recommend an appropriate source without fully hearing the query. An active listener resists that temptation.

Trained reference employees apply active listening to the reference interview by giving the patron full attention and maintaining eye contact. While directing the interview, they indicate their understanding by responding to the patron's explanation with nods and short "yes" and "OK" responses. Then it is useful to paraphrase the query back to the patron to ensure both parties that they are on the same wavelength.

Putting the Customer at Ease

Asking for assistance in a library setting is not something that everyone feels comfortable doing. Putting into play some basic tenets of good customer service can help alleviate some of that discomfort. When staff present a friendly, informal, yet businesslike demeanor, people sense that library staff are there to help them. This same combination of friendliness and efficiency has been cited as being helpful in successful virtual reference exchanges as well. Moving out from behind the reference service counter and walking to the computers or stacks with the patron removes the physical barrier of a desk or counter. The increasing use of large, thin computer screens with swivel capability also decreases barriers and facilitates the sharing of search results between librarian and patron. Keeping the reference desk clear and free from clutter also sends the message that staff are available and not otherwise distracted. Many reference librarians and technicians wear name tags indicating their job title and company logo while on duty. This encourages customers to approach them, instead of a student aide, volunteer, or other library staff not specially trained in reference assistance.

Nonverbal behavior, or body language, also plays an important part in putting the customer at ease. A pleasant, even tone of voice, not too loud or condescending, is optimal. A patient and courteous manner is much more welcoming than an abrupt, easily annoyed demeanor. Unconscious gestures such as placing hands on the hips or folding the arms can be interpreted as negative, aggressive gestures. Prefer a neutral stance, with both hands to the side or placed behind the back in the "actor's grip."

Maintaining eye contact is an important cue that expresses interest and a willingness to assist. In contrast, averting eye contact with a customer conveys the distinct feelings of inattention or boredom. When a staff member and a patron are at different levels, making eye contact can be difficult—for example, when the staff member is seated at a desk and a customer is standing, or, conversely, when a staff member walks up to assist a wheelchair patron or a customer seated at a computer. Computer screens themselves, though indispensable, can also present a barrier to eye contact. Instead of directly communicating with one another, all eyes are on the monitor. Selecting counter height reference desks and computer tables is one method of putting both parties on the same eye level.

Being aware of cross-cultural differences is of growing importance as the library-using community increases in diversity. Issues such as personal space, reluctance to approach strangers for help, reluctance to make eye contact with a perceived authority figure, and other cultural customs or behaviors can prevent direct communication. Some libraries with distinctive ethic populations provide cultural sensitivity training to staff as a means of breaking down such barriers.

Burnout is a problem in any public contact job. At a busy reference desk it is important to schedule staff for shifts that reduce the chance for burnout. Usually two hours without a break or without a variety of other tasks is about the longest most staff can maintain the highest level of service orientation.

Occasionally, longer shifts may be tolerable, but, over the long haul, prolonged shifts lead to stressed staff members and less than optimal service. Many libraries offer their virtual reference as part of a geographically dispersed consortium in order to share coverage of evening, night, and weekend service hours. Digital reference shift patterns and problem areas are still emerging, but issues such as repetitive use syndrome and patron rudeness to reference staff in the (anonymous) virtual environment have been identified to date. Potential for burnout also applies here as well.

Learning the Reference Interview

One of the best methods for novices to learn the ins and outs of the interview process is to observe reference librarians in action. If possible, shadowing, or following the librarian-patron interaction from the initial query to the completion of the search, is particularly helpful. Afterwards, discussing the search strategy chosen and its pitfalls or successes will reinforce the actions observed. Shadowing more than one staff person is especially valuable because each individual has a unique approach. Role playing in a classroom or workshop situation and viewing training videos or YouTube tutorials are other effective instructional methods.

Several Library/Information Technology student interns from the authors' college were recently based in academic library reference departments for fieldwork and spent their initial days shadowing seasoned staff interacting with students. Their comments on reference training bears out the effectiveness of this method:

- "The concept of the reference interview is becoming clearer as the students come in with their questions. Even a simple directional question, such as 'Where are the current periodicals?' may need some clarification."

- "It's interesting to see the different approaches each librarian takes to a search and what their favorite databases and search engines are."

- "While covering reference [with the college librarian], I found out how much I enjoy helping people narrow down their huge, expansive topics. They often start with something completely unmanageable."

- "I am feeling more and more comfortable in assisting students with their search needs. I get started by conducting the Reference Interview, get them started on Polycat or appropriate databases and then seek further assistance, if necessary."

- "These [business] questions are once again a reminder that it is vital and time-saving if you can query the student and qualify their exact needs. One student started out wanting to know information about 'the restaurant business in California.' As it turned out, he needed the numbers of wine and beer licenses issued in California."

Reference Service Policies

Clear-cut policies for reference services are essential to good customer service. Among the policy issues to consider are the level of staff (professional or paraprofessional or both) that will answer reference requests; which format of inquiry has priority (e.g., walk in, e-mail, telephone, fax, and, when conducted by in-house reference staff, virtual); and what time limitations, if any, are imposed per individual question. As with all policies, these issues should be re-evaluated as reference tools, habits, and customer preferences change. Traditionally, in most publicly accessed libraries, walk-in customers receive first priority over telephone or other electronic requests. Perhaps in the future, e-mail requests will be of such volume that they take priority over walk-in traffic. In that case, staffing patterns and service policies would need to be adjusted accordingly for a new customer preference.

REFERENCE: ART OR SCIENCE?

Is good reference work an art or a science? Actually, it is a combination of both. Certain core elements are present in any successful reference transaction. Success is based on a skillful reference interview combined with an efficient and appropriate matching of the customer's needs with available or attainable information sources.

The science of reference is in the ability to understand and characterize an inquiry by subject category and amount and type of information sought. For example, does the patron's request regard sociology or social work, social policy, or religious teaching? Does the person want a definition, an overview, a list of sources, everything on the topic, or only one specific fact? The right referral might be to a dictionary of social work or a religious encyclopedia, a specialized bibliography, or a website.

The art of reference is in the conduct of the interview. Personal style that is comfortable for the interviewer is important. The other end of the process, recommendation of a source, is also an art based on the experience of the staff member. There really is not a single right way to do it. That is why even very experienced reference staff like to observe other staff members. Each person develops pet information sources that work well for him or her. They may also specialize by subject areas and personal interests. It is not a sign of weakness to turn to another staff member for collaboration in the process of trying to answer a patron's query. In fact, it is a sign of confidence and maturity. No staff member can know everything about every subject.

REFERENCE REALITY CHECK AND THE FUTURE

Of course, quality reference service is always dependent on adequate staffing and funding. Expectations of service must be adjusted when these resource levels are not optimal. For example, with limited numbers of workers, reference staff may be too busy to return to on-site patrons for follow-up assistance or may be able to offer chat reference only during selected hours (not the full 24/7). If that is the case, staff should use common sense shortcuts where possible: get patrons started on their searches and recommend that they check back if they need more help or find a staff member if they need further assistance. Another technique is batching reference requests. For example, a staff member shows two or three people at once how to use the library OPAC. For chat lines, the use of pre-scripted answers for commonly asked questions can help with speedy and timely replies.

In understaffed libraries, strong emphasis needs to be placed on the goal of teaching patrons how to be more self-sufficient in their library skills. The use of trained library science or library technology interns, docents, or other seasoned volunteers should be considered to augment permanent staff where appropriate.

Especially in facilities that are open to the general public, problem patrons are a daily reality of life. Problem patrons require patience and special attention whether they are the homeless, lonely seniors, people with mental illness, latch-key children, or other populations. Here again, staff training is commonplace to prepare and educate library workers in techniques for diffusing difficult, awkward, or potentially violent situations. Information centers and libraries often develop policies specifically to deal with recurring problem-patron issues. Having security staff on-site and cultivating a good rapport with the local police are also common approaches.

With the percentage of Americans who use a library's website increasing (as documented in a recent major study conducted by the respected Pew Research Center's Internet & American Life Project)[6] it makes sense that the likelihood increases for patrons to also avail themselves of virtual reference or chat services more often. Some industry watchers feel that the steady decline in the volume of telephone reference calls coincides with an organic shift to the usage of virtual reference options—especially for easily answered queries about hours, access, logins, policies, and services. Just as consumers now expect chat lines for help with online retail purchases or other Web businesses, and as people in the workplace continue to shift more business communication to electronic rather than direct phone conversations, library patrons, too, are making that shift over to virtual reference.

Transforming Library Spaces

As overall usage of hard copy reference book collections has been declining with the ever-increasing shift to virtual reference sources, e-books, and web resources, the decision of how to make the best use of this newly available floor space in libraries has been undergoing discussion and action. Changes in the publishing world and society in general all add to this challenge for library planners to serve their communities in fresh ways.

As Librarian Wright Rix of Santa Monica Public Library, in southern California and always a trending library, put it in 2009: "Trimming collections is always a sobering task, but one that also presents several opportunities and choices. After dusty volumes are removed, what to do with the newly free space?"[7]

Additionally, the trend of consolidating service desks within a smaller library or on a given floor or level of a larger library facility is regaining popularity. The authors regularly receive listserv posts seeking advice on making this consolidation. The single point-of-service model can reduce staffing, costs, and free up floor space—as long as it does not negatively impact the quality of service. Space freed up by consolidating service desks can be repurposed for creative or more in-demand uses (e.g., makerspaces, art exhibits, computer labs/stations). A shared-service-desk model might mean combining circulation and reference points; another example might be merging a children's desk with adult reference or a tech help counter with general reference.

Thus there are several emerging trends—all of which foster creativity, learning and sharing in the repurposed space. While personnel at many libraries have already started to implement these innovations, time will tell just how varied the re-invention of stack areas and floor spaces will be.

Flexible, Multi-Purpose Areas

Whether it is live sessions at the annual Internet Librarian or ALA conferences, virtual continuing education workshops, or graduate courses in library science, innovative ideas for remaking library space is a hotly discussed topic.

The names for these new spaces may range from Makerspace, Hackerspace, Learning Commons, Media Lab, Library Arts Center, to Science Café; but the concepts have a lot in common. Emphasis is on flexible, multi-purpose spaces that promote exposure to new technologies, collaborative learning, and creation.

These multi-functional spaces housed inside a library facility accentuate community partnerships and involvement. The concept thrives on collaboration between town and gown, academia and private industry, public agencies and local businesses, library staff and local artists/creators/experts. Spaces may be venues for academic or cultural use, as well as formal and informal meetings and workshops. Hands-on learning, creating, and "making" are possible with computers and other technology including touchable interfaces, 3D printers, on-demand book printing kiosks, sewing machines, and other tools. The makerspace may also include an adjacent café or coffee bar, showing a newer tolerance for allowing limited food/drinks inside library buildings.

One high profile example of such a creative space is the Digital Commons and Dream Lab found at the Martin Luther King Jr. Memorial Library, the downtown branch of the Washington, DC Public Library. Part of a recent major remodel project and funded in part by IMLS funds, this space is part computer lab, innovative design space, and tech classroom.[8]

Another instance of an exciting and ambitious project is the new 21st Century Library facility in Colorado's Pikes Peak Library District. Tagged "Library 21c," it showcases the community's vision of a forward-looking regional public library. In addition to core services of books, DVDs, and e-books, it features a computer commons area, video production and editing equipment, 3D printers, sewing machines, video conferencing rooms, and other free public workspaces. By purchasing a building, then renovating it to desired specifications, the library district has designed a customized environment emphasizing creative spaces, community engagement, and lifelong learning for all ages.[9]

As the makerspace movement grows in numbers and variety in the library world, more attention is being paid to the legal considerations that go hand in hand with these creative partnerships on library premises. Issues of liability, awareness of copyright and trademark infringements, appropriate signage on scanners, waivers for use of heavy equipment, and permission-to-use forms all need to be considered by the host library or agency. Webinars and conference sessions on these topics abound and can provide a helpful overview to those embarking on makerspace projects.

Exhibiting Art in the Library

Featuring art in a library facility is not a new concept, but it is certainly undergoing a rebirth and morphing into more sophisticated interpretations than past practices. With the advent of a new energy that showcases libraries as community and cultural centers, there are many examples of spaces formerly used for book storage that are being repurposed to feature artwork. Especially since the widespread decrease of reference book stacks, square footage is freed up for new uses that expand the concept of the cultural experience a library has to offer beyond books.

Traditionally, college and university libraries as well as public libraries could be counted on to squeeze rotating exhibits of student art projects, works by local artists, traveling exhibits, mixed media crafts, and other displays into available lobby space, entrance areas, hallways, and multi-purpose program rooms. Community rooms that by morning housed toddlers' story hour or staff meetings were booked on weekends and evenings for poetry readings, small musical events, and club meetings.

A growing recent trend is to have art of all types (e.g., larger-scale installation art, faculty and art student paintings and sculpture, children's art, original public art commissioned for a new building) integrated into a facility's space. As libraries are remodeled, expanded, repurposed and for those with the fortunate opportunity to construct a new facility such as the Central Library in San Diego, California, dedicated space for displaying art is becoming more commonplace. Just as retail spaces, restaurants, offices often serve as adjunct galleries for the exhibit of paintings and other artwork in a community, librarians at facilities of all sizes can encourage and formally recruit displays that provide visual interest and encourage artistic awareness. As a library information/technology student exclaimed to one of the authors after a family visit to the architecturally notable Seattle Public Library: "It's great there are so many public libraries that are remodeling their spaces for the 21st Century!"

In addition to beautifying the space, this movement inspires minds, showcases local and regional talent, and creates an engaging collaboration with the larger community. In terms of the impact on library personnel, staff's tasks can now be found to include the recruiting of artist submissions, reviewing of proposals, working with exhibitors, compiling policy statements, crafting press releases, and dealing with insurance/liability issues. For an example of one public library system's exhibits policy and agreement, see: http://friends ofheatascaderolibrary.org/documents/artpolicy.pdf.

As for the future, reference service in libraries and information centers will continue to be very visible, and staff will continue to have high levels of inter-action with customers, though more may be in a virtual setting rather than primarily face to face. The anticipated ongoing growth in distance education courses and training, with its anytime/anyplace philosophy and capability, is already impacting existing reference service traditions. And the concept of focusing reference service on users who live within a local political or geo-graphical funding area may also be challenged with the growth in electronic communication and research where traditional physical boundaries are overlooked.

STUDY QUESTIONS

1. Do you use the reference department of your local public library? Why or why not? If yes, did you visit the reference librarian in person or use their virtual help desk? How would you characterize the service you received?

2. As a student, do you use the reference department of your college library? How does it compare to the local public library? What kind of a reputation does it have among students on campus? Do they have a 24/7 virtual help desk or e-mail reference service for students?

3. Is it important to offer reference services 24/7? Why or why not? How do libraries work cooperatively to make this happen?

4. To see firsthand how a typical reference department operates, visit the reference department of a large, local library, preferably a university, college, or central public library. Spend about 30 minutes to an hour observing the reference desk operation. Summarize your observations in a one- to two-page report. Some things to discuss in your summary include the following: the number of personnel staffing the desk, the physical layout, the amount and type of customer activity, print and electronic reference materials on hand at the desk, number of computer stations, and the proximity to larger reference collections in the library. Do staff offer virtual or e-mail reference services? If possible, note sample questions asked by patrons during your visit.

5. Nonverbal communication plays a subtle but important role in the reference interview. List five positive nonverbal cues that are helpful to exhibit when working the reference desk (in person).

6. What approach would you suggest for dealing with a patron who repeatedly poses reference queries that perplex the librarian?

7. Is there an archives or special collections department in your college library or hometown? If so, visit it and observe the level of reference

service provided. How does it differ from the general information desk in your college library?

8. Have you attended art showings or viewed art exhibits that were on display in your local library? What was your impression of the experience?

NOTES

1. Kathryn Zickuhr, Lee Rainie, Kristen Purcell, and Maeve Duggan, "How Americans Value Public Libraries in Their Communities," *Pew Research Center*, December 2013, accessed January 26, 2015, http://libraries.pewinternet.org/2013/12/11/libraries-in-communities/.
2. Kathryn Zickuhr, Lee Rainie, and Kristen Purcell, "Library Services in the Digital Age," *Pew Research Center*, January 22, 2013, 40, accessed January 26, 2015, http://libraries.pewinternet.org/2013/01/22/Library-services/.
3. Nicole Fawcett, "Patients Need Help Finding Medical Information, U-M Study Finds: Librarians Provided New Information, Resources for 95 Percent of Patients," *University of Michigan Health System Press Release*, May 22, 2006, accessed February 1, 2015, http://www.med.umich.edu/opm/newspage/2006/healthinfo.htm.
4. William A. Katz, *Introduction to Reference Work, Vol. II: Reference Services and Reference Processes*, 8th ed. (New York: McGraw-Hill, 2002), 125.
5. William A. Katz, *Introduction to Reference Work, Vol. I: Basic Information Services*, 8th ed. (New York: McGraw-Hill, 2002), 16–19.
6. Kathryn Zickuhr and Lee Rainie, "Younger Americans and Public Libraries: How Those Under 30 Engage with Libraries and Think about Libraries' Role in Their Lives and Communities," *Pew Research Center*, September 10, 2014, accessed January 26, 2015. http://www.pewinternet.org/2014/09/10/younger-americans-and-public-libraries/.
7. Wright Rix, "Reference Collections and Staff: Retaining Relevance." *The Reference Librarian* 50, no. 3 (2009): 302–505.
8. "Digital Commons: About Us," *District of Columbia Public Library*, accessed February 1, 2015, http://dclibrary.org/digitalcommons/about.
9. Robin Intemann, "Library of Future Ready to Open in Colorado Springs," *The Gazette* (Colorado Springs, CO), May 25, 2014, accessed February 1, 2015, http://gazette.com/library-of-future-ready-to-open-in-colorado-springs/article/1520530#p4IwkAfZm6KBHLeQ.99.

RESOURCES

Books and Articles

Bielskas, Amanda and Kathleen M. Dreyer. *IM and SMS Reference Services for Libraries: THE TECH SET® #19*. Chicago: ALA Neal-Schuman, 2012.

Bopp, Richard E. and Linda C. Smith, eds. *Reference and Information Services: An Introduction*. 4th ed. Santa Barbara, CA: Libraries Unlimited, 2011.

Breitbach, William. "Your Guide to Meebo Options: Libraries That Are Looking for New Virtual Reference Services Have Some Nice, Affordable Options to Select

From." *Computers in Libraries*, October 2012. http://www.infotoday.com/cil mag/oct12/Breitbach—Your-Guide-to-Meebo-Options.shtml. (accessed February 1, 2015)

Carlson, Scott. "Are Reference Desks Dying Out?" *The Chronicle of Higher Education*, April 20, 2007: A37.

Cassell, Kay Ann and Uma Hiremath. *Reference and Information Services in the 21st Century: An Introduction*. 2nd rev. ed. Chicago: Neal-Schuman Publishers, 2011.

Cirasella, Jill. "You and Me and Google Makes Three: Welcoming Google into the Reference Interview." *Library Philosophy and Practice* (e-journal). Paper 122. (2007), http://digitalcommons.unl.edu/libphilprac/122/. (accessed February 1, 2015)

Farkas, Meredith G. *Social Software in Libraries: Building Collaboration, Communication, and Community Online*. Medford, NJ: Information Today, 2007.

Head, Alison and John Wihbey. "At Sea in a Deluge of Data." *The Chronicle of Higher Education*, July 7, 2014. http://chronicle.com/article/At-Sea-in-a-Deluge-of-Data/147477/. (accessed February 1, 2015)

Hysell, Shannon Graff, ed. *Recommended Reference Books for Small and Medium-Sized Libraries and Media Centers*, Santa Barbara, CA. Libraries Unlimited, 2013.

Knoer, Susan. *The Reference Interview Today*. Santa Barbara, CA: Libraries Unlimited, 2011.

Kovacs, Diane Kaye. *The Virtual Reference Handbook: Interview and Information Delivery Techniques for the Chat and E-Mail Environments*. New York: Neal-Schuman Publishers, Inc., 2007.

Lankes, R. David, and Philip Nast. *Virtual Reference Service: From Competencies to Assessment*. New York: Neal-Schuman Publishers, 2008.

Lindbloom, Mary-Carol et al. "Virtual Reference: A Reference Question Is a Reference Question . . . Or Is Virtual Reference a New Reality? New Career Opportunities for Librarians." *Reference Librarian* 45, no. 93 (2006): 3–22.

Poparad, Christa E. "Staffing an Information Desk for Maximum Responsiveness and Effectiveness in Meeting Research and Computing Needs in an Academic Library." *Reference Librarian* 56, no. 2 (2015): 83–92.

Ross, Catherine Sheldrick, Kirsti Nilsen, and Marie L. Radford. *Conducting the Reference Interview: A How-To-Do-It Manual for Librarians*. 2nd ed. Chicago: ALA Neal-Schuman, 2009.

Schmidt, Aaron and Michael Stephens. "IM me." *Library Journal*, April 2005: 34–35.

Thomsett-Scott, Beth C., ed. *Implementing Virtual Reference Services: A LITA Guide*. Chicago: ALA TechSource, 2013.

Zabel, Diane, ed. *Reference Reborn: Breathing New Life into Public Services Librarianship*. Santa Barbara, CA: Libraries Unlimited, 2010.

Film

Best Practices in Virtual Reference Panel. *Way Sweet or Just Wrong: Users and Librarians Reveal Critical Factors for Virtual Reference Service Excellence*. (87 minutes) Chicago, IL: ALA Annual Conference, 2009. http://player.multi castmedia.com/player.php?p=g9674k0g. (accessed February 1, 2015)

Conducting the Reference Interview. (29 minutes) Towson, MD: Library Video Network, 2004. DVD.

Quick Tips for Successful Virtual Reference. (6 minutes) Tampa, FL: Tampa Bay Library Consortium Continuing Education Training Videos, 2013. http://www.youtube.com/watch?v=pJMSDzv5WEE. (accessed February 1, 2015)

Websites

American Library Association. "Readers' Advisory 101: Reference and Users Services Association (RUSA) Course." March 2014.
http://www.ala.org/rusa/development/readersadvisory101
(accessed February 1, 2015)
Online course provides an introduction to readers' advisory; target audience is librarian technicians and new-hire reference librarians.
American Library Association, *Guide to Reference*: Essentials Webinar/Archive
http://www.guidetoreference.org/
(accessed April 1, 2015)
Guide to Reference is a subscription-based database of 16,000 entries describing essential print and Web reference sources. A current subscription is required to access the dynamic database, but the *Guide to Reference* Essentials webinars are free and open to everyone. Follow the links to the archived slides and video from these helpful presentations. Effective as staff training tool, in collection development, and for LIBT or LIS curriculum.
Answerland. "Oregon Virtual Reference Summit." May 2014.
https://www.answerland.org/2014-oregon-virtual-reference-summit
(accessed February 1, 2015)
Oregon's initiative for statewide online reference service is called "Answerland." They sponsor an annual one-day conference focusing on reference, service, and technology. Open to all skill levels, library types, and experiences. Provides an opportunity to network with virtual reference staff.
OCLC WebJunction.org. "Readers Advisory." 2015.
http://webjunction.org/explore-topics/readers-advisory.html
(accessed February 1, 2015)
Portal page from WebJunction—"the learning place for libraries"—serves as a tutorial on readers' advisory. Links to current news articles, webinars, recommended websites on this topic.
OCLC WebJunction.org. "Reference." 2015.
http://www.webjunction.org/explore-topics/reference.html
(accessed February 1, 2015)
Links to current news articles, webinars, recommended websites on this ever-evolving topic with emphasis on virtual or digital reference innovations.
Ohio Library Council. "ORE Module Two: Readers' Advisory, Web Based Training for Reference Services." June 2008.
http://www.olc.org/ore/2readers.htm
(accessed February 1, 2015)
Succinct overview of skills and interview techniques for implementing readers' advisory service with library patrons. Material adapted from MORE (Minnesota Opportunities for Reference Excellence), 2003.
Pearl, Nancy. "The Official Website of Nancy Pearl."
http://www.nancypearl.com/
(accessed February 1, 2015)
Formal Seattle Public Library librarian Nancy Pearl is the diva of book groups, shared reading, and recommended titles. Website continues the discussions about her recommended lists as found in her various compilations of works beginning with *Book Lust* (2003).

Sullivan, Danny. Editor. "Search Engine Watch." 23 April 2014.
http://searchenginewatch.com/
(accessed February 1, 2015)
Since the early days of the Web (1997), SEW has continued to provide a wealth of news, analysis, and discussion about the search engines we all rely on. While today's site focuses heavily on marketing and optimization trends, it is still a great place for librarians and researchers to keep up on search engine trends, redesign, ownership. Look for overview articles on the status of major search engines. Constantly updated.

Chapter 8

Ethics in the Information Age

Ethics apply to all aspects of our lives. This chapter addresses ethical issues and dilemmas regarding access to information in library settings. For decades, librarians have been in the forefront of ethical issues related to information access and management, including intellectual freedom, censorship, user privacy, and adhering to intellectual property laws. The ease with which digital information is shared has amplified these long-standing issues. As philosophy professor Hans Jonas wrote in *The Imperative of Responsibility*, "[M]odern technology has introduced actions of such novel scale, objects, and consequences, that the framework of former ethics can no longer contain them."[1]

Opinions differ as to what constitutes ethics, both in theory and application. Many equate law with ethics. Law and ethics are not *un*related. However, if they were always the same, there would be no reason to study ethics. In many cases, the law is merely society's attempt to codify elements of ethical beliefs. Ethics may also demand a higher standard than the law. At other times ethical beliefs have caused individuals to break the law. Examples include the nonviolent civil disobedience campaigns led in India by Mahatma Gandhi and in the United States by Dr. Martin Luther King, Jr., and environmental protests by Greenpeace and others.

Lawrence Lessig, lawyer and founder of the Stanford Law School's Center for Internet and Society, is one of the most influential thinkers on ethical issues related to cyberspace. Lessig sees laws as only one method, and not necessarily the most effective one, influencing how individual behavior is regulated online. His model includes the following forces shaping our actions:

- Laws
- Social norms

- Market forces
- Architecture (technology infrastructure)

Of these, *laws* are self-explanatory. *Social norms,* as Lessig uses the term, refer to the ways communities modify individual behavior. *Market forces* include all the economic activities that stimulate or hinder human activity. *Architecture* refers to the ways technology, such as coded software, helps or hinders online activity. Each factor may be based on ethical values, but none are synonymous with ethics.[2]

What then are the governing principles that should guide library workers in the digital environment? Activities that enable or constrain the flow of information are the most important defining concerns of those in the library field. Ethical values within the library community are often discussed within the context of increasing or impeding access to information. Some values, such as intellectual freedom and freedom of information are generally values that increase access to information. Other values, such as the right to privacy, the right to intellectual property, and the need to protect children tend to restrict information.

Most information workers would enthusiastically embrace each of these rights in the abstract. In practice, however, as the "Code of Ethics of the American Library Association" (Appendix C) notes, "Ethical dilemmas occur when values are in conflict."[3] What is the relationship between ethics and behavior? One theory is that individual ethics are most clearly defined when no one is watching. Library workers may be called upon to overlay their personal ethics with both the values adopted by the library profession and the library's written policies.

Each person considering ethical issues must decide whether there are absolute ethical principles that can be applied universally, or whether situational ethics make the answer vary from one setting to another. Are there some absolutes upon which we all can agree? Is it possible that two people both trying to do the ethical thing will adopt very different courses of action? In applied ethics, often it is necessary to decide what RIGHT is and what WRONG is. However, the real tension comes in situations where two or more RIGHT concepts appear to be in conflict.

ETHICS IN CYBERSPACE

Ethics can be considered to be professional standards of conduct. When individuals take actions in cyberspace, certain common courtesies have come to be expected. One such list can be found in "The Core Rules of Netiquette."[4] While these rules form a good foundation for appropriate behavior in cyberspace, often issues are more complex for library workers.

Within the context of this chapter, many of the situations we will be considering place us in greater roles than that of one private individual relating to another. These additional roles include:

- Professionals relating to library users
- Employees relating to fellow employees

- Supervisors relating to subordinates
- Agents of the government

Although we may not often think of ourselves as such, most library employees are agents of the government because we work in tax-supported public institutions. Many concepts, such as justice, truth, honesty, and morality apply, whether we are considering individual-to-individual interaction or workplace transactions. Within the workplace, additional concepts such as informed decisions and client confidentiality come into play.

INFORMATION IS POWER

Information is power. So the questions become who has the power and who controls the information? In a democracy, the citizens, individually and collectively, are assumed to be in control. In a totalitarian state, the government is in control, in part because it controls the flow of information.

In the 21st century, information is fluid. Think of information as being able to flow from one location to another, or from one person to another. Some factors encourage and enable this flow; others impede it. Many of the dilemmas in this chapter are based on whether concerns of the state or individual citizens control the flow of information.

For our purposes, assume that the players are divided into three categories, much like three sides of a triangle:

- Individuals
- Corporations
- Governments

Each of these players impedes or encourages the flow of information, affecting the other two players. Each of the three groups asserts that they have certain rights. Any one of these three groups can enhance its rights, but usually at the expense of one or both of the other groups of players.

If information is power, then power is freedom. The freedom or power to act in the self-interest of any of these three groups is constrained or counterbalanced by the freedom or power to act possessed by the other two entities. For example, as the power of government increases, the freedom of corporations and/or of individuals decreases. The FBI crackdown on the protest group Occupy Wall Street is an example of government increasing its power by restricting individual freedom of expression. The USA PATRIOT Act is another example of government increasing its power by restricting privacy of individuals, through records searches and surveillance of citizens.

Where should the balance point of freedom be located within the triangle above? Each of us may arrive at a different answer to this question. However, each of the groups can make compelling arguments as to why their power needs to be increased, usually rationalizing it as being in the interest of all of us. However, that power can only be increased if the other groups give up some freedom.

THE CONFLICT OF RIGHTS

The conflict of ownership of information can best be understood by an examination of various rights that are often claimed by one or more of the players. In this chapter, the following issues related to rights are discussed:

- Access to information
- Keeping information private
- Intellectual property rights
- Surveillance of citizens

When one of these rights is emphasized, other rights are affected. For example, the impact of the events of September 11, 2001, resulted in new surveillance programs, which diminished individuals' right to privacy.

The French philosopher Émile Chartier once stated, "Nothing is more dangerous than an idea, when it's the only one we have."[5] This is particularly true with decisions about ethical behavior in the Information Age. Those who try to define behavior from the perspective of only one right are doing all of us a disservice. In doing so, they often discredit their own point of view by pushing a single-theme agenda well beyond the point where it can be considered to be credible.

INTELLECTUAL FREEDOM

Individual freedom to access information is essential to the effective functioning of a democratic society. Libraries and the Internet are key institutions that provide individuals with access to the vast array of information they need to function as citizens. These institutions also have the potential to be powerful agents in a capitalist economy. Both have the potential to deliver power to citizens by providing them with the information they need to control their lives.

By contrast, Chinese, North Korean, and Middle Eastern citizens are restricted by their governments from access to reading materials and to the Internet, particularly on specific topics. Influential technologists Eric Schmidt and Jared Cohen have warned against a "Balkanization of the Internet." Nations censoring or filtering information "would transform what was once the global Internet into a connected series of nation-state networks. The Web would fracture and fragment, and soon there would be a 'Russian Internet' and an 'American Internet' and so on, all coexisting and sometimes overlapping but, in important ways, separate. Information would largely flow within countries but not across them."[6]

Library workers have both the opportunity and the responsibility to protect democratic rights by ensuring access to information, so that citizens are able to make informed decisions about their lives. The oath taken by all new citizens, members of the armed services, and holders of federal office include the words, "I will support and defend the Constitution and laws of the United

States of America against all enemies, foreign and domestic." Although no one has suggested an oath of office for library workers, we find ourselves consistently defending the right of citizens to access the information they need to freely exercise their Constitutional rights.

First Amendment

The First Amendment to the U.S. Constitution is actually only one sentence long. The germane part consists of only 10 words—the following two phrases in bold:

Congress shall make no law respecting an establishment of religion, or prohibiting the free exercise thereof; or **abridging the freedom of speech,** or of the press; or the right of the people peaceably to assemble, and to petition the government for a redress of grievances.

From this brief statement has grown a set of laws, court decisions, and practices that have shaped the development of our country. The American Civil Liberties Union (ACLU) is a national nonprofit organization that opposes regulation of any form of speech. The organization defends the rights of all citizens to express their views, even if the ACLU disagrees with the content of the expression and even finds that expression distasteful. The organization states:

Freedom of speech, of the press, of association, of assembly and petition— this set of guarantees, protected by the First Amendment, comprises what we refer to as freedom of expression. The Supreme Court has written that this freedom is "the matrix, the indispensable condition of nearly every other form of freedom." Without it, other fundamental rights, like the right to vote, would wither and die.[7]

In spite of the First Amendment's prime position in our constitutional hierarchy, the nation's commitment to freedom of expression has been tested over and over again. Especially during times of national crisis, such as war abroad or social upheaval at home, people exercising their First Amendment rights have been censored, fined, even jailed. Those with unpopular political ideas have always borne the brunt of government repression. During World War I, a U.S. citizen could be jailed just for giving out anti-war leaflets. Out of those early cases, modern First Amendment law evolved. Many struggles and many cases later, ours is the most speech-protective country in the world.

Free speech rights still need constant, vigilant protection. New questions arise and old ones return. Should flag burning be a crime? How do we protect children from exploitation or predation on the Internet? What about government or private censorship of works of art relating to sensitive subjects like religion or sexuality? Should the Internet be subject to any form of governmental or corporate control? How do we deal with those who espouse racist, sexist, or other offensive opinions? In answering these questions, the history and the core values of the First Amendment must be our guide.

Libraries and the First Amendment

Various policy statements and guidelines of the American Library Association (ALA) are the result of careful deliberation on the part of the library profession and are quoted or referred to in this section. It is important to note that these policies have no legal standing and individual libraries are not required to follow them. Library or school boards, city councils, academic committees, and corporate executive committees set policy for various individual libraries; it is at this level that decisions are made about which ALA policies are used, adopted, revised, or even ignored.

The first clause of ALA's "Code of Ethics" (see Appendix C) states:

I. We provide the highest level of service to all library users through appropriate and usefully organized resources; equitable service policies; equitable access; and accurate, unbiased, and courteous responses to all requests.

To adhere to this first ethical guideline, information must be available to those who are citizens or striving to become citizens. Tax-supported libraries bear a particular burden to ensure that all library users are treated similarly, and that everyone has access to the same information resources and services. No single patron should be treated as being more important than another. The defining ethic for librarians and library workers is the obligation to provide information to library users. This driving force is only slightly different from those who work in bookstores, publishing houses, broadcast media, and other profit-driven, information-related occupations.

However, one difference in role between profit and nonprofit organizations remains significant. The library worker is committed first to the user, and then to the information needed by that individual. Further, neither the library worker nor the library directly profit from successful transactions that help users.

Within the context of libraries, the First Amendment is expressed in terms of the intellectual freedom of citizens to enquire about any subject at any time. Intellectual freedom is defined by ALA as "the right of every individual to both seek and receive information from all points of view without restriction. It provides for free access to all expressions of ideas through which any and all sides of a question, cause or movement may be explored."[8]

The second clause of ALA's "Code of Ethics" (see Appendix C) states:

II. We uphold the principles of intellectual freedom and resist all efforts to censor library resources.

The "Freedom to Read Statement" (see Appendix D) was originally drafted in 1953 by librarians, bookstore owners, teachers, and publishers and was last revised in 2004. This statement has been endorsed by numerous organizations promoting in reading, literacy, and freedom of access to information. Links to a number of policies related to censorship of library materials are listed at the end of this chapter, including videotapes, materials for children, electronic information, meeting room scheduling, exhibits and bulletin boards, and the labeling of materials as to their age appropriateness.

From these clauses, it is clear that intellectual freedom is a right of library users. The ethical obligation of library workers is to ensure that library users can exercise their intellectual freedom. The Florida Library Association's "Intellectual Freedom Manual" includes the following introduction:

> Intellectual Freedom is the ability to think, to reason, and to consider both ideas and actions. It includes the ability to seek information to help form opinions as well as the ability to express that opinion in speech or in writing. It is an essential part of our democratic government because it helps insure an informed electorate and allows the public to assist in forming public opinion through debate and discussion.
>
> Library workers and supporters have long understood the close tie that exists between libraries and a strong, democratic society. They know that libraries must be able to provide access to a wide range of materials on many different subjects and from many points of view. They understand that access must be provided without restriction or outside scrutiny. And they know that the true answer to requests to restrict, or censor, is more speech, not less speech. In a true democracy, ideas are tested through examination and discussion and libraries provide access to information on all sides of controversial issues.[9]

Therefore, it is the role of library staff to enable citizens to secure the information they need to make informed decisions for themselves. Free democratic societies are based on the premise that educated and informed citizens are capable of governing themselves. Libraries are an embodiment of this belief. Providing information resources to help maintain an educated and informed citizenry is a central role of public and academic libraries. To visibly demonstrate this role, the ALA launched the "Libraries Change Lives" initiative in 2013, which is designed to build public will and sustained support for America's right to libraries of all types: academic, special, school, and public. To articulate the following goals, ALA passed the "Declaration for the Right to Libraries" (Appendix A):

- Increase public and media awareness about the critical role of libraries in communities around the country
- Inspire ongoing conversations about the role of the library in the community
- Cultivate a network of community allies and advocates for the library
- Position the library as a trusted convener to help in the response to community issues[10]

Access to information and the right to know are basic premises upon which democracy, libraries, and the Internet are based. And yet these rights must be balanced: a person's right to know may be limited by another person's right to privacy.

PRIVACY

Fourth Amendment

The legal basis for our privacy rights flows from the Fourth Amendment to the U.S. Constitution, although the word *privacy* does not appear. Privacy, said Supreme Court Justice Louis Brandeis, is "the right to be left alone—the most comprehensive of rights, and the right most valued by a free people."[11]

The Fourth Amendment states:

> The right of the people to be secure in their persons, houses, papers, and effects, against unreasonable searches and seizures, shall not be violated, and no Warrants shall issue, but upon probable cause, supported by Oath or affirmation, and particularly describing the place to be searched, and the persons or things to be seized.

The Right to Privacy

Author and computer scientist Dr. Joseph S. Fulda argues, "If no one knows what I do, when I do it, and with whom I do it, no one can possibly interfere with it. . . . A society cannot be free if citizens do not have a right to privacy. Privacy is essential because a government that is ignorant of an individual's thoughts and deeds cannot act to impinge on his or her rights."[12]

Stacey L. Bowers, in her 2006 article entitled "Privacy and Library Records," writes:

> Libraries are built on the concept of freedom, freedom for individuals to use the library and freedom for individuals to access and read any information that they desire and for those activities to be kept confidential. In general, individuals view the library as a place where they can perform research, locate information, ask questions, check out books, and more with the expectation that these matters will be kept confidential and private. *If a person does not have an expectation that their library records will be kept confidential, they may be unwilling to ask questions, perform a search, read a book on the premises, or check out a book on a controversial subject for fear of judgment by the community they live in or society at large, or for fear of retribution by the government.* [emphasis added][13]

Threats to Privacy

Threats to our privacy can come from governments; corporations and private organizations; and/or individuals. These threats are real. Science fiction author and privacy advocate David Brin observes that whenever a conflict arises between privacy and accountability, people demand the former for themselves and the latter for everybody else. He applies this observation to governments and corporations as well as to individuals.

Threats from the Government

While the government can be the protector of individual citizens, it also has the potential to be the biggest threat to their privacy. George Orwell wrote the most famous fictional threat of government trumping individual privacy. In his seminal book, *1984*, Orwell described a nation in which the government, "Big Brother," exercised almost total thought control over the citizens. His book was such a profound wakeup call that his prediction to some extent became a self-defeating prophecy.

Privacy issues in libraries gained new prominence in the wake of John Hinckley's attempted assassination of President Ronald Reagan in 1981. The library director in Hinckley's hometown had been told previously by the county attorney that circulation records were not confidential. Although accounts differ about how the information was obtained, the director released Hinckley's information to the FBI and later to a newsmagazine reporter.[14] In the aftermath of these events, the Colorado Library Association spearheaded successful state legislation to make library records confidential, and other state associations followed with similar measures.

After the terrorist attacks in the United States on September 11, 2001, Congress passed the USA PATRIOT Act ("Uniting and Strengthening America by Providing Appropriate Tools Required to Intercept and Obstruct Terrorism Act of 2001"). This legislation expanded surveillance of U.S. citizens while reducing Constitutional checks and balances. Among other provisions, this legislation enabled governmental monitoring of individual reading habits, commonly known as "the library provision." The Federal USA PATRIOT Act also trumps individual states' laws on the confidentiality of library records. Some libraries have responded by scrubbing patron circulation records from library data files once materials are returned. In 2003, John Ashcroft, President George W. Bush's attorney general, accused ALA of fueling "baseless hysteria" about the government's ability to access library circulation records of users. "Mr. Ashcroft mocked and condemned the American Library Association and other Justice Department critics for believing that the FBI wants to know 'how far you have gotten on the latest Tom Clancy novel.'"[15]

The Electronic Frontier Foundation (EFF) is the "leading nonprofit organization defending civil liberties in the digital world." At the time the PATRIOT Act was passed, the Electronic Frontier Foundation stated:

> With this law we have given sweeping new powers to both domestic law enforcement and international intelligence agencies and have eliminated the checks and balances that previously gave courts the opportunity to ensure that these powers were not abused. . . . The civil liberties of ordinary Americans have taken a tremendous blow with this law, especially the right to privacy in our online communications and activities. Yet there is no evidence that our previous civil liberties posed a barrier to the effective tracking or prosecution of terrorists. In fact, in asking for these broad new powers, the government made no showing that the previous powers of law enforcement and intelligence agencies to spy on U.S. citizens were insufficient to allow them to investigate and prosecute acts of terrorism.[16]

More than ten years after it was passed, the PATRIOT Act has survived not only criticism by ALA, ACLU, EFF, and other organizations, but also several court challenges. The USA PATRIOT Act, other post-9/11 responses to terrorism, and recent revelations about the surveillance of private citizens by the National Security Administration (NSA), makes it even more critical for library workers to understand ethical issues relating to the library profession and library users. ALA's Office for Intellectual Freedom maintains a comprehensive resource page, "USA PATRIOT Act and Intellectual Freedom," with links to the latest iterations of the legislation, resolutions opposing the PATRIOT Act, and links to outside resources on libraries and national security issues, and relevant ALA guidelines on privacy and confidentiality.[17]

The New York Times brought the warrantless surveillance of U.S. citizens by the NSA to public attention in December 2005. At the time, the George W. Bush Administration appeared to bow to public and Congressional pressure and promised not to pursue such surveillance in the future without court approval.

In June 2013, Edward Snowden disclosed thousands of classified documents that he acquired while working as an NSA contractor. Snowden's leaked documents revealed sweeping global surveillance programs instigated by the NSA in cooperation with telecommunications companies. Snowden, a controversial figure, has alternately been labeled a hero or traitor for bringing to light the pervasive clandestine surveillance of private citizens in the United States and abroad. The disclosures he made have emphasized the Fourth Amendment concerns of U.S. citizens and the imbalance between national security and individual privacy. Two court rulings have split on the constitutionality of the NSA's bulk collection of telephone metadata.[18]

Two years after Snowden's revelations, Congress is debating the USA Freedom Act, a bill to halt the NSA's collection of data from millions of Americans' phones. Passage of this bill, however, would mean that other provisions of the 2001 PATRIOT Act, including government access to library records, would be extended to 2019.

Threats from Corporations

While the government has long been called Big Brother when invading the privacy of individuals, corporations are now considered Little Brothers. Corporations that track our computer use create Big Data. The use to which this information is put is sometimes benign, such as Amazon using purchase histories to make targeted book recommendations to users. But there is a darker side to corporate-controlled Big Data.

A 2012 *C|Net* article baldly stated, "In the world of Big Data, privacy invasion is the business model. Apps snooping on your address book, sneaky ad cookies, and social networking are bad. But the real privacy demon is the shadowy data brokers slurping up every last byte about you."[19]

Websites such as Spokeo, Pipl, Zabasearch, and CVGadget aggregate public records into one easy-to-search portal. These sites and others like them compromise the privacy of individuals and provide users who are willing to pay with a disturbingly complete profile of individuals gleaned from public records, including birthdates, people living at the same address, campaign contributions, property values, and magazine subscriptions. Regarding these aggregators, *PCWorld* reported:

> I know things about my lawyer I absolutely should not know. He's 55 years old, listens to the music of the band Creed, and screams like a little girl when riding roller coasters. He also relaxes with New Age spa treatments and is thinking about getting an electronic nose hair trimmer. And that's just the start. . . . I learned all of these details by tracking his social footprint across the Web—and he probably has no idea that he has left such a vivid trail behind. In our age of social sharing, we expect some of our thoughts to be public. But as we slowly put more and more pieces of ourselves online, specialized search engines are making it easier than ever to pull them together into a highly detailed (and potentially invasive) profile of our virtual lives.[20]

Some companies charge for access to this aggregated information, while others permit limited access as a teaser. Many websites, whether open or protected a paywall (a barrier that restricts information without a paid subscription) continue to track your movements through the Web once you log in.

The differences between digital and print environments are stark. Previously, a newspaper employee could tell that you either subscribed to or did not subscribe to the newspaper, but had no idea whether or not you even opened it. With the online version, it is possible to trace the sections you visit, how long you have each page open, and in what order you visit the pages.

Some companies see the invasion of online privacy as a business opportunity: Lessig's market forces at work. Others see the same opportunities by offering privacy. DuckDuckGo bills itself as the "search engine that doesn't track you," in sharp contrast to Google. The new social media player Ello is billed as the "anti-Facebook," promising to protect users from data mining and advertising.

Americans give very mixed signals as to whether they really care about their online privacy. Poll results suggest that online privacy is a big concern, but actions contradict these findings. The issue is further clouded by individuals not understanding the extent to which their personal information is being retained, repackaged, and sold by both government and businesses.

Threats from Individuals

Corporations and governments may be keen to track and aggregate Big Data about our lives and habits. But they have been less than vigilant about protecting these massive data sets from hackers. Data breaches of businesses are revealed more and more frequently and not always by the business or agency that has been hacked. Identity theft is one of the biggest threats we face from other individuals. According to the nonprofit consumer organization Privacy Rights Clearinghouse, 4,488 data breaches have occurred since 2005, with 816 million individual records containing sensitive personal information falling into the hands of hackers.[21]

What steps put you at risk and what you can do to protect yourself and library patrons who ask about this issue? The Federal Trade Commission (FTC) is the nation's consumer protection agency, playing a vital role protecting consumers' privacy through both enforcement and education. The FTC has also posted a variety of resources to help consumers protect their information from identity theft from unscrupulous individuals as well as from corporations and the government.

In 2012, the FTC issued a report including best practices for businesses to protect the privacy of Americans and give them greater control over the collection and use of their personal data by business, including a "framework for consumer privacy in light of new technologies that allow for rapid data collection and sharing that is often invisible to consumers. The goal is to balance the privacy interests of consumers with innovation that relies on information to develop beneficial new products and services."[22]

Privacy Versus Free Speech

Free speech and the right to privacy can collide. We are not free to express information we know to be false about individuals or other entities, such as the classic example of shouting "Fire!" in a crowded theater. Legal precedents, as well as ethical principles, define libel and defamation. There is growing concern about the availability and use of private information about individuals. The balance of this chapter highlights the issues in libraries related to the two fundamental rights of free speech and the right to privacy.

Privacy in Libraries

The third clause of ALA's "Code of Ethics" (Appendix C) states:

III. Protect each library user's right to privacy and confidentiality with respect to information sought or received and resources consulted, borrowed, acquired or transmitted."

To reinforce this third clause of the "Code of Ethics," ALA's "Freedom to Read Statement" (Appendix D) states, in part:

The freedom to read is essential to our democracy. It is continuously under attack. Private groups and public authorities in various parts of the country are working to remove or limit access to reading materials, to censor content in schools, to label "controversial" views, to distribute lists of "objectionable" books or authors, and to purge libraries. These actions apparently rise from a view that our national tradition of free expression is no longer valid; that censorship and suppression are needed to avoid the subversion of politics and the corruption of morals. We, as citizens devoted to reading and as librarians and publishers responsible for disseminating ideas, wish to assert the public interest in the preservation of the freedom to read.

The ALA strongly recommends that libraries formally develop policies stating circulation records of library users remain private, and "shall not be made available to any agency of state, federal, or local government except pursuant to such process, order or subpoena as may be authorized under the authority of, and pursuant to, federal, state, or local law relating to civil, criminal, or administrative discovery procedures or legislative investigative power." ALA further recommends that individual libraries should "consult with their legal counsel to determine if such process, order, or subpoena is in proper form and if there is a showing of good cause for its issuance; if the process, order, or subpoena is not in proper form or if good cause has not been shown, they will insist that such defects be cured."[23]

Staff members, particularly those at public service desks, should be trained so that they will not be intimidated if an authority figure demands to see any records of a specific library user. The same would apply to requests for the names of anyone who has checked out books on any given subject. Should classroom teachers have access to what books students check out? In a college setting the answer is clearly no. In practice at K-12 settings, the policies may be more nuanced.

Library staff members should not have access to such information unless that data is needed to perform a legitimate library function (e.g., processing of overdue notices). In addition, library staff members need to be vigilant about protecting other personal information that is on record about patrons such as telephone numbers, mailing addresses, age, identification numbers, borrowing record, and so forth. Staff members have no business giving out this patron information to anyone and may be placing the library in jeopardy of legal liability of invasion of privacy by doing so.

In addition to respecting the privacy of library users, librarians and library staff should never disclose to anyone what another person has been researching. Confidentiality applies equally when library users consult staff. To the extent possible, reference queries should be conducted in an environment in which questions can be asked and answered in a confidential manner.

Much of the information collected by publicly supported libraries may be considered to be public information, and therefore, subject to disclosure under Freedom of Information Act requests, a direct conflict between the right of access to information and the right of privacy. Sometimes it is better not to collect information that the library might not wish to disclose that links specific patrons to the information they access. We also need to consider carefully how long we should keep backups of the information we do need to collect.

According to Stacey Bowers in "Privacy and Library Records," 48 states have enacted some type of law that protects the privacy of a patron's library records. Thirty-five states offer protection through an exception to their open records act. For example, California's legislation on the privacy of library circulation records reads:

> In enacting this chapter, the Legislature, mindful of the right of individuals to privacy, finds and declares that access to information concerning the conduct of the people's business is a fundamental and necessary right of every person in this state.

All registration and circulation records of any library which is in whole or in part supported by public funds shall remain confidential and shall not be disclosed to any person, local agency, or state agency except as follows:

(a) By a person acting within the scope of his or her duties within the administration of the library.
(b) By a person authorized, in writing, by the individual to whom the records pertain, to inspect the records.
(c) By order of the appropriate superior court.[24]

Professional ethics and state laws make clear the legal and ethical requirements to uphold both patron privacy and confidentiality of library records. However, if presented with a legitimate order by law enforcement, librarians are compelled to turn over the specified documents, hard drives, and disks.

Librarians can best prepare for these possibilities by adopting policies and procedures regarding privacy, using ALA guidelines as a starting point. "Confidentiality and Coping with Law Enforcement Inquiries: Guidelines for the Library and its Staff" is an excellent resource for staff training, as well as drafting policies and procedures.

INTELLECTUAL PROPERTY

The fourth clause of ALA's "Code of Ethics" (Appendix C) states:

IV. We respect intellectual property rights and advocate balance between the interests of information users and rights holders.

Intellectual property is "generally characterized as non-physical property that is the product of original thought."[25] There are four types of intellectual property in the United States with legal protection: copyright, trademark, patents, and trade secrets. Of greatest concern to librarians and staff is copyright. Even though the concept of intellectual property law has existed for hundreds of years, the phrase itself did not appear in the seminal *Black's Law Dictionary* until 1999:

A category of intangible rights protecting commercially valuable products of the human intellect. The category comprises primarily trademark, copyright, and patent rights, but also includes trade-secret rights, publicity rights, moral rights, and rights against unfair competition.[26]

This definition has not evolved that far from an 1845 court case, which is the first recorded usage of the term: "Only in this way can we protect intellectual property, the labors of the mind, productions and interests as much a man's own . . . as the wheat he cultivates."[27]

Copyright

Copyright is based in the U.S. Constitution:

> Congress shall have the power **to promote the Progress of Science and useful Arts,** by securing **for limited Times** to **Authors** and **Inventors** the exclusive right to their Respective Writings and Discoveries. (Article 1, Section 8, U.S. Constitution)

Copyright, therefore, balances the "exclusive rights" of creators with the desire to "promote progress" in the United States. Creator(s) are granted the "exclusive right to reproduce, distribute, publicly perform, and publicly display their works, and to make 'derivative works' (such as translations and adaptations) based on their works. Copyright law covers creative works such as books, movies, music, photographs, poetry, plays, paintings, sculpture, architecture, websites, blogs, and software code. A work is protected by copyright as soon as it is fixed in a 'tangible medium of expression'—whether by writing it down, recording it, pressing the shutter button, hitting 'save,' etc. Neither a copyright notice nor registration is required for copyright protection."[28] In a 1991 case, U.S. Supreme Court Justice Sandra Day O'Connor summed up the purpose of copyright:

> The primary objective of copyright is not to reward the labor of authors, but [t]o promote the Progress of Science and useful Arts. To this end, copyright assures authors the right to their original expression, but encourages others to build freely upon the ideas and information conveyed by a work. This result is neither unfair nor unfortunate. It is the means by which copyright advances the progress of science and art.[29]

Over time, Congress has passed a series of laws extending the term of copyright, particularly the Copyright Term Extension Act and the Digital Millennium Copyright Act (DMCA), both passed in 1998. Until 1978, the copyright term was 28 years from the date of publication, renewable once for another 28 years. According to the Center for the Study of the Public Domain, "Estimates are that 85 percent of copyrights were not renewed (93 percent in the case of books), most likely because the works were no longer commercially valuable. . . . Fast forward to 1998, and the copyright term was increased to an extraordinary 70 years after the death of a creator, and to 95 years after publication for works owned by corporations."[30]

The series of copyright extensions is parallel and a direct benefit to the Walt Disney Company. Copyright on Mickey Mouse would have expired and rights to the animated character would have fallen into the public domain without the DMCA. A further consequence is that most copyrighted works created from the late 1970s to the present will probably not enter the public domain in our lifetimes. Therefore, it is difficult to see how the provisions of the DMCA encourage the progress of science and useful arts.

What Works Are Protected?

Copyright protects "original works of authorship" that are fixed in a tangible form of expression. The fixation need not be directly perceptible so long as it may be communicated with the aid of a machine or device. Copyright protection exists from the time the work is created in fixed form. The copyright in the work of authorship immediately becomes the property of the creator of the work. Only the author or those deriving their rights through the author can rightfully claim copyright. Physical ownership of a book, manuscript, or photograph does not give the possessor the copyright. The law provides that transfer of ownership of any material object containing copyrighted work does not convey any rights to the copyright.

What Is Not Protected by Copyright?

The following cannot be copyrighted:

- Works that have not been fixed in a tangible form of expression
- Titles, names, short phrases, and slogans; familiar symbols or designs; mere variations of typographic ornamentation, lettering, or coloring; mere listings of ingredients or contents
- Ideas, procedures, methods, systems, processes, concepts, principles, discoveries, or devices, as distinguished from a description, explanation, or illustration
- Works consisting entirely of information that is common property and containing no original authorship (calendars, height and weight charts, tape measures and rulers, and lists or tables taken from public documents)
- Works by the U.S. government

Because works "prepared by an officer or employee" of the federal government are not copyrightable in the United States, state and local governments tend to follow this practice.

Notice of Copyright

The use of a copyright notice is now no longer required to preserve rights under U.S. law, although it can be beneficial. Use of the copyright notice is the decision of the copyright owner and no longer requires advance permission from, or registration with, the United States Copyright Office. Although no longer legally required, registration may clarify rights should a possible infringement occur. An individual copyright notice is used to:

- Assert that the work is protected by copyright
- Identify the copyright owner
- Show the year of first publication

A sample copyright notice reads:

© [Author or Legally Recognized Entity] [Year]. All Rights Reserved.

How Long Does Copyright Endure?

Copyright terms in the United States depend on several factors, including whether works were registered, when works were published, and the format of the material under copyright. Generally, copyright extends from the life of the author plus a certain number of years after his or her death (or *pma: post mortem auctoris*). In the United States and the European Union, the copyright terms for works created after January 1, 1978, expire 70 years *pma*; in Canada and New Zealand, copyright ends 50 years *pma*.

Before 1978, the copyright term in general was 28 years from the date of publication, renewable once for another 28 years, but vary depending on the factors mentioned earlier. Cornell University's detailed chart "Copyright Term and the Public Domain in the United States" is updated annually on January 1, providing an essential and thorough overview of prior copyright provisions and works leaving copyrighted status and entering the public domain.[31]

Public Domain

There are three kinds of public domain works:

- Works that automatically enter the public domain upon creation, because they are not copyrightable, such as
  - Titles, names, short phrases and slogans, familiar symbols, numbers
  - Ideas and facts
  - Processes and systems
  - Government works and documents
- Works that have been assigned to the public domain by their creators
- Works that have entered the public domain because their copyright has expired.

Therefore, public domain works are not restricted by copyright and do not require royalties or licenses for use. Generally speaking, works published in the United States before 1977 without a copyright notice or formal registration have entered the public domain. The Center for the Study of the Public Domain at Duke University Law School states:

Artists of all kinds rely on the public domain—Homer's *The Odyssey* has given us Twain's *The Adventures of Huckleberry Finn*, Joyce's *Ulysses*, and the Coen Brothers' *O Brother Where Art Thou?*, to name only a few; and the twelve bar blues influenced genres from country to jazz to soul to rock and roll. Journalists and activists use facts and symbols in the public domain to inform the public and spur debate. Wikipedia relies on public domain information and images. Hobbyists screen forgotten films and collect old recordings. Commercial publishers reprint public domain works and sell them at discounted prices. Teachers, libraries, museums, historians, archivists, and database operators use the public domain to collect, preserve, and teach us about our past. Scientific and technical research would be impossible without access to data and discoveries. Youth orchestras and church choirs perform public domain works for their communities.[32]

The first day of each year is designated Public Domain Day, to celebrate the role of public domain in worldwide culture and highlight works that enter the public domain on that date. As of this writing, the following are in the public domain in the United States:

- All works published in the United States before 1923
- All works published with a copyright notice from 1923 through 1963 without copyright renewal
- All works published without a copyright notice from 1923 through 1977
- All works published without a copyright notice from 1978 through March 1, 1989, and without subsequent registration within five years.[33]

The benefits of the public domain are manifold. However, as Center for the Study of the Public Domain succinctly notes, "The public domain has been dramatically eroded in recent years" because of the passage of the Digital Millennium Copyright Act and other copyright law changes.

Fair Use

Copyright is always balanced by the principle of fair use. Users of copyrighted works are permitted to make "fair use" of that work. Fair use means that the work is being used in a legally acceptable manner that does not require the specific permission of the copyright holder or payment of royalties to the author or publisher. For it to apply, the use generally must be personal or educational and not for profit, such as reviews of the copyrighted work.

The most common example of legitimate fair use is to make a single copy of a work for personal use. Personal use means that the copy will not be shared with others in any way. Any shared use or further dissemination of information is restricted by copyright law. The fair-use provision permits self-service copiers for patron use. Although the patron has the right to make a copy for personal use, the library does not have the right to systematically make multiple copies for patrons.

Additional factors that determine whether fair use applies include the nature of the work, the amount and percentage of the original to be used, and the effect of the use on potential sales of the original. The most important issue is whether the proposed use of the work will diminish the commercial value of the copyright for its holder. If the proposed use would replace sales that otherwise might take place, then the owner of the copyright deserves compensation. If the use is so inconsequential that no sales could be reasonably expected to be affected, then this would suggest a fair use of the item. Other specific guidelines apply if the item is for classroom use or for library reserve desk use. Copyright holders are often very generous in granting permission for clearly specified and limited educational use of their materials. However, one should never presume that this is the case. Foregoing compensation does not negate the need to recognize authors for their work.

Even for copyrighted materials there are fair uses that can be made. Under the fair use doctrine of the U.S. copyright statute, it is permissible to use limited portions of a work including quotes, for purposes such as commentary, criticism, news reporting, and scholarly reports. How long the quotations can be is a highly technical issue that is beyond the scope of our discussion here.

This doctrine has been codified in Section 107 of the copyright law, which stipulates the various purposes for which the reproduction of a particular work may be considered "fair," such as criticism, comment, news reporting, teaching, scholarship, and research. Section 107 also sets out four factors to be considered in determining whether or not a particular use is fair:

1. Purpose and character of the use, including whether such use is of commercial nature or is for nonprofit educational purposes;

2. Nature of the copyrighted work;

3. Amount and substantiality of the portion used in relation to the copyrighted work as a whole; and

4. Effect of the use upon the potential market for or value of the copyrighted work.

The distinction between fair use and infringement may be unclear and not easily defined. There is no specific number of words, lines, or notes that may safely be taken without permission. Acknowledging the source of the copyrighted material does not substitute for obtaining permission.

Much more latitude is given to fair use in nonprofit educational settings, in which most libraries are found. Even more latitude for fair use is allowed within the classroom setting, a scope that the Teach Act has extended to online classes with registered students.

Copyright in Libraries

Legally, copyright is intended to balance the rights of authors and other creators with those of the general public. This places library workers and administrators in the crux between the rights of the authors and other creators and those of library users. The intellectual property rights enshrined in copyright are complex, but library workers can benefit in particular from an understanding of the concepts of both public domain and fair use.

It is often difficult for a citizen, even with the best of intentions, to know what is appropriate to for a particular use and what is not. While librarians and library staff should never give legal advice, it is possible to point patrons in the direction of copyright resources for laypeople. A number of Internet-based and up-to-date resources exist to help you assist patrons. The

University of Maryland University College provides an excellent summary of fair use in a library setting at its page "Copyright and Fair Use in the UMUC Online or Face-to-Face Classroom." Cornell University's "Copyright Term and the Public Domain in the United States" is updated annually, providing an essential overview of copyright provisions and detailed information by year of publication on the status of published works, sound recordings, architectural works, and other formats.

Fair use in a library setting is an important concept to master. In addition to the resources listed earlier, library workers should consult "Reproduction of Copyrighted Works by Educators and Librarians," from the U.S. Copyright Office at the Library of Congress. Among the topics covered in this document are duplication of books and articles, audiovisual materials, music, and periodical articles for other libraries as interlibrary loans and for classroom use.[34]

Sometimes the distinctions are rather subtle to the uninitiated. For example, individuals are generally authorized to make a single copy of copyrighted materials for their own use as long as they do not share it with others. If the library staff makes the copy and then sells it to the patron for a dime, this could be considered a violation of the law. However, if the patron makes the photocopy at a coin-operated machine, this is generally considered to be within the fair use provision of the law. The same 10¢ changes hands, but the library is not legally considered to be involved in the transaction. However, the library does have an obligation to comply with this provision:

> *Form and Manner of Use.* A Display Warning of Copyright shall be printed on heavy paper or other durable material in type at least 18 points in size, and shall be displayed prominently, in such manner and location as to be clearly visible, legible, and comprehensible to a casual observer within the immediate vicinity of the place where orders are accepted.[35]

School library workers in particular may wish to consult "Reproduction of Copyrighted Works by Educators and Librarians" to better understand the ways in which copyrighted materials are permissible for classroom use. If you work in a library you are often considered to be the on-site expert on copyright. Be careful about falling into the trap of trying to interpret law that is very complex—especially in the area of multimedia and electronic information. The level of expertise to make fine legal distinctions is seldom included in library job descriptions. Mistakes can be costly. When in doubt refer questions to a district expert or legal counsel. Academic librarians should consult with campus copyright staff to advise on specific intellectual property questions, particularly related to copyrighted materials in coursepacks, reserves, and classroom use in a library setting.

Intellectual Property in the Digital Age

Intellectual property issues are magnified by new and more fluid digital formats. Who owns what information on the Internet? How can these rights of ownership be protected in cyberspace? Electronic publishing is making it possible to sell works on a per-use basis. Journal articles or individual issues of journals can now be downloaded on demand. Publishers do not have to guess in advance what the demand for a particular item will be. Royalties can be collected and text and graphics downloaded on demand. Not only is this changing the landscape of copyright and licensing, it also may change the role of the library as a repository. In the 20th century, librarians had to try to anticipate future need and acquire items just in case someone wanted access to them at some future time. Now it is increasingly possible for library staff to find and download information very quickly, at the "point of need" when requested by a user.

Traditionally, libraries operated by buying containers of information (e.g., a book, a video, or a periodical). Although this work was usually framed as libraries acquiring the physical item, what we were in fact doing was acquiring the information embedded within that item. This distinction may seem abstract. However, in understanding our role in the Information Age, it is a very important one.

Lawyers, legal scholars, judges, lawmakers, and Internet users disagree about how the existing set of legal rules should be applied to this new medium—and disagree even more about whether and how those rules should be modified to manage the medium better. The DMCA discussed previously was the first comprehensive attempt to codify new rules. Fair use took a beating in the passage of that law. Previously, if one bought a book, the author retained the copyright, but the buyer was free to resell the physical object. Purchasing an e-book or digital edition of a work does not convey the right to the buyer to resell the work. Some provisions of DMCA have already been reversed in legislation like the Teach Act, which allows distance education and online classes to exercise essentially the same fair use latitude already in place for physical classrooms.

Creative Commons is a "global nonprofit organization that enables sharing and reuse of creativity and knowledge through the provision of free legal tools."[36] Founded by the aforementioned Lawrence Lessig, the mission of this organization is to help both "those who want to make creative uses of works" and authors who want to "realize the full potential of the Internet." As a tangible symbol of its mission, the logo for Creative Commons is an adaptation of the © symbol for copyright. The organization has expanded authors' options from "all rights reserved" to "some rights preserved." Creative Commons offers legal tools to stipulate which rights digital authors are asserting and which rights they are forgoing in terms easy to understand for authors and users. Creative Commons has "affiliates all over the world who help ensure our licenses work internationally and who raise awareness of our work." The Creative Commons website offers an infographic to illustrate clearly the Spectrum of Rights at http://creativecommons.org/about/licenses/comics1.

ETHICS IN THE WORKPLACE

The fifth clause of ALA's "Code of Ethics" (see Appendix C) states:

V. We treat co-workers and other colleagues with respect, fairness and good faith, and advocate conditions of employment that safeguard the rights and welfare of all employees of our institutions.

The fifth clause of ALA's "Code of Ethics," stipulates that library workers are expected to treat each other with fairness and consideration, which reflects the helping nature of the library profession. Library work attracts people who have an active concern for the welfare of others and colleagues are no exception.

The sixth clause of ALA's "Code of Ethics" (see Appendix C) states:

VI. We do not advance private interests at the expense of library users, colleagues, or our employing institutions.

To follow the sixth clause of the "Code of Ethics," administrators in particular need to write and enforce policies and procedures to ensure that no personal gain by library employees from patrons is possible. Liability concerns are causing employers to pay attention to how e-mail is being used. Courts have held that any e-mail, however frivolously intended or by what level of staff it was authored, has the potential to subject employers to harassment and other claims.

The seventh clause of ALA's "Code of Ethics" (see Appendix C) states:

VII. We distinguish between our personal convictions and professional duties and do not allow our personal beliefs to interfere with fair representation of the aims of our institutions or the provision of access to their information resources.

In the seventh clause of the "Code of Ethics" lies one of the greatest professional dilemmas for many library workers. Although most are able to hold to the fairness suggested in this article, it is often personally traumatic to offer unbiased information on topics on which they have very strong personal views. It is difficult to keep personal feelings from slipping out, even with the best of intentions. Continual self-monitoring is needed to ensure that personal beliefs do not color fair and balanced advice that allows users to find the information they need to allow them to make decisions and to further their ends.

In the United States, libraries offer individuals access to a vast array of information on almost any conceivable topic, using the following principles:

- All views may be presented
- Readers must weigh different points of view and evaluate the credibility of the authors
- Readers, not the library, decide what they wish to believe

Relevant questions for those who aspire to work in the library field include:

- How much information should be available?
- Who wants more information to be available?
- Who wants less information to be available?
- Do individuals change their positions on these questions depending on what information is being considered?

- What is really in the public interest?
- Who gets to decide?

Those who work in the library industry should constantly examine their own actions to ask themselves in what ways they are increasing or impeding the flow of information to their library users, their coworkers, and their organizations.

These criteria are espoused not just in the United States. The preamble of *The Universal Declaration of Human Rights*, adopted by the United Nations General Assembly in 1948, states:

> . . . Recognition of the inherent dignity and of the equal and inalienable rights of all members of the human family is the foundation of freedom, justice, and peace in the world [and] the advent of a world in which human beings shall enjoy freedom of speech and belief and freedom from fear and want has been proclaimed as the highest aspiration of the common people.
>
> . . . Everyone has the right to freedom of opinion and expression; this right includes freedom to hold opinions without interference and to seek, receive and impart information and ideas through any media regardless of frontiers."[37]

The ALA's "Freedom to Read Statement" (see Appendix D) further elaborates on these ideas:

1. It is in the public interest for publishers and librarians to make available the widest diversity of views and expressions, including those that are unorthodox or unpopular with the majority.

2. Publishers, librarians, and booksellers do not need to endorse every idea or presentation contained in the books they make available. It would conflict with the public interest for them to establish their own political, moral, or aesthetic views as a standard for determining what books should be published or circulated.

3. It is contrary to the public interest for publishers or librarians to determine the acceptability of a book on the basis of the personal history or political affiliations of the author.

4. There is no place in our society for efforts to coerce the taste of others, to confine adults to the reading matter deemed suitable for adolescents, or to inhibit the efforts of writers to achieve artistic expression.

5. It is not in the public interest to force a reader to accept with any book the prejudgment of a label characterizing the book or author as subversive or dangerous.

6. It is the responsibility of publishers and librarians, as guardians of the people's freedom to read, to contest encroachments upon that freedom by individuals or groups seeking to impose their own standards or tastes upon the community at large.

7. It is the responsibility of publishers and librarians to give full meaning to the freedom to read by providing books that enrich the quality and diversity of thought and expression. By the exercise of this affirmative responsibility, they can demonstrate that the answer to a bad book is a good one; the answer to a bad idea is a good one.[38]

Links to a number of policies related to censorship of various types of materials are listed at the end of this chapter. These include policies about films, materials for children, electronic information, meeting room scheduling, information on sexual orientation, exhibits and bulletin boards, and the labeling of materials as to their suitability.

The eighth clause of ALA's "Code of Ethics" (see Appendix C) states:

VIII. We strive for excellence in the profession by maintaining and enhancing our own knowledge and skills, by encouraging the professional development of co-workers, and by fostering the aspirations of potential members of the profession.

Supporting and encouraging lifelong learning is a fundamental part of the ethos of library work. Because of their commitment to education, library workers and administrators have a mutual responsibility to ensure that all library workers develop and advance their knowledge and skills. Without a strong and ongoing commitment on the part of library administrators for continuing education to build skills and abilities of all staff, libraries cannot provide users with the level of service they deserve. Many of us were first attracted to the library profession by the caring attention of library workers. Fostering aspirations on the part of users to join the profession helps attract the most committed workers at every level of library employment. Librarians present at high school career days on the information professions or at colleges to represent a library and information science graduate program. Everyone in the library profession needs to be ambassadors for librarianship and lifelong learning.

To meet this ethic completely, librarians are expected to actively recruit for the profession. Encouraging promising high school student works in the library is one group. Attending career days at high schools to explain the information professions or at colleges to represent a library and information science graduate program are excellent places to promote the profession

CHALLENGED MATERIALS AND BANNED BOOKS

Censorship is often defined as the suppression of materials considered by specific groups to be objectionable, harmful, insensitive, or blasphemous. While censorship of library resources has occurred in various parts of the country, it is important to know that United States does not and has never banned books. The American Library Association does not and has never banned books. Challenges and bans of library materials most often are imposed at the local level by individual school districts, library boards, churches, or other organizations.

The ALA states, "A challenge is an attempt to remove or restrict materials, based upon the objections of a person or group. A banning is the removal of those materials. Challenges do not simply involve a person expressing a point of view; rather, they are an attempt to remove material from the curriculum or library, thereby restricting the access of others."[39]

Banning books, unfortunately, is not new in America. *The Meritorious Price of Our Redemption* by William Pynchon, was banned in 1650 in the Massachusetts Bay Colony as heretical to prevailing Puritan doctrine. In today's more complex society, challenges are often mounted to protect children from sexual content or profanity. Ninety-seven percent of the books challenged from 2000–2009 were materials in schools, school libraries, or public libraries. Of these, almost three-fourths were in schools or school libraries. Parents (2,535) initiated the most challenges by far, followed by patrons (516) and administrators (489).[40]

The ALA's Office of Intellectual Freedom (OIF) has received and analyzed information from libraries, schools, and the media about challenges books and library materials since 1990. The OIF compiled lists of challenged books to inform the public about censorship efforts that affect libraries and schools through their website, "Missing: Find a Banned Book," at http://www.ala.org/bbooks. From 2000 to 2009, more than 5,000 challenges were reported to the Office for Intellectual Freedom for the following:

- 1,577 challenges due to "sexually explicit" material
- 1,291 challenges due to "offensive language"
- 989 challenges due to materials deemed "unsuited to age group"
- 619 challenged due to "violence"
- 361 challenges due to "homosexuality"
- 274 challenges due to "occult" or "Satanic" themes
- 119 challenges for "anti-family"[41]

The OIF also compiles lists of challenged books to inform the public about censorship efforts that affect libraries and schools. In 2013, the top 10 challenged books were:

1. *Captain Underpants* (series), by Dav Pilkey
   Reasons: Offensive language, unsuited for age group, violence

2. *The Bluest Eye*, by Toni Morrison
   Reasons: Offensive language, sexually explicit, unsuited to age group, violence

3. *The Absolutely True Diary of a Part-Time Indian*, by Sherman Alexie
   Reasons: Drugs/alcohol/smoking, offensive language, racism, sexually explicit, unsuited to age group

4. *Fifty Shades of Grey*, by E. L. James
   Reasons: Nudity, offensive language, religious viewpoint, sexually explicit, unsuited to age group

5. *The Hunger Games,* by Suzanne Collins
   Reasons: Religious viewpoint, unsuited to age group

6. *A Bad Boy Can Be Good for A Girl,* by Tanya Lee Stone
   Reasons: Drugs/alcohol/smoking, nudity, offensive language, sexually explicit

7. *Looking for Alaska,* by John Green
   Reasons: Drugs/alcohol/smoking, sexually explicit, unsuited to age group

8. *The Perks of Being a Wallflower,* by Stephen Chbosky
   Reasons: drugs/alcohol/smoking, homosexuality, sexually explicit, unsuited to age group

9. *Bless Me Ultima,* by Rudolfo Anaya
   Reasons: Occult/Satanism, offensive language, religious viewpoint, sexually explicit

10. *Bone* (series), by Jeff Smith
    Reasons: Political viewpoint, racism, violence

Classics are also not immune to challenges and censorship. According to the OIF, at least 46 of the *Radcliffe Publishing Course Top 100 Novels of the 20th Century* have been challenged or banned. The top 10 challenged literary classics are:

1. *The Great Gatsby,* by F. Scott Fitzgerald

2. *The Catcher in the Rye,* by J.D. Salinger

3. *The Grapes of Wrath,* by John Steinbeck

4. *To Kill a Mockingbird,* by Harper Lee

5. *The Color Purple,* by Alice Walker

6. *Ulysses,* by James Joyce

7. *Beloved,* by Toni Morrison

8. *The Lord of the Flies,* by William Golding

9. *1984,* by George Orwell

10. *Lolita,* by Vladimir Nabokov[42]

ALA policies on intellectual freedom are not only supported by most library professionals and staff, but also have been endorsed by numerous library agencies and organizations promoting reading and literacy. However, it is important for those entering the library field to realize that encounters with parents, groups, families, or constituents who feel strongly about specific library materials are likely. Among some organizations, the very name of the American Library Association conjures the image of outspoken librarians pushing materials on unwitting users.

In the final analysis, each community defines its values and standards. Library workers can play a positive role in helping to articulate these standards. Librarians should also be prepared to respond professionally to challenges. Librarian Valerie Nye offers the following concrete steps:

- Maintain a collection development policy and make sure all staff know about the policy.
- Have a procedure in place for dealing with challenges—handle all complaints in the same way and in writing, and make sure all staff members know about the procedure.
- Have a form that patrons can fill out when there is a challenge to material—and again, make sure all staff members know about the form.
- Develop good relationships with local librarians, politicians, and the media so that when a challenge does arise, relationships are already in place that can provide support. (Developing a good relationship with the community in general is also important; educating the community about the role of libraries has dramatically reduced the number of challenges libraries experience.)[43]

Specific Internet use policies are also necessary in all types of libraries before a challenge is received. They are absolutely critical in public libraries. Special and academic libraries for the most part serve only clients who are chronologically adults. The primary focus of school libraries is to serve the needs of children. Policies can be crafted for one age group or the other much more easily than can policies that attempt to meet the needs of both groups.

Free Speech

In reviewing whether expression is protected free speech, courts generally have ruled that the rights of the individual take precedence over the preferences of the majority. Often this ruling is not popular with the general public. Supreme Court Justice Anthony M. Kennedy described this difficult concept of the rights of the individual when he wrote:

When a student first encounters our free speech jurisprudence, he or she might think it is influenced by the philosophy that one idea is as good as any other, and that in art and literature objective standards of style, taste, decorum, beauty, and esthetics are deemed by the Constitution to be inappropriate, indeed unattainable. Quite the opposite is true. The Constitution no more enforces a relativistic philosophy or moral nihilism than it does any other point of view.

The Constitution exists precisely so that opinions and judgments, including esthetic and moral judgments about art and literature, can be formed, tested, and expressed. What the Constitution says is that these judgments are for the individual to make, not for the Government to decree, even with the mandate or approval of a majority. Technology expands the capacity to choose; and it denies the potential of this revolution if we assume the Government is best positioned to make these choices for us.

It is rare that a regulation restricting speech because of its content will ever be permissible. Indeed, were we to give the Government the benefit of the doubt when it attempted to restrict speech, we would risk leaving regulations in place that sought to shape our unique personalities or to silence dissenting ideas. When First Amendment compliance is the point to be proved, the risk of non-persuasion—operative in all trials—must rest with the Government, not with the citizen.[44]

Pornography

Whether pornography should be protected under the First Amendment or restricted on moral grounds has been debated in and outside of courtrooms for generations. Some feminists agree with attempts to suppress pornography, believing it promotes violence against women.

According to case law, pornography that is not protected by the First Amendment includes:

- Obscenity
- Child pornography
- Material "harmful to minors"

Obscenity

Obscenity is not protected free speech and can therefore be regulated by the state. As defined in *Miller v. California*, and upheld by the Supreme Court in 1973, for the state to declare materials obscene, each of the following three criteria must be met:

1. Whether the average person, applying contemporary community standards, would find that the work, taken as a whole, appeals to the prurient interest;

2. Whether the work depicts or describes, in an offensive way, sexual conduct or excretory functions, specifically defined by applicable state law; and

3. Whether the work, taken as a whole, lacks serious literary, artistic, political, or scientific value.[45]

Child Pornography

Child pornography is also not protected by free speech. Child pornography is legally defined as "any visual depiction . . . whether made or produced by electronic, mechanical, or other means, of sexually explicit conduct" that involves the use of a minor, is indistinguishable from that of a minor, or "has been created, adapted, or modified to appear that an identifiable minor is engaging in sexually explicit conduct."[46]

Harmful to Minors

Although children have First Amendment rights, states may enact laws regulating sexually explicit materials as not legal for minors, even though the items are not legally obscene. "Harm-to-minors" legislation has proved difficult to craft and more often than not has been overturned by the courts. Not all states have harmful-to-minors laws, but those that do must:

- Use the least restrictive means to limit expression
- State a compelling need
- Offer a clear definition of what is restricted
- Allow adults access

PROTECTING CHILDREN

Should some people in our society be restricted in their ability to exercise rights and responsibilities generally given to adults? Should children have a protected environment in which to thrive? If so, should the community, state, or parents provide it?

Certainly the community as a whole has an interest in seeing that children grow into responsible adults. Advocates of restricting access to library materials frequently do so with the best of intentions, often believing their actions are justified by the need to protect children. Sometimes the justification is to protect everyone. Other times, the rationale is to prevent the misuse of public funds.

Protecting children is a legitimate goal of civilized society. But is it the responsibility of the state, through its schools and libraries, to determine what children access? The ALA's position is that only parents should restrict their children's materials, but a library should not restrict access for children of any age from information that some might find offensive or inappropriate. ALA's "Access to Library Resources and Services for Minors" states:

> Libraries are charged with the mission of providing services and developing resources to meet the diverse information needs and interests of the communities they serve. Services, materials, and facilities that fulfill the needs and interests of library users at different stages in their personal development are a necessary part of library resources. The needs and interests of each library user, and resources appropriate to meet those needs and interests, must be determined on an individual basis. Librarians cannot predict what resources will best fulfill the needs and interests of any individual user based on a single criterion such as chronological age, educational level, literacy skills, or legal emancipation. Equitable access to all library resources and services shall not be abridged through restrictive scheduling or use policies.

Libraries should not limit the selection and development of library resources simply because minors will have access to them. Institutional self-censorship diminishes the credibility of the library in the community and restricts access for all library users.

The mission, goals, and objectives of libraries cannot authorize librarians or library governing bodies to assume, abrogate, or overrule the rights and responsibilities of parents and guardians. As "Libraries: An American Value" states, "We affirm the responsibility and the right of all parents and guardians to guide their own children's use of the library and its resources and services." Librarians and library governing bodies cannot assume the role of parents or the functions of parental authority in the private relationship between parent and child. Librarians and governing bodies should maintain that only parents and guardians have the right and the responsibility to determine their children's—and only their children's—access to library resources. Parents and guardians who do not want their children to have access to specific library services, materials, or facilities should so advise their children.[47]

For most people, it is easier to discuss these issues in the abstract than it is to deal with specific application in public or library policy. Librarians have the greatest personal difficulty with issues regarding information sources are suitable for children, mirroring the society in which we live. In our communities there are sometimes very vocal citizens who demand that all people be protected from ideas and expression with which they do not personally agree. However, Article V of the ALA's "Library Bill of Rights" states in absolute terms:

A person's right to use a library should not be denied or abridged because of origin, age, background, or views. The "right to use a library" includes free access to, and unrestricted use of, all the services, materials, and facilities the library has to offer. Every restriction on access to, and use of, library resources, based solely on the chronological age, educational level, literacy skills, or legal emancipation of users violates Article V.

As the Internet increasingly transforms our economy and our culture, its rough edges become more widely known. As we enter the third decade of the Web, scholarly research of childhood and adolescent use of the Web lends insight into both safe and risky online behavior.

Concerned citizens usually pursue two remedies. The first is filtering, or content-control, software that attempts to block offending sites or messages. The second is attempts to legislate what can or cannot be communicated over the World Wide Web.

Filtering or Content-Control Software

Filtering software uses a variety of methods to identify potentially objectionable sites. Some employ a Web rating system, asking information specialists, parents, and teachers to classify and rate sites. Others block keywords or entire sites. Most use a combination of these methods. Filters also can screen for categories other than pornography. It also flags other terms that give you clues as to the values of its creators.

Mandated implementation of filters in libraries can be problematic. In one author's experience using filtering software, a resource was flagged for the repeated use of word *sex*. However, the file flagged was a federal population census record in which the column indicating the gender of people enumerated was labeled "Sex." These and other examples of false flagging results question the efficacy of filtering software in practice.

As an aid to parents in managing home access, filtering software has matured significantly in the past few years. Filtering can be implemented in browsers, e-mail, operating systems, or search engines. Both commercial and free filtering app providers focus on blocking and restricting Web content. Other functions may include monitoring Internet-based activities such as video and game usage, social media, and chats, while notifying parents of ongoing computer habits.

Parents clearly have the right and the responsibility to protect their children. However, the issues change significantly when government attempts to mandate a solution that will apply to all. Public libraries have become battlefields for the resolution of the issue of state-mandated limits to inquiry. Public libraries often serve very diverse communities, different segments of which have very different views of what information is acceptable and what is unacceptable.

The final word has yet to be spoken on how best to protect children from the hazards in the online world while using its obvious educational advantages. Filtering software continues to evolve. Legislation continues to be proposed, adopted, and subjected to judicial review. Through these processes, we grow closer to the goal of protecting children while preserving the rights of adults to free speech. Debate will continue on the effectiveness and drawbacks of specific measures as they are implemented. Meanwhile, libraries remain on the front lines of this battle.

Legislation

On the political front, major legislative initiatives have been crafted to address this complex issue, with support for the legislation often framed as measures to protect children.

Communications Decency Act (CDA), 1996

The Communications Decency Act was Congress's first attempt to regulate online speech. The CDA prohibited posting "indecent" or "patently offensive" materials in a public forum on the Internet, including Web pages, newsgroups, chat rooms, or online discussion lists. Section 230 stated that Internet service and content providers were not liable for content posted by others on the Internet.[48] This Act attempted to extend controls for broadcast television to the Internet. A panel of three federal judges unanimously struck down key parts of this Act in 1996. In his opinion Federal Judge Stewart R. Dalzell wrote, "The

Internet may fairly be regarded as a never-ending worldwide conversation. The Government may not, through the CDA, interrupt that conversation. As the most participatory form of mass speech yet developed, the Internet deserves the highest protection from governmental intrusion."[49]

The Supreme Court upheld the challenges to this legislation, stating that the indecency provisions were an unconstitutional abridgement of the First Amendment right to free speech because "they did not permit parents to decide for themselves what material was acceptable for their children, extended to non-commercial speech, and did not define 'patently offensive,' a term with no prior legal meaning."[50]

Child Online Protection Act (COPA), 1998

After portions of the CDA were declared unconstitutional, Congress attempted to craft a somewhat narrower version with the same intent. The COPA made it a crime for anyone, by means of the World Wide Web, to make any communication for commercial purposes that is "harmful to minors," unless the person had restricted access by minors by requiring a credit card number.[51] Possession of a credit card is thus presumed to be an indicator that the holder of that card is an adult—a questionable assumption in today's society. Free speech advocates found this law flawed in many of the same ways the courts found CDA to be deficient. This law never took effect. Three separate rounds of litigation led to a permanent injunction in 2009.

Children's Internet Protection Act (CIPA), 2000

Legislators successfully changed their strategy by attaching legislation to federal funding. The Children's Internet Protection Act (CIPA) requires that U.S. K-12 schools and libraries use Internet filters and implement other measures to protect children from harmful online content, as a condition for federal funding. Signed into law in 2000, and upheld by the Supreme Court in 2003, CIPA requires libraries and K-12 schools receiving federal e-Rate discounts to acquire and use a "technology protection measure" on every computer connected to the Internet. Libraries receiving a subset of grants authorized through the Library Services and Technology Act (LSTA) also complied. CIPA did not provide any funds for the purchase of the mandated "technology protection measure," so the financial burden was borne only by libraries. Some public libraries refused to accept e-Rate discounts to avoid the restrictions of CIPA. In early 2001, the Federal Communications Commission (FCC) issued rules to clarify implementation of CIPA and provided updates to those rules in 2011.[52]

Deleting Online Predators Act (DOPA), 2006

If enacted, DOPA would amend the Communications Act of 1934, requiring schools and libraries that receive certain federal funds to protect minors from online predators in the absence of parental supervision when using

"Commercial Social Networking Websites" and "Chat Rooms." Although passed by the House, the bill has languished in committee in the senate.

Both ALA and its Young Adult Library Services Association oppose DOPA. Educational sites with sharing functions, discussion boards, and chat functions could be construed to be in violation of this bill as it is currently worded.

ALA Access Policies

Perhaps no other issue in libraries attracts more debate than protecting children while providing access to library materials. Most of the challenges reported to ALA came from parents, who want to protect children from content they consider inappropriate or offensive. Other challenges come from conservative organizations, often aligned with the Religious Right. As one watchdog site noted:

> Eagle Forum . . . has objected to Common Core elementary school readings that deal with wind power and the impact of climate change on polar bears.
> In August 2013, One Million Moms, a project of the American Family Association, called for Toni Morrison's *The Bluest Eye* to be removed from a Common Core list of 11th-grade English texts. One Million Moms director Monica Cole claimed the novel by the Nobel Prize-winning author was "no different than pornography," and that by including villainous characters, it encouraged children to be villainous. Focus on the Family claimed that the American Library Association was "manufacturing a national crisis" in order to push an "anti-family agenda.[53]

The question of what children should have access to in libraries is one of the most difficult to deal with for library workers. Whatever the motivation for challenges, ALA's firm position is parents must govern what their children access, rather than libraries and librarians. This issue challenges library workers to carefully examine professional ethics, and the policies of their employers and ALA. Updated in July 2014, the "Access to Library Resources and Services for Minors" merits quoting at length:

> Library policies and procedures that effectively deny minors equal and equitable access to all library resources and services available to other users violate the American Library Association's "Library Bill of Rights." The American Library Association opposes all attempts to restrict access to library services, materials, and facilities based on the age of library users.
> Article V of the "Library Bill of Rights" states, "A person's right to use a library should not be denied or abridged because of origin, age, background, or views." The "right to use a library" includes free access to, and unrestricted use of, all the services, materials, and facilities the library has to offer. Every restriction on access to, and use of, library resources,

based solely on the chronological age, educational level, literacy skills, or legal emancipation of users violates Article V.

Libraries are charged with the mission of providing services and developing resources to meet the diverse information needs and interests of the communities they serve. Services, materials, and facilities that fulfill the needs and interests of library users at different stages in their personal development are a necessary part of library resources. The needs and interests of each library user, and resources appropriate to meet those needs and interests, must be determined on an individual basis. Librarians cannot predict what resources will best fulfill the needs and interests of any individual user based on a single criterion such as chronological age, educational level, literacy skills, or legal emancipation. Equitable access to all library resources and services shall not be abridged through restrictive scheduling or use policies.

Libraries should not limit the selection and development of library resources simply because minors will have access to them. Institutional self-censorship diminishes the credibility of the library in the community and restricts access for all library users.

Children and young adults unquestionably possess First Amendment rights, including the right to receive information through the library in print, sound, images, data, games, software, and other formats. Constitutionally protected speech cannot be suppressed solely to protect children or young adults from ideas or images a legislative body believes to be unsuitable for them. Librarians and library governing bodies should not resort to age restrictions in an effort to avoid actual or anticipated objections because only a court of law can determine whether or not content is constitutionally protected.

The mission, goals, and objectives of libraries cannot authorize librarians or library governing bodies to assume, abrogate, or overrule the rights and responsibilities of parents and guardians. As "Libraries: An American Value" states, "We affirm the responsibility and the right of all parents and guardians to guide their own children's use of the library and its resources and services." **Librarians and library governing bodies cannot assume the role of parents or the functions of parental authority in the private relationship between parent and child. Librarians and governing bodies should maintain that only parents and guardians have the right and the responsibility to determine their children's—and only their children's—access to library resources**. [emphasis added] Parents and guardians who do not want their children to have access to specific library services, materials, or facilities should so advise their children.

Librarians and library governing bodies have a public and professional obligation to ensure that all members of the community they serve have free, equal, and equitable access to the entire range of library resources regardless of content, approach, or format. This principle of library service applies equally to all users, minors as well as adults. Lack of access to information can be harmful to minors. Librarians and library governing bodies must uphold this principle in order to provide adequate and effective service to minors.[54]

DIGITAL DIVIDE

The *digital divide* is the gulf between those who have ready access to computers and the Internet, and those who do not. This gulf is often expressed and studied as the gap between specific demographic populations and geographic regions with little or no access to modern information technology, and those populations and regions with robust access. Although the concept is simple to express, solving it is more difficult.

How is the digital divide important?

- Politically?
- Economically?
- Morally?

Because of the resulting polarization of our society into two extremes—the information haves and have-nots—librarians, public-policymakers, and information technological professionals study this divide and work to alleviate it. Although divisions in our society are not new, the digital divide has the potential to widen the traditional gap between the rich and the poor and to make it more difficult for the poor to take part in the new digital economy. In addition to the goals of economic growth and equality, those who work to close the digital divide believe it would also improve literacy, further job skills, inform citizen-voters, promote social advancement, and improve health.

The digital divide typically exists between the:

- Educated and the uneducated
- City-dwellers and those in rural areas
- Young users and the elderly
- Socioeconomic groups, particularly related to income
- Industrial nations and developing countries

To help individuals understand the concept of the digital divide, the TechTarget website notes:

> Even among populations with some access to technology, the digital divide can be evident in the form of lower-performance computers, lower-speed wireless connections, lower-priced connections such as dial-up, and limited access to subscription-based content. . . . And while adoption of smartphones is growing, even among lower-income and minority groups, the rising costs of data plans and the difficulty of performing tasks and transactions on smartphones continue to inhibit the closing of the gap.[55]

A 2013 recent White House poll showed that only 71 percent of American homes have adopted broadband, a figure lower than in other countries with comparable gross domestic product.[56]

Tracking Internet statistics can be a rather slippery pursuit because of the medium's ever-changing nature, but some usage milestones and trends are evident. In 1998, there were 147 million people worldwide using the Internet and more than half of these users resided in the United States. By 2014, worldwide use numbers increased to nearly 3 billion, with the United States in third place with 199 million users. China with 458 million users and Europe with 430 million users were in first and second places.[57]

Meanwhile, resource-poor developing countries with limited access to technology are decidedly behind in Internet usage. Factors that keep these numbers low include illiteracy, lack of computers, aging or nonexistent infrastructures, and political structures that do not embrace the concept of freedom of information.

The digital divide is also a gender gap. Worldwide, men have many more opportunities to access the Internet than women, according to a new report issued by the United Nations' Broadband Commission Working Group. In the developing world, the report estimates that 16 percent fewer women use the Internet than men, but in developed countries, use by gender is virtually equal. Worldwide, 37 percent of women are connected to the Internet as opposed to 41 percent of men. This represents a gap of at least 200 million more men having access to the Internet than women, due particularly to countries where Internet access is politically restricted.[58] The UN report also notes that facilitating Internet access for women would have an immensely positive global economic impact.

Online harassment and threats aimed at women users also factor into this gender gap. "Caroline Criado-Perez, the journalist heading up the campaign to make British author Jane Austen the face of England's £10 note, was bombarded with abusive comments and rape threats via Twitter. On Facebook, sexism had become such a pervasive issue that earlier this year the company announced new efforts to crack down specifically on content that 'targets women with images and content that threatens or incites gender-based violence or hate.'"[59] See Chapter 10 for a fuller discussion of these issues.

Digital Divide or Digital Inequality?

Frequently the digital divide is expressed as a binary problem: those who "have" access and those who "have not," including the disadvantaged, disabled, low-income, homeless, poorly educated, immigrant, or elderly. Some researchers have suggested that the digital divide is perhaps better expressed as *digital inequality*, focusing "not just on providing affordable and universal access to the Internet, but also on increasing interest in the use of the resulting access."[60] This more nuanced picture of those who "have-not" reveals a gulf between those who are interested in getting online, and those who are not. The Internet Society's "Global Internet Report 2014: Open and Sustainable Access for All" revealed that "more non-Internet users indicate that they are not online because of a lack of interest, understanding or time, rather than the affordability or availability of access."[61] The Internet Society suggests that creating and promoting more local content in local languages on local servers would help develop interest in using the Internet. The Internet Society summarizes the current issues and outline work to be done:

> . . . It is important to differentiate those who could afford to go online, but choose not to, from those who do not have access or could not afford it anyway. It is also important to consider the issues that impact those already online, such as improved security and privacy measures. Addressing those concerns will not just impact those already online, but improve the experience for those considering going online.

- Have Internet already
  - Resilience: Increase cross-border projects between countries to enhance physical connectivity
  - Security and privacy: Use technology to promote trust and privacy
  - Content availability: Make sure content is widely and legally available
- Could have Internet
  - Content access: Provide access to locally relevant content
  - Content creation: Government leads in developing applications and creating demand for hosting infrastructure
- Cannot have Internet
  - Access: Remove barriers to deployment, and government invests where costs are high or incomes are low
  - Affordability: Remove taxes on equipment and services to lower costs; subsidize demand in targeted fashion[62]

Is the digital divide important economically? Can the rest of us afford to pay the cost of bringing along those who don't have the resources for or the interest in going digital? Can the rest of us afford not to pay the cost of staying connected economically and socially with those on the other side of the digital divide?

Is the digital divide important morally? What about individuals having a responsibility for taking care of themselves? What about the children on the wrong side of the divide? Do they get left behind?

Is the digital divide narrowing? It depends on what you are measuring. Personal computers are in more and more homes. Internet connectivity at home has changed dramatically in just the last couple of years. But is bandwidth adequate to span the gap so that all have access to the digital economy? And what will be the next barrier? Will the digital divide always be a moving target? First it was a home computer. Next it was an Internet connection. Now it's a broadband connection. Will there always be a new technology hurdle? What can be done to narrow or bridge the digital divide? Which of these are worth the economic cost to society?

- Education in schools
- Work force training

- Public access terminals in libraries and in other public places
- Government tax deductions for purchasing home computers and Internet connectivity
- Corporations subsidizing employees to purchase home technology
- Individuals volunteering to teach skills to those who otherwise might be left behind

Libraries and the Digital Divide

Now, as ever, libraries play a central role in extending the political and economic benefits of our free society and economic prosperity to all residents of our country. School and public libraries are at the forefront of providing free access to the Internet, particularly to members of their communities who are unable to afford a computer or online service. As more government and commercial information is distributed online, libraries need to make sure that their policies of acquiring and disseminating information shrink rather than widen this gap. Free and unfettered access to information for all is critical to the strengthening of our democracy.

NET NEUTRALITY

The principle that transmission of data on the Internet must be treated equally and not restricted in any way is called *net neutrality*. Also known as *network neutrality* or *net equality*, this means Internet service providers (ISPs) and telecommunications companies should not block, discriminate, or interfere with data transmission to end users. How this neutrality is protected—or if it's even necessary—is the subject of continuing debate. Those in favor of net neutrality believe ISPs and other providers should be regulated like utilities. Opponents believe the issue is best resolved in the marketplace.

Proponents, including the American Library Association, believe that net neutrality is vital to an uncensored and open Internet, embracing and protecting both free speech and intellectual freedom. To these supporters, net neutrality "means your broadband provider, which controls your access to the Internet, can't block or slow down your ability to use services or applications or view Web sites. It also means your Internet service provider—whether it's a cable company or telephone service—can't create so-called 'fast lanes' that force content companies like Netflix to pay an additional fee to deliver their content to customers faster," according to *C|Net*.[63]

Net neutrality advocates believe the cost of these "fast lanes" will be passed on to consumers, while data transmission in the resulting "slow lanes" could be as sluggish as early Internet dial-up connections. Innovation will also suffer, advocates believe, if small companies and start-ups are unable to compete with established corporations whose deep pockets can pay to deliver their content faster than smaller competitors.

Perhaps of greatest concern to proponents of net neutrality is the power that telecommunications companies would have to dictate what their customers can access and how quickly or slowly it loads. Such incidents have already occurred. In 2007, Verizon blocked text messages from a pro-choice group to its members. Believing Verizon's censorship set a dangerous precedent, a broad coalition of groups ranging from Planned Parenthood to the Christian Coalition pressed Verizon to relent and won. In 2012, AT&T blocked Apple's FaceTime video chat app unless customers paid extra fees. After protests by users who believed that AT&T feared Apple's competition with its own voice services, the company backed down. However, AT&T specifically retained the right to decide which applications customers can run on their network.[64]

Opponents of net neutrality, including AT&T, Verizon, IBM, Intel, and other giant corporations, see the issue in economic and political terms. Some academic economists believe that broadband regulation would impede innovation and restrict competition. Conservative politicians warn against unnecessary government intrusion and unfair burdens on corporations, stating that net neutrality "is not an economically appropriate goal of public policy, which instead should focus on maximizing consumer welfare."[65] Opponents believe competition with rivals would push telecom corporations to build better networks. "Consumer welfare" would improve when pauses in streaming media are eliminated for customers of media companies who pay the telecoms for "fast lane" access.

After fierce debate, in February 2015, the Federal Communications Commission (FCC) voted to uphold net neutrality and regulate broadband Internet service and mobile data service as a public utility. FFC chairman Tom Wheeler said the commission was using "all the tools in our toolbox to protect innovators and consumers" to preserve an open Internet. Wheeler said that Internet access was "too important to let broadband providers be the ones making the rules."[66] Lawsuits from telecom and cable television companies are likely, ensuring that net neutrality remains a contentious issue.

SUMMARY

Ethical issues in libraries, as we have seen in this chapter, are often complex. However, as your career progresses, it is useful to recall the concept that began this chapter. The three basic players—individuals, corporations, and governments—remain the same. Freedom and accountability are both finite. You can move them around, but you can't make more or less of either.

STUDY QUESTIONS

1. Why is access to information particularly valuable to our society?

2. Why is privacy valuable to individuals?

3. What level of privacy control do you prefer to use for social media sites and why?

4. Why should individuals be able to profit from their ideas?

5. Under what conditions should details about the information sought by library patrons be made available to others?

6. What does "fair use" have to do with copyrighted materials?

7. Do parents or the state know better how to protect children from harmful influences?

8. What motivated challenges to schools and public libraries for books listed in this chapter? Were you surprised by some of the titles listed?

9. Is filtering appropriate and effective to protect children using the Internet?

10. Is resolution of the digital divide important to our society? To the world?

11. How can libraries work to promote access to the Internet and to technology for populations that do not have their own access (homeless, elderly, undereducated, migrant workers, and others)?

12. Do you have any friends or family members who do not use the Internet? If so, what are their reasons?

13. If you had created original content (artwork, a play, a novel, a book, a film) what would be the benefits to you of using a Creative Commons license for that work? How would you feel about retaining full copyright, or "all rights reserved," for the same work instead?

14. After reading the ALA "Library Bill of Rights," what are your thoughts on Article V, especially in relation to children and minors?

15. What is your opinion on net neutrality? Explain why you are for or against it.

NOTES

1. Hans Jonas, *The Imperative of Responsibility: In Search of an Ethics for the Technological Age* (Chicago: University of Chicago Press, 1984), 6.
2. Lawrence Lessig, *Code and Other Laws of Cyberspace* (New York: Basic Books, 1999). Lessig has continued to develop his ideas on this topic in *Code v2*, a wiki-based e-book available at http://codev2.cc under a Creative Commons Attribution-ShareAlike 2.5 License.
3. "Code of Ethics of the American Library Association," adopted by the ALA Council, June 28, 1995; amended January 22, 2008.
4. "The Core Rules of Netiquette," accessed March 4, 2015, http://www.albion.com/netiquette.
5. "Émile Chartier," *Wikiquote,* accessed March 4, 2015, http://en.wikiquote.org/wiki/Émile_Chartier.
6. Eric Schmidt and Jared Cohen. "Web Censorship: The Net Is Closing In," *The Guardian,* April 23, 2013, accessed March 4, 2015, http://www.theguardian.com/technology/2013/apr/23/web-censorship-net-closing-in.
7. American Civil Liberties Union, "Freedom of Expression," excerpted from the ACLU position paper, January 2, 1997, accessed March 4, 2015, http://www.aclu.org/freespeech/gen/21179pub20051031.html.
8. American Library Association, "Intellectual Freedom and Censorship Q & A," accessed March 4, 2015, http://www.ala.org/ala/aboutala/offices/oif/basics/ifcensorshipqanda.pdf.

9. Florida Library Association, "Intellectual Freedom Manual 2014," May 9, 2014, accessed March 4, 2015, http://www.flalib.org/int_Freedom_Manual.php.

10. American Library Association, "Libraries Change Lives: Declaration for the Right to Libraries," accessed March 4, 2015, http://www.ala.org/advocacy/declaration-right-libraries-text-only.

11. Justice Louis D. Brandeis, *Olmstead v. United States,* 277 U.S. 438 (1928).

12. Joseph S. Fulda, "A Loss of Privacy Harms Society," in "Liberty and Privacy: Connections," *The Freeman,* December 1996.

13. Stacey L. Bowers, "Privacy and Library Records," *Journal of Academic Librarianship* 32, no. 4 (July 2006): 377–383, doi:10.1016/j.acalib.2006.03.005.

14. "Colo. Library Grants Access to Hinckley's Reading Records," *Library Journal,* July 1, 1981, 1366, and "Interview with Bill Knott," Jefferson County Public Library Digital History Collection in Jefferson County Public Library Digital Repository, 2008, accessed March 4, 2015, http://jcpl.coalliance.org/fedora/repository/colwjcpl:65.

15. Eric Lichtblau, "Ashcroft Mocks Librarians and Others Who Oppose Parts of Counterterrorism Law," *The New York Times,* September 16, 2003, accessed March 4, 2015, http://www.nytimes.com/2003/09/16/politics/16LIBR.html.

16. Electronic Frontier Foundation, "EFF Analysis of the Provisions of the USA PATRIOT Act That Relate to Online Activities," October 31, 2001; updated October 27, 2003, accessed March 4, 2015, https://w2.eff.org/Privacy/Surveillance/Terrorism/20011031_eff_usa_patriot_analysis.php.

17. American Library Association, "USA PATRIOT Act and Intellectual Freedom," accessed March 4, 2015, http://www.ala.org/offices/oif/ifissues/usapatriotact.

18. Matthew Cole and Mike Brunker, "Edward Snowden: A Timeline," *NBC News,* May 26, 2014, accessed March 4, 2015, http://www.nbcnews.com/feature/edward-snowden-interview/edward-snowden-timeline-n114871.

19. Molly Wood, "In the World of Big Data, Privacy Invasion Is the Business Model," *C|Net,* February 29, 2012, accessed March 4, 2015, http://www.cnet.com/news/in-the-world-of-big-data-privacy-invasion-is-the-business-model/.

20. J.R. Raphael, "People Search Engines: They Know Your Dark Secrets . . . And Tell Anyone," *PCWorld,* March 10, 2009, accessed March 4, 2015, http://www.pcworld.com/article/161018/people_search_engines.html.

21. Privacy Rights Clearinghouse, "Chronology of Data Breaches," accessed March 4, 2015, http://www.privacyrights.org/data-breach.

22. Federal Trade Commission, "Protecting Consumer Privacy in an Era of Rapid Change: Recommendations for Businesses and Policymakers," March 2012, accessed March 4, 2015, http://www.ftc.gov/reports/protecting-consumer-privacy-era-rapid-change-recommendations-businesses-policymakers. FTC, "Identity Theft," accessed March 8, 2015, http://www.consumer.ftc.gov/features/feature-0014-identity-theft.

23. American Library Association, "Policy on Confidentiality of Library Records," amended July 2, 1986, accessed March 4, 2015, http://www.ala.org/advocacy/intfreedom/statementspols/otherpolicies/policyconfidentiality.

24. *California Code,* Section 6267, accessed March 4, 2015, http://www.leginfo.ca.gov/cgi-bin/displaycode?section=gov&group=06001-07000&file=6250-6270.

25. "Intellectual Property," *Stanford Dictionary of Philosophy,* March 8, 2011; rev. September 22, 2014; accessed March 4, 2015, http://plato.stanford.edu/entries/intellectual-property.

26. Bryan A. Garner, ed., *Black's Law Dictionary,* 7th ed. (St. Paul, MN: West Group, 1999), 813.

27. J.A. Simpson and E.S.C. Weiner, *The Oxford English Dictionary,* Vol. VIII, 2nd ed. (Oxford: Clarendon, 1989), 1068.

28. Center for the Study of the Public Domain, Duke University School of Law, "Public Domain Day—Frequently Asked Questions," accessed March 4, 2015, http://web.law.duke.edu/cspd/publicdomainday/2015/.

29. *Feist Publications, Inc. v. Rural Tel. Service Co.,* 499 U.S. 340 (1991), accessed March 4, 2015, http://caselaw.lp.findlaw.com/scripts/getcase.pl?court=US&vol=499&invol=340.

30. Cornell University Copyright Information Center, "Copyright Term and the Public Domain in the United States, 1 January 2015," accessed March 4, 2015, http://copyright.cornell.edu/resources/publicdomain.cfm. This chart was first published by Peter B. Hirtle, "Recent Changes to the Copyright Law: Copyright Term Extension," *Archival Outlook,* January/February 1999. For information on using the chart, see Peter B. Hirtle, "When Is 1923 Going to Arrive and Other Complications of the U.S. Public Domain," *Searcher* (Sept 2012). Hirtle also notes that the chart is based in part on Laura N. Gasaway's chart, "When Works Pass into the Public Domain," at http://www.unc.edu/~unclng/public-d.htm, and similar charts found in Marie C. Malaro, *A Legal Primer on Managing Museum Collections* (Washington, DC: Smithsonian Institution Press, 1998): 155-156. A useful copyright duration chart by Mary Minow, organized by year, is found at http://www.librarylaw.com/Digitization Table.htm. For an excellent discussion of the evolution of U.S. copyright law and the impact of the Internet, see Louis Menard, "Crooner in Rights Spat: Are Copyright Laws Too Strict?" *The New Yorker,* October 14, 2014, accessed May 19, 2015, http://www.newyorker.com/magazine/2014/10/20/crooner-rights-spat.

31. Center for the Study of the Public Domain, Duke University School of Law, "Public Domain Day—Frequently Asked Questions," accessed March 4, 2015, https://web.law.duke.edu/cspd/publicdomainday/2015/faqs

32. Ibid.

33. Ibid.

34. U.S. Copyright Office, "Reproduction of Copyrighted Works by Educators and Librarians," accessed March 7, 2015, http://www.copyright.gov/circs/circ21.pdf.

35. As required by law, the copyright statement posted on or by copiers states: "NOTICE WARNING CONCERNING COPYRIGHT RESTRICTIONS The copyright law of the United States (Title 17, United States Code) governs the making of photocopies or other reproductions of copyrighted material. Under certain conditions specified in the law, libraries and archives are authorized to furnish a photocopy or other reproduction. One of these specified conditions is that the photocopy or reproduction is not to be "used for any purpose other than private study, scholarship, or research." If a user makes a request for, or later uses, a photocopy or reproduction for purposes in excess of "fair use," that user may be liable for copyright infringement. This institution reserves the right to refuse to accept a copying order if, in its judgment, fulfillment of the order would involve violation of copyright law." U.S. Copyright Office, "Fair Use," accessed March 4, 2015, http://www.copyright.gov/fls/fl102.html.

36. "What Is Creative Commons?," *Creative Commons.org,* accessed March 7, 2015, http://creativecommons.org/about.

37. United Nations, "The Universal Declaration of Human Rights," accessed March 7, 2015, http://www.un.org/en/documents/udhr/.

38. American Library Association, "The Freedom to Read Statement," accessed March 7, 2015, http://www.ala.org/advocacy/intfreedom/statementspols/freedomreadstatement.

39. Office of Intellectual Freedom, American Library Association, "About Banned & Challenged Books," accessed March 7, 2015, http://www.ala.org/bbooks/about.

40. Office of Intellectual Freedom, American Library Association, "Challenges by Reason, Initiator & Institution for 1990–99 and 2000–09," accessed March 7, 2015, http://www.ala.org/bbooks/frequentlychallengedbooks/statistics. Of the 5,220 challenges received from 2000–2009, 1,639 were in school libraries; 1,811 were in classrooms; 1,217 took place in public libraries. There were 114 challenges to materials used in college classes; and 30 to academic libraries. There are isolated cases of challenges to library materials made available in or by prisons, special libraries, community groups, and students.

41. Ibid.

42. Office of Intellectual Freedom, American Library Association, "Top Ten Challenged Books Lists by Year: 2001–2013," accessed March 7, 2015, http://www.ala.org/bbooks/frequentlychallengedbooks/top10 and "Banned and Challenged Classics," accessed March 30, 2015, http://www.ala.org/bbooks/frequentlychallengedbooks/classics.

43. American Library Association, "State of America's Libraries Report 2014: Intellectual Freedom," accessed March 7, 2015, http://www.ala.org/news/state-americas-libraries-report-2014/intellectual-freedom, quoting Valerie Nye, co-editor of *True Stories of Censorship Battles in America's Libraries* (ALA Editions, 2012).

44. *United States et al. v. Playboy Entertainment Group, Inc.* (2000), accessed March 8, 2015, http://caselaw.lp.findlaw.com/scripts/getcase.pl?court=US&vol=529&invol=803.

45. *Miller v. California*, 413 U.S. 15 (1973), accessed March 7, 2015, http://caselaw.lp.findlaw.com/scripts/getcase.pl?court=US&vol=413&invol=15.

46. 18 U.S.C. § 2256: *US Code—Section 2256: Definitions for Chapter.* See more at: http://codes.lp.findlaw.com/uscode/18/I/110/2256-sthash.yeeAVFGc.dpuf

47. American Library Association, "Access to Library Resources and Services for Minors," accessed March 7, 2015, http://www.ala.org/advocacy/intfreedom/librarybill/interpretations/access-library-resources-for-minors.

48. Electronic Privacy Information Center, "Communications Decency Act," accessed March 8, 2015, https://epic.org/free_speech/cda/cda.html.

49. Thomas J. DeLoughry and Jeffrey R. Young, "Federal Judges Rule Internet Restrictions Unconstitutional: In Striking Down Law That Many Said Violated Academic Freedom, The Jurists Call For 'The Highest Protection' for the Internet," *The Chronicle of Higher Education,* June 21, 1996.

50. *Reno v. American Civil Liberties Union* 521 U.S. 844 (1997), accessed March 7, 2015, https://supreme.justia.com/cases/federal/us/521/844/case.html.

51. 47 U.S.C. § 231: *US Code—Section 231: Restriction of Access by Minors to Materials Commercially Distributed by Means of World Wide Web That Are Harmful to Minors,* accessed March 7, 2015, http://codes.lp.findlaw.com/uscode/47/5/II/I/231.

52. Federal Communications Commission, "Children's Internet Protection Act," accessed March 7, 2015, http://www.fcc.gov/guides/childrens-internet-protection-act.

53. People for the American Way, "Book Wars: The Right's Campaign to Censor Literature," accessed March 7, 2015, http://www.pfaw.org/sites/default/files/BookWars_The_Rights_Fight.pdf.

54. American Library Association, "Access to Library Resources and Services for Minors," accessed March 7, 2015, http://www.ala.org/advocacy/intfreedom/librarybill/interpretations/access-library-resources-for-minors.

55. "Digital Divide," *TechTarget.com,* accessed March 8, 2015, http://whatis
.techtarget.com/definition/digital-divide.
56. White House Blog, "Four Years of Broadband Growth," accessed March 8,
2015, http://www.whitehouse.gov/blog/2013/06/14/four-years-broadband-
growth.
57. "Number of Internet Users in Selected Countries and Regions as of May
2014 (in Millions)," accessed March 8, 2015, http://www.statista.com/
statistics/271411/number-of-internet-users-in-selected-countries.
58. United Nations Educational, Scientific and Cultural Organization, "Doubling
Digital Opportunities: Enhancing the Inclusion of Women & Girls in the Information Society: A Report by the Broadband Commission Working Group on
Broadband and Gender," accessed March 8, 2015, http://www.broadbandcom
mission.org/Documents/working-groups/bb-doubling-digital-2013.pdf.
59. Colin Neagle, "U.N. Report Highlights Massive Internet Gender Gap," *Net-
workWorld,* September 24, 2013, accessed March 8, 2015, http://www.net
workworld.com/article/2170200/lan-wan/un-report-highlights-massive-
internet-gender-gap.html.
60. Michael Kende, "The Digital Divide Is Not Binary," *Wired,* January 2015, accessed April 8, 2015, http://www.wired.com/2015/01/the-digital-divide-is-
not-binary/.
61. Internet Society, "Global Internet Report 2014: Open and Sustainable Access for All" accessed March 8, 2015, http://www.internetsociety.org/doc/
global-internet-report.
62. Internet Society, "Global Internet Report 2014: Open and Sustainable Access
for All, Executive Summary," accessed March 8, 2015, http://www.internet
society.org/sites/default/files/IS_ExSummary_30may.pdf.
63. Marguerite Reardon, "FCC Got Net Neutrality 'Right,' But Fight Isn't Over, Frank-
en Says," *C|Net,* March 3, 2015, accessed April 8, 2015, http://www.cnet.com/
news/the-fcc-got-net-neutrality-right-but-the-fight-isnt-over-franken-says/.
64. Aaron Sankin, "The Worst Net Neutrality Violations in History," *Daily Dot,*
May 21, 2014, accessed April 8, 2015, http://www.dailydot.com/politics/net-
neutrality-violations-history/.
65. Gary S. Becker, Dennis W. Carlton, and Hal S. Sider, "Net Neutrality and
Consumer Welfare," *Journal of Competition Law & Economics* 6, no. 3 (2010):
497–519, accessed April 8, 2015, http://faculty.chicagobooth.edu/dennis
.carlton/research/pdfs/NetNeutralityConsumerWelfare.pdf.
66. Rebecca R. Ruiz and Steve Lohr. "F.C.C. Approves Net Neutrality Rules, Classifying Broadband Internet Service as a Utility," *The New York Times,* February 26, 2015, accessed April 8, 2015, http://www.nytimes.com/2015/02/27/
technology/net-neutrality-fcc-vote-internet-utility.html.

RESOURCES

Websites

Ethics for Libraries

American Library Association—Core Values of Librarianship. http://www.ala.org/
advocacy/intfreedom/statementspols/corevalues.
American Library Association—Digital Divide. http://www.ala.org/advocacy/
access/equityofaccess/digitaldivide.
American Library Association—"Library Bill of Rights" and Its Interpretations.
http://www.ala.org/advocacy/intfreedom/librarybill/.

American Library Association—Office for Intellectual Freedom. http://www.ala .org/offices/oif.

American Library Association—Office for Intellectual Freedom—About Banned & Challenged Books. http://www.ala.org/bbooks/about.

American Library Association—Office for Intellectual Freedom—Banned Books Week. http://www.ala.org/bbooks/bannedbooksweek.

American Library Association—Policy on Confidentiality of Library Records. http://www.ala.org/advocacy/intfreedom/statementspols/otherpolicies/ policyconfidentiality.

American Library Association—Privacy Toolkit. http://www.ala.org/advocacy/ privacyconfidentiality/toolkitsprivacy/privacy.

American Library Association. *Questions and Answers: Access to Digital Information, Services, and Networks: An Interpretation of the Library Bill of Rights.* http://www.ala.org/advocacy/intfreedom/librarybill/interpretations/ qa-accesstodigital

American Library Association—USA PATRIOT Act. http://www.ala.org/advocacy/ advleg/federallegislation/theusapatriotact.

Florida Library Association—Intellectual Freedom Manual, 2014. http://www.flalib .org/int_Freedom_Manual.php.

Hill, Jacob and Johanna Delaney—The USA PATRIOT Act in 2013: What It Currently Means for Libraries—Illinois Library Association. http://www.ila.org/ the-usa-patriot-act-in-2012-what-it-currently-means-for-libraries.

Infopeople—Internet Filtering. https://infopeople.org/resources/filtering.

Minow, Mary—Specific Issues for Libraries. http://www.librarylaw.com

Minow, Mary—Library Digitization Projects: U.S. Copyrighted Works That Have Expired into the Public Domain. http://www.librarylaw.com/Digitization Table.htm.

New York Public Library—Internet Safety Tips for Children and Teens. http:// www.nypl.org/help/about-nypl/legal-notices/internet-safety-tips.

Young Adult Library Services Association (YALSA)—Social Networking and DOPA. http://www.leonline.com/yalsa/positive_uses.pdf.

Intellectual Freedom

American Civil Liberties Union—Free Speech. https://www.aclu.org/free-speech.

American Family Association. http://www.afa.net.

Electronic Frontier Foundation. https://www.eff.org.

Federal Communications Commission—Children's Internet Protection Act. http:// www.fcc.gov/guides/childrens-internet-protection-act.

Internet Society—Internet Issues. http://www.internetsociety.org/what-we-do/ internet-issues.

Privacy

American Civil Liberties Union—Protecting Civil Liberties in the Digital Age. https://www.aclu.org/protecting-civil-liberties-digital-age.

Anderson, Janna and Lee Rainie. "Net Threats." Pew Internet Research Center. July 3, 2014. http://www.pewinternet.org/2014/07/03/net-threats/.

Electronic Privacy Information Center. http://www.epic.org/.

Federal Trade Commission—Identity Theft. http://www.consumer.ftc.gov/features/ feature-0014-identity-theft.

Privacy Rights Clearinghouse. http://www.privacyrights.org.

Copyright

Cornell University—Copyright Term and the Public Domain in the United States. http://copyright.cornell.edu/resources/publicdomain.cfm.

Creative Commons. http://creativecommons.org/.

Duke University School of Law—Center for the Study of the Public Domain. http://web.law.duke.edu/cspd/.

University of Texas System Administration Office of the General Counsel—Copyright Management Center. http://www.utsystem.edu/OGC/IntellectualProperty/cprtindx.htm.

U.S. Copyright Office. http://www.copyright.gov/.

U.S. Copyright Office—Reproduction of Copyrighted Works by Educators and Librarians. http://www.copyright.gov/circs/circ21.pdf.

Net Neutrality

Net Neutrality—President Obama's Plan for a Free and Open Internet. https://www.whitehouse.gov/net-neutrality.

New York Times—Net Neutrality. http://topics.nytimes.com/top/reference/times topics/subjects/n/net_neutrality/index.html

Articles and Reports

Mannapperuma, Menesha A., Brianna L. Schofield, Andrea K. Yankovsky, Lila Bailey, and Jennifer M. Urban. *Is It in the Public Domain? A Handbook For Evaluating the Copyright Status of a Work Created in the United States between January 1, 1923 and December 31, 1977.* Berkeley, CA: University of California Law School, Samuelson Law, Technology & Public Policy Clinic, 2014. https://www.law.berkeley.edu/files/FINAL_PublicDomain_Handbook_FINAL%281%29.pdf.

Smith, Aaron. "Older Adults and Technology Use." *Pew Internet Research Center.* April 3, 2014. http://www.pewinternet.org/2014/04/03/older-adults-and-technology-use/.

Sullivan, Gail. "What the Heck Is Net Neutrality?" *Washington Post,* May 15, 2014. http://www.washingtonpost.com/news/morning-mix/wp/2014/05/15/everything-you-need-to-know-about-net-neutrality/.

Zickuhr, Kathryn and Aaron Smith. "Digital Differences." *Pew Internet Research Center.* April 13, 2012. http://pewinternet.org/Reports/2012/Digital-differences.aspx.

Books

Beckstrom, Matthew. *Protecting Patron Privacy: Safe Practices for Public Computers.* Santa Barbara, CA: Libraries Unlimited, 2015.

Crews, Kenneth D. *Copyright Essentials for Librarians and Educators.* 3rd ed. Chicago: American Library Association, 2011.

Doyle, Robert P. *Banned Books: Challenging Our Freedom to Read, 2014 Edition.* Chicago: American Library Association, 2014.

Lewis, Anthony. *Freedom for the Thought That We Hate: A Biography of the First Amendment.* New York: Basic Books, 2010.

Spinello, Richard. *Cyberethics: Morality and Law in Cyberspace.* 5th ed. Burlington, MA: Jones & Bartlett Learning, 2013.

Warburton, Nigel. *Free Speech: A Very Short Introduction.* New York: Oxford University Press, 2009.

Chapter 9

Job Search Basics

The array of professional knowledge and skills you possess are of the most value to you and to others once you can find an appropriate setting in which to put them to use. As job hunters reading this chapter, many of you will be searching for openings in a library or information industry organization, but there is a growing need in the field for contractors and freelance employees who can work independently. Finding the appropriate setting requires a well-planned and carefully executed job search strategy.

GETTING READY FOR THE JOB SEARCH

According to news reports and personnel experts, current American workplace trends include fundamental change, outsourcing of staff, increasing dependence on sophisticated technology, a rise in working from home or remotely, and changing demographics as the workforce ages and the baby-boomer generation retires. Additionally, in the wake of the Great Recession, employers who have had to shrink their workforce are cautious about adding new positions and can afford to be choosy with a large pool of applicants.

As a result of these trends, workers can expect multiple job changes throughout their careers and the need for continual updating of their skills. The days of working solely for one employer until retirement are as *passé* as hard-wired computer workstations. As Richard Bolles, author of the perennial best seller *What Color Is Your Parachute? A Practical Manual for Job Hunters and Career-Changers*, advises: "Our typical work history now is going to be three careers over our lifetime and at least eight jobs."[1]

These general workplace trends are also true in the library and information center sector as well. Whether you are a new graduate or re-entering the workplace after time away, a seasoned library professional or someone looking for a mid-career shift, you should keep your job-hunting skills honed; you will most likely put them to use several times during the course of your working life.

21st-Century Library and Information Center Job Markets

The field has entered a very dynamic period, such that the librarian or library technician of today can only speculate on how the profession will continue to

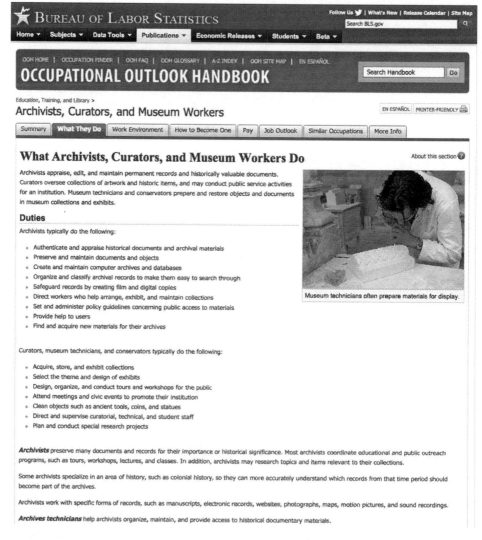

FIGURE 9.1 Both on the Web and in print format, the annual *Occupational Outlook Handbook* is a useful tool for those seeking an overview of the job outlook in libraries and information centers, as well as in other related fields such as archives. Courtesy *Occupational Outlook Handbook.*

change given future technological advances and the increasing importance placed on innovation. For those uncomfortable with continual change, this pattern may cause dissatisfaction or a departure from the field.

An important source for nation-wide job category projections, changing trends, median salaries, and overall career data is the U.S. Department of Labor's annual *Occupational Outlook Handbook* website (see Figure 9.1). According to its 2014 publication, the job outlook for the field overall is mixed, with slower-than-average job growth predicted for professional librarian positions in traditional environments. However, employment growth is forecast in related occupations with a strong emphasis on computer and organizational skills, such as private corporations, consulting firms, and information brokers. Another factor in the field is that a large number of librarians are expected to retire in the next 10 years, while the number entering the profession has been declining; the end result is that job opportunities overall should be good for librarians.[2]

For library technicians, according to the *Occupational Outlook Handbook,* jobs are expected to rise on average or above all occupations through the year 2022. Also, as some school districts continue to downsize librarian positions to the paraprofessional level due to budgetary issues, this results in growth in the number of library technicians in the school market.[3]

Regardless of the level of employment, technological competency is mandatory for entering the library and information field; once employed, the need for ongoing learning, upgrading of skills, and innovation in this area continues.

Who Am I, Professionally Speaking?

Before embarking on a job search or compiling a résumé, serious job seekers need to spend time thoughtfully taking stock of their own skill sets and consider what an ideal job situation would be. This self-assessment may well be the hardest part of the job search process, even though filling out multiple-page job application forms can seem onerous.

Before beginning your search, consider the following logistical issues:

- Do you have a preference for working in a particular type or size of library or information center?
- Are you willing to relocate? If not, what are your geographical limitations?
- Are you seeking a part-time or full-time position? Temporary or permanent employment?
- Are you able and willing to work out of your home or to telecommute? Do you have the discipline and self-motivation needed to work independently and remotely?
- Do you prefer traditional office hours? Are you willing to work evenings, weekends, on-call, or variable hours?
- Are you an entrepreneur? Would you enjoy starting your own business?
- Are several steps needed to reach your ultimate career goal?

Your Skill Set

Enumerate your unique set of skills. For what are they best suited? Creative adult programming and outreach? Designing and maintaining Web pages? Teaching? Instructing and working with elementary school children? Some of each? Is a lot of public interaction or public speaking appealing to you or a turnoff? For guidance in taking stock of your skills and interests, browse the current print edition of Deborah Hunt and David Grossman's *The Librarian's Skillbook: 51 Essential Career Skills for Information Professionals*.

Another recommended source for stretching your mind as to the varieties of employment within the library and information business is *Working in the Virtual Stacks: The New Library and Information Science*, by Laura Townsend Kane. Many traditional and non-traditional career paths are featured in short chapters written by real people who are employed in public, school, academic, special libraries, archives, museums, Web design, and in careers outside of the familiar such as working for outsourcing companies, vendors, or publishers, serving as independent consultants, and technical writing and teaching. (See the Resources section for complete citations to titles mentioned here). For an overview of the mechanics of employee recruitment and job hiring from an employer's point of view see *What Do Employers Want? A Guide for Library Science Students*, by Priscilla K. Shontz and Richard A. Murray.

The Other Side of the Job Market

Filling a vacant or newly created position is very costly both in time and money. Thus, employers do not take this activity lightly. Too often job seekers focus almost exclusively on their own needs, and give short shrift to the goals of the employer. Making an effort to understand and respond to the reasons employers seek to fill positions provides the job seeker with competitive insight.

Even though many library employers are caring individuals, they do not make hiring decisions based on whether you are behind on your rent, your child needs $3,500 worth of orthodontic work next year, or you need just six more quarters to qualify for full Social Security benefits. Although these may be powerful motivators for you, these are not convincing reasons for an employer to hire you. In fact, sharing these needs too early in the employment process can be counterproductive.

A more productive job-seeking strategy is to look at the situation from the perspective of potential employers. Why are they looking for new employees? Do they need to add fresh talent, knowledge, and skills not currently present in their organization? Do they need additional people with the same skills as existing staff? How much of the desired knowledge and skills can the employer afford to teach you on the job? What expertise must the new staff member possess on day one? Is the employer attempting to maintain current operation levels or to go in new directions?

A frequently heard comment voiced by employers today is that finding job candidates with key education and technical know-how is not difficult. However, many applicants—whether brand new graduates or re-entry workers—often lack what are known as "soft skills," or crucial workplace competencies for time management, interpersonal and communications skills, and the ability to work cooperatively with others.

Some investigation will help you to be realistic about how you match up with the needs of the employer. This is an opportunity to demonstrate your research skills and to reach out to your network of colleagues and acquaintances to assist you to achieve your goal. In addition, most employers will appreciate the thoughtful initiative and analytical ability that you demonstrate by exploring their organization and goals in advance.

First, collect the public data, such as the official position description, posting, or advertisement; information about the library agency; and data about employment conditions and benefits with the parent organization of that library. Next, contact your network of friends and colleagues who might know something about the position and the library. After you have absorbed this information, you may want to contact the immediate supervisor directly, either by telephone or e-mail. Do this with care. Some supervisors may be reluctant to have contact with applicants outside the formal selection process; there may also be organizational policies forbidding this. Others may welcome the opportunity to do some recruiting. Remember that the impression you make will carry over to the formal selection process. Nothing is off the record. Therefore, call with a specific purpose. Ask some questions that, when answered, will affect whether you apply or how you target your formal application. Do not call just to chat or to shoot the breeze. The underlying purpose is to establish the foundation of a business relationship.

Once you have a good idea of what expectations the employer has for the prospective employee, you will have a more realistic view of your suitability for the position. If it appears that you match up well with the expectations for the position, you will have a good starting point for how best to present yourself as the candidate who can solve the issues that led to the current recruitment.

Carefully analyze the job description. Is it specific to an individual position, or is it for a class of jobs? Stated another way, is this an application process to fill a specific opening or is it merely to establish eligibility to be placed on a list (possibly in ranked order of priority) for any hiring decisions made during the next six months or the next year? Or is it a recruitment to identify a candidate pool for possible future assignments as they become available? This last scenario is most common in academic teaching settings.

The Competition

As you enter the next step in your job seeking plan, you need to focus on another element in the employment process: the competition. Your competitors are not prospective employers. Rather, they are other potential employees with similar skills, degrees, interests, and aspirations. When you write your cover letter to introduce yourself as the best fit for an employer's vacancy, you need to think about who your competition is likely to be for this specific job. It's not good enough to simply be qualified for the job. You must appear better qualified than the other qualified candidates. Of all the people who may apply for the job and meet the minimum qualifications, why should employers think that you are a better solution for this position than any of the other applicants? Is your education more relevant? Have you demonstrated better skills? If so, which ones? Do you have more applicable experience? Find at least one area where you should have an advantage over most other candidates for the job and build a convincing application package to sell to that potential employer.

Internships and Volunteer Experience

If relevant work experience is not one of your most competitive job assets, you may want to consider the benefits of an internship or volunteer stint before completing your formal educational program or as you prepare to embark on a job search. An internship can offer a valuable sneak preview into the world of work. As an intern in a library or information center, you can sample various working environments, network with library personnel in your geographical region, and gain valuable hands-on experience. Interning in the field can be quite eye-opening and can provide a very different learning experience from the traditional classroom venue (whether a virtual classroom or face-to-face learning). A successful internship can also serve as an important source for job referrals and letters of recommendation in the future. Remember that each experience should be a building block to your ultimate career objective. It should be taken seriously so that you not only learn all that you can, but also leave behind an advocate who will want to help you succeed in future steps down your chosen career path.

Internships typically come in two forms: (1) paid internships, and (2) practicums. Paid internships are most often available at a business, nonprofit, or government agency that has set aside funds to hire students for summer or other short-term periods as a learning experience. Often, these are not widely advertised, and the hiring agencies may rely on word of mouth to recruit candidates. Professors, counselors, fellow students, and job placement personnel are good sources to contact about potential paid internships. Querying library-related listservs or blogs can also be productive.

Unpaid internships or practicums are usually set up as academic courses with enrolled students earning college credit for their field hours. Practicums are frequent and valuable components in both community college level library/media technician programs and in graduate library and information school curricula. Many educational programs, at both levels, require students to complete official internship courses prior to completion of their certificate or degree. Other programs will be willing to try to set up such opportunities.

In the event that no formal internship opportunities are available, serving as a volunteer staffer in a library, archives, museum, or information center can provide some beneficial work experience for the novice, student, or re-entry worker. Many public library agencies and academic facilities have ongoing placement of volunteers. Begin by discussing your career goals and educational background with the department head or branch librarian where you would like to volunteer in order to explore what opportunities might best serve their needs and yours. It is not unusual for these agencies to require their volunteers to undergo a background check, to be fingerprinted and to update appropriate inoculations prior to beginning their assignment.

As with an employer filling a paid staff position, the internship site will be looking for a volunteer who can dig in and provide help where needed within their organization; don't make the mistake of thinking that an internship opportunity exists solely to fit your interests or needs. Flexibility, reliability, enthusiasm, and being open to learning new things are very attractive qualities in an intern. Successfully completed internships and volunteer situations can provide relevant experience to place on résumés when entering a field or changing careers.

THE JOB HUNT

Employment openings are advertised in a variety of media: job search websites, newspapers, job hotlines, and industry newsletters, as well as informally through word of mouth. Subscribing via e-mail to listservs that focus on your special area of employment interest—for example, law libraries, business information centers, or school libraries—is one way to find out about openings regionally, nationwide, and beyond. E-mail lists that focus on library industry openings in a particular geographic area or state (or allow filtering by area or state) are also very helpful in a job search. Traditional job classified ads are published in local and regional newspapers primarily in their digital versions, with limited notices showing up in print editions. Digital job postings are often dynamic; in addition to detailed job descriptions, they may allow job seekers to create customized job alerts or submit interest profiles; upload a résumé (for free or for a fee) for recruiters to review; and/or offer services for résumé review and editing.

Well-developed general job sites—such as the job search engine Indeed.com and the job posting/career resource site Monster.com—provide a variety of resources for managing the job search, application process, and career pathways. Business networking leader LinkedIn.com offers members the ability to see professional profiles and résumés of other members, thus providing a job seeker with many avenues for networking instantly with people in the field. Job hunters search for positions here, employers post current openings, and members endorse the skills of colleagues on this social media site. If you identify someone in the field on LinkedIn who could be rewarding for you to know, be specific when making requests of them and above all, be polite and respectful of their time.

Agencies such as city and county public libraries, universities, colleges, museums, and private companies post their openings on their organization's website, and via flyers, newspapers, listservs, and e-mail lists. Online submission of applications, cover letters, and other supporting materials, usually through a human resources department, is the norm for all but the smallest businesses and nonprofits.

Trade publications such as *Library Journal, School Library Journal, American Libraries, Chronicle of Higher Education,* and many others carry regular job announcements on their websites and in their print editions. EdJoin is the preferred online job board for openings in public education including teacher librarians and library technicians. Larger professional associations such as the American Association of Law Libraries, the ALA, and the Society of American

Archivists maintain active career centers and job listings through their web-sites (see Resources section). Librarian positions tend to be advertised over a wider area than do library technician positions. It is generally assumed that paraprofessionals are recruited from within the local commuting area, but that librarians may be willing to relocate for the right job. Whether or not these presumptions are correct, most employers will formulate their recruiting efforts on this basis. Therefore, paraprofessionals who are willing to relocate may have to exercise greater initiative to locate employment listings than do librarians.

For example, to become aware of appropriate job openings library tech-nicians may need to study local and regional newspaper websites in a geo-graphical area they want to relocate to. Browsing websites of organizations and libraries in targeted cities within your geographic area of job interest is another key component for all levels of job seekers.

Proactive Job Searching

Regularly scanning employment listings and signing up for e-mail alerts is one approach, but creative and energetic job searchers will also want to target and directly approach agencies for whom they are interested in working. Tools such as the annual *American Library Directory* are indispensable for locating major library agencies in a given geographical area and gleaning some very basic information about their collections, budgets, staffing, goals, users, and so forth. Most state libraries also publish a directory of library agencies within their borders. However, neither of these tools will include all of the smaller, private companies or agencies with internal information centers or libraries.

Visiting the websites of library agencies is a vital means of learning about the organizations and how they present themselves to their clientele and the world at large. For agencies open to the public, there is still nothing like an in-person visit to observe, explore, and get a feel for services, staffing, and facilities. In addition, many part-time or temporary positions are not formally advertised and may be discovered only through an on-site visit or inquiry.

Any prospective library or information industry employee should be well equipped with the research skills needed to locate background information on a potential employer. This situation provides a test case for putting your reference skills to work by searching for company or agency profiles, statis-tics, news coverage, press releases, floor plans, or mission statements to help further your job search.

Outsourcing

Many first-time employees tend to seek traditional full-time, permanent positions in library agencies, private industry, government information cen-ters, and schools. However, jobs with outsourcing firms are an area of growth in the field.

What is outsourcing? Basically, it is supplementing an in-house workforce by hiring outside contractors from the private sector. Outsourcing may mean hiring a freelance consultant, turning to a temporary employment agency for staffing needs, or going out to bid to contract with a private company that will perform certain specified services. Historically, libraries have used automation, architecture, public relations, and management consultants, and have contracted out services such as book approval plans and cataloging.

Contracting out library services has gone on quietly since at least the 1960s, especially in military and government libraries. In the last decade or so, several smaller city library systems or public library agencies, especially those with fiscal shortages, have contracted with private firms to staff, manage, and operate their entire library systems. On a much smaller scale, libraries of all types regularly turn to outside sources for short-term employee needs, consulting, or special skills. Some commonplace examples of outsourcing include operating special libraries, such as those on military bases, providing staffing to relocate a collection to a new facility, disaster cleanup after a flood or fire, or hiring a consultant to prepare a specialized report.

In terms of career options, this type of non-traditional employment translates into diverse opportunities for entrepreneurs. Freelance librarians and library technicians, information brokers, consultants, Web masters, Web-page designers, and others may serve as independent contractors to library agencies, private industry, or consumers. Typically, they work independently, supply their own work space and equipment, and are paid per hour or per project. They may also be considered short-term staff, depending on the hiring arrangements. The last U.S. Bureau of Labor report specifically tallying freelance workers in every field estimated that in total there were 10.3 million freelance workers in the United States as of 2005.[4] A more recent 2014 report commissioned by the nonprofit group Freelancers Union estimated up to 53 million independent workers in the nation.[5]

Although there are no definite figures available for the library and information field, overall outsourcing trends and the growing reliance on remote work indicate continued opportunities here. Temporary employees, on the other hand, may be hired by the library through a personnel agency that specializes in supplying trained staff for short-term, project-based, or temporary needs—such as the startup of a new branch library, a move to new quarters, a collection inventory, or weekend staffing.

The Appeal of Outsourcing

Outsourcing appeals to library managers because it allows a company or library to meet a sudden or unusual demand; provides flexibility in staffing; reduces personnel costs for fringe benefits; and allows permanent staff to focus on interactions with patrons or deliver customized services that do not lend themselves well to outsourcing.

What does outsourcing offer to the employee? For those who prefer flexible or part-time hours, a variety of changing work venues, project-based assignments, or a steady stream of new challenges, outsourcing may be the answer. It can also be an effective way to sample or preview the field when considering a career change or shifting to a different focus within the profession. For those with lifestyle needs such as retirement or parenthood, outsourcing can be an attractive option.

In addition to featuring general job listings, the leading professional networking site, LinkedIn.com, is heavily used by members as a source for those seeking freelance or consulting jobs in their area of expertise.

Conferences

Whether searching for outsourcing opportunities or for a permanent job with a library or information center, attending conferences is another key means of networking and data gathering in your job search. State and national library industry trade associations (e.g., Illinois Library Association, New York Library Association, Medical Library Association, Special Libraries Association, Society of American Archivists, American Society for Information Science, ALA, and many others) typically have free career information centers or placement services as part of their annual conventions, where employers may conduct on-site interviews of potential candidates or staff a recruitment booth. These services and opportunities are geared to assist both job seekers and employers. Some of the larger conferences provide on-site photography services for attendees at a minimal price for those job seekers desiring a high-quality professional headshot image to post on LinkedIn or their own portfolios.

While job-hunting, consider attending such a conference in your state or region to tap these services as well as to sit in on presentations and hear the current issues under discussion by practitioners. One of the biggest reasons for attending trade shows and conferences for workers at all levels is the networking value in making new professional contacts. These same associations maintain websites with information on current job openings. See the Resources section for some examples.

JOB SEARCH TOOLS

Three standard documents typically comprise the job application packet: the résumé, a cover letter, and the application form. Each is different in format and in the data they convey about an applicant; effectively done, each should complement the other. Because the hiring process today has become increasingly paperless, expect to be submitting these documents to the prospective employer electronically.

Additionally, online portfolios or *e-portfolios* are becoming more commonplace in many industries. These provide a more visual and in-depth method to showcase work projects, experience, creativity, and other skills. Potential employers can view your presentation as a way of further investigating your abilities. At this time, the industry norm in the library and information profession does not require e-portfolios from job applicants. But forward-looking applicants would be wise to learn how to use online tools to create and host e-portfolios as a career advancement tool. A Web-based portfolio can also function as a personal repository of your work achievements, certificates, awards, press coverage, photo-ops, and can serve as a prompt to refer to when creating or revising a résumé.

Résumé

The résumé is a canvas upon which you paint a portrait of the demon-strated skills and knowledge you are offering to employers. Each brush stroke (i.e., word) should be added for a purpose—to convey to employers a particular message about how you will be able to help that library be successful after you are employed. Keep it focused on what they want to know, not what you want to brag about.

Compiling a résumé represents a large investment of time and energy. It should represent you. Once you have that base résumé assembled, proofed, and saved, it can then be easily updated as needed to keep it current. Addi-tionally, it is wise to consider modifying your résumé and cover letter to best match the specifics of each job opening that you apply for. For example, if you are applying for very different positions (e.g., a job in a public library or a position in a university archives), you may want to tailor your materials to closely address those attributes and skills reflected in the specific job descrip-tion. Increasingly, larger organizations rely on automated scanners that check words and phrases from the job description against résumés and cover letters. This frees human resources staff to review smaller but more relevant pools of applicants for positions.

Data Sheet, Curriculum Vitae, or Résumé?

In this chapter, the term *résumé* is used in its broadest connotation. There are actually three different résumé types that vary in length: the data sheet, the curriculum vitae, and the résumé. The data sheet is a bare bones outline with no embellishments. It usually comprises less than a page and gives little flavor for you and your style. An example of information on a data sheet would be "A.S., Library/Information Technology, Cuesta College, 2015." Because your purpose in creating a résumé is to communicate your attributes in a way that makes you stand out from your competitors in the job market, the data sheet is not nearly long enough to accomplish your purpose.

At the other extreme, the curriculum vitae is too much information for most library positions. On the other hand, if you are applying for a librarian posi-tion in a university, many colleges, and some private research organizations, this is exactly what is expected to be competitive. You should list professional papers you have presented, articles you have published, committees you have served on, and funded or in-progress research you have conducted. The vitae cannot be too lengthy if each item is legitimately professional and verifiable. However, if the job does not fall into the above categories, such activities—no matter how relevant in your mind—should be summarized or limited to only the most recent. An overly lengthy résumé outside of the academic or research environment could actually work against you. You may be viewed as not gen-uinely committed to libraries outside the academic or research sector or too "nerdy" to relate to the clientele at hand.

For most positions, the true résumé or summary is the appropriate model to follow. In using the résumé, unless you have considerable professional experience—generally, more than 5 or 10 years—you should keep this summary to one page or two at the maximum. As mentioned previously, this is the place to describe yourself in terms that will encourage employers to see you as a good fit for their organization.

To Include or Not to Include Information

When crafting your résumé, the real question you should address is what knowledge and skills you are trying to market at this point in your career. You may possess knowledge and skills that you do not want to pursue at this stage in your life. Focus your attention on where you want to go, rather than where you have been. For example, if you are going through a career change, too much emphasis on the field you are leaving may give the impression that you are not truly committed to your new chosen field. However, many skills are transferable.

As you progress through your vocational self-analysis, you will be ready to start drafting a résumé. The purpose of the résumé is to sketch an honest picture of the person you are marketing. Every phrase in the résumé should be another brush stroke portraying the professional knowledge and skills you can apply in your new job. Facts about you that do not add to this persona, however proud of them you are, have no place in the résumé; many résumé writers forget this important rule of thumb and, as a result, end up with a muddled, unfocused résumé. At the same time, some of the images you paint can be subtle. For example, one of the qualities employers need on the job is the ability to work as a member of a team. If possible, you should list something on your résumé that indicates that you have demonstrated teamwork in the workplace. However, if you have not yet had an opportunity to document this in a paid job setting, perhaps success in community organizations, student clubs, or group assignments in relevant classes may suffice. This is but one example of many small impressions that can be conveyed with a well-constructed résumé. If you have compiled a professional e-portfolio of your achievements, be sure to include the website address in your résumé.

Common attributes that employers look for are listed at the end of this chapter. The checklist can serve as a tool to evaluate whether you have included something in your résumé to spark the interest of a potential boss about the kinds of skills you are prepared to bring to their organization.

Résumé Formatting

Résumé preparation books, guides, and templates provide differing advice about the sequence of the sections of your résumé. Sometimes it makes sense to decide on the particular area in which you are likely to have an advantage over your competitors for the position. Again, the point is not to prove that you are qualified for the position. Several others may also be qualified. Your goal is to show that you are the *best* qualified person for the job. Ask yourself, are you likely to have more work experience than your fellow job applicants? If so, then your job history should be the lead item in your résumé. If your advantage is education, that section should come first. If your expertise is computer skills or a foreign language, make sure these are prominently displayed. Arrange your résumé so that employers can look it over and quickly zero in on whatever item interests them most.

A good résumé should showcase your skills, education, and relevant work experience and echo the qualifications spelled out in the job advertisement. Regardless of the method you choose for compiling a résumé or the finished format, experts recommend starting the process by compiling a personal data list. You will need to gather the pertinent facts and dates about your prior job history, education, and training before you can start organizing these data into a selling tool.

Computer screening of résumés is becoming more popular, especially in the high-tech industry. A résumé is electronically submitted by the candidate, then searched for the number and occurrence of key vocabulary and phrases relevant to the employer's job description. Based on the ranking from this keyword analysis, a candidate may or may not warrant an interview.

Many websites, software, and books exist to help you format or lay out your résumé. Some of the best have hundreds of samples to illustrate good and bad résumés. Your college career center or local public library is likely to stock many titles. We have provided addresses of several helpful websites and recommended titles in the Resources section at the end of this chapter. In addition, here are some basic tips that apply to all résumés:

- Check spelling and grammar in the document and have at least one other person proof it before sending it out. Spelling and grammar count, show attention to detail, and should be impeccable.

- Present your contact information (i.e., home, work, cellular, fax numbers; e-mail addresses) clearly. Use your school e-mail address or create a professional-sounding e-mail account, rather than relying on personal accounts, such as foxxxy69@hotmail.

- Check at least twice to be sure all company and place names, contact information and phone numbers, and citations for your projects or publications are listed correctly.

- Use a standard word processing program or résumé template; never submit a typed (on a typewriter) or handwritten résumé;

- Use an attractive and uncluttered format.

- Choose a standard business font, not an artsy or hard-to-read typeface.

- Leave out personal information about hobbies, age, marital status, health, and religion.

- Use action verbs, words and phrases throughout the résumé.

- Ask a professional in the field to review it and make comments on your draft.

Cover Letter

A cover letter included along with your résumé provides an opportunity to highlight the most important items from your application and résumé in narrative form. It also serves as a sample of your written communication skills and lets you demonstrate that you know something about the agency or company. The purpose is to make a connection between the job opening and you, the person described in the résumé. The letter should be brief—normally one page. Your intent should be to guide a reader through the cover letter as quickly as possible and make them eager to read your résumé to learn more about you.

If possible, address a cover letter to a specific individual, if the name is available. The opening sentence should indicate very clearly for which job classification you are applying, including the formal title and position number, if applicable. Remember that the first review may most likely be via scanner or human resources clerk. That person may not care about your wonderful qualifications, but you do want the HR technician to place your application submission into the correct file. Organizations often recruit simultaneously for many positions. In addition, HR offices receive a high volume of incoming e-mail and phone communications every day. Do not make them work to decipher what job you're applying for.

Your next task is to demonstrate to the personnel who screen applications that you have thoughtfully and thoroughly read their job posting. Veteran library personnel officers often get cover letters that appear to have been sent to them by mistake or to have been recycled from a very different, previous job search with no modification. Applicants should be sincerely interested in the position and qualified for it before they apply. Be enthusiastic, but remain professional; carefully check all spelling of personal names, place names, and library agencies mentioned in the document. One of the authors received two separate applications from the same person for two very different jobs. Each letter claimed that the advertised vacancy was a perfect fit for which the applicant had patterned all of his education and years of experience. Avoid such hyperbole.

Next, show that you have carefully analyzed your skills compared to the requirements of the position. Use key phrases from the actual posting to highlight the most important areas in which you meet or exceed the requirements. Suggest that as employers read the attached résumé, they will see additional areas in which your knowledge and skills are appropriate to meet their needs.

Close by stating your eagerness (within reason) to discuss further with them how you are prepared to meet the needs of the organization through this open position. Keep the entire cover letter to a single page.

Application Form

These are tools used to screen applicants and to narrow the pool to those who merit an interview. Especially for civil service jobs, such as public libraries, schools districts, and public colleges and universities, be sure to follow application instructions *precisely*. If you omit some information or a required part of the supporting materials, this alone can disqualify you, regardless of how wonderful your skills are.

Often, application forms are generic, gathering the most basic employment history and background information from applicants at all levels and for multiple job categories within an organization. This is where the importance of a résumé as a personalized statement comes into play.

In summary, the purpose of the cover letter is to stimulate the reader to carefully examine your résumé. The purpose of the résumé is to procure an interview. The résumé is the primary tool of the job search, and you should expect to work through several drafts before arriving at a finished product.

Electronic submission of completed application forms or application packets has become the standard for most public sector agencies (city or county libraries; colleges and universities; school districts) and for all but the smallest private companies and nonprofits. Here again, follow specific formatting and submission instructions very carefully.

Online Reputation Management

It is important not to overlook this aspect of job searching. Whether you like it or not, potential employers, recruiters, HR analysts, and interviewers can and will check out candidates through searches of the Web and social media. This may not be an official part of the applicant screening process, but it is easy to do and very commonplace. It is best to investigate your online footprint well before beginning a serious job hunt.

What is your own online reputation? Using your favorite search engine, conduct a "vanity" search for yourself, using any variant names, nicknames, or previous names. What do you find? What type of impression would a potential employer have if they found this same information when searching for your name? Many names are not unique, so it is also possible that someone else with the same name in your geographical area may be confused with you.

It pays to be aware and mindful of your online presence. The Internet has a long, long memory and whether it's social media postings, personal photographs, YouTube clips, Twitter exchanges, Facebook activity, blog entries, or other data, your online presence has the potential to influence your career for good or for bad. Best practices advise that you use personal social media wisely and employ privacy settings to narrow your viewing audience. Periodically "Google" your name to see what appears. Monitor all privacy settings on sharing sites—options change often without notice. Alternately, lack of an online presence may cause you to be perceived as out of touch, not involved in virtual communities or networking sites, and avoiding the use of current technology. In all cases, review the online locations of capstone projects, theses, and other student work to ensure that your intellectual work is readily available.

References and Letters of Recommendation

Most application forms request a list of references from previous employers— that is, names, position titles, and current contact information of people who can vouch for your work experience, job performance, education, or all three. As a courtesy to your reference person and as a safeguard for yourself, *always* ask first before listing someone as a job reference. Be sure that your reference person is comfortable about giving you a positive endorsement if called or contacted by the recruiting employer. When asking someone to write a letter of recommendation for you, allow adequate lead time for its preparation. (Contacting a potential reference for a letter the night before the application deadline is never a smart idea.) Although not always required, an appropriate, well-written letter of recommendation from a former employer, an intern supervisor, or an instructor can be another asset in your application packet. Be prepared to furnish them with pertinent dates worked, projects assigned, course names, and semesters attended if needed. You will also want to provide them with the detailed description of the job for which you are applying. Refrain from listing reference contacts on your résumé, which is not the appropriate place for such information.

INTERVIEWING SKILLS

Once selected for an interview, the wise candidate takes time to prepare. Be aware that you are likely to be interviewed with a group of staff members, who will ask you questions in turn. The crux of the interview is to persuade the panel or group that you are the best person for the job in question. You can be persuasive in several ways, through your appearance, demeanor, presentation, and interpersonal skills, and crafting thoughtful responses to the questions posed. From the panel's perspective, there is much more going on than just hearing a right or wrong answer. This is a chance for them to evaluate how you think on your feet, your personality, your job philosophy, and your technical knowledge. This holds true whether you are interviewing for a civil service list, with a private sector employer, or with an outsourcing agency.

Today, the use of remote interviews via conference call, Skype, or other modalities is very commonplace for initial interviews. If a remote interviewee makes the cut and is included in the set of serious contenders, they are usually invited to a traditional in-person, on-site interview.

Numerous books, videos, and websites are available on interviewing skills. A few resources are listed in the Resources section; public libraries, college career centers, local bookstores, and online booksellers also carry many titles on this topic. Although every job interview is different, there are some standard questions that a candidate can anticipate and thus can prepare thoughtful, appropriate answers for. Some typical interview questions include the following:

- Describe your qualifications for this job.
- Why are you interested in this position?
- Why do you want to work for our company/organization?
- Describe your strengths.
- Describe your weaknesses.
- What are your career goals; where do you see yourself in five years?

- How would you deal with the following situation? (Usually a scenario where you need to solve a problem, assist customers, enforce a policy, demonstrate sensitivity to patrons or staff, etc.)
- What accomplishment in your work life are you the most proud of and why?
- Describe a difficult work or personnel situation and how you handled it.
- What have you learned about this library and its goals today?

In the course of the interview, you may also be asked questions to test your knowledge of library technology, information science, Internet skills, recognition of key author names, and so on. You may also be expected to perform demonstrations of computer skills, speak knowledgeably about an emerging library issue, or answer specific questions to determine your proficiency with software programs, library systems and products, and Internet resources, among others.

Although many interviews will be structured in such a way as to make this impossible, the book *The Five-Minute Interview* outlines a method for beginning an interview in a positive way. The strategy is for the candidate to ask the first significant question. That question might be framed as: "It would help me to focus my responses to your questions if you could take just a minute and share with me your key expectations for the successful candidate." Don't try to force this question if the opening is not there. It can be asked at the end of the interview. However, the earlier it is asked and answered, the more advantageous the information will be.[6]

Do take advantage of all opportunities to pose questions to your interviewers. Come prepared with a list of questions about the job, the library, and the parent organization based on the research you've done on this specific library and position. Listen and observe during your time with the interviewer(s). Ask substantive questions of the interviewer(s) and do not focus solely on questions about paid leave or fringe benefits at this stage of the interview. Be fully prepared to sum up your key qualifications, reaffirming your enthusiasm for the position and ability to help the library achieve its goals. This is your last chance to make an impression on the interviewers and is all too often overlooked by applicants in their eagerness to conclude the session.

Your college or university career center may also help with résumé reviews, mock interviews, and other strategies to help you put your best foot forward. If you need practice with interviews, consider applying for a job opening or two just to gain experience with the application process and interview sessions. Such practice will provide you exposure to the process and can serve as a dry run for future interviews for highly desired positions. Be sure to prepare well and take these test-run applications and interviews seriously since you will be making first impressions and potential contacts in a field with extensive networks.

Questions about a candidate's personal life, sexual orientation, ethnicity, age, health, religion, political views, and so on, are all examples of illegal interview questions. Be tactful in your responses; try to steer the conversation to another topic. If you are asked inappropriate or suspect questions, report them to the personnel analyst or board after your interview.

If you are not the chosen candidate, you may want to call the human resources department and ask for feedback on your interview performance. Constructive comments noted by the panel may help you improve in your next interview. At the same time, be understanding if local policy does not allow them to provide this information to you.

The following lists include interview tips that can help you accomplish a successful interview:

Interview dos

- Dress professionally. This may vary from organization to organization. As a rule of thumb, you should dress a step more conservatively than you would if you were already working in the job.

- Ask in advance for clarification on directions to reach the campus or specific building, any parking permits needed, availability of WiFi access, or other logistics for your interview.

- Be on time (or early) for the interview. Aside from the rudeness of being late, the interview committee may be on a tight schedule and may not have the opportunity to make up the time. Also, arrive early enough to allow a visit to the restroom for any last-minute preparation.

- Answer questions concisely, using specific illustrations or examples to make your point.

- If asked a complex or multipart question, attempt to answer it. Do not hesitate to look straight at the person who posed the question and ask if you have covered all parts of it.

- Bring extra copies of your résumé.

- Be attentive and polite.

- Be confident. Remember to smile.

Interview don'ts

- Don't drink too much caffeine prior to the interview. Your natural adrenaline flow will be sufficient stimulation.

- Don't ramble on. Answer each question efficiently and move on.

- Don't make negative comments about yourself, or any present or former supervisors, employers, or coworkers.

- Don't focus on any health or personal problems you may have.

- Don't chew gum.

- Don't answer your cell phone during the interview. Best to mute it during your interview.

- Don't wear overly strong cologne or aftershave; many people have sensitivity to certain scents.

- Don't initiate a conversation about salary at this point.

- Do not argue with or correct interviewers or assume you know more about the library than they do.

For further consideration, realize that potential employers are looking for staff members who can:

- learn quickly
- organize work and time
- set priorities and focus on what is important
- analyze complicated problems
- generate several potential solutions
- concentrate on complex details
- work harmoniously with coworkers with different skill levels
- interact well with diverse kinds of people and meet the public with courtesy
- make it easier for coworkers, superiors, and subordinates to do their own jobs well
- follow through on long, complex procedures
- think linearly
- write and speak well
- work independently
- work collaboratively on a group or team project
- see the big picture
- balance many activities simultaneously
- teach and train others
- think well on their feet
- listen well with both their ears and their eyes
- understand the environment in which they work
- keep focused on the library user
- be goal oriented
- be responsible
- look for better ways to do things
- be computer literate
- be intellectually curious
- be service oriented
- be emotionally secure
- be intelligent
- be creative
- be team players
- be dependable
- be self-starters
- be flexible
- be fast workers
- be accurate
- be honest
- actively seek opportunities to grow both personally and professionally
- have a thorough knowledge of their profession in general and their specialty in particular
- have high professional standards; and
- enjoy learning new things.

STUDY QUESTIONS

1. Why is it important to keep your job hunting skills updated?

2. What are some of the trends predicted for the library and information center workforce? What trends do you see in your geographic region?

3. What is outsourcing? Can you find examples of outsourcing companies in your state or of a public library that is managed by an outsourcing company? Do contract jobs appeal to you?

4. How do the résumé, cover letter, and application form differ in the information they present about a candidate?

5. What value does an internship provide? How would you go about trying to locate a paid or unpaid internship in a library, archival, or other information industry setting?

6. Use role-playing with your classmates to practice a mock job interview. Choose one person to be the interview candidate and have three others role-play as the interview panel. Have the panelists devise several typical questions and pose them to the candidate in a mock interview situation. Afterwards, give feedback to the interviewee on his or her performance.

7. Why is networking important to a job seeker? Describe some opportunities for networking in the library and information science field. Have you developed a network of personal contacts yet?

8. Investigate your own online reputation. Using your favorite search engine, conduct a search for yourself, using any variant names or previous names. What do you find? What type of impression would a potential employer have if they found this same information when searching for "your name"? Are there steps you can take to improve or better position your online presence?

NOTES

1. Richard Nelson Bolles, *What Color Is Your Parachute? 2015; A Practical Manual for Job Hunters and Career-Changers* (Berkeley, CA: Ten Speed Press, 2014), 5.
2. Bureau of Labor Statistics, U.S. Department of Labor, "Librarians," *Occupational Outlook Handbook, 2014–15 Edition,* accessed June 30, 2015, http://www.bls.gov/ooh/education-training-and-library/librarians.htm.
3. Bureau of Labor Statistics, U.S. Department of Labor, "Library Technicians and Assistants," *Occupational Outlook Handbook, 2014–15 Edition,* accessed June 30, 2015, http://www.bls.gov/ooh/education-training-and-library/library-technicians-and-assistants.htm.
4. Bureau of Labor Statistics, U.S. Department of Labor, "Independent contractors in 2005," *The Economics Daily,* July 29, 2005, accessed June 30, 2015, http://stats.bls.gov/opub/ted/2005/jul/wk4/art05.htm.
5. Daniel J. Edelman, "Freelancing in America: A National Survey of the New Workforce," September 2014, accessed June 30, 2015, https://fu-web-storage-prod.s3.amazonaws.com/content/filer_public/c2/06/c2065a8a-7f00-46db-915a-2122965df7d9/fu_freelancinginamericareport_v3-rgb.pdf and http://www.slideshare.net/oDesk/global-freelancer-surveyresearch-38467323/1.
6. Richard H. Beatty, *The Five Minute Interview: A Jobhunter's Guide to a Successful Interview,* 3rd ed. (New York: John Wiley & Sons, 2002).

RESOURCES

Books

Bastian, Jeannette A. and Donna Webber. *Archival Internships: A Guide for Faculty, Supervisors, and Students.* Chicago: Society of American Archivists, 2008.

Bolles, Richard Nelson. *What Color Is Your Parachute? 2015; A Practical Manual for Job Hunters and Career-Changers.* Berkeley, CA: Ten Speed Press, 2014.

Dority, G. Kim. *LIS Career Sourcebook: Managing and Maximizing Every Step of Your Career* Santa Barbara, CA: Libraries Unlimited, 2012.

Elad, Joel. *LinkedIn For Dummies.* 3rd ed. Hoboken, NJ: John Wiley & Sons, 2014.

Gordon, Rachel Singer. *What's the Alternative? Career Options for Library and Info Pros.* Medford, NJ: Information Today, 2008.

Hunt, Deborah and David Grossman. *The Librarian's Skillbook: 51 Essential Career Skills for Information Professionals.* San Leandro, CA: Information Edge, 2013.

Hurst-Wahl, Jill and Ulla de Stricker. *The Information and Knowledge Professional's Career Handbook: Define and Create Your Success.* Wintey, UK: Chandos Publishing, 2011.

Ireland, Susan. *The Complete Idiot's Guide to the Perfect Résumé.* 5th ed. Indianapolis, IN: Alpha Books, 2010.

Kane, Laura Townsend. *Working in the Virtual Stacks: The New Library and Information Science.* Chicago: American Library Association, 2011.

Latham, Kiersten F. and John E. Simmons. *Foundations of Museum Studies.* Santa Barbara, CA: Libraries Unlimited, 2014,

Lawson, Judy, Joanne Kroll, and Kelly Kowatch. *The New Information Professional: Your Guide to Careers in the Digital Age.* New York: Neal-Schuman Publishers, Inc., 2010.

Shontz, Priscilla K. and Richard A. Murray. *What Do Employers Want? A Guide for Library Science Students.* Santa Barbara, CA: Libraries Unlimited, 2012.

Stickell, Lois and Bridgette Sanders, eds. *Making the Most of Your Library Career.* Chicago: American Library Association, 2014.

Websites

The American Association of Law Libraries
http://www.aallnet.org/mm/Careers
   (accessed July 9, 2015)
   Leading source of job postings for legal information professionals. Search job database by state or keyword. Some portions of the site are available to members only.

American Library Association
http://www.ala.org/
   (accessed July 9, 2015)
   ALA maintains an extensive, up-to-date website that features career resources, conference dates, legislation updates, and current employment openings on their JobLIST.

Chronicle of Higher Education
http://chronicle.com/
   (accessed July 9, 2015)
   The leading publication for news, trends, and job searching in academia; job listings include library-related administrative, teaching, professional librarian,

and library technician level openings as well as career-building tools. Search job database by state, institution, or job title. Available online and in print.

Indeed

http://www.indeed.com/

(accessed July 9, 2015)

Leading general job search engine that includes postings in the United States and internationally.

Job Placement/Outsourcing Firms

http://lac-group.com/

http://www.lssi.com/

http://www.aimusa.com/

(accessed July 9, 2015)

Just as in any other industry the library and information field has private firms dedicated to recruitment, personnel placement, and staffing. A few examples include the LAC Group, LSSI and AIM. Search their websites for job openings at various levels.

LibGig

http://www.libgig.com/

(accessed July 9, 2015)

Specific to library careers of all levels and other information industry-related fields. Resource for employers and job seekers; helpful career building content.

Library Job Postings

http://www.libraryjobpostings.org/

(accessed July 9, 2015)

Writer, academic librarian, and blogger Sarah L. Johnson's Library Job Postings on the Internet debuted in 1995 and has been going strong since then. A detailed Web-based portal to library-related jobs and employment sites on the Internet. A professor at Booth Library, Eastern Illinois University, Johnson maintains this service for free. Organized by job type (e.g., archives and records management, federal libraries, academic positions, etc.) or by geographic region.

Monster

http://www.monster.com/

(accessed July 9, 2015)

One of the best-known general job search sites on the Web. Besides its job search function, content includes articles and advice on all facets of the job search—résumés, interviews, cover letters, job references, dressing for success, ethics, salary calculations, and more.

Society of American Archivists Online Career Center

http://www2.archivists.org/groups/saa-online-career-center

(accessed July 23, 2015)

The seminal location for job postings in government, corporate, academic archival settings, and for freelance or grant-funded temporary positions.

Special Libraries Association

http://www.sla.org/

(accessed July 9, 2015)

The SLA website features job listings, webinars, and many other career resources; some portions of the site are available to members only.

Chapter 10

Evolving Library Services

Not since the introduction of moveable type has the library field been enveloped in such dramatic change as that of the digital revolution that began in the 1990s. All aspects of library operations have been affected, from daily staffing needs to the skills and abilities needed to be effective library workers. Information technology professionals and library professionals and staff are now integral members of the same teams. Even the design of new libraries and remodeling of existing buildings reflect these changes.

Many of the long-promised benefits of the information technology revolution were realized with the development of the World Wide Web, which is built upon a specific kind of data communication called *hypertext transfer protocol* (HTTP). Web designers use *hypertext mark-up language* (HTML) to unite text, images, graphics, fonts, and colors into the content of Web pages and sites. A *browser,* formally known as a *user agent* (UA), permits users to navigate to specific Internet addresses called *uniform resource locators* (URLs), and to click or hover over *hyperlinks* to load content. Other UAs for accessing the Web include mobile apps and voice-command assistants, such as Siri, built into Apple's mobile operating system, and Google Voice Search, part of Android's operating system. The Web's ease of use, graphical nature, and accessibility are an incredible improvement over earlier text-based interfaces, such as telnet and gopher.

With the advent of user-friendly (and usually free) site builders, such as Weebly, Wix, Squarespace, and Jimdo, creating a website can be as simple as selecting a template and using drag-and-drop commands. For individuals who want more features, a *content management system* (CMS), such as WordPress, or *blogging tools,* such as Google's Blogger, are also available for free.

The ease of use to access information and create content on the Web has raised library users' expectations. Library leaders stress that to remain

301

relevant, the modern library needs to be, in the words of Stacey A. Aldrich and Jarrid P. Keller, "everywhere and somewhere."[1] Core on-site services still include children's story hours, walk-in reference assistance, print book and periodical collections, public-access computers, author events, and other cultural programs. But what were once building-bound traditional services, such as reference, have been transformed not just by digitization, but also by the ways in which the services are promoted and delivered.

So, yes, maintain valued core services in physical libraries that draw patrons inside. But at the same time, be prepared to meet users where they spend much of their leisure, study, and research time: online.

WEB 2.0, LIBRARY 2.0, AND INTERNET2

Web 2.0 was conceptualized at a conference brainstorming session in the aftermath of the burst of the dot.com bubble in the fall of 2001. Technologists Tim O'Reilly and John Battelle defined Web 2.0 in part as using the Web to harness collective intelligence and create rich user experiences.[2]

A parallel concept is Library 2.0, incorporating Web 2.0 elements into daily library operations. Web 2.0 in libraries commonly refers to using second-generation Internet tools, such as blogs, wikis, and other means of encouraging, sharing, and promoting content. As Web 2.0 matured, librarians have moved to integrate their services with social networks. Only a few years ago, having a library blog or employing social media, such as Facebook or Twitter, was considered novel. Many library users have now come to expect a library presence on Facebook and Twitter and to easily share library content with others.

However, as David Stuart of the Centre for e-Research at King's College London warns, the "huge popularity of social media today has led us to lose sight of the bigger Web 2.0 picture. . . . The Web provides a constantly evolving landscape of sites and services that the library and information professional needs to survey regularly. Does the latest site offer a new way to share content? Is it likely to be a flash in the pan—here today, gone tomorrow? What are the implications of not joining a particular site now? Too often these decisions are being made at the soft, user-friendly end of the spectrum, when the library and information professional should be paying more attention to the technical aspects. How open is the service? How easily can other services be integrated into it? Is it making use of open standards?"[3]

Begun in 1996, Internet2 today is a global computer-networking consortium of leaders in research, academia, industry, and government who are building upon and improving the technology of the original Internet. The non-profit operates the Internet2 Network, an Internet Protocol (IP) network using optical fiber to deliver network services for research and education, and provide a secure network testing and research environment.

Internet2 combines the financial support and advanced research efforts of some 200 leading universities and private sector companies, along with global government partners to develop and deploy advanced network applications and technologies, accelerating the creation of tomorrow's Internet. Ever-increasing traffic on the Web, the need for improved connectivity, and the growth in e-commerce have led these sophisticated Internet researchers to look for alternate routes for data delivery. Believing that the current network is too clogged by commercial and personal users, Internet2 members are committed to paying for the research, technology upgrades, and organizational structure needed to provide a more reliable, faster network for intensive research use. They also expect that the newer network applications they pioneer will eventually benefit all levels of Internet users.[4]

INFORMATION ACCESS AND PUBLISHING TRENDS

"Disruptive innovation" creates new markets and transforms existing ones, usually by displacing earlier technology or media. The pace of disruption seems to be growing: think of the progress from 8-inch floppy drives to CDs to flash drives to cloud data storage. Photographs captured on film and developed on paper have given way to digital images, while cellphone cameras are supplanting traditional ones. Stand-alone global positioning system (GPS) units, popular just a few years ago, face a shrinking market because of navigation apps on mobile devices.

The world of publishing has been turned upside down by a variety of disruptors. Wikipedia has altered the market for traditional encyclopedias. The advent of small appealing electronic readers, such as Kindle and iPad Mini, finally made e-books viable. Chain bookstores have disappeared before the Amazon juggernaut. Amazon may be good for readers, but publishers are in almost constant conflict with the online retailing giant as Amazon controls more and more of the market for books.[5]

Electronic Resources

Libraries offer instant and often free access to databases, journals, magazines, newspapers, government documents, legal codes, and images. More hard-copy materials are digitized every day, reaching wider audiences, and gaining greater exposure for authors. For periodicals, simultaneous publication in hard copy and on the Web is commonplace for both scholarly journals and popular magazines, although the two versions may differ. The Internet has also yielded e-zines and e-journals, *born-digital* content created and located exclusively on the Web.

Commercial e-book services, such as those offered by vendors EBSCO and ebrary, bundle collections of electronic books and audio recordings to libraries for an annual subscription price. Overdrive is another digital distributor delivering e-books, as well as video and audiobook files, to library users. EBSCO, ebrary, and Overdrive manage content containing Digital Restrictions Management (DRM), a technology built into electronic files to control use during borrowing.

Many popular titles in the public domain, such as those by Jane Austen, Nathaniel Hawthorne, William Shakespeare, Herman Melville, and others, can be downloaded as full-text PDFs or e-book files from the Web, thanks to the efforts of Project Gutenberg, Internet Archive, and other sites that make public domain content accessible.

Digital content from Google Partners and Google Books Library Project comprise Google Books (formerly Google Book Search). If a book is out of copyright and in the public domain, the entire book is available for downloading at no cost; if not, small passages are made available to the searcher along with a search function. Primarily accomplished by massive scanning of works in the collections of major libraries, Google Books Library Project is not without controversy as authors and publishers protest the infringement of intellectual property rights and resulting loss of revenue. Protracted litigation between Google and the Authors Guild and other writing and publishing groups began in 2005. As of the spring of 2014, the Authors Guild is appealing a ruling in favor of Google that declares the scanning to be fair use. They are also lobbying Congress to set up a National Digital Library to license and deliver copyrighted out-of-print books digitally.[6]

HathiTrust Digital Library is the collaborative repository of content from the top-tier research libraries via the Google Books Library Project, plus the Internet Archive, and Microsoft. As of 2010, it included about 6 million volumes, over 1 million of which are public domain in the United States. While the latter public domain titles are available in Google Books search results, access to the remainder of the content in HathiTrust is restricted to only the top-tier contributing libraries. The Authors Guild is also suing HathiTrust for intellectual property rights infringement.[7]

The Internet is still young, but its original emphasis on current and contemporary information is changing. Commercial vendors, such as Newspapers .com and ProQuest Historical Newspapers have digitized newspapers from the 18th through the 20th centuries. The Library of Congress (LC) provides free access to U.S. historical newspapers from many states and time periods at *Chronicling America* (http://chroniclingamerica.loc.gov/newspapers).

A related issue for libraries is that of perpetual access to periodicals. Will an online commercial database, even for scholarly journals, create and maintain permanent access to back issues? If a library cancels a digital subscription, will they lose access to past issues? Will commercial publishers suddenly drop or omit older files, leaving a huge gap of back issues within the library collection? Or will they impose a separate annual fee for access to archival files? This issue is critical for all learning institutions as they transition to electronic journals and indexes. Professors, students, scholars, and researchers expect libraries to be repositories for non-current periodicals, books, and government documents. As library networks or consortia negotiate licenses with commercial publishers of online products, perpetual access is a major point of negotiation. A related problem is the extent to which professional organizations, through their libraries or other archival sources, have a responsibility to preserve information that was born digital and published only on their websites.

Information is clearly a commodity in demand. Yet it has never been entirely free; digitization and the Web will not alter that. There are real costs associated with creating or acquiring digital information, and delivering it to users on demand. Yet misperceptions persist that digital resources are cheaper than print and all information should be free. When students, faculty, taxpayers, and other library users learn about the actual subscription costs that libraries pay to publishers for "free" electronic resources, they are often very surprised.

The considerable costs of digitizing and delivering archival materials are often possible only with external grant funding. Promoting value-added library collections and services to school, public, and academic library users helps them understand the bargains libraries provide.

Digital Collections

Digital Asset Management (DAM) and *Digital Resource Management* (DRM) are umbrella terms for the policies, procedures, and workflow needed to ingest, catalog, store, and retrieve digital content. DAM encompasses such evolving terms as digital archiving and digital preservation. Libraries, archives, and museums use digital *collection management software,* such as open-source CollectionSpace (collectionspace.org), or commercial CONTENTdm (contentdm .org) from OCLC. These software suites manage and deliver digital text, audio, visual, and streaming files. While it isn't necessary for library or archives users to know (or care) what collection management software is in use, staff members should remain conversant with the tools that support and deliver digital resources at their libraries or archives.

GLAM (Galleries, Libraries, Archives, and Museums) is an acronym embracing institutions that create and provide access to digital collections of unique materials. In the push to digitize primary sources, cultural heritage institutions recognized the increasing convergence between their collections and their missions. Initially known as LAM (Libraries, Archives, and Museums), leadership in this area was provided in the mid-2000s by OCLC Research, a 2008 report describing new ways LAM partnerships were converging.[8]

As pioneering digital archivist Deborah Wythe noted, libraries and archives could learn more from museums about education, while museums could take a page from libraries to provide better access to collections.[9] The Digital Library Federation, part of the Council on Library and Information Resources, has continued to promote best practices and standards for creation, aggregation, and preservation of digital materials, and perhaps most importantly, serve as a collaboration space where digital archivists, librarians, and technologists can turn theory into practice.[10]

Digital Finding Aids and Archives

Archives have also been transformed with the advent of the Web, making it possible to share unique materials with researchers across the globe. Encoded Archival Description (EAD) and Encoded Archival Context (EAC) are professional standards created by archivists to share finding aids and even collections themselves on the Web. Finding aids may vary somewhat because the collections they describe are unique, but EAD and EAC provide a uniform standard, much as MARC bibliographic records do for library cataloging. A subcommittee of the Society of American Archivists (SAA) maintains and updates EAD, while insuring its compatibility with ISAD(G), or General International Standard Archival Description.

The leap from delivering digital finding aids to providing full-text archival documents was dependent not just on advances in computing capability, but also on development of additional standards for delivering digital media. Commonly defined as "data about data," metadata serves many purposes. "Administrative metadata may include the date and source of acquisition, disposal date, and disposal method. Descriptive metadata may include information about the content and form of the materials. Preservation metadata may record activities to protect or extend the life of the resource, such as reformatting. Structural metadata may indicate the interrelationships between discrete information resources, such as page numbers."[11]

Archival portals—often created between multiple institutions—provide researchers with a single interface to search multiple digital repositories. *ArchiveGrid*, a commercial product of OCLC Research, provides access to over 4 million "detailed archival collection descriptions such as documents, personal papers, family histories, and other archival materials held by thousands of libraries, museums, historical societies, and archives. It also provides contact information for the institutions where these collections are kept."

Other portals are organized by location, such as the *Online Archive of California* (www.oac.cdlib.org), providing access to finding aids from 200 California libraries, special collections, archives, historical societies, and museums, plus digital archival collections maintained by the 10 University of California (UC) campuses. *Archives Portal Europe* (www.archivesportaleurope.net) offers more than 62 million records about archival collections from 905 institutions in European countries. An example of an organizational portal in an OPAC is the Archives, Manuscripts and Photographs Catalog (http://sirisarchives.si.edu), part of the Smithsonian Institution Research Information System (SIRIS), which facilitates searches for archival materials across all of the Smithsonian institutions.

An example of a subject portal is *The Greene & Green Virtual Archives* (http://www.usc.edu/dept/architecture/greeneandgreene/) offering digital archives by or about noted architects Charles Sumner Green and Henry Mather Greene. Finding aids and a searchable image database are aggregated from four major partners: Columbia University; University of California, Berkeley; The Gamble House, University of Southern California, in Pasadena; and the Greene and Greene Archives, USC at The Huntington Library in San Marino, California.

Digital Libraries

The term *digital libraries* was popularized by the Digital Libraries Initiative (DLI) of 1994, a combined effort from the National Science Foundation, Defense Advanced Research Projects Agency, and National Aeronautics and Space Administration. DLI helped legitimize digital libraries as scholarly resources and focused on the need for additional research and development. One of the oldest digital libraries is the American Memory Project (memory .loc.gov) at the Library of Congress. When it was launched in 1990, collections were distributed on CDs and laserdiscs. By 1994, when the Web became robust enough to share digital files more easily, *American Memory* migrated to that platform as part of the second iteration of DLI. Two years later, LC funded grants to non-federal cultural agencies to digitize American history collections and make them available on LC's *American Memory* site. This competition produced 23 digital collections that complement *American Memory*, including Memory Projects for Arizona, Florida, Indiana, Kansas, Maine, Montana, Ohio, Virginia, West Virginia, and Wyoming.[12]

Granting agencies particularly encourage multi-institutional digital library collaborations. Notable examples include:

Digital Public Library of America (DPLA) (http://dp.la) is a large-scale, collaborative project across government, research institutions, museums, libraries, and archives to build a digital library platform to make America's cultural and scientific history free and publicly available anytime, anywhere, online through a single access point. The National Archives and Records Administration (NARA), Harvard, the Smithsonian, New York Public Library, and others are working with DPLA directly to identify and prepare their collections for aggregation. DPLA is also launching "digital hubs" and "service hubs," to aggregate content from existing state libraries.

Digital Collection Celebrating the Founding of the Historically Black College and University (http://contentdm.auctr.edu/cdm) highlights the contributions of Historically Black Colleges and Universities (HBCU) to American history, while encouraging scholarship and a broader collaboration between HBCU libraries and other organizations. Partners include the HBCU Library Alliance, Cornell University Library, HBCU Institutions, and the Southeastern Library Network.

Digital Library of Appalachia (http://dla.acaweb.org/cdm) is a collaboration of Appalachian College Association member libraries. Institutions from Kentucky, North Carolina, Tennessee, Virginia, and West Virginia provide online access to collections related to the culture of the southern and central Appalachian region.

Western Waters Digital Library (http://westernwaters.org) is a collaborative project from Arizona, Colorado, Nebraska, New Mexico, Oregon, Utah, and Washington. The site is dedicated to providing free public access to classic water literature, legal transcripts, maps, reports, personal papers, water project records, photographs, audio recordings, videos, and other resources on water in the western United States.

Institutional Repositories

An *institutional repository* (IR) acquires, stores, and preserves the intellectual capital of an organization and shares it with an increasingly global community. The crisis in *scholarly communication*, arising from the unsustainable economics of commercial scholarly publishing, spurred the growth and development of IRs. As library budgets were cut and the cost of journal subscriptions from commercial publishers rapidly escalated in the mid-1980s, new methods of sharing scholarship were needed. This crisis was further fueled by underlying concerns about limited accessibility of government-funded research, together with the desire of scholarly authors and editors to retain the rights to their work published in the peer-reviewed journals required for tenure.

Digital institutional repositories gained increasing attention in 2002, when top-tier universities began offering in-house services to manage and disseminate digital content created by faculty. That same year, MIT and Hewlett-Packard launched Dspace, open-source institutional repository software. At present, IRs are generally delivered using either commercial software, such as OpenText or DigitalCommons; or open-source systems, such as Fedora or the aforementioned Dspace. The former is often the choice of libraries with little or no dedicated information technology support, while the latter is used at campuses with on-staff library technologists who can customize sites.

Implementing the technology necessary to launch an IR may present initial hurdles, but greater challenges lie in securing content from faculty and students and clearing rights. Libraries often promote their IRs in traditional ways, such as linking to the main campus website, and creating brochures and press releases. In their examination of the use of social networking to advance institutional repositories, library scholars Robin Bedenbaugh and Holly Mercer also emphasize "embeddedness," or the need for librarians to engage students and faculty directly, often outside the library.[13]

In 2007–2008, the first year of operation of DigitalCommons@CalPoly, the IR for California Polytechnic State University, librarians reported that efforts to secure and clear rights for content were paramount:

- Citing teaching loads as the primary reason for non-response, most faculty wanted to participate, but lacked citations or current bibliographies of their publications for repository staff.

- Some academic publishers failed to respond or refused to grant non-exclusive licenses for IR use, delaying and/or limiting content ingestion.

- Open-access benefits were sometimes perceived as redundant by faculty who already shared their research via professional organizations.[14]

During the first year of operation of the DigitalCommons@CalPoly, there were just over 36,000 downloads. Seven years later, downloads exceed 3 million per year. Cal Poly librarians, who manage the IR from the library's Special Collections and University Archives department, took advantage of the IR's implementation to create a larger digital archive of university records. Beyond faculty scholarship, the scope of DigitalCommons@CalPoly soon broadened to include student capstone projects and master's theses; proceedings from the university's centers, institutes, and conferences; and institutional documents, including master plans, architectural drawings, accreditation reports, department journals, student and alumni publications, and press releases.

The benefits of IRs clearly address many continuing issues in scholarly communication, digital collection delivery, and resource sharing, such as:

- Including the full range of research conducted at the institution, illustrating the coherence, depth, and scope of the institution's research and teaching disciplines

- Solving chronic information management issues for faculty and academic units

- Providing 24/7 worldwide access to institutionally created digital content

- Demonstrating the library's value to the parent institution
- Increasing search engine optimization (SEO) for improved and reliable search results
- Supporting various file formats, including streaming media
- Offering persistence of data via stable URLs
- Integrating Web 2.0 abilities, including RSS feeds, automated links to blogs and social networking sites, and customized e-mail alert options for users
- Providing effective digital rights management and ADA compliance by trained library staff

IRs also benefit alumni outreach, fundraising and academic development, and faculty and administrator search committees. These repositories, at nonprofit organizations, research institutions, and government, public, and academic libraries, are the foundation for the new model of scholarly communication.

USER SERVICES

The Web has opened up an enticing smorgasbord of information to consumers. Although many sources now available online, such as *WorldCat* or the *Occupational Outlook Handbook* have long been familiar resources to librarians, accessibility on the Web makes them novel and useful to the student or casual searcher.

The information search itself has become much easier for patrons. Ferreting out information from cranky microfilm, heavy bound volumes, indexes with tiny print, or clunky computer programs can be exchanged for the point-and-click ease, visual appeal, and 24/7 access of the Web. Information once only available in print—whether back issues of newspapers, daily stock quotes, current job listings, or government documents—receives much greater exposure to consumers when made available on the Web and aggregated by libraries.

Virtual Branches

Libraries, particularly public ones, have embraced the concept of the virtual branch. Transforming original library websites into virtual branches using content management systems (CMSs) and Web 2.0 tools offers new ways to serve first-time and experienced library users, gives users a voice, and makes it easier for staff to offer dynamic content by continually updating pages and highlighting services.

Librarian Kay Cahill has documented the implementation of a virtual branch at the Vancouver (Canada) Public Library. Pre-planning emphasized the importance of "extending the library's online presence beyond the boundaries of its own Web site." Describing their traditional library website as a "walled garden," librarians implementing the virtual branch invited users to "participate actively in the site: conversing, contributing content, and interacting with staff and with each other." The library had contemplated custom computer coding to engage users, but shifted their strategy to "mash-up versus build-up," based on user surveys. "Patrons were more interested in engaging with the library on existing social networking sites than in seeing content such as discussion forums or wikis developed on www.vpl.ca."[15]

Virtual Reference

Virtual reference is an excellent example of the transformative nature of computer-mediated communication in libraries. Virtual reference is defined by the American Library Association (ALA) as "reference service initiated electronically, often in real-time, where patrons employ computers or other Internet technology to communicate with reference staff, without being physically present."[16]

In practice, most virtual reference takes place via the following methods:

- Chat-based inquiries using commercial software, such as OCLC's QuestionPoint
- Webforms via the library's website
- Short Message Service (SMS) or text, such as Mosio or Google SMS
- Instant Message (IM) (may offer more open-source or lower-cost alternatives to commercial applications), such as Libraryh3lp, Trillian, and Adium
- Voice Over Internet Protocol (VOIP) or co-browsing services, such as Skype or Unyte

The "Online Reference" page at *Library Success: A Best Practices Wiki* is an excellent resource for virtual reference information, offering guidelines, links to libraries providing online reference services and to software and outsourcing vendors, and blogs and websites that discuss implementation.[17]

OPACs and Interlibrary Services

Many library-specific services are improved and more convenient since the traditional card-based card catalog has given way to online public access catalogs (OPACs). Union catalogs and portals permit patrons to search, browse, initiate holds on desired books, or request interlibrary services from a local library or a regional consortium.

From the smallest to the largest library, and for all categories of researchers, the Internet revolution has resulted in a tremendous increase of available resources. Gone are the days of strolling through a library's book stacks and thinking, "This is all that's available." Collections now extend well beyond local shelves to both physical and digital repositories.

Enrolled students and researchers with access to commercial databases can locate journal articles online and either download full-text or request it via digital interlibrary loan. This improves fill rates while providing faster service. Many academic institutions, larger public libraries, and special libraries offer e-mail-based alert services or updates via RSS (Really Simple Syndication)

Web feeds, which alert library users to new publications in their interest areas or research specialties.

Electronic reserve reading is a reality for college students. Instructors' lecture notes, sample quizzes, articles, and readings that are compliant with copyright can be viewed by students on their library's website or within a Moodle, Canvas, or Blackboard course shell, rather than having to visit the library.

Accessibility Services

Library users may have sensory, learning, and/or mobility disabilities, and within each of these is a spectrum of differing abilities. Sensory disabilities can include visual impairment, blindness, hearing impairment, and/or deafness. Learning disabilities can include neurological differences that affect reading, writing, speaking, and calculating. Mobility impairments can include difficulty physically accessing a computer, keyboard, or print materials.

The Internet has made great inroads changing the lives of those who live with disabilities. New assistive devices, accessibility features built into operating systems, dedicated campus or community services, and protection under the Americans with Disabilities Act have all expanded the resources available to those with disabilities.

Homebound individuals formerly reliant on library shut-in services now have access in their homes to an enormous global resource with home computers and broadband access. Those with motor and dexterity impairments are able to navigate the Web with voice recognition software. Web accessibility—designing and editing websites to be equally accessible to all users—is not just legally required but also benefits the library by reaching the widest possible audience.

Resources abound for guiding librarians and staff to provide access to collections and assist users with impairments and limitations. Staff training is one of the most effective ways to serve users with disabilities. At the local level, library staff members participate in efforts to improve collections' accessibility. ALA's Association of Specialized and Cooperative Library Services has released specific policy recommendations for "Library Services for People with Disabilities."[18]

Family History Services

Genealogists constitute a reliable and ever-growing population of library users. The evolution of digital archives, software to manage complex family history data, and the leisure time available to retired baby boomers, has yielded a prime library user group marked by repeat visits and a desire to access resources, regardless of format. Fueling demand are many commercial vendors, including Ancestry.com, Fold3.com, MyHeritage.com, FindMyPast.com, Geni.com, and others, delivering indexes, abstracts, and even full-text family history records. Public libraries often license the library edition of Ancestry for their patrons who may not be able to afford access to these sites on their own. Other commercially licensed databases, such as ProQuest

Historical Newspapers, are priced out of the realm of individual users, but may be provided by libraries.

Free sites that can help library users doing genealogy research include WikiTree.org, Geneanet.org, RootsWeb.Ancestry.com, and FamilySearch.org, the latter of which is produced by the Church of Jesus Christ of Latter-day Saints (LDS). Founded in 1894 as the Genealogical Society of Utah, Family-Search has pioneered industry standards for identifying, microfilming, scanning, indexing, and providing free access to full-text family history records from around the world. FamilySearch.org site now unites their databases and services in one location, including the OPAC for Family History Library collections in Salt Lake City, containing records for 2.4 million rolls of microfilm, 727,000 microfiche, 356,000 books, and 3.725 electronic resources from the United States, Canada, the British Isles, Europe, Latin America, Asia, and Africa. Genealogists also use the FamilySearch OPAC to identify and order microforms from the Family History Library for a modest fee. Thousands of local family history centers in LDS churches, staffed by volunteers, provide access to rented microfilm, as well as selected commercial genealogy sites.

PHYSICAL LIBRARIES

Reduced demand to house physical collections in library buildings has prompted librarians to reevaluate the role of the library building within their communities and campuses. As librarians and technologists think about library spaces in new ways, it is clear that libraries are evolving from the traditional role of book repository to more dynamic roles.

In academic libraries, student enrollment growth and demand for physical space on campuses have prompted the development of *learning commons* spaces in libraries. Beginning with the integration of computer labs into library space, academic libraries added cafés to offer refreshments for library users spending long hours in the library for study and group work assignments.

These learning commons spaces have now moved beyond the café-bookstore model to include student-centered services such as tutoring, advising, and adaptive technology support services. Group presentation space, as well as exhibition and event areas, are also often included. One-stop shops staffed by technologists introduce teaching faculty to these new learning environments and help them integrate technology into their courses and assignments.

Lessons learned from implementation of learning commons spaces are now being applied by IT professionals and librarians to experimental classrooms in libraries. *Flipped courses*, embracing active learning and collaborative work between faculty and student groups, demand technology-rich environments. Academic libraries are uniquely positioned for these experimental classrooms, offering collaborative space for related academic disciplines in a neutral campus environment, robust technology backbones, and access to subject-based resources.

Helen Chu, director of Academic Technology at the University of Oregon, notes that integrating active learning classrooms into the library not only creates additional opportunities for the embedded librarian to partner meaningfully with teaching faculty, but also leads to new collaborative opportunities with other campus units. Through such initiatives, academic libraries partner with campus planning, technology service delivery, student success, faculty development, and research and innovation. By embedding not only the librarian into the curricula, but also the library itself, the role of the academic library evolves from a passive book repository to a key partner in every aspect of the core teaching and research missions of the parent institution.[19]

Public library administrators, realizing that the traditional "no food, no drink" library policies are no longer viable, are combining collections and services with cafés. Santa Monica Public Library's headquarters library remodel offers an attractive compromise. The rehabbed library building wraps around an outdoor patio with a detached café, where patrons sip coffee, eat breakfast, and read outside on the patio as they wait for the library to open. Staff members also benefit from having an on-site restaurant for quick lunches, impromptu meetings, or work breaks.

As librarians, technologists, and administrators think holistically about what physical library spaces should be, new opportunities arise. Is the physical library becoming a *third place*, as described in Ray Oldenburg's book *The Great Good Place*—that is, somewhere other than work/classroom or home?[20] Some of the characteristics of a third place include a neutral and welcoming atmosphere, free or inexpensive services, and highly accessible space where users feel a sense of belonging. Physical libraries—within their respective

FIGURE 10.1 With flexible furnishings and cutting-edge technology resources, the University of Oregon library's collaborative learning classroom offers a welcoming space for students and faculty to engage in active learning. Reprinted with permission of University of Oregon Active Learning Classroom. Photo: Amanda Garcia, University of Oregon Libraries.

communities of campus, neighborhood, or school—are increasingly and deliberately offering elements of third places.

"Interestingly (and tellingly) the index to *The Great Good Place* lists fifteen entries for tavern, nineteen entries for coffee houses, but no entries for libraries," notes University of Iowa Librarian James Elmborg. In his thoughtful and comprehensive article on libraries and theories about public spaces, he writes:

> We can choose to become more like commercial entities with products and customer bases, or we can aim to be socially meaningful institutions with a higher role and calling. We can become bookstores in an effort to beat bookstores, or we can work to build libraries and librarianship around the concept of shared social space where real people engage in real struggle for meaning and purpose in a landscape of increasingly rapid human movement and social change. . . . [M]ost of all, it is crucial for libraries and librarians to continue to "market" the library, in the sense that we need to make sure libraries are seen as an important presence in our communities, especially to those who fund us. However, it is crucial that in our competition with commercial entities we keep our focus on being libraries and librarians, and it is especially crucial that we not give up on the search for understanding what those concepts mean. A library is a fundamentally different place than a bookstore or the cloud, and one profound difference is the presence of librarians.[21]

LIBRARY OUTREACH AND MARKETING

Traditional library services and buildings have been transformed not just by digitization, but also in the ways services are promoted and delivered. Although digitizing collections and creating new learning spaces may seem to be worthy goals in themselves, ensuring that these collections and services play a crucial role for users and parent institutions is the ultimate purpose. A 2012 EDUCAUSE article, "If You Build It, Will They Come? Library Learning Spaces and Technology," found that providing new collaborative hardware and remodeled library learning spaces was not enough. Rather, the crucial step was reaching out to users, employing four basic principles:

1. Make it obvious

2. Market it

3. Model it

4. Modify as needed[22]

Reaching out to faculty and students, and integrating digital resources, are essential to position academic librarians and services effectively in campus knowledge creation cycles. The days when academic and public libraries relied on a few press releases to promote building-bound services are over.

ROBIN A. BEDENBAUGH
Coordinator of Library Marketing
& Communication

INGRID RUFFIN
Student Success Librarian
for First-Year Programs

JUDY LI
Business Librarian

LIBRARIES

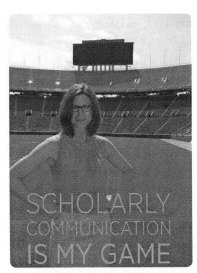

HOLLY MERCER
Associate Dean for Scholarly
Communication & Research Services

FIGURES 10.2, 10.3, 10.4, 10.5 The libraries of the University of Tennessee, Knoxville, reach out to students and faculty with a series of personalized librarian profiles entitled "Information Is Our Game." Reprinted with permission of University of Tennessee Libraries, Knoxville.

Now government, public, and academic libraries frequently dedicate full-time outreach positions to librarians with specializations in marketing. Communication and outreach job descriptions in public and academic libraries reflect this shift, including new responsibilities for:

- Developing and maintaining the library's brand, with unified graphics and logos
- Creating library media and marketing campaigns and assessing results
- Encouraging librarians to meet with user groups, leave the library to visit academic units, attend academic department meetings and events, and stay in touch via chat, e-mail, and social media
- Determining the most effective social media vehicles and securing content
- Coordinating with the institution's public affairs/marketing staff, fundraising officers, upper-level administrators, local press, and media outlets

Using the university's catchphrase, "Big Orange, Big Ideas," the University of Tennessee Libraries attracts faculty and students to library services in innovative ways. A Web page called "Information Is Our Game" introduces academic librarians to students and faculty by discipline, using a colorful and appealing trading-card format.[23]

The University of Tennessee Libraries also has a YouTube channel offering videos of special collections and library events, as well as "Information Is Our Game" videos. Featuring academic librarians and their subject expertise, the videos convey a great deal of information about library services in an engaging and humorous way.[24]

LIBRARY WORKERS AND EVOLVING SERVICES

For library staffers at all levels, the Internet has brought fundamental change to their responsibilities. Online ordering from vendor or publisher websites has streamlined acquisitions. Electronic journals have reduced the need for serials check-in and binding. Patrons may check out their selections themselves. In addition to changes such as these, new positions and responsibilities are being developed.

New Careers and New Training

The rise of the Internet and reliance on digital information has created new job classifications in libraries. The need for digital librarians and digital technicians is on the rise. Knowledge of imaging technologies, markup languages, metadata schemas, and Web technology go hand-in-hand with an understanding of library operations and a user-centered focus. Academic and public library employers expect successful candidates for these positions to understand traditional resources and services, and translate them into digital collections and services that meet user demands, library goals, and demonstrate the library's value to the parent institution. In schools and colleges, librarians and technicians work closely with instructors to identify and create multimedia resources for classroom presentations or distance education. The Web is increasingly being used as the mechanism for delivering instruction to students and content to users.

These imperatives emphasize the critical need for constant retraining and updating of skills for all library personnel, from seasoned staffers to new recruits just entering the library field. These trends and innovations require not only staff members who are committed to growth, but also an equal institutional commitment to ongoing library staff development. Staff training possibilities are now richer because of teleconferencing and Webinars, expanding continuing education access for those staff members who may not have been eligible in the past for limited travel funds.

Electronic discussion groups, professional listservs, and librarian blogs provide convenient venues for problem solving and information sharing among colleagues. These tools provide fresh avenues for discussion among library and media center employees. Because e-mail and the Web are not geographically bound, requests for problem solving or responses to a query are just as likely to come from halfway around the world as they are from a nearby librarian. Staff can also go online for the latest industry news. Library trade periodicals have sprouted Web versions, and there are numerous specialty e-journals that cater to specialties, such as data curation, IT systems, knowledge management, and library instruction. Issues facing library support staff are addressed via the pioneering *Associates* newsletter.[25]

Teaching Users

Information managers, librarians, and library technicians have always drawn from their teaching skills as they walk library users through the mysteries of catalogs, call numbers, periodical indexes, shelf locations, and other tools essential to locating information. In the Internet era, add to that basic skill set the need to train novice users in keyboarding, computer basics, Web use, e-mail access, and specific programs, along with the ability to differentiate between reliable and spurious information sources.

A continuing challenge in the 21st century is conveying critical thinking skills to library users to sort out the proverbial wheat from the chaff of information. Often, electronic information has not passed through the filtering process to which information published on paper is subjected. Welcome gains in timely distribution may be offset by a lack of quality. Fact checking and editing are no longer guarantees when information is made available immediately. How to best help patrons learn to locate reliable information on the Web is an ongoing priority.

Instructional presentations to small groups, entire classrooms, and computer labs are daily duties that require a thorough grounding in library resources and services, public speaking and teaching abilities, plus understanding of different learning styles. In addition, strong research skills, patience, and an ability to solve problems are musts.

Teaching Research Skills

As with any information source, Internet data requires both novice and experienced researchers alike to evaluate and apply critical thinking skills to their search results. To publish digital editions around the clock, editorial and reporting standards for newspapers may fall by the wayside, as proliferating media outlets and aggregators rush to scoop competitors. Traditional journalistic standards can be lost in the rush to be first, creating a fertile ground for inaccuracies that fuel gossip and innuendo. Academic sites that appear to be scholarly may have skipped the lengthy editorial processes common to publishing peer-reviewed articles in scholarly journals. Websites, articles, comments, and redirects may masquerade as legitimate, but may have been created entirely by online marketing firms.

Researchers, especially younger students, have a tendency to think exclusively in terms of the Internet as a source. In many cases, they are unaware of reference books, subscription databases, or other vetted sources and are forsaking tools that could help and instead defaulting to a general Google search. A corollary of this dependence on Web resources is that novice researchers have less tolerance for using print- or microfilm-based resources.

Surveys conducted by Project Information Literacy (PLI) reveal troubling data. Employers expect college graduates hired today to be able to search and find resources online, yet one PLI study found that most students relied almost exclusively on course readings, Google, and Wikipedia. Nearly all employers also said they expected successful job candidates "to be patient and persistent researchers and to be able to retrieve information in a variety of formats, identify patterns within an array of sources, and dive deeply into source material." These employers are often disappointed to find their "fresh-from-college hires frequently lack deeper and more traditional skills in research and analysis. Instead, the new workers default to quick answers plucked from the Internet. That method might be fine for looking up a definition or updating a fact, but for many tasks, it proved superficial and incomplete."[26]

Librarians should perhaps shoulder part of the responsibility for this gap in research skills. The average library user success rate for finding journal articles or article databases is only 52 percent, according to *Library Journal*.[27] In a review of 51 usability studies primarily undertaken by university libraries, UC Berkeley reference librarian John Kupersmith found that users don't know what librarians are talking about. Acronyms and brand names, subject categories, and the words *database, library catalog, e-journals, index, interlibrary loan, periodical, serial, reference,* and *resource* were major sources of confusion. Kupersmith discovered successful terms used natural language, such as "find books" or "find articles," that focused on what resources users were seeking. Kupersmith lists seven best practices, including usability testing, using natural language on top-level pages, and using mouse-overs or tooltips to define terms that confuse.[28]

Reaching Readers

Numerous studies show that for Americans (and likely others worldwide), less time is spent on sustained, in-depth reading, with browsing and scanning on the rise. The number of adults who read at least one novel, play, or poem within the past 12 months fell to 47 percent in 2012, from 50 percent in 2008, according to a National Endowment for the Arts survey of 37,000 Americans. Fiction reading rose from 2002 to 2008, but has been dropping ever since, and is now back to 2002 levels. By comparison, 30 years ago 56 percent of Americans read fiction. The decline in fiction reading last year occurred mostly among white Americans, including women and men of various educational backgrounds; rates held steady among persons of color and Latino groups, the report found.[29]

Technology author Nicholas G. Carr has written extensively about his growing problem remaining engaged both with books he reads for work and books he reads for pleasure. Carr posits that the Internet diminishes the capacity for concentration and contemplation found in "deep reading." He writes, "Once I was a scuba diver in the sea of words. Now I zip along the surface like a guy on a Jet Ski."[30] A *Chicago Tribune* reviewer of Carr's work concurs:

> . . . If you've ever had the feeling Carr writes about, you know that . . . he is onto something. Like transformative information technologies before it, the Internet just might be rewiring us, luring us with its seemingly limitless flow of data, then shattering our attention spans into a hundred little shards, turning us from readers into gleaners, from writers, metaphorically speaking, into bloggers.
>
> That feeling? You used to be a voracious reader, almost nestling inside the typeface, but now you skitter along the surface of a page, ready to be distracted by a light bulb going off in another room or the sudden thought that you need to TiVo a show that airs next week.[31]

This decline understandably creates great concern among librarians and other professionals who promote reading and literacy. One response comes from ALA's Young Adult Library Services Association (YALSA) and their wiki devoted to teen outreach. The Summer Reading page includes ways to promote Teen Read Week and Teen Tech Week, based on studies that prove "summer reading and learning programs help ensure that children and teens retain critical reading and academic skills they acquired during the school year." Librarians are also examining strategies that appeal to dedicated adult readers, while reaching out to non-readers by promoting downloadable audiobooks and e-books.[32]

THE INTERNET AND HEALTH

So is there a downside to the Internet, this remarkable global network, the devices, the apps that have so transformed our lives? Any new technology is invariably accompanied by new issues and unforeseen situations. In the meantime, controversial aspects of the Internet provide plenty of fodder for discussion among the media, educators, technologists, futurists, and users.

Managing Constant Change

Multitasking on computers and mobile devices not only affects the way people process information, but can also lead workers to feeling overwhelmed.

New apps, new sites, new gadgets, new software, new ways to connect with others seem to appear daily. When these tools promise to make our lives and the lives of library users easier, it may be difficult to resist. According to *The State of Workplace Productivity Report,* "Fifty percent of employees said they experience some type of work overload, with 34 percent claiming information overload and 25 percent technology overload. Furthermore, 38 percent of respondents said there isn't enough collaboration in their workplace."[33]

"The average person today consumes almost three times as much information as what the typical person consumed in 1960, according to research at the University of California, San Diego," NPR reports. "And *The New York Times* reports that the average computer user checks 40 Web sites a day and can switch [television] programs 36 times an hour. 'It's an onslaught of information coming in today,' says *Times* technology journalist Matt Richtel. 'At one time a screen meant maybe something in your living room. But now it's something in your pocket so it goes everywhere—it can be behind the wheel, it can be at the dinner table, it can be in the bathroom. We see it everywhere today.'"[34]

One documented downside is technology overload. The proliferation of newer, better, faster, cheaper, more convenient electronic apps and devices is an amazing convenience from which we all benefit, but it can also be a mixed blessing. In a business environment that assumes that one is always available by text, e-mail, pager, cell phone, fax, or other invention, where are the boundaries between constant access and being "un-plugged" in our personal lives? Managing the use of modern communication tools and technology to prevent anxiety and psychological stress from the constant pressure to be on duty is an important contemporary issue. Do we skillfully use our iPhones and Androids to manage our lives, or are they managing us?

Another issue of concern is the divide created by those who are skilled at using the Internet and those who are not. Although divisions in our society are not new, the *digital divide* has the potential to widen the already looming gap between the poor and the rich. In addition to the goals of economic growth and equality, those working to bridge the digital divide believe it would also improve literacy, further job skills, inform citizen-voters, promote social advancement, and improve health.

The digital divide typically exists between:

- Educated and the uneducated
- City-dwellers and those in rural areas
- Younger users and the elderly
- Socioeconomic groups
- Industrial nations and developing countries

Remedies to this chronic situation are mostly grant-funded individual projects. An example is a grant the city of Boston received in 2010 to reach three underserved groups: (1) parents and children learning about technology together (Technology Goes Home), (2) those living in three senior communities (Connected Living), and (3) out-of-work adults enrolled in technology programs at job assistance centers (On Line Learning Readiness).[35] Given the scale of the issues involved, more coherent and coordinated programs, perhaps at the state level, are indicated to reach those who are negatively affected by the digital divide. For a fuller discussion of the digital divide, see Chapter 8.

Physical and Psychological Effects

Scientists are researching the mental and physical health effects from the increasing amount of time humans now spend in front of computer screens, some days logging more hours in cyberspace than in the real world. But certain trends are apparent. Carpal tunnel syndrome and repetitive-use injuries have long been commonplace among data-entry operators, and are on the rise among youth who have grown up with substantial keyboarding use—on desktops, laptops, and smaller portable devices, such as tablets and cell phones.

In addition to physiological effects, there are psychological effects as well. As use of the Internet has become pervasive in Americans' daily lives, so has the rise of various Web-based addictions. Some professionals suggest "6 percent to 10 percent of the Internet users in the U.S. have a dependency that can be as destructive as alcoholism and drug addiction, and [doctors] are rushing to treat it."[36]

Other research has focused on whether use of the Internet presents an increased risk of isolation or depression. Studies show that use of online community/chat and websites that are sexually gratifying or offer gaming correlate with Internet addiction. "The concept of Internet addiction is emerging as a construct that must be taken seriously. . . . Those who regard themselves as dependent on the Internet report high levels of depressive symptoms . . . [and] are likely to engage proportionately more than the normal population in sites that serve as a replacement for real-life socialising."[37]

Cyberbullying—preteens and teenagers using electronic technology to bully others—is a dismaying trend arising from digital anonymity in the hands of children. Many K-12 school districts now have policies specifying disciplinary actions for offenders in an attempt to dissuade this new, uglier version of playground taunting. School library workers in particular should be well versed about bullying, cyberbullying, who is at risk, and how to prevent and respond to bullying.[38]

Teenage girls are significantly more likely to be cyberbullied than boys. Online harassment and threats aimed at women users also are on the rise. "Just appearing as a woman online, it seems, can be enough to inspire abuse. In 2006, researchers from the University of Maryland set up a bunch of fake online accounts and then dispatched them into chat rooms. Accounts with feminine usernames incurred an average of 100 sexually explicit or threatening messages a day. Masculine names received 3.7."[39]

In 2014, the first Pew Research Center survey on online violence found that young women ages 18 to 24, "experience certain severe types of harassment at disproportionately high levels: 26 percent of these young women have been stalked online, and 25 percent were the target of online sexual harassment. In addition, they do not escape the heightened rates of physical threats and sustained harassment common to their male peers and young people in general."[40]

Twitter-based campaigns, such as #TakeBackTheTech and #16Days, try to prevent online gender-based violence. Sexism on Facebook is such a pervasive issue that the company announced new efforts to crack down specifically on posts that target "women with images and content that threatens or incites gender-based violence or hate."[41]

Increased reliance on computers, whether for work or for pleasure, can't help but further compete for our discretionary time and make it that much harder to engage in exercise or physical fitness activities. Children are especially at risk as they may develop early behavior patterns with less time spent in daily physical activity and more time spent in inactive forms of play, such as watching TV, playing video games, text messaging, and using computers.

As the Internet usage matures, future inventions will help resolve some of these current issues while simultaneously ushering in a host of new challenges. Count on the Internet to spark discussion among the old and the young, the technological gurus, Luddites, and novices as to its virtues and vices. But the changes ushered in by the Internet, and particularly by the World Wide Web, are here to stay. And the pace of change will only continue to accelerate.

SUMMARY

If the dynamic environment described in the preceding chapters seems attractive to you, you may have a future in library science. If you are over 30 and contemplating a career change, you will not be alone. In the 20th century, librarians and library technicians alike typically chose their careers after spending some time in other endeavors.

The average age of students in post-baccalaureate certificate programs was 36.8; the average age of library school graduate students was 36.6.[42] Historically, students in library technology programs primarily have been females in their forties.

Whatever the gender and age demographics of those employed in the library field, their mission remains solving information problems for library users. In this quest, the only predictable constant appears to be change. The cascading development of technology and the resulting explosion of both formats and quantity of information will make problem-solving skills in this field more necessary than ever.

STUDY QUESTIONS

1. Spend some time browsing one of the "digital libraries" mentioned in the text. Name and describe three documents or resources that you located which especially impressed you.

2. Take the Pew Research Center's test to find out your engagement level with the local public library. Do you feel this is an accurate characterization of your habits? http://www.pewinternet.org/quiz/library-typology/

3. Would you consider your public library to be a comfortable and welcoming place to go? If so, describe three features that contribute to this positive environment. If not, name three drawbacks to the facility.

4. What is a genealogist? Why are they noteworthy as users of library resources?

5. Name your favorite social networking sites. Why do you prefer these? Are you using them for business promotion or for recreation?

6. Can you recommend a specific library outreach campaign or effort (other than those mentioned earlier) that you find effective? How are they promoting their services and to what audiences?

7. How are modern academic libraries involved in building collections of and providing access to scholarly communication for their institution?

8. What are the disadvantages of using the Web? Have you had any negative personal experiences?

9. Do you think libraries are obsolete because of the Internet? Why or why not? Are libraries doing a good job of repositioning themselves? What else should be done to remain relevant?

10. What are your thoughts on the decline in "deep reading"? What steps can librarians take on this issue?

NOTES

1. Stacey A. Aldrich and Jarrid P. Keller, "IV: Place," in *The Library 2020: Today's Leading Visionaries Describe Tomorrow's Library*, ed. Joseph Janes (Lanham, MD: The Scarecrow Press, Inc., 2013), 107.

2. Tim O'Reilly, "What Is Web 2.0: Design Patterns and Business Models for the Next Generation of Software," *O'Reilly Media*, 2009, accessed March 9, 2015, http://www.oreilly.com/pub/a/web2/archive/what-is-web-20.html?page=1.

3. David Stuart, "Web 2.0 in Libraries Should Be More Than Social Media Research Information," *Research Information*, June/July 2012, accessed March 9, 2015, http://www.researchinformation.info/features/feature.php?feature_id=367.

4. Internet2, *About Internet2*, accessed March 11, 2015, http://www.internet2.edu/about-us/.

5. George Packer, "Cheap Words: Amazon Is Good For Customers. But Is It Good For Books?" *The New Yorker*, February 14, 2014, accessed March 9, 2015, http://www.newyorker.com/magazine/2014/02/17/cheap-words.

6. Gary Price, "The Authors Guild Files Brief in Google Books Appeal & Proposes That Congress Establish a National Digital Library," *InfoDocket/Library Journal*, April 11, 2014, accessed March 9, 2015, http://www.infodocket.com/2014/04/11/authors-guild-files-brief-in-google-books-appeal-says-congress-should-create-a-national-digital-library. "The Authors Guild proposes that Congress establish a collective management organization, similar to ASCAP, to license digital rights to out-of-print books. Authors, publishers and other rights holders would be paid for the use of their works, and they would have the right to exclude their books from any or all uses. . . . It would not license e-book or print book rights (only the author or other rights holder could

do that), and it wouldn't collect its administrative fee until it paid the rights holder."

"The National Digital Library would display full book pages, not mere "snippets." It would be the equivalent of a great research library that anyone can view from their dorm room or through access to a high school, public library or other subscribing institution. It would be a level-the-playing-field leap for small colleges, remote libraries and communities everywhere. . . . The National Digital Library's digitized text and digital page images would be fully accessible to the visually impaired."

7. "Authors Guild v. HathiTrust," Electronic Frontier Foundation, accessed March 9, 2015, https://www.eff.org/cases/authors-guild-v-hathitrust.

8. Diane Zorich, Günter Waibel and Ricky Erway, "Beyond the Silos of the LAMs: Collaboration among Libraries, Archives and Museums. *OCLC Research*, (2008), accessed March 11, 2015, http://www.oclc.org/content/dam/research/publications/library/2008/2008-05.pdf?urlm=162914.

9. Deborah Wythe, "New Technologies and the Convergence of Libraries, Archives, and Museums," *RBM: A Journal of Rare Books, Manuscripts, and Cultural Heritage*, 8:1 (Spring 2007), accessed March 11, 2015, rbm.acrl.org/content/8/1/51.full.pdf.

10. Digital Library Federation, accessed March 11, 2015, http://www.diglib.org.

11. Society of American Archivists, *Metadata*, accessed March 11, 2015, http://www2.archivists.org/glossary/terms/m/metadata.

12. Library of Congress, *American Memory*, http://memory.loc.gov/ammem/index.html and *State Digital Resources: Memory Projects, Online Encyclopedias, Historical & Cultural Materials Collections*, accessed March 11, 2015, http://www.loc.gov/rr/program/bib/statememory/American Memory.

13. Robin Bedenbaugh and Holly Mercer, "The Embedded Repository: Introducing an Institutional Repository to a New Audience Via Location-Aware Social Networking," *Practical Academic Librarianship: The International Journal of the SLA Academic Division*. 2:1 (2012), 26–402.

14. Kennedy Library, California Polytechnic State University. *Institutional Repository Annual Report to the Provost AY 2007–2008*, (September 2008), accessed March 29, 2015, http://works.bepress.com/nloe/39.

15. Kay Cahill. "Building a Virtual Branch at Vancouver Public Library Using Web 2.0 Tools," *Program*. 43: 2 (2009), 140–155, accessed March 11, 2015, http://dx.doi.org/10.1108/00330330910954361.

16. American Library Association, *Guidelines for Implementing and Maintaining Virtual Reference Services*, accessed March 11, 2015, http://www.ala.org/rusa/resources/guidelines/virtrefguidelines.

17. "Online Reference," *Library Success: A Best Practices Wiki*, accessed March 11, 2015, http://www.libsuccess.org/Online_Reference.

18. Association of Cooperative and Specialized Library Agencies, *Library Services for People with Disabilities Policy*, (January 16, 2001), accessed March 29, 2015, http://www.ala.org/ascla/asclaissues/libraryservices.

19. Helen Y. Chu, "UO Libraries Shape the Student Academic Experience" (presentation, University of Oregon Libraries Advancement Council, Eugene, OR, May 2015), accessed May 18, 2015, http://works.bepress.com/helen_chu/9/.

20. Ray Oldenburg, *The Great Good Place: Cafés, Coffee Shops, Bookstores, Bars, Hair Salons, and Other Hangouts at the Heart of a Community*. Cambridge, MA: Da Capo Press, 1989, rev. 1999.

21. James Elmborg, "Libraries as the Spaces Between Us: Recognizing and Valuing the Third Space," *Reference & User Services Quarterly* (2011), 338–350,

accessed March 29, 2015, http://ir.uiowa.edu/cgi/viewcontent.cgi?article= 1008&context=slis_pubs.

22. Megan McGlynn, Amanda Peters, and Shae Rafferty, "If You Build It, Will They Come? Library Learning Spaces and Technology," *EDUCAUSE Review,* November 1, 2012, accessed March 29, 2015, http://www.educause.edu/ero/ article/if-you-build-it-will-they-come-library-learning-spaces-and-technology.

23. University of Tennessee Libraries, *Information Is Our Game,* accessed March 29, 2015, http://www.lib.utk.edu/news/category/information-is-our-game/.

24. University of Tennessee Libraries, "Information Is Our Game—Episode 2" *YouTube* video, 1:15. July 18, 2014, accessed March 29, 2015, https://youtu .be/sFu8J8ExY_Y. See also https://www.youtube.com/user/UTKLibraries.

25. *Associates: The Electronic Library Support Staff Journal,* accessed March 11, 2015, http://associates.ucr.edu/index.html.

26. Alison J. Head and John Wihbey, "At Sea in a Deluge of Data," *The Chronicle of Higher Education,* accessed March 12, 2015, http://chronicle.com/article/ At-Sea-in-a-Deluge-of-Data/147477/.

27. Meredith Schwartz, "Users Don't Know What Libraries Are Talking About, Studies Find," *Library Journal,* March 15, 2012, accessed March 12, 2015, http://lj.libraryjournal.com/2012/03/academic-libraries/users-dont-know- what-libraries-are-talking-about-studies-find/.

28. John Kupersmith, *Library Terms That Users Understand,* University of California eScholarship, 2012, accessed March 12, 2015, http://escholarship.org/ uc/item/3qq499w7.

29. National Endowment for the Arts, *A Decade of Arts Engagement: Findings from the Survey of Public Participation in the Arts, 2002–2012,* accessed March 15, 2015, http://arts.gov/sites/default/files/2012-sppa-jan2015-rev.pdf.

30. Nicholas Carr, "Is Google Making Us Stupid? What the Internet Is Doing to Our Brains," *Atlantic Monthly,* July 1 2008, accessed April 8, 2015, http:// www.theatlantic.com/magazine/archive/2008/07/is-google-making-us- stupid/306868/. See also Carr's *The Big Switch: Rewiring the World, from Edison to Google,* New York: W.W. Norton & Company, 2008, rev. ed. 2013. His blog, Rough Type, is available at http://www.roughtype.com/.

31. Steve Johnson, "Read This If You're Easily Distracted Lately," *Reading Eagle,* August 22, 2008, http://www2.readingeagle.com/article.aspx?id=103183.

32. Young Adult Library Services Association, *Summer Reading,* accessed April 8, 2015, http://wikis.ala.org/yalsa/index.php/Summer_Reading.

33. Cornerstone OnDemand. *The State of Workplace Productivity Report,* 2013, accessed March 11, 2015, http://www.cornerstoneondemand.com/sites/ default/files/research/csod-rs-state-of-workplace-productivity-report_0.pdf.

34. National Public Radio, "Digital Overload: Your Brain on Gadgets," accessed March 11, 2015, http://www.npr.org/templates/story/story.php?storyId= 129384107.

35. "City of Boston Receives $4.3 Million Grant That Will Give Training, Computers and Opportunity to Underserved Communities," City of Boston press release, September 14, 2010, accessed March 12, 2015, http://www.cityof boston.gov/news/Default.aspx?id=4765.

36. Sarah Kershaw, "Hooked on the Web: Help Is on the Way," *The New York Times,* December 1, 2005, accessed March 12, 2015, http://www.nytimes .com/2005/12/01/fashion/thursdaystyles/01addict.html.

37. Catronia M. Morrison and Helen Gore, "The Relationship Between Excessive Internet Use and Depression: A Questionnaire-Based Study of 1,319 Young People and Adults," *Psychopathology* 43, no. 2 (2010), 121–126. dx.doi.org/

10.1159/000277001, accessed March 29, 2015, http://www.gnmhealthcare
.com/pdf/01-2010/22/1867841_TheRelationshipbetweenExc.pdf.

38. StopBullying.gov. *What Is Cyberbullying?*, accessed March 29, 2015, http://
www.stopbullying.gov/index.html and https://www.youtube.com/watch?v=
lN2fuKPDzHA.

39. Amanda Hess, "Why Women Aren't Welcome on the Internet," *Pacific Standard,* January 6, 2014, accessed March 29, 2015, http://www.psmag.com/
health-and-behavior/women-arent-welcome-internet-72170.

40. Maeve Duggan, *Online Harassment,* Pew Research Center for Internet, Science and Tech June 2014 accessed March 29, 2015, http://www.pewinternet
.org/2014/10/22/online-harassment/.

41. "Facebook Bows to Campaign Groups Over 'Hate Speech,'" *BBC News,* May 20,
2013, accessed March 29, 2015, http://www.bbc.com/news/technology-227
01082. Also "Controversial, Harmful and Hateful Speech on Facebook," *Facebook
Safety,* accessed March 29, 2015, https://www.facebook.com/notes/facebook-
safety/controversial-harmful-and-hateful-speech-on-facebook/574430
655911054.

42. Council of Graduate Schools, "Data Sources: Non-Traditional Students in Graduate Education," *Communicator,* December 2009, accessed March 12, 2015,
http://www.cgsnet.org/ckfinder/userfiles/files/DataSources_2009_12.pdf.

RESOURCES

Books

Alman, Sue, Christinger Tomer, and Margaret L. Lincoln, eds. *Designing Online
Learning: A Primer for Librarians.* Santa Barbara, CA: Libraries Unlimited,
2012.

Almquist, Sharon G., ed. *Distributed Learning and Virtual Librarianship.* Santa
Barbara, CA: Libraries Unlimited, 2011.

Bonn, Maria and Mike Furlough, eds. *Getting the Word Out: Academic Libraries as
Scholarly Publishers.* Chicago: Association of College and Research Libraries,
2015.

Davis-Kahl, Stephanie and Merinda Kaye Hensley. *Common Ground at the Nexus
of Information Literacy and Scholarly Communication.* Chicago: Association of
College and Research Libraries, 2015.

Describing Archives: A Content Standard. 2nd ed. Chicago: Society of American
Archivists, 2013. Also at: http://files.archivists.org/pubs/DACS2E-2013
.pdf.

Hartsell-Gundy, Arianne, Laura Braunstein, and Liorah Golomb. *Digital Humanities
in the Library: Challenges and Opportunities for Subject Specialists.* Chicago:
American Library Association, 2015.

Papers/Articles/Presentations

Allen-Barker, Jennifer, Nikki DeMoville, Nancy E. Loe, Deborah McArdle, Michael
Price, and Frank Vuotto. "Increasing Accessibility of Kennedy Library Materials for Individuals with Disabilities: A Task Group Report." *Office of the Dean,
Kennedy Library, California Polytechnic State University.* June 2009. http://
works.bepress.com/nloe/40.

Chu, Helen Y., Franz Kurfess, David Gillette, et al. "Toward a User-Centered I2-Enabled Collaborative Learning and Teaching Environment: The Cal Poly Scandinavian Style Participatory Design Project." Presentation, Internet2 Fall 2005 Member Meeting, Philadelphia, PA, September 2005, http://works.bepress.com/helen_chu/11.

Cox, Andrew M. and Sheila Corrall. "Evolving Academic Library Specialties." *Journal of the American Society for Information Science and Technology* 64, no. 8 (May 2013): 1526–1542. http://dx.doi.org/10.1002/asi.22847.

Diamond, David. "Library Science, Not Library Silence." *CMSWire.com.* August 19, 2014. http://www.cmswire.com/cms/digital-asset-management/library-science-not-library-silence-026230.php.

Fanslow, Deborah. "Who Needs a DAM Librarian?" *DAM News: Digital Asset Management News, Reviews, Trends, and Opinion.* 2014–2015. http://digitalassetmanagementnews.org/category/dam-for-librarians/.

Richards, Lisa. "Computer and Software Accessibility for the Disabled." *Mapcon: The Original CMMS.* http://www.mapcon.com/computer-and-software-accessibility-for-the-disabled.

Salem, Susan and Kenning Arlitsch. "The Western Waters Digital Library: Providing Solutions through Collaboration and Technology." Paper and presentation, ACRL Twelfth National Conference, Minneapolis, MN April 7–10, 2005, http://www.ala.org/acrl/sites/ala.org.acrl/files/content/conferences/pdf/salem05.pdf.

Websites

American Library Association—Library Instruction Round Table (LIRT). http://www.ala.org/lirt/front.

Associates: The Electronic Library Support Staff Journal. http://associates.ucr.edu/journal/.

California State Library—*Library Literacy Services.* http://libraryliteracy.org.

Cyberbullying Research Center. http://cyberbullying.us/.

Young Adult Library Services Association. http://wikis.ala.org/yalsa/index.php/Main_Page.

Appendix A: Declaration for the Right to Libraries

In the spirit of the United States Declaration of Independence and the Universal Declaration of Human Rights, we believe that libraries are essential to a democratic society. Every day, in countless communities across our nation and the world, millions of children, students, and adults use libraries to learn, grow, and achieve their dreams. In addition to a vast array of books, computers and other resources, library users benefit from the expert teaching and guidance of librarians and library staff to help expand their minds and open new worlds. We declare and affirm our right to quality libraries—public, school, academic, and special—and urge you to show your support by signing your name to this Declaration for the Right to Libraries.

LIBRARIES EMPOWER THE INDIVIDUAL. Whether developing skills to succeed in school, looking for a job, exploring possible careers, having a baby, or planning retirement, people of all ages turn to libraries for instruction, support, and access to computers and other resources to help them lead better lives.

LIBRARIES SUPPORT LITERACY AND LIFELONG LEARNING. Many children and adults learn to read at their school and public libraries via story

Adopted June 30, 2013, by the ALA Council. Used with permission from the American Library Association.

times, research projects, summer reading, tutoring, and other opportunities. Others come to the library to learn the technology and information skills that help them answer their questions, discover new interests, and share their ideas with others.

LIBRARIES STRENGTHEN FAMILIES. Families find a comfortable, welcoming space and a wealth of resources to help them learn, grow and play together.

LIBRARIES ARE THE GREAT EQUALIZER. Libraries serve people of every age, education level, income level, ethnicity, and physical ability. For many people, libraries provide resources that they could not otherwise afford—resources they need to live, learn, work, and govern.

LIBRARIES BUILD COMMUNITIES. Libraries bring people together, both in person and online, to have conversations and to learn from and help each other. Libraries provide support for seniors, immigrants and others with special needs.

LIBRARIES PROTECT OUR RIGHT TO KNOW. Our right to read, seek information, and speak freely must not be taken for granted. Libraries and librarians actively defend this most basic freedom as guaranteed by the First Amendment.

LIBRARIES STRENGTHEN OUR NATION. The economic health and successful governance of our nation depend on people who are literate and informed. School, public, academic, and special libraries support this basic right.

LIBRARIES ADVANCE RESEARCH AND SCHOLARSHIP. Knowledge grows from knowledge. Whether doing a school assignment, seeking a cure for cancer, pursuing an academic degree, or developing a more fuel efficient engine, scholars and researchers of all ages depend on the knowledge and expertise that libraries and librarians offer.

LIBRARIES HELP US TO BETTER UNDERSTAND EACH OTHER. People from all walks of life come together at libraries to discuss issues of common concern. Libraries provide programs, collections, and meeting spaces to help us share and learn from our differences.

LIBRARIES PRESERVE OUR NATION'S CULTURAL HERITAGE. The past is key to our future. Libraries collect, digitize, and preserve original and unique historical documents that help us to better understand our past, present, and future.

Appendix B:
"Library Bill of Rights"

The American Library Association affirms that all libraries are forums for information and ideas, and that the following basic policies should guide their services.

I. Books and other library resources should be provided for the interest, information, and enlightenment of all people of the community the library serves. Materials should not be excluded because of the origin, background, or views of those contributing to their creation.

II. Libraries should provide materials and information presenting all points of view on current and historical issues. Materials should not be proscribed or removed because of partisan or doctrinal disapproval.

III. Libraries should challenge censorship in the fulfillment of their responsibility to provide information and enlightenment.

IV. Libraries should cooperate with all persons and groups concerned with resisting abridgment of free expression and free access to ideas.

Adopted June 18, 1948, by the ALA Council; amended February 2, 1961; amended June 28, 1967; amended January 23, 1980; inclusion of "age" reaffirmed January 24, 1996. Used with permission from the American Library Association.

331

V. A person's right to use a library should not be denied or abridged because of origin, age, background, or views.

VI. Libraries which make exhibit spaces and meeting rooms available to the public they serve should make such facilities available on an equitable basis, regardless of the beliefs or affiliations of individuals or groups requesting their use.

Appendix C:
Code of Ethics of the American Library Association

As members of the American Library Association, we recognize the importance of codifying and making known to the profession and to the general public the ethical principles that guide the work of librarians, other professionals providing information services, library trustees, and library staffs.

Ethical dilemmas occur when values are in conflict. The American Library Association Code of Ethics states the values to which we are committed, and embodies the ethical responsibilities of the profession in this changing information environment.

We significantly influence or control the selection, organization, preservation, and dissemination of information. In a political system grounded in an informed citizenry, we are members of a profession explicitly committed to intellectual freedom and the freedom of access to information. We have a special obligation to ensure the free flow of information and ideas to present and future generations.

Adopted at the 1939 Midwinter Meeting by the ALA Council; amended June 30, 1981; June 28, 1995; and January 22, 2008. Used with permission from the American Library Association.

333

The principles of this Code are expressed in broad statements to guide ethical decision making. These statements provide a framework; they cannot and do not dictate conduct to cover particular situations.

I. We provide the highest level of service to all library users through appropriate and usefully organized resources; equitable service policies; equitable access; and accurate, unbiased, and courteous responses to all requests.

II. We uphold the principles of intellectual freedom and resist all efforts to censor library resources.

III. We protect each library user's right to privacy and confidentiality with respect to information sought or received and resources consulted, borrowed, acquired or transmitted.

IV. We respect intellectual property rights and advocate balance between the interests of information users and rights holders.

V. We treat co-workers and other colleagues with respect, fairness, and good faith, and advocate conditions of employment that safeguard the rights and welfare of all employees of our institutions.

VI. We do not advance private interests at the expense of library users, colleagues, or our employing institutions.

VII. We distinguish between our personal convictions and professional duties and do not allow our personal beliefs to interfere with fair representation of the aims of our institutions or the provision of access to their information resources.

VIII. We strive for excellence in the profession by maintaining and enhancing our own knowledge and skills, by encouraging the professional development of co-workers, and by fostering the aspirations of potential members of the profession.

Appendix D:
The Freedom to
Read Statement

The freedom to read is essential to our democracy. It is continuously under attack. Private groups and public authorities in various parts of the country are working to remove or limit access to reading materials, to censor content in schools, to label "controversial" views, to distribute lists of "objectionable" books or authors, and to purge libraries. These actions apparently rise from a view that our national tradition of free expression is no longer valid; that censorship and suppression are needed to counter threats to safety or national security, as well as to avoid the subversion of politics and the corruption of morals. We, as individuals devoted to reading and as librarians and publishers responsible for disseminating ideas, wish to assert the public interest in the preservation of the freedom to read.

Most attempts at suppression rest on a denial of the fundamental premise of democracy: that the ordinary individual, by exercising critical judgment, will select the good and reject the bad. We trust Americans to recognize propaganda and misinformation, and to make their own decisions about what they read and believe. We do not believe they are prepared to sacrifice their heritage of a free press in order to be "protected" against what others think may be bad for them. We believe they still favor free enterprise in ideas and expression.

Used with permission from the American Library Association.

335

These efforts at suppression are related to a larger pattern of pressures being brought against education, the press, art and images, films, broadcast media, and the Internet. The problem is not only one of actual censorship. The shadow of fear cast by these pressures leads, we suspect, to an even larger voluntary curtailment of expression by those who seek to avoid controversy or unwelcome scrutiny by government officials.

Such pressure toward conformity is perhaps natural to a time of accelerated change. And yet suppression is never more dangerous than in such a time of social tension. Freedom has given the United States the elasticity to endure strain. Freedom keeps open the path of novel and creative solutions, and enables change to come by choice. Every silencing of a heresy, every enforcement of an orthodoxy, diminishes the toughness and resilience of our society and leaves it the less able to deal with controversy and difference.

Now as always in our history, reading is among our greatest freedoms. The freedom to read and write is almost the only means for making generally available ideas or manners of expression that can initially command only a small audience. The written word is the natural medium for the new idea and the untried voice from which come the original contributions to social growth. It is essential to the extended discussion that serious thought requires, and to the accumulation of knowledge and ideas into organized collections.

We believe that free communication is essential to the preservation of a free society and a creative culture. We believe that these pressures toward conformity present the danger of limiting the range and variety of inquiry and expression on which our democracy and our culture depend. We believe that every American community must jealously guard the freedom to publish and to circulate, in order to preserve its own freedom to read. We believe that publishers and librarians have a profound responsibility to give validity to that freedom to read by making it possible for the readers to choose freely from a variety of offerings.

The freedom to read is guaranteed by the Constitution. Those with faith in free people will stand firm on these constitutional guarantees of essential rights and will exercise the responsibilities that accompany these rights.

We therefore affirm these propositions:

1. It is in the public interest for publishers and librarians to make available the widest diversity of views and expressions, including those that are unorthodox, unpopular, or considered dangerous by the majority.

Creative thought is by definition new, and what is new is different. The bearer of every new thought is a rebel until that idea is refined and tested. Totalitarian systems attempt to maintain themselves in power by the ruthless suppression of any concept that challenges the established orthodoxy. The power of a democratic system to adapt to change is vastly strengthened by the freedom of its citizens to choose widely from among conflicting opinions offered freely to them. To stifle every nonconformist idea at birth would mark the end of the democratic process. Furthermore, only through the constant activity of weighing and selecting can the democratic mind attain the strength demanded by times like these. We need to know not only what we believe but why we believe it.

2. Publishers, librarians, and booksellers do not need to endorse every idea or presentation they make available. It would conflict with the public interest

for them to establish their own political, moral, or aesthetic views as a standard for determining what should be published or circulated.

Publishers and librarians serve the educational process by helping to make available knowledge and ideas required for the growth of the mind and the increase of learning. They do not foster education by imposing as mentors the patterns of their own thought. The people should have the freedom to read and consider a broader range of ideas than those that may be held by any single librarian or publisher or government or church. It is wrong that what one can read should be confined to what another thinks proper.

3. It is contrary to the public interest for publishers or librarians to bar access to writings on the basis of the personal history or political affiliations of the author.

No art or literature can flourish if it is to be measured by the political views or private lives of its creators. No society of free people can flourish that draws up lists of writers to whom it will not listen, whatever they may have to say.

4. There is no place in our society for efforts to coerce the taste of others, to confine adults to the reading matter deemed suitable for adolescents, or to inhibit the efforts of writers to achieve artistic expression.

To some, much of modern expression is shocking. But is not much of life itself shocking? We cut off literature at the source if we prevent writers from dealing with the stuff of life. Parents and teachers have a responsibility to prepare the young to meet the diversity of experiences in life to which they will be exposed, as they have a responsibility to help them learn to think critically for themselves. These are affirmative responsibilities, not to be discharged simply by preventing them from reading works for which they are not yet prepared. In these matters values differ, and values cannot be legislated; nor can machinery be devised that will suit the demands of one group without limiting the freedom of others.

5. It is not in the public interest to force a reader to accept the prejudgment of a label characterizing any expression or its author as subversive or dangerous.

The ideal of labeling presupposes the existence of individuals or groups with wisdom to determine by authority what is good or bad for others. It presupposes that individuals must be directed in making up their minds about the ideas they examine. But Americans do not need others to do their thinking for them.

6. It is the responsibility of publishers and librarians, as guardians of the people's freedom to read, to contest encroachments upon that freedom by individuals or groups seeking to impose their own standards or tastes upon the community at large; and by the government whenever it seeks to reduce or deny public access to public information.

It is inevitable in the give and take of the democratic process that the political, the moral, or the aesthetic concepts of an individual or group will occasionally collide with those of another individual or group. In a free society individuals are free to determine for themselves what they wish to read, and each group is free to determine what it will recommend to its freely associated members. But no group has the right to take the law into its own hands, and to impose its own concept of politics or morality upon other members of a democratic society. Freedom is no freedom if it is accorded only to the accepted and the inoffensive. Further, democratic societies are more safe, free, and creative when the free flow of public information is not restricted by governmental prerogative or self-censorship.

7. It is the responsibility of publishers and librarians to give full meaning to the freedom to read by providing books that enrich the quality and diversity of thought and expression. By the exercise of this affirmative responsibility, they can demonstrate that the answer to a "bad" book is a good one, the answer to a "bad" idea is a good one.

The freedom to read is of little consequence when the reader cannot obtain matter fit for that reader's purpose. What is needed is not only the absence of restraint, but the positive provision of opportunity for the people to read the best that has been thought and said. Books are the major channel by which the intellectual inheritance is handed down, and the principal means of its testing and growth. The defense of the freedom to read requires of all publishers and librarians the utmost of their faculties, and deserves of all Americans the fullest of their support.

We state these propositions neither lightly nor as easy generalizations. We here stake out a lofty claim for the value of the written word. We do so because we believe that it is possessed of enormous variety and usefulness, worthy of cherishing and keeping free. We realize that the application of these propositions may mean the dissemination of ideas and manners of expression that are repugnant to many persons. We do not state these propositions in the comfortable belief that what people read is unimportant. We believe rather that what people read is deeply important; that ideas can be dangerous; but that the suppression of ideas is fatal to a democratic society. Freedom itself is a dangerous way of life, but it is ours.

This statement was originally issued in May of 1953 by the Westchester Conference of the American Library Association and the American Book Publishers Council, which in 1970 consolidated with the American Educational Publishers Institute to become the Association of American Publishers.

Adopted June 25, 1953, by the ALA Council and the AAP Freedom to Read Committee; amended January 28, 1972; January 16, 1991; July 12, 2000; June 30, 2004.

A Joint Statement by:

American Library Association

Association of American Publishers

Subsequently endorsed by:

American Booksellers Foundation for Free Expression

The Association of American University Presses, Inc.

The Children's Book Council

Freedom to Read Foundation

National Association of College Stores

National Coalition Against Censorship

National Council of Teachers of English

The Thomas Jefferson Center for the Protection of Free Expression

INDEX

339

About the Authors

DENISE K. FOURIE, MLS, is the lead instructor for the library/information technology distance education curriculum at Cuesta Community College, San Luis Obispo, California. She has more than 25 years' experience in the library field, including serving as a reference librarian in public and academic libraries, as a consultant, and as an instructor. Fourie received her bachelor's degree from the University of California, Berkeley, and her master's in library science from the University of Southern California. Some of her favorite projects have included working with the Julia Morgan architectural drawings and papers, mentoring interns, developing community reads programs, and experimenting with virtual reference.

NANCY E. LOE, MLS, is librarian emerita at California Polytechnic State University, where she managed Special Collections and Archives for 30 years. She received a master's degree in American history and a master's in library science with specialization in archives administration from the Catholic University of America. Loe has managed local history, genealogy, and special collections in public and academic libraries and taught women's history at the University of Colorado. She has written and directed three NEH grants for public library outreach and archival arrangement of architectural records. Loe appeared on PBS's *American Experience* and has presented at library, archives, and genealogy conferences. In addition to consulting on institutional archives and digital asset management, she now works as a professional genealogist and manages an award-winning website, sassyjanegenealogy.com.